CB129976

STEM INVESTIGATIONS

for MIDDLE PRIMARY

integrating SCIENCE, MATHS and TECHNOLOGIES for real-world learning

Charlotte Forwood

macmillan education

TEACHER RESOURCE BOOK

CONTENTS

→ INTRODUCTION

→ STEM INVESTIGATIONS

BUILT WORLD

MANAGED WORLD

NATURAL WORLD

SUSTAINABLE WORLD

WHO WE ARE

→ GENERIC REPRODUCIBLES

ABOUT *STEM INVESTIGATIONS FOR MIDDLE PRIMARY*

STEM Investigations for Middle Primary **is designed to enable educators to implement inquiry-based investigations with a STEM approach. This resource provides 20 'real-world' challenges to inspire and motivate students. Each challenge is supported by an investigation into the key issues around the project, scaffolded by a comprehensive teaching plan and instructional model.**

STEM stands for Science, Technology, Engineering and Mathematics. *STEM Investigations* helps students use skills and learnings from all four STEM disciplines to question and problem solve in real-world contexts, using an inquiry-based instructional model. Each STEM investigation links explicitly to Science content and inquiry skills in the curriculum, as well as to Mathematics and Digital and/or Design Technologies. The Engineering component – that is, the practical application of science to solve real-world problems – is facilitated through a five-step design thinking process used in each investigation (see page 8).

REAL-WORLD CHALLENGES, DESIGN THINKING AND VOCABULARY BUILDING

By focusing on authentic real-world challenges and problems, *STEM Investigations* allows students to engage in a transdisciplinary approach to learning and problem solving – just as we all do in real life. Student challenges range from building an arcade game with reused materials to designing living pods for tourists in Antarctica.

For each STEM investigation, students must first explore the key scientific concepts relating to the investigation before completing the challenge using a design thinking process (see pages 7–8). This process guides students through the different stages necessary to produce an end product or process relating to the original challenge. Stages include:

- empathising through learning about different points of view
- defining the issue
- ideating/creating different possible solutions
- prototyping
- testing their designs.

A key part of each STEM investigation is the development of students' subject-specific vocabulary (see pages 9–12). Students are encouraged to monitor their learning throughout the investigation and engage in evaluation and self-reflection at the conclusion of the challenge.

→ COMPONENTS OF STEM INVESTIGATIONS

STUDENT CARDS

For each STEM investigation, students are given a student card that sets out their challenge. They can work individually, in pairs or in groups. The student card outlines a description of the challenge, plus the key understandings, key skills, key actions, key vocabulary and definitions, and design thinking stages involved.

TEACHER RESOURCE BOOK

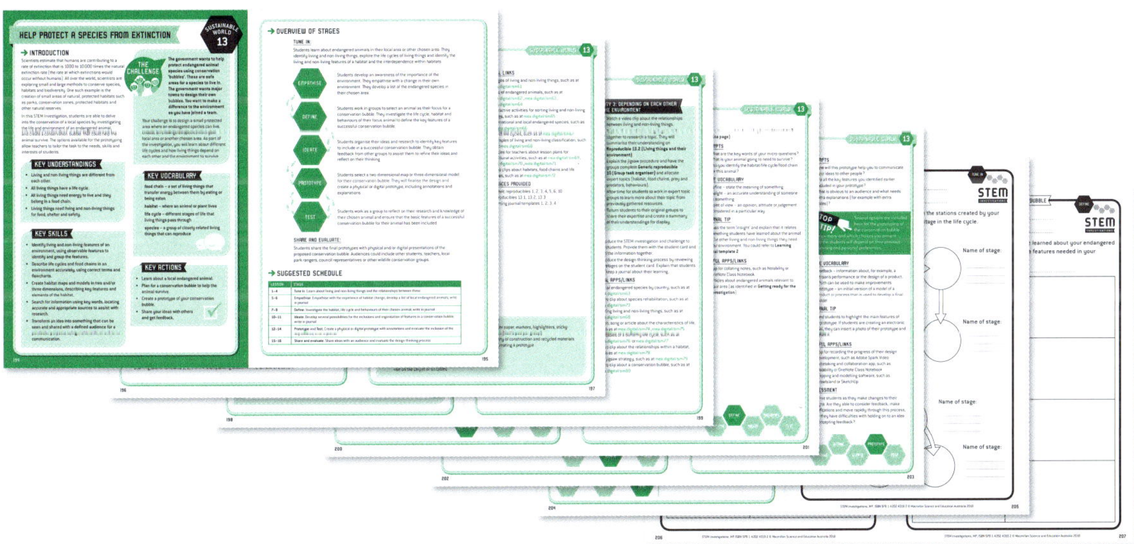

Each investigation is outlined in the Teacher Resource Book. The educator is provided with an overview of the challenge, and with curriculum links and detailed lesson plans, including suggestions for resources, technology use and assessment. Generic and investigation-specific reproducibles are also included.

DIGITAL RESOURCES

Digital resources include PDFs of the student cards and Teacher Resource Book, templates so that educators can create their own STEM projects, and learning journal templates that can be printed or filled in electronically by students. They can be accessed online using the instructions on the inside front cover of this Teacher Resource Book.

STEM SKILLS AND KNOWLEDGE, IN SCHOOL AND BEYOND

Discussions about the role of STEM in schools are ongoing, involving academics, business leaders and educators. Concern is widespread about the low levels of engagement in STEM subjects at school and university, and about poor performance compared with other countries, and the potential impact that this might have on the economic outlook. At the same time, there is real growth in STEM-related job opportunities, particularly in the fields of information and communications technology (ICT) and engineering.

THE BENEFITS OF BUILDING STEM SKILLS AND KNOWLEDGE

STEM knowledge and skills drive innovation and are important for economic growth, today and in the future. Employers are seeking graduates with a range of transdisciplinary skills, such as those developed in STEM subjects, and will continue to do so. In order to ensure today's students have the required skills for a changing future, schools need to develop students' STEM knowledge and skills from an early age. *STEM Investigations* offers a way to develop students' interdisciplinary STEM thinking.

The benefits of STEM are not just in the knowledge and skills specific to the individual disciplines of STEM. Benefits also include the learnings developed through the interplay of two or more of the STEM areas, as well as the development of general capabilities such as Critical and Creative Thinking.

Another benefit of engagement in STEM education is the development of collaborative skills. *STEM Investigations* encourages collaboration through small group work and regular peer feedback, and also through opportunities to interact with and interview school and local community members as part of the design thinking process.

Schools are addressing STEM competencies and attitudes in many different ways. Some programs incorporate the Arts and are referred to as STEAM, or other similar acronyms. Many of the STEM investigations in this resource require artistic or visual design input.

THE IMPORTANCE OF REAL-WORLD RELEVANCE

As well as developing STEM knowledge and skills, students need to be aware of the importance of STEM in their lives. Many Middle Primary students may not have been exposed explicitly to STEM learning, and they may perceive Science and Maths subjects as too difficult or even irrelevant. Students are naturally curious from an early age. Harnessing and nurturing this curiosity throughout the primary years may lead to students having greater levels of confidence to engage with STEM subjects in secondary and tertiary education.

STEM Investigations tackles the issue of relevance by presenting authentic contexts. Real-world investigations provide students with opportunities to apply their knowledge and skills through sustained investigation and provide learning experiences that increase students' ability to transfer theoretical knowledge to the real world. Authentic experiences allow students to develop the four domains of learning:

- **cognitive** (associated with developing problem-solving skills)
- **affective** (relating to emotion and feeling)
- **psychomotor** (including expressing ideas through physical movement)
- **conative** (to do with striving and effort).

Authentic learning incorporates collaborative practices with opportunities for reflection, scaffolding and feedback at key points. *STEM Investigations for Middle Primary* provides authentic challenges that can be modified to consider the unique context and interests of the students and address such things as local conservation issues.

STEM AND THE WORKFORCE

Today, the STEM workforce covers a diverse range of jobs, including scientific and technical services, manufacturing, public administration and safety, and education and training. The unemployment rate for STEM-qualified adults is lower than for people with no STEM qualifications.

STEM jobs are growing at a faster rate than non-STEM jobs, and many current primary students will, in the future, work in STEM jobs that have not even been imagined today. The many benefits of a STEM education will be obvious, regardless of the future career a student chooses. Even employers in sectors that are not STEM-focused value the skill set of STEM-qualified professionals. *STEM Investigations for Middle Primary* helps prepare students for the workforce of the future.

USEFUL RESOURCES

- **ACARA STEM report:** mea.digital/sm248
- **STEM NSW resources, Australia:** mea.digital/sm249
- **Students Fir st, Australian Government initiative:** mea.digital/sm250
- **STEM Learning UK resources:** mea.digital/sm251
- **The STEM Strategy, UK:** mea.digital/sm252
- **STEM education data, National Science Foundation, USA:** mea.digital/sm253
- **Science, Technology, Engineering & Math (STEM), National Education Association, USA:** mea.digital/sm254
- **STEM education resources, New Zealand:** mea.digital/sm255

THE DESIGN THINKING PROCESS

Design thinking is a process for developing solutions to problems. The design thinking process involves considering different points of view, exploring possibilities, thinking broadly but also within the scope of a challenge, and creating a solution that meets the needs of the people, group or organisation with the original problem.

Some of the key skills students develop through engagement with the design thinking process are:

- **observational skills** – learning to look carefully, make observations and identify patterns and trends
- **empathy** – considering something from different points of view
- **flexible thinking** – willingness to change ideas, opinions and solutions
- **narrative skills** – using language effectively to create a story to explain an issue, process, solution or product
- **creative thinking** – using imagination to generate a range of diverse ideas and solutions
- **evaluation skills** – reflecting on engagement with content, processes and product, and making constructive suggestions
- **synthesising skills** – using imagination to create new ideas, solutions and products
- **collaboration** – working with others, considering different ideas and opinions, compromising and being committed to a group task.

THE FIVE STAGES OF THE DESIGN THINKING PROCESS

There are many variations of the design thinking process. All involve creative solution-based thinking, but the stages of the process vary. The version used in *STEM Investigations for Middle Primary* was made famous by the Stanford University Design School, which used it to scaffold their students' learning and design approach. Five design thinking stages are used in *STEM Investigations for Middle Primary*: empathise, define, ideate, prototype and test.

EMPATHISE

During this stage, students focus on finding out different points of view. They look for patterns and trends in the information they initially find out.

DEFINE

The main focus of this stage is reframing the challenge. The initial challenge is usually quite open, so at this stage students learn how to define what needs to be done. This includes noting insights that have been generated.

IDEATE

The Ideate stage is all about generating lots of ideas. Students need to be flexible in their thinking and able to move beyond obvious ideas. At this stage, ideas are not judged, just generated and gathered.

PROTOTYPE

At this stage, students are asked to create a physical prototype of a solution. It is the stage where students need to get their ideas out of their heads and present them in a way that engages other students and helps them to understand the concept. When students create, it helps them to think and solve problems and disagreements. Students can role-play, make storyboards or use sticky notes. The most important feature is that viewers can interact with whatever is produced.

TEST

At this stage, students test their prototype to see if it meets the requirements of the audience or users. Students check to see if their prototype meets the criteria set at the start of the design process. They are given the opportunity to cycle through the Prototype and Test stages again.

USEFUL RESOURCES

- **Stanford University Design School:** mea.digital/sm256
- **A Virtual Crash Course in Design Thinking:** mea.digital/sm257

UNDERSTANDING AND USING STEM VOCABULARY

The understanding and use of terms relating to an area of study, whether it be Science, Mathematics or another discipline, are incredibly important. Specific vocabulary is used to describe abstract scientific concepts, such as 'reversible' and 'absorption'. Discipline-specific vocabulary is also used to describe specific concrete objects, such as the science terms 'pipette' and 'LED'. One of the strengths of *STEM Investigations* is its emphasis on subject-specific vocabulary growth, which should result in improved comprehension and engagement.

ORAL LANGUAGE

Oral vocabulary has a key role in the development of comprehension and literacy skills. Students need to use oral language effectively. It has a considerable impact on literacy and numeracy development, curriculum access, academic success and social interactions (Snow, Eadie, Connell, Dalheim, McCusker & Munro, 2014). Rich oral language experiences are critical for vocabulary growth. Opportunities for speaking new vocabulary are a vital part of the vocabulary learning process, not only for general vocabulary acquisition but also for general academic vocabulary development. Students need multiple opportunities to read, hear and use words in multiple contexts in order to own the words they see, hear and use (Forwood, 2013). When teachers are providing students with vocabulary instruction, they are helping students to build their lexicon (vocabulary that they use) rather than teaching a word. Key components of lexicon building include understanding word meanings, relationships between words, parts of speech and uses in different contexts.

LEVELS OF KNOWING VOCABULARY

Words are not simply known or unknown. Dale (1965) outlined four stages of vocabulary development, ranging from no knowledge of a word to an ability to use and remember a word. These stages were later placed on a continuum by Stahl (1999), whereby students moved between no knowledge of a word's meaning to full and flexible knowledge of a word's meaning. Each of the four components makes a long-term contribution to vocabulary growth. Developing a deep understanding of new terms is a gradual process and requires students to be able to use words in different contexts.

The four levels of knowing vocabulary are:

DON'T KNOW THE WORD → HEARD OF THE WORD BUT DON'T KNOW WHAT IT MEANS → KNOW THE MEANING OF THE WORD IN ONE CONTEXT → KNOW THE MEANING OF THE WORD IN MULTIPLE CONTEXTS

VOCABULARY AND COMPREHENSION

Students need to know at least 95 per cent of words in a text in order to engage with and understand it (Schmitt, Jiang & Grabe, 2011). Science, along with History and Geography, is one of the subject areas with the highest number of subject-specific, or technical, terms. Many scientific terms are infrequently used and rarely used beyond the classroom.

Considerable research has shown that vocabulary levels are linked to general comprehension, reading comprehension, high-level thinking skills and attitude to school. Isabel Beck's three-tier model of vocabulary (see page 10) divides words into three levels (Beck & McKeown, 1985).

THREE-TIER MODEL OF VOCABULARY

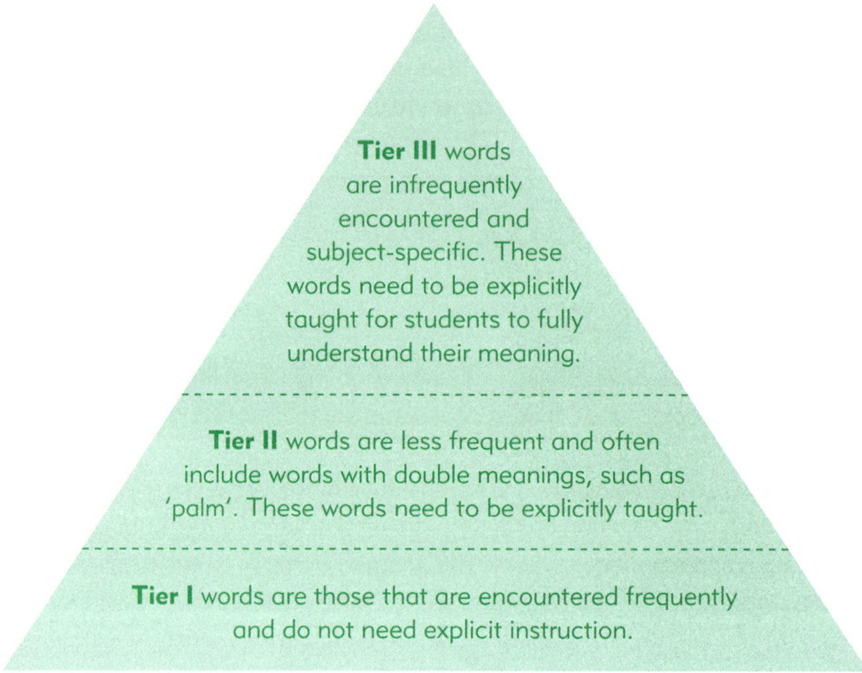

Understanding a word is more than just knowing its meaning. Understanding is also about knowing a word's associations with other words; for example, its category, synonyms, antonyms and word family. Students need multiple exposures to words, over time. They need to hear, see and write new words. Most importantly, words must be verbalised in order to be stored and retrieved correctly.

Students also need a well-developed vocabulary to use the high-level thinking skills necessary for developing STEM-related skills. A broad internalised vocabulary is important for a student to think about their thinking (metacognition) and articulate their ideas and observations with precision.

→ CONCEPTUAL AND INSTRUCTIONAL VOCABULARY

Understanding of conceptual and instructional science vocabulary has been linked to student attitudes to science. *STEM Investigations* includes the explicit teaching of key instructional and conceptual vocabulary, focusing on functional words relating to each investigation, encouraging enhanced student engagement with the topic.

→ PRE-TESTING AND POST-TESTING VOCABULARY

STEM Investigations pre-tests key vocabulary knowledge at the Tune-in stage of each investigation and post-tests the same vocabulary at the Share and evaluate stage. Pre-testing understanding of key vocabulary relating to a unit of work provides information about the level of understanding of terminology for individual students, as well as that of the whole class. This can assist with targeting specific words for explicit instruction and additional practice. Including a post-test of the same words at the end of a unit of work provides students with tangible evidence of their learning and is also a way for teachers to monitor progress.

→ WAYS OF DEVELOPING VOCABULARY AND ORAL LANGUAGE

As already highlighted, it is important to develop students' STEM-related vocabulary and oral language skills. The following suggestions can support this skill development.

Marzano and Pickering (2005) provide a useful framework for building subject-specific vocabulary in their book *Building Academic Vocabulary: Teacher's Manual*. First, new words need to be discussed, with anecdotes and examples provided. Then students should write their own description of a word's meaning before drawing a picture or symbol that links to the word. The next stage is to compare terms, through different activities.

STEM Investigations can be used to develop subject-specific vocabulary in the following ways:

- **Key vocabulary list**: Before beginning a new unit of work, gauge students' understandings of words by providing them with a list of key words and asking them to indicate their level of understanding (see **Generic reproducible 1 – Key vocabulary table**).
- **Discuss and examine terms**: After the words have been identified, discuss them, providing anecdotes and examples. Then ask students to write their own description of a word's meaning before drawing a picture or symbol that links to the word.
- **Compare terms**: Various activities can be used to compare terms (see example activities below, such as sentence stems and semantic gradients).
- **Review words**: After students have been provided with opportunities to explore new words, they should review their initial descriptions and revise them, where relevant.

SENTENCE STEMS

Use sentence stems such as 'These two words are similar because' and 'These two words are different because'. For example:

'Hot' and 'cold' are similar because they are both to do with temperature.
'Hot' and 'cold' are different because 'hot' relates to a high temperature and 'cold' relates to a low temperature.

SEMANTIC GRADIENTS

Sort words according to 'degrees' of meaning. For example:

hottest/boiling, warm, lukewarm, cold, freezing/coldest

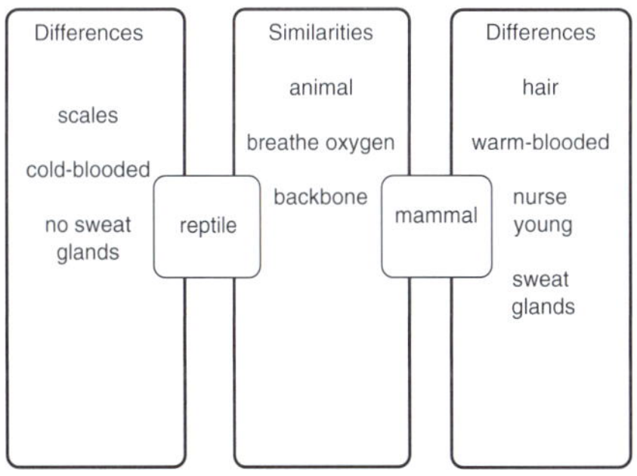

▲ Double Bubble activity

DOUBLE BUBBLE

Identify similarities and differences between words (see **Generic reproducible 7 – Double bubble**).

SEMANTIC MAPS

Make connections between the key word and other words or phrases.

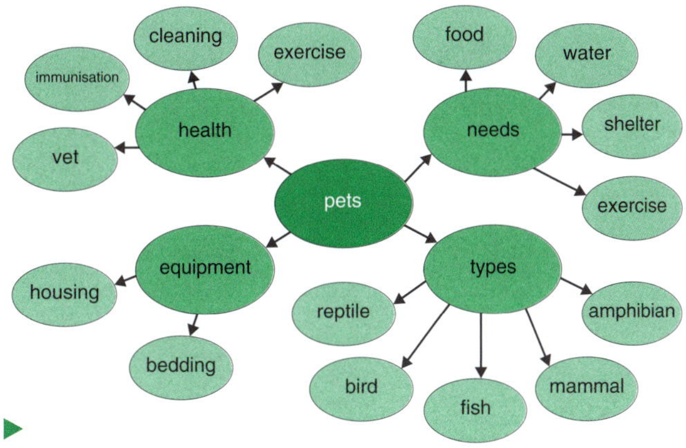

Semantic map ▶

WORD MATRIX

A word matrix (table) can be used to compare the features of different words.

Material	Magnetic?	Waterproof?	Flexible?	Natural or synthetic?
Iron	yes	yes	no	natural
Plastic	no	yes	can be	synthetic
Wood	no	yes	no	natural

VOCABULARY HEXAGONS

Create a paper-based or software-generated mind map, or provide students with several copies of **Generic reproducible 8 (Vocabulary hexagons)**. Students write each word they have generated onto a hexagon. They cut out and arrange the hexagons to connect related words. Create a wall display with the words and concepts. Students can add hexagons as they learn more related words and concepts.

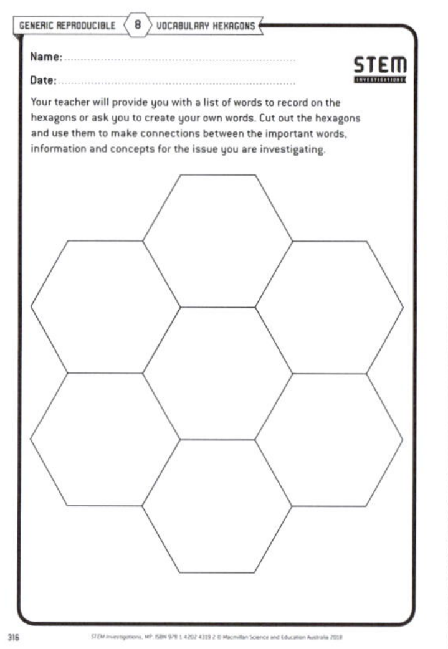
GENERIC REPRODUCIBLE 8 VOCABULARY HEXAGONS

Name:

Date:

STEM

Your teacher will provide you with a list of words to record on the hexagons or ask you to create your own words. Cut out the hexagons and use them to make connections between the important words, information and concepts for the issue you are investigating.

316

▲ Generic reproducible 8

OTHER WORD GAMES

Many word games can be played to increase word knowledge and consciousness. For examples, see the free vocabulary resources at the Marzano Research website.

REFERENCES AND RESOURCES

- Beck, IL & McKeown, MG 1985, 'Teaching vocabulary: Making the instruction fit the goal', *Educational Perspectives*, vol. 23(1), pp. 11–15
- Carrier, SJ, *Effective Strategies for Teaching Science Vocabulary*, mea.digital/sm258
- Dale, E 1965, 'Vocabulary measurement: Techniques and major findings', *Elementary English*, vol. 42, pp. 395–401
- Forwood, C 2013, 'Investigating Differences in Understanding of Vocabulary in Secondary Science', Curtin University of Technology, Perth, Australia, mea.digital/sm259
- Marzano, RJ & Carleton, L 2010, *Vocabulary Games for the Classroom*. Bloomington, IN: Marzano Research Laboratory
- Marzano, RJ, *Vocabulary Games for the Classroom Reproducibles*, Marzano Research, mea.digital/sm260
- Marzano, RJ & Pickering, DJ 2005, *Building Academic Vocabulary: Teacher's Manual*, Alexandria, VA: Association for Supervision and Curriculum Development
- Reading Rockets, *STEM Literacy*, mea.digital/sm261
- Schmitt, N, Jiang X, & Grabe, W 2011, 'The percentage of words known in a text and reading comprehension', *The Modern Language Journal*, vol. 95(1), pp. 26–43. DOI: 10.1111/j.1540-4781.2011.01146.x
- Snow, PC, Eadie PA, Connell, J, Dalheim, B, McCusker, HJ & Munro JK, 2013, 'Oral language supports early literacy: A pilot cluster randomised trial in disadvantaged schools', *International Journal of Speech-Language Pathology*, vol. 16(5), pp. 495–506
- Stahl, SA 1999, *Vocabulary Development*, Brookline, MA: Brookline Books

USING *STEM INVESTIGATIONS*

STEM Investigations **brings together three elements – student cards, a Teacher Resource Book and online digital resources – to facilitate 20 individual investigations for Middle Primary students.**

Each investigation includes a set of student cards, which outline the challenge, the key learning, the important vocabulary and the main focus for each stage of the design thinking process. The accompanying Teacher Resource Book provides a framework for each of the 20 STEM investigations, including a range of resources and tasks to support the development of critical and creative thinking skills, design thinking skills, practical literacy and numeracy, visual literacy and digital technology use. Online digital resources include digital copies of reproducibles, templates and rubrics, plus links to curated, third-party digital resources, to help teachers guide students through the investigations.

STUDENT CARDS

Each investigation consists of six copies of a double-sided student card. The card presents the challenge and guides students through the design thinking process.

The challenge
Gives the challenge parameters and general guidance, including questions to consider. Also outlines the key scientific learning linked to the task.

Investigation theme and number

Key vocabulary
Lists key terms that are important for understanding the concepts explored in the investigation, plus their definitions. Ideas for developing challenge-related vocabulary are provided in the Teacher Resource Book.

Key actions
Gives an overview of the main actions students will be expected to perform. Actions may also form part of student assessment.

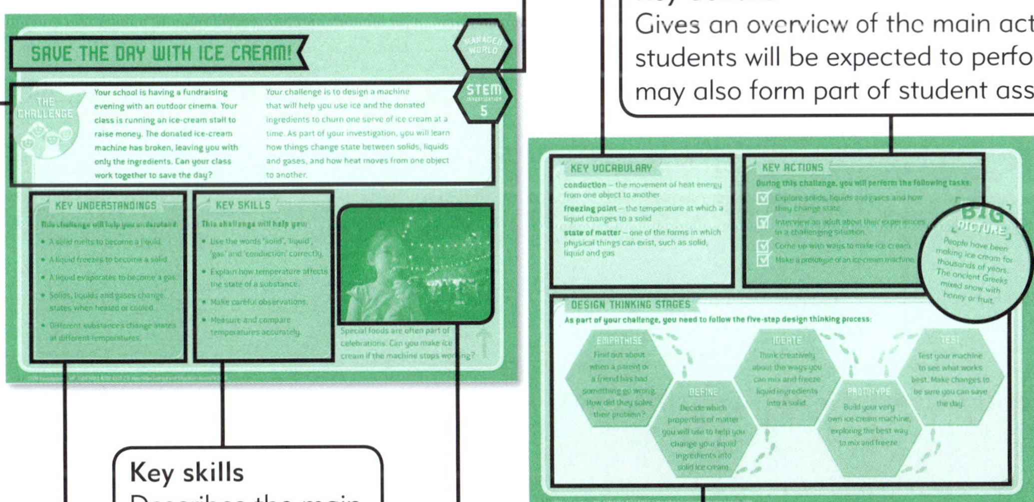

Key skills
Describes the main skills that will be developed. Also provides general information about the skills that will be assessed, formally or informally.

Image
Engages and hooks students into the investigation.

Big picture
A relevant quirky or light-hearted snippet of information that will spark student interest.

Key understandings
Identifies the key curriculum-linked understandings associated with the challenge.

Design thinking stages
Gives an overview of the main activities associated with each stage of the design thinking process.

→ TEACHER RESOURCE BOOK

The Teacher Resource Book provides teachers with background information about each of the investigations, as well as structured activities and resources to teach the key concepts required for students to complete the challenge.

Investigation theme and number

Introduction
Gives background information relating to the challenge, including the focus of the investigation.

Key understandings
Information from the student card is repeated, for ease of use. Identifies the key curriculum-linked understandings associated with the challenge.

Key skills
Information from the student card is repeated, for ease of use. Describes the main skills that will be developed. Also provides general information about the skills that will be assessed, formally or informally.

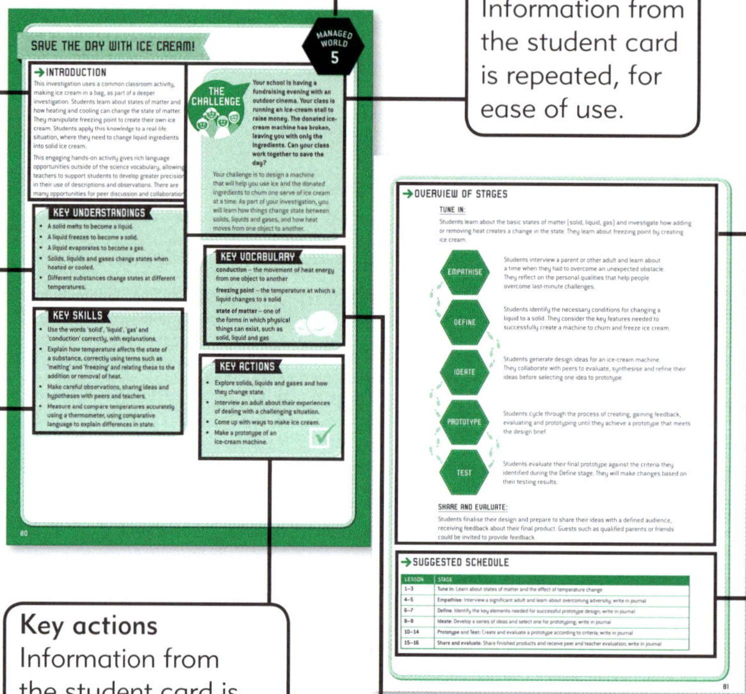

Key actions
Information from the student card is repeated, for ease of use. Gives an overview of the main actions students will be expected to perform. Actions may also form part of student assessment.

The challenge
Information from the student card is repeated, for ease of use.

Overview of stages
Gives an overview of the design thinking stages, with key actions for the investigation highlighted. Also gives an overview of the main components of the Tune-in stage, plus a final evaluation stage.

Key vocabulary
Lists the key vocabulary and definitions from the student card.

Suggested schedule
Helps teachers timetable the investigation. The initial sessions tune in the students to the investigation and introduce and/or develop the key science concepts required for the investigation. The rest of the sessions involve exploring, creating, evaluating and sharing solutions.

LESSON PLANNING AND DIFFERENTIATION

Each STEM investigation should take 15 to 21 sessions, depending on its scope, and the investigation can be completed over an extended period of time. This allows students time to reflect between sessions. Alternatively, the investigations could be completed as an intensive program of work over a one- or two-week period, although this depends on the focus of the investigation. Some investigations may require a specific amount of time to observe changes.

The open-ended nature of each STEM investigation lends itself to differentiation. The initial sessions are clearly scaffolded to develop understanding of key science concepts, and they set up the criteria and limitations of the challenges clearly. The design thinking process provides scope to work at a pace and level suitable to individual skill and interest levels while still engaging in collaborative tasks.

INVESTIGATION THEMES

The 20 STEM investigations are grouped into five themes for ease of use and navigation:

- **BUILT WORLD** — Topics such as town planning and infrastructure design
- **MANAGED WORLD** — Topics such as product design, manufacturing and human-made systems
- **NATURAL WORLD** — Topics such as life cycles, habitats and ecosystems, animal classification, day and night, and seasons
- **SUSTAINABLE WORLD** — Topics such as sustainable projects and communities, and interactions between the natural world and humans
- **WHO WE ARE** — Topics such as community and cultural celebrations, identity and expression, art and creativity

Curriculum links
Lists major STEM links, along with links to other parts of the curriculum.

Getting ready for the investigation
A checklist to consider before beginning the investigation with students. Includes considerations for organisation, grouping of students, storage of materials for construction, sourcing of materials and preparation of resources.

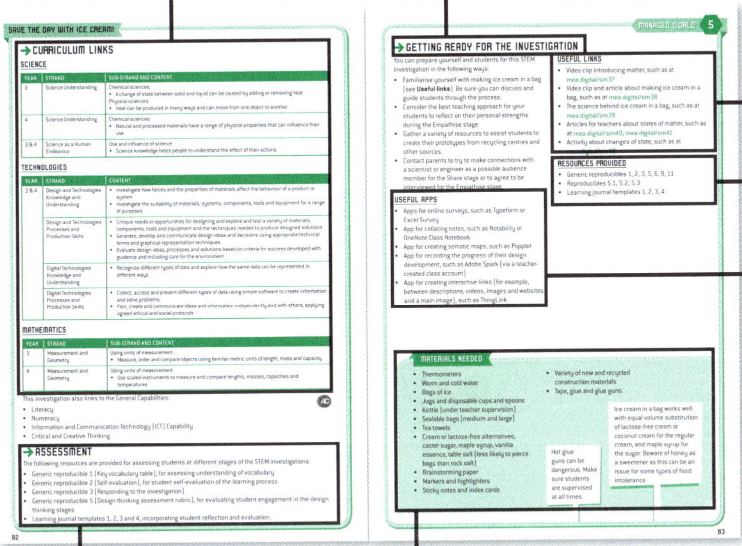

Useful links
Provides managed hyperlinks to third-party resources, including texts, images and videos that can be incorporated into activities.

Resources provided
Lists all generic reproducibles, investigation-specific reproducibles and learning journal templates used in the investigation.

Assessment resources
Lists resources for assessing students at different stages of the investigation.

Materials needed
Lists materials required for activities and to make prototypes or models.

Useful apps
Suggests specific apps, but alternatives can be substituted. Most recommendations are free, although some require sign-up; in these cases, a class account could be created by the teacher to cover any age limitations.

Key science knowledge
An overview of the key science knowledge that is required for the investigation. Provides descriptions and elaborations of key concepts, as well as images, diagrams and infographics.

Tune-in session
Establishes students' prior knowledge and understanding of key concepts and vocabulary. Introduces the key understandings involved in the challenge.

Activities
Used to develop understanding of the key scientific concepts required for the challenge.

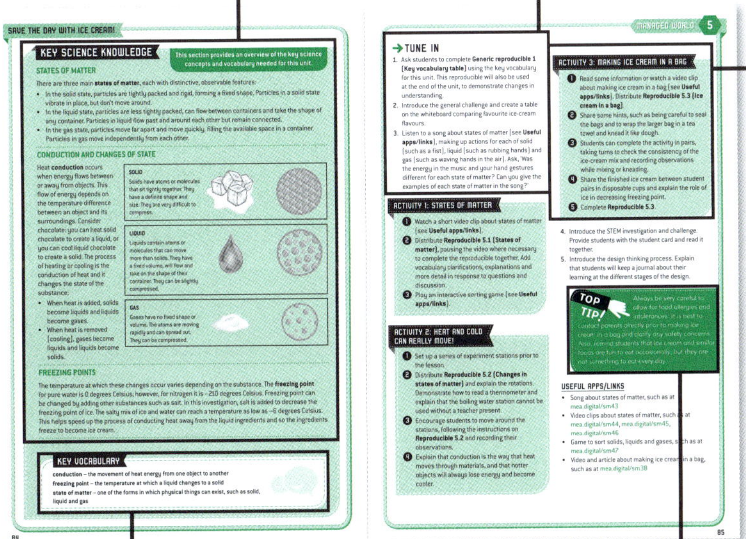

Key vocabulary
Definitions of key terms.

Top tip
Offers advice and tips, such as further activities and helpful resources.

BEGINNING THE INVESTIGATION

It is important to establish students' current knowledge and understandings of concepts and terminology at the start of the investigation. This will give teachers an insight into the prior knowledge students are bringing to the challenge.

At the Tune-in stage, students are asked to indicate their level of understanding of key conceptual and/or instructional vocabulary relating to the investigation. Following a Tune-in session or two, students are provided with a student card outlining their investigation. It is useful to review each section of the student card and link the information provided to the investigation.

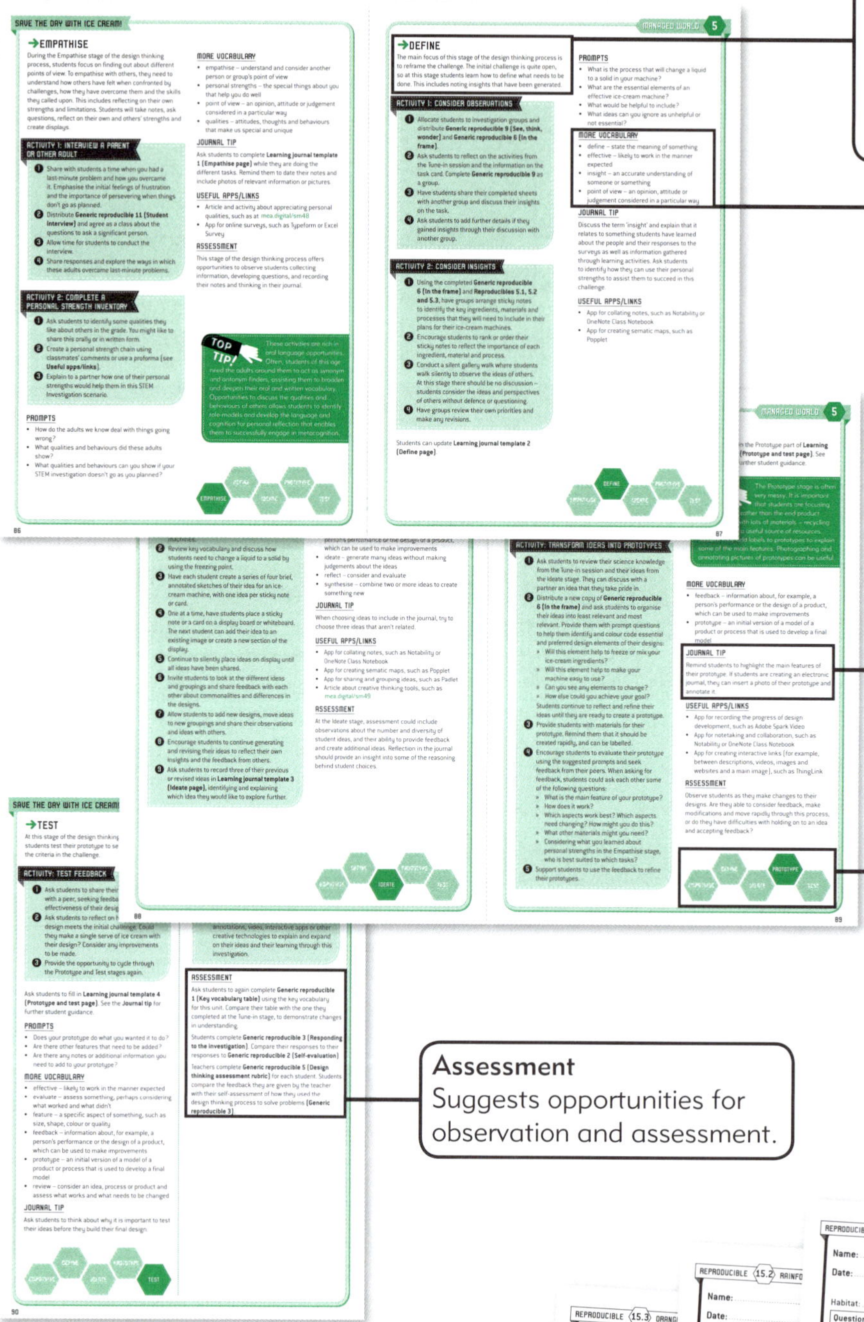

Design thinking stages
Each stage includes activities, including cross-references to reproducible activity sheets and prompts.

More vocabulary
Defines design thinking vocabulary.

Journal tip
Students complete a learning journal template at each stage to show what they are learning and how they are reflecting on their learning.

Design thinking diagram
Shows what stage the student is at in the design thinking process.

Assessment
Suggests opportunities for observation and assessment.

REPRODUCIBLES

Investigation-specific reproducibles are included with the relevant investigation. Generic reproducibles and assessment rubrics can be found at the end of the Teacher Resource Book (see table opposite).

Each of the reproducibles can be used as an assessment task. These can be assessed informally, through observation and anecdotal records, or using rubrics, peer evaluation or self-evaluation.

GENERIC REPRODUCIBLE NUMBER	GENERIC REPRODUCIBLE NAME	DESCRIPTION
1	Key vocabulary table	Used by students at the start and end of the investigation to determine their level of understanding of key vocabulary relating to the investigation. It provides tangible evidence of vocabulary development over the course of the investigation.
2	Self-evaluation	Focuses on the content, learning process and products produced with the investigation. Resources cater for a variety of purposes and student ability. Focuses on how a student's learning has changed, helps them evaluate their end product and provides them with the opportunity to consider improvements.
3	Responding to the investigation	Focuses on the content, learning process and products produced with the investigation. Resources cater for a variety of purposes and student ability. Focuses on feedback about the investigation topic and the design thinking process.
4	Key question table	Provides a template for guiding research. Students create micro-questions prior to beginning their research. These assist students to engage in focused searches by providing key words. The template provides space for note-taking and recording the source of information.
5	Design thinking assessment rubric	Used to evaluate student engagement in the different design thinking stages throughout the investigation.
6	In the frame	Used by students to assist with classifying and identifying relevant ideas.
7	Double bubble*	Used by students to scaffold comparisons between two objects, concepts or ideas. Students identify both similarities and differences.
8	Vocabulary hexagons**	Used by students to demonstrate their understandings of the relationships between words or concepts.
9	See, think, wonder***	Used by students when making observations and interpreting the information they see.
10	Group task organiser	Assists students to organise roles when completing collaborative tasks.
11	Student interview	Provides question starters for interviewing and space for recording responses.
12	Prototype and test	Used by students to highlight key inclusions, checking process and changes made.

* A term coined by David Hyerle: dft.designsforthinking.com
** A SOLO Hexagons app is now available
*** A thinking routine from Harvard University's Project Zero: Visible Thinking: visiblethinkingpz.org

DIGITAL RESOURCES

Online digital resources include PDFs of the cards and Teacher Resource Book, templates so that educators can create their own STEM projects, learning journal templates and a glossary booklet.

Learning journal templates
Can be printed out and filled in by students, or PDFs can be filled in electronically.

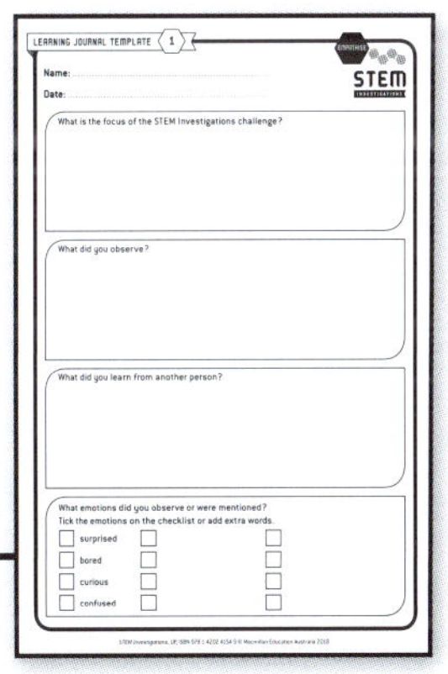

LEARNING JOURNAL TEMPLATES

Students can document and evaluate their learning at each stage of the investigation using the learning journal templates. They can be used to provide evidence of students' learning across the investigation.

TEMPLATE NUMBER	LEARNING JOURNAL STAGE	DESCRIPTION
1	Empathise	Used by students to record some of the observations they make at the start of the investigation. They describe some of the things they have learned at the start of the investigation.
2	Define	Used by students to define the investigation by identifying relevant insights and actions.
3	Ideate	Used by students to record four different ideas that they have generated during the Ideate stage of the investigation.
4	Prototype and test	Used by students to choose one idea to develop and test. They record their evaluations, as well as feedback from others.

INVESTIGATION OVERVIEWS AND CURRICULUM LINKS

THEME	NO.	PAGE	INVESTIGATION OVERVIEW	RESOURCES PROVIDED	SCIENCE CURRICULUM ALIGNMENT			TECHNOLOGY AND ENGINEERING CURRICULUM ALIGNMENT		MATHEMATICS CURRICULUM ALIGNMENT	OTHER CURRICULUM LINKS
					SCIENCE UNDERSTANDING	SCIENCE AS A HUMAN ENDEAVOUR	SCIENCE INQUIRY SKILLS	DIGITAL TECHNOLOGIES	DESIGN AND TECHNOLOGIES		
BUILT WORLD	**1**	22	**Plan an attractive bus shelter** In this STEM investigation, students are challenged to create a bus shelter that is practical and inexpensive. As part of the investigation, they will explore the properties of different materials and consider the importance of strong structures in their designs.	• Generic reproducibles 1, 2, 3, 5, 6, 12 • Reproducibles 1.1, 1.2, 1.3 • Learning journal templates 1, 2, 3, 4 (online)	**Chemical sciences:** Natural and processed materials have a range of physical properties that can influence their use (Year 4)	✓	✓		✓	Measurement and Geometry	**General Capabilities:** Literacy, Numeracy, Information and Communication Technology (ICT) Capability, Critical and Creative Thinking **Cross-curriculum priority:** Sustainability
BUILT WORLD	**2**	36	**Design a playground for playing and learning** In this STEM investigation, students are challenged to create an exciting, engaging and instructional playground. As part of the investigation, they learn about simple machines and forces, and consider the range of play needs of students from Foundation to Year 6.	• Generic reproducibles 1, 2, 3, 5, 10 • Reproducibles 2.1, 2.2, 2.3, 2.4, 2.5 • Learning journal templates 1, 2, 3, 4 (online)	**Physical sciences:** Forces can be exerted by one object on another through direct contact or from a distance (Year 4)	✓		✓	✓	Measurement and Geometry	**General Capabilities:** Literacy, Numeracy, Information and Communication Technology (ICT) Capability, Critical and Creative Thinking
BUILT WORLD	**3**	52	**Bridge the gap to help a town** In this STEM investigation, students are challenged to create a simple model of a bridge. As part of the investigation, they will learn about the impact of flooding on infrastructure and explore how strong structures are designed and built.	• Generic reproducibles 1, 2, 3, 4, 5, 12 • Reproducibles 3.1, 3.2, 3.3 • Learning journal templates 1, 2, 3, 4 (online)	**Earth and space sciences:** Earth's surface changes over time as a result of natural processes and human activity (Year 4)	✓	✓	✓		Measurement and Geometry	**General Capabilities:** Literacy, Numeracy, Information and Communication Technology (ICT) Capability, Critical and Creative Thinking **Cross-curriculum priority:** Sustainability
BUILT WORLD	**4**	66	**Design an amazing maze for your school fair** In this STEM investigation, students are challenged to design and create a maze using computer software. As part of the investigation, they will consider materials that could be used to create a full-scale model and how the materials could be reused.	• Generic reproducibles 1, 2, 3, 5, 12 • Reproducibles 4.1, 4.2, 4.3 • Learning journal templates 1, 2, 3, 4 (online)	**Chemical sciences:** Natural and processed materials have a range of physical properties that can influence their use (Year 4)	✓	✓	✓	✓	Measurement and Geometry	**General Capabilities:** Literacy, Numeracy, Information and Communication Technology (ICT) Capability, Critical and Creative Thinking
MANAGED WORLD	**5**	80	**Save the day with ice cream!** In this STEM investigation, students are challenged to design an ice-cream machine that will churn one serve of ice cream at a time. As part of the investigation, they will learn about how heating and cooling can change the states of matter.	• Generic reproducibles 1, 2, 3, 5, 6, 9, 11 • Reproducibles 5.1, 5.2, 5.3 • Learning journal templates 1, 2, 3, 4 (online)	**Chemical sciences:** A change of state between solid and liquid can be caused by adding or removing heat (Year 3) Natural and processed materials have a range of physical properties that can influence their use (Year 4) **Physical sciences:** Heat can be produced in many ways and can move from one object to another (Year 3)	✓		✓	✓	Measurement and Geometry	**General Capabilities:** Literacy, Numeracy, Information and Communication Technology (ICT) Capability, Critical and Creative Thinking

THEME	NO.	PAGE	INVESTIGATION OVERVIEW	RESOURCES PROVIDED	SCIENCE CURRICULUM ALIGNMENT: SCIENCE UNDERSTANDING	SCIENCE CURRICULUM ALIGNMENT: SCIENCE AS A HUMAN ENDEAVOUR	SCIENCE CURRICULUM ALIGNMENT: SCIENCE INQUIRY SKILLS	TECHNOLOGY AND ENGINEERING CURRICULUM ALIGNMENT: DIGITAL TECHNOLOGIES	TECHNOLOGY AND ENGINEERING CURRICULUM ALIGNMENT: DESIGN AND TECHNOLOGIES	MATHEMATICS CURRICULUM ALIGNMENT	OTHER CURRICULUM LINKS
MANAGED WORLD	6	94	**Keep the water taps cool** In this STEM investigation, students are challenged to create a solution for keeping the water in drinking taps cool during warmer months. As part of the investigation, they will explore heat transfer and materials that are good conductors.	• Generic reproducibles 1, 2, 3, 5, 12 • Reproducibles 6.1, 6.2, 6.3 • Learning journal templates 1, 2, 3, 4 (online)	**Physical sciences:** Heat can be produced in many ways and can move from one object to another (Year 3) **Chemical sciences:** Natural and processed materials have a range of physical properties that can influence their use (Year 4)	✓	✓		✓	Measurement and Geometry	**General Capabilities:** Literacy, Numeracy, Information and Communication Technology (ICT) Capability, Critical and Creative Thinking
MANAGED WORLD	7	108	**Design an energy-efficient pet house** In this STEM investigation, students are challenged to design a pet house that could be used to look after a small animal during short-term stay in their backyard. As part of the investigation, they will explore different materials and ways to insulate their design.	• Generic reproducibles 1, 2, 3, 4, 5, 6, 8, 10, 12 • Reproducibles 7.1, 7.2, 7.3 • Learning journal templates 1, 2, 3, 4 (online)	**Physical sciences:** Heat can be produced in many ways and can move from one object to another (Year 3) **Biological sciences:** Living things depend on each other and the environment to survive (Year 4)	✓	✓		✓	Measurement and Geometry	**General Capabilities:** Literacy, Numeracy, Information and Communication Technology (ICT) Capability, Critical and Creative Thinking **Cross-curriculum priority:** Sustainability
MANAGED WORLD	8	122	**Sort things with a compost system** In this STEM investigation, students are challenged to design a simple community compost system to fit a tall, narrow space. As part of the investigation, they will learn about grouping living, non-living and once-living things.	• Generic reproducibles 1, 2, 3, 4, 5, 6 • Reproducibles 8.1, 8.2, 8.3, 8.4, 8.5 • Learning journal templates 1, 2, 3, 4 (online)	**Biological sciences:** Living things can be grouped on the basis of observable features and can be distinguished from non-living things (Year 3)	✓			✓	Measurement and Geometry	**General Capabilities:** Literacy, Numeracy, Information and Communication Technology (ICT) Capability, Critical and Creative Thinking **Cross-curriculum priority:** Sustainability
NATURAL WORLD	9	138	**Sort the bulls from the chickens** In this STEM investigation, students are challenged to create a map or diorama that demonstrates the different classifications of plants and animals at an agricultural show. As part of the investigation, they will explore the differences between animal and plant classification, with a specific focus on vertebrate animals.	• Generic reproducibles 1, 2, 3, 5, 7, 10, 12 • Reproducibles 9.1, 9.2, 9.3 • Learning journal templates 1, 2, 3, 4 (online)	**Biological sciences:** Living things can be grouped on the basis of observable features and can be distinguished from non-living things (Year 3)	✓	✓		✓	Measurement and Geometry	**General Capabilities:** Literacy, Numeracy, Information and Communication Technology (ICT) Capability, Critical and Creative Thinking
NATURAL WORLD	10	152	**Make a movie about the Earth's movement** In this STEM investigation, students are challenged to produce a movie that shows that the Earth is a sphere that rotates on its axis and revolves around the Sun. As part of the investigation, they will learn how the Earth's rotation on its axis causes regular changes.	• Generic reproducibles 1, 2, 3, 4, 5, 6 • Reproducibles 10.1, 10.2, 10.3 • Learning journal templates 1, 2, 3, 4 (online)	**Earth and space sciences:** Earth's rotation on its axis causes regular changes, including night and day (Year 3)	✓	✓	✓	✓	Measurement and Geometry	**General Capabilities:** Literacy, Numeracy, Information and Communication Technology (ICT) Capability, Critical and Creative Thinking **Cross-curriculum priority:** Sustainability

THEME	NO.	PAGE	INVESTIGATION OVERVIEW	RESOURCES PROVIDED	SCIENCE CURRICULUM ALIGNMENT: SCIENCE UNDERSTANDING	SCIENCE AS A HUMAN ENDEAVOUR	SCIENCE INQUIRY SKILLS	TECHNOLOGY AND ENGINEERING CURRICULUM ALIGNMENT: DIGITAL TECHNOLOGIES	DESIGN AND TECHNOLOGIES	MATHEMATICS CURRICULUM ALIGNMENT	OTHER CURRICULUM LINKS
NATURAL WORLD	**11**	166	**Help tourists sleep in the 'midnight sun'** In this STEM investigation, students are challenged to design a portable living pod that could be used by visitors to Antarctica. As part of the investigation, they will learn about the rotation of the Earth and how it causes night and day.	• Generic reproducibles 1, 2, 3, 4, 5, 7, 9 • Reproducibles 11.1, 11.2, 11.3 • Learning journal templates 1, 2, 3, 4 (online)	**Earth and space sciences:** Earth's rotation on its axis causes regular changes, including night and day (Year 3) **Physical sciences:** Heat can be produced in many ways and can move from one object to another (Year 3)				✓	Statistics and Probability Measurement and Geometry	**General Capabilities:** Literacy, Numeracy, Information and Communication Technology (ICT) Capability, Critical and Creative Thinking **Cross-curriculum priority:** Sustainability
NATURAL WORLD	**12**	180	**Bring bees back to the city** In this STEM investigation, students are challenged to show how cities could be transformed to attract bees. As part of the investigation, they will explore the relationship between bees and flowering plants, and how living things depend on each other.	• Generic reproducibles 1, 2, 3, 4, 5, 6, 11 • Reproducibles 12.1, 12.2, 12.3 • Learning journal templates 1, 2, 3, 4 (online)	**Biological sciences:** Living things have life cycles Living things depend on each other and the environment to survive (Year 4)	✓			✓	Measurement and Geometry	**General Capabilities:** Literacy, Numeracy, Information and Communication Technology (ICT) Capability, Critical and Creative Thinking **Cross-curriculum priority:** Sustainability
SUSTAINABLE WORLD	**13**	194	**Help protect a species from extinction** In this STEM investigation, students are challenged to design a small protected area where a local endangered species can live. As part of the investigation, they will learn about different life cycles and how living things depend on each other and the environment.	• Generic reproducibles 1, 2, 3, 4, 5, 6, 10 • Reproducibles 13.1, 13.2, 13.3 • Learning journal templates 1, 2, 3, 4 (online)	**Biological sciences:** Living things can be grouped on the basis of observable features and can be distinguished from non-living things [Year 3] Living things have life cycles Living things depend on each other and the environment to survive (Year 4)	✓		✓	✓	Measurement and Geometry	**General Capabilities:** Literacy, Numeracy, Information and Communication Technology (ICT) Capability, Critical and Creative Thinking **Cross-curriculum priority:** Sustainability
SUSTAINABLE WORLD	**14**	208	**Create an arcade game by reusing materials** In this STEM investigation, students are challenged to build a cardboard games arcade to demonstrate their understanding of the properties of different materials, simple machines and forces. As part of the investigation, they will learn about reusing materials that otherwise may end up in landfill.	• Generic reproducibles 1, 2, 3, 4, 5, 7, 9, 10, 12 • Reproducibles 14.1, 14.2, 14.3 • Learning journal templates 1, 2, 3, 4 (online)	**Physical sciences:** Forces can be exerted by one object on another through direct contact or from a distance (Year 4) **Chemical sciences:** Natural and processed materials have a range of physical properties that can influence their use (Year 4)	✓	✓		✓	Measurement and Geometry Number and Algebra	**General Capabilities:** Literacy, Numeracy, Information and Communication Technology (ICT) Capability, Critical and Creative Thinking **Cross-curriculum priority:** Sustainability
SUSTAINABLE WORLD	**15**	222	**Show how engineering helps save habitats** In this STEM investigation, students are challenged to invent and present one design or process to help stop the destruction of a habitat. As part of the investigation, they will explore how living things depend on each other and the environment to survive.	• Generic reproducibles 1, 2, 3, 5, 6 • Reproducibles 15.1, 15.2, 15.3 • Learning journal templates 1, 2, 3, 4 (online)	**Biological sciences:** Living things depend on each other and the environment to survive (Year 4)	✓			✓	Statistics and Probability	**General Capabilities:** Literacy, Numeracy, Information and Communication Technology (ICT) Capability, Critical and Creative Thinking **Cross-curriculum priority:** Sustainability

THEME	NO.	PAGE	INVESTIGATION OVERVIEW	RESOURCES PROVIDED	SCIENCE CURRICULUM ALIGNMENT			TECHNOLOGY AND ENGINEERING CURRICULUM ALIGNMENT		MATHEMATICS CURRICULUM ALIGNMENT	OTHER CURRICULUM LINKS
					SCIENCE UNDERSTANDING	SCIENCE AS A HUMAN ENDEAVOUR	SCIENCE INQUIRY SKILLS	DIGITAL TECHNOLOGIES	DESIGN AND TECHNOLOGIES		
SUSTAINABLE WORLD	16	236	**Help protect a river for years to come** In this STEM investigation, students are challenged to create a plan to protect a river. As part of the investigation, they will learn how human activities, such as irrigation, can have major effects on the Earth's surface.	• Generic reproducibles 1, 2, 3, 4, 5, 6 • Reproducibles 16.1, 16.2, 16.3 • Learning journal templates 1, 2, 3, 4 (online)	**Earth and space sciences:** Earth's surface changes over time as a result of natural processes and human activity (Year 4)	✓			✓	Measurement and Geometry	**General Capabilities:** Literacy, Numeracy, Information and Communication Technology (ICT) Capability, Critical and Creative Thinking, Ethical Understanding **Cross-curriculum priority:** Sustainability
WHO WE ARE	17	250	**Give new life to old clothes** In this STEM investigation, students are challenged to transform an old item of clothing into something new. As part of the investigation, they will explore the different properties of materials, and sustainability in the fashion industry.	• Generic reproducibles 1, 2, 3, 4, 5, 6 • Reproducibles 17.1, 17.2, 17.3 • Learning journal templates 1, 2, 3, 4 (online)	**Chemical sciences:** Natural and processed materials have a range of physical properties that can influence their use (Year 4)	✓			✓	Measurement and Geometry Statistics and Probability	**General Capabilities:** Literacy, Numeracy, Information and Communication Technology (ICT) Capability, Critical and Creative Thinking **Cross-curriculum priority:** Sustainability
WHO WE ARE	18	264	**Make an attractive toy for children** In this STEM investigation, students are challenged to build a game or toy that demonstrates their understanding of magnetic forces and the properties of different materials. As part of the investigation, they will learn about magnetic forces and the properties of different materials.	• Generic reproducibles 1, 2, 3, 5, 10, 12 • Reproducibles 18.1, 18.2, 18.3 • Learning journal templates 1, 2, 3, 4 (online)	**Physical sciences:** Forces can be exerted by one object on another through direct contact or from a distance (Year 4)	✓	✓		✓	Measurement and Geometry	**General Capabilities:** Literacy, Numeracy, Information and Communication Technology (ICT) Capability, Critical and Creative Thinking
WHO WE ARE	19	278	**Create art to celebrate the passing of time** In this STEM investigation, students are challenged to design an art installation that incorporates a sundial or other sun clock that represents their community. As part of the investigation, they will explore how objects in sunlight cast shadows.	• Generic reproducibles 1, 2, 3, 4, 5, 6 • Reproducibles 19.1, 19.2, 19.3, 19.4, 19.5 • Learning journal templates 1, 2, 3, 4 (online)	**Earth and space sciences:** Earth's rotation on its axis causes regular changes, including night and day (Year 3)	✓			✓	Measurement and Geometry Statistics and Probability	**General Capabilities:** Literacy, Numeracy, Information and Communication Technology (ICT) Capability, Critical and Creative Thinking, Personal and Social Capability
WHO WE ARE	20	294	**Keep people cool at big events** In this STEM investigation, students are challenged to design an exciting climate-proof stadium of the future that includes features that make it suitable for sport and entertainment in all weather. As part of the investigation, students will learn about the effects of heat on different materials.	• Generic reproducibles 1, 2, 3, 4, 5, 6, 12 • Reproducibles 20.1, 20.2, 20.3, 20.4 • Learning journal templates 1, 2, 3, 4 (online)	**Chemical sciences:** A change of state between solid and liquid can be caused by adding or removing heat (Year 3) Natural and processed materials have a range of physical properties that can influence their use (Year 4)	✓		✓	✓	Statistics and Probability Measurement and Geometry	**General Capabilities:** Literacy, Numeracy, Information and Communication Technology (ICT) Capability, Critical and Creative Thinking

PLAN AN ATTRACTIVE BUS SHELTER

→ INTRODUCTION

Buses are a popular form of transport in many countries. Some services run frequently and others less regularly. Some bus routes have bus shelters along the way to protect passengers from bad weather and to provide a place to sit while they are waiting.

This investigation provides students with the opportunity to consider the needs of others, especially elderly people, when using public transport. They are challenged to create a bus shelter that is practical and inexpensive. They explore the properties of different materials and consider the importance of strong structures in their designs.

This task could be differentiated to consider the needs of specific passengers, such as someone in a wheelchair, or a parent with a small child.

THE CHALLENGE

Your elderly neighbour often catches a bus to see his sister. He sometimes waits for 30 minutes at the bus stop. The bus stop has no seating or shelter. The local council is thinking about building a bus shelter but hasn't decided on a design.

Your challenge is to convince the council to build a simple bus shelter that meets the needs of local people. The design should use as few materials and pieces as possible. You should focus on simple shapes and the users' needs. As part of your investigation, you will learn how the physical properties of different materials affect their use.

KEY UNDERSTANDINGS

- Different materials have different properties.
- The properties of a material affect its use.
- Properties such as weather resistance, durability, strength and flexibility are important when building small outdoor structures.

KEY SKILLS

- Make careful observations, learning about how bus shelters are constructed and some of the features that are included.
- Think about the needs of other people, by interviewing others.
- Choose the best materials for a task.
- Choose the best shapes for your design.
- Transform ideas into something that can be seen – discuss, write, draw and build ideas.

KEY VOCABULARY

durability – ability to last

flexibility – ability of something to bend without breaking

property – feature of a material, such as strength or ability to change shape

resistance – ability to not be affected by something else, such as rain or sunshine

KEY ACTIONS

- Interview people about their experiences.
- Find out about different types of bus shelters.
- Explore properties of different materials.
- Design a bus shelter and pitch it to the local council.

→ OVERVIEW OF STAGES

TUNE IN:

Students consider their responses to different weather conditions; they will explore issues relating to human exposure to high temperatures, wind and rain. Students explore properties of different materials and find out about the best shapes to use to create strong structures.

EMPATHISE

Students find out about bus travellers' experiences at bus stops. They observe and research different types of bus shelters.

DEFINE

Students analyse the results of their interviews and observations. They gather information about the needs of different people who may need to wait for a bus, particularly elderly people. Students decide on the most important features to include and create a list of things to include in their bus shelter design.

IDEATE

Students come up with creative ideas for using different materials and shapes to create a useful, attractive and inexpensive bus shelter.

PROTOTYPE

Students choose two ideas to develop further and prototype. These may include drawing and constructing.

TEST

Students test the design of their bus shelter by asking for feedback from peers and bus travellers. They make changes to their designs based on the feedback and reviews.

SHARE AND EVALUATE:

Students create their final design as well as a short pitch to promote their design. They share their designs and evaluate both their own and others' solutions.

→ SUGGESTED SCHEDULE

LESSON	STAGE
1–4	**Tune in:** Find out about issues relating to human exposure to different weather conditions; explore properties of different materials; find out about the best shapes to use to create strong structures
5–7	**Empathise:** Interview others to find out about bus travellers' experiences at bus stops; observe and research different types of bus shelters; write in journal
8–9	**Define:** Analyse results of the survey and observation; gather information about the needs of different people who use buses; determine the most important features to include and create a design brief; write in journal
10–11	**Ideate:** Come up with creative ideas for using different materials and shapes to create a useful, attractive and inexpensive bus shelter; write in journal
12–16	**Prototype** and **Test:** Develop two ideas, including drawing and constructing designs; write in journal
17–20	**Share and evaluate:** Provide time to complete the final design; create a short pitch to promote design; share final designs; evaluate self and others

→ CURRICULUM LINKS

SCIENCE

YEAR	STRAND	SUB-STRAND AND CONTENT
4	Science Understanding	Chemical sciences: • Natural and processed materials have a range of physical properties that can influence their use
3 & 4	Science as a Human Endeavour	Nature and development of science: • Science involves making predictions and describing patterns and relationships
	Science Inquiry Skills	Questioning and predicting Planning and conducting Processing and analysing data and information Communicating

TECHNOLOGIES

YEAR	STRAND	CONTENT
3 & 4	Design and Technologies Knowledge and Understanding	• Investigate the suitability of materials, systems, components, tools and equipment for a range of purposes
		• Recognise the role of people in design and technologies occupations and explore factors, including sustainability, that impact on the design of solutions to meet community needs
	Design and Technologies Processes and Production Skills	• Select and use materials, components, tools, equipment and techniques and use safe work practices to make designed solutions • Generate, develop and communicate design ideas and decisions using appropriate technical terms and graphical representation techniques

MATHEMATICS

YEAR	STRAND	SUB-STRAND AND CONTENT
3	Measurement and Geometry	Using units of measurement: • Measure, order and compare objects using familiar metric units of length, mass and capacity Shape: • Make models of three-dimensional objects and describe key features
4	Measurement and Geometry	Using units of measurement: • Use scaled instruments to measure and compare lengths, masses, capacities and temperatures

This investigation also links to the General Capabilities:

- Literacy
- Numeracy
- Information and Communication Technology (ICT) Capability
- Critical and Creative Thinking.

This investigation also links to the Cross-Curriculum Priority of Sustainability (if a recyclable materials component is incorporated).

→ ASSESSMENT

The following resources are provided for assessing students at different stages of the STEM investigations:

- Generic reproducible 1 (Key vocabulary table), for assessing understanding of vocabulary
- Generic reproducible 2 (Self-evaluation), for student self-evaluation of the learning process
- Generic reproducible 3 (Responding to the investigation)
- Generic reproducible 5 (Design thinking assessment rubric), for evaluating student engagement in the design thinking stages
- Learning journal templates 1, 2, 3 and 4, incorporating student reflection and evaluation.

→ GETTING READY FOR THE INVESTIGATION

You can prepare yourself and students for this STEM investigation in the following ways:

- Identify groups of students who will work well together. Organise the class into pairs.
- Review the **Key science knowledge** that supports this investigation, and look at the **Useful links**.
- Investigate the **Useful apps**.
- Gather materials for the science activities about properties and structures during the Tune-in session.
- Create some visualisation passages about hot weather, wet weather and windy weather.
- Collect pictures of different buildings that show different shapes in their design (see **Useful links**).
- Start collecting additional materials for prototyping (as shown on the **Materials needed** list).
- Determine where prototypes will be kept.
- Create a wall space where students can share their ideas in the Ideate stage.
- Start thinking about:
  - » sourcing information about bus shelters, including a bank of pictures (see **Useful links**)
  - » inviting someone to speak about materials, structures and/or public transport
  - » making connections with a community organisation, local council or public transport organisation
  - » finding people in the school community who travel by bus who would be willing to be interviewed, particularly elderly people if possible
  - » gathering a panel of advisors or mentors to assist students when testing their designs
  - » time constraints for the task
  - » how, when and where the designs will be shared and evaluated.

USEFUL APPS

- App for creating interactive links (for example, between descriptions, videos, images and websites and a main image), such as ThingLink
- App for creating semantic maps (links between different words and/or concepts), such as Popplet
- App for creating multimedia presentations, such as Adobe Spark Video (via a teacher-created class account), Prezi or iMovie
- App for drawing shapes, inserting images and making annotations or adding to the inserted image, such as DrawIsland
- App for sharing ideas, thoughts, questions and images, such as Padlet or Lino
- App for engaging in collaborative tasks, such as OneNote Class Notebook or SharePoint
- App for modelling, such as SketchUp

USEFUL LINKS

- Pictures of iconic buildings, such as at mea.digital/sm100
- Information and guidelines for bus shelters, such as at mea.digital/sm101, mea.digital/sm107
- Sample bus shelter survey, such as at mea.digital/sm102
- Information and pictures about unusual bus shelters, such as at mea.digital/sm104
- Information about sustainable bus shelters, such as at mea.digital/sm105
- Video showing a bus shelter entertaining commuters, such as at mea.digital/sm106

RESOURCES PROVIDED

- Generic reproducibles 1, 2, 3, 5, 6, 12
- Reproducibles 1.1, 1.2, 1.3
- Learning journal templates 1, 2, 3, 4

MATERIALS NEEDED

- Recycled materials, such as assorted cardboard boxes, cardboard offcuts, tubes, string, ribbon
- Scissors
- Paperclips
- Straws
- Droppers
- Water
- Weights
- Staplers and staples
- Tape – different widths, strengths, materials
- PVA glue
- Hot glue guns and glue (optional)
- Materials for exploring properties, such as plastic, aluminium, metals
- Drinking glasses (e.g. plastic shot glasses)
- Cardboard and coloured paper
- Transparent plastic

Hot glue guns can be dangerous. Make sure students are supervised at all times.

KEY SCIENCE KNOWLEDGE

This section provides an overview of the key science concepts and vocabulary needed for this unit.

STRONG SHAPES

Different geometric shapes can be used to create outdoor structures. When shapes are exposed to different forces, they need to be able to remain standing.

Triangles are the strongest geometric shape. The Egyptian pyramids have a triangular structure. Triangles can be seen in bridges around the world, such as the Sydney Harbour Bridge and Golden Gate Bridge. Another strong structure is the cylinder. It was used structurally in ancient Greek buildings such as the Acropolis, many of which are still standing. Modern buildings use combinations of different shapes for strength and visual appeal.

Almost 7500 triangular panes of glass were used in the construction of the Gherkin in London.

A square can be made stronger by adding a triangular supporting framework called a truss. Bridges and other buildings contain triangular trusses to support beams and other elements.

The best bus shelters are those that are designed to meet the needs of users.

PROPERTIES OF BUILDING MATERIALS

Materials have different **properties**, which include:

- strength – ability to withstand certain forces
- hardness – ease with which a material can be scratched
- **flexibility** – ability to change shape without breaking
- being waterproof – ability to repel water.

Materials can be natural (made from plants or animals) or synthetic (made from chemicals). Common materials include metals, plastics, glass, wood and fabrics. The properties of these materials determine how they can be best used.

The design of a building is very important, and so is the choice of materials. If a structure needs to be strong, then materials such as wood and steel are often used. If a structure needs to be flexible, then materials such as plastic and aluminium are chosen for their ability to be bent easily. Different features of a building may require different materials.

It is important to consider the properties of materials when designing an outside structure. It needs to have **durability**, and **resistance** to extreme temperatures and weather conditions as well as to human activity.

KEY VOCABULARY

durability – ability to last, for example in extreme conditions
flexibility – ability of something to bend without breaking
property – feature of a material, such as strength or ability to change shape
resistance – ability to not be affected by something else, such as rain or sunshine

TUNE IN

1. Ask students to complete **Key vocabulary table (Generic reproducible 1)** using the key vocabulary for this unit. This reproducible will also be used at the end of the unit, to demonstrate changes in understanding.
2. Engage in a visualisation task with students. First, ask them to close their eyes and imagine a hot day. They could think about being at the beach, school or at home. Guide them to imagine the temperature, the effect it has on their skin and how they are feeling.
3. Have students describe the feeling to a partner.
4. Repeat the visualisation task twice, considering a very windy day and then wet weather.
5. Provide students with **Generic reproducible 7 (Double bubble)**. Have them compare similarities and differences of two weather types (such as hot day and windy day). Have students share their ideas.
6. Students need to understand about the properties of different building materials and strong shapes for construction before beginning the challenge.

ACTIVITY 1: STRONG SHAPES

1. Provide students with paper, tape, scissors, straws, paperclips and a book.
2. Challenge students to build a freestanding structure that will support the book.
3. Have students discuss their observations.
4. Set up a gallery walk of different buildings and highlight some of the shapes that have been used in the buildings, including triangular trusses, if visible. Explain that the triangle is the strongest shape and the cylinder or tube is also a strong shape. Some good examples include Sydney Harbour Bridge, Hagia Sophia, the Acropolis, the Great Pyramids and Centre Georges Pompidou.
5. Provide students with the opportunity to create a different structure to support the book. Students could find out the maximum number of books their structure can hold.
6. Discuss students' designs, highlighting the shapes they have incorporated.

TOP TIP!

Encourage students to photograph the different structures they build in Activity 1. This can be referred to later when they are designing the bus shelter.

ACTIVITY 2: PROPERTIES OF MATERIALS

1. Set up and provide students with time to complete each of the following three activities. Discuss the different test designs and the results.

Strength:

a. Have students design a simple test to explore the strength of different materials such as plastic, wood and metal. This could involve materials spanning two blocks and then weights made of similar materials being placed on top (under supervision) until the material being tested breaks or bends.
b. Provide them with **Reproducible 1.1 (Materials and their properties)** to record their results and summarise their observations in a couple of sentences.

Durability:

a. Provide students with different materials such as metal, plastic and wood.
b. Ask them to design a simple test to see how durable the materials are. This could include tearing the materials or scratching them.
c. Provide them with **Reproducible 1.1** for planning and recording.

Resistance to water (waterproof):

a. Provide students with droppers, water and a selection of materials including plastic, wood, metal and cardboard.
b. Have students design a simple test to see which materials are the most waterproof.
c. Students use **Reproducible 1.1** to plan their test and record their results.

7. Introduce the STEM investigation and challenge to the students. Provide them with the student card and read the information together.
8. Introduce the design thinking process by reviewing the stages on the student card. Explain that students will keep a journal about their learning at the different stages of the design.

USEFUL APPS/LINKS

- Pictures of iconic buildings, such as at mea.digital/sm100

→ EMPATHISE

During the Empathise stage of the design thinking process, students focus on finding out about different points of view. To empathise with others, they need to research some of the points of view associated with waiting at bus stops. This includes finding out about different types of bus shelters. Students will take notes, ask questions, draw diagrams and take photos where relevant.

ACTIVITY 1: INTERVIEWS ABOUT BUS STOPS

1. Have students design some interview questions to ask bus travellers about their experiences at bus stops with and without bus shelters.
2. Have students consider:
   - » when it is important to have a bus shelter at a bus stop
   - » what features all bus shelters should have
   - » issues for specific groups such as people who are elderly, or who have a disability or a young family
   - » weather-related events, such as rain.
3. After students have created their interview questions, have them practise interviewing each other before they collect information more formally.
4. If possible, arrange for some parents, friends or other members of the community to visit the school and be interviewed by the students. It may also be possible to interview via teleconferencing. Some students could interview family or friends at home.

PROMPTS

- Do all bus stops in your area have bus shelters?
- What were some of the most common features of the bus shelters you found out about?
- What was one interesting feature you saw?
- Do bus travellers think it is important for bus stops to have bus shelters?
- What were some of the materials used to build bus shelters?

MORE VOCABULARY

- empathise – understand and consider another person or group's point of view
- point of view – an opinion, attitude or judgement considered in a particular way

ACTIVITY 2: OBSERVING BUS SHELTERS

1. Students observe features of bus shelters, incorporating a visit to local bus shelters and online research. If possible, arrange for groups of students to visit nearby bus shelters and note the dimensions, shapes, features and materials. They should also note how many people can fit into the shelter. Alternatively, guide students in their online research.
2. Provide students with **Reproducible 1.2 (Features of bus shelters)** to record the information they collect about bus shelters. Alternatively, they could use a collaborative app such as OneNote Class Notebook or SharePoint. Remind them to include links to sources.

JOURNAL TIP

Ask students to complete **Learning journal template 1 (Empathise page)** while they are doing the different tasks. Remind them to date their notes and include photos of relevant information or pictures.

USEFUL APPS/LINKS

- App for creating shared documents, such as OneNote Class Notebook or SharePoint
- App for sharing ideas, thoughts, questions and images, such as Padlet
- Website with information about bus shelters, such as at mea.digital/sm107

ASSESSMENT

This stage of the design thinking process offers opportunities to observe students collecting information, developing questions, and recording their notes and thinking in their journal.

TOP TIP! Set up a Padlet for students to collect images of interesting bus shelters from around the world.

EMPATHISE | DEFINE | IDEATE | PROTOTYPE | TEST

→ DEFINE

The main focus of this stage of the design thinking process is to reframe the challenge. The initial challenge is quite open, so at this stage students learn how to define what needs to be done. This includes noting insights that have been generated.

ACTIVITY 1: CONSIDER INFORMATION FROM INTERVIEWS

1. Have students consider the information collected about bus stops and bus shelters.
2. Show students how to collect the information using a spreadsheet.
3. Differentiate between numerical (quantitative) data, such as the number of people who thought that a seat should be provided at all bus shelters, and descriptive (qualitative) data, such as information about the key issues for bus travellers.
4. Have students create a graph or infographic to share the results of the interviews.

ACTIVITY 2: CONSIDER INFORMATION ABOUT BUS SHELTERS

1. Review the information collected about bus shelters locally and around the world.
2. Identify the common features of the bus shelters, such as materials used, provision of seats (or not), types of shapes incorporated in the design of the structure, and size.

Students can update **Learning journal template 2 (Define page)**.

JOURNAL TIP

Discuss the term 'insight' and explain that it relates to something students have learned from the information gathered through research or excursions. You could refer to **Learning journal template 2**.

MORE VOCABULARY

- define – state the meaning of something
- insight – an accurate understanding of someone or something
- point of view – an opinion, attitude or judgement considered in a particular way

ACTIVITY 3: CREATE A DESIGN BRIEF

1. Have groups of students make a list of important considerations, having considered the information collected from the interviews and initial research.
2. Write each consideration on a separate piece of paper. Ask students to rank them and discuss their rankings. They should choose their top five.
3. Have two groups of students share their top five considerations. As a combined group, they then decide on four key considerations to be included in the bus shelter design brief. These are shared with the class.
4. Have the class make a final decision about what must be included in the bus shelter design, such as a seat and roof, and which features are optional, such as side walls and timetables. Use **Reproducible 1.3 (Bus shelter design brief)** to record the compulsory features, optional features, time constraints and any materials constraints. It should also include information about the final pitch, and whether or not it will be created using an app, recorded or presented live.

PROMPTS

- How will you decide on the most important features to include?
- How will you make sure that you have thought about the information collected in the interviews?
- Which features do you think should be optional? Why?
- What other information do you need?

USEFUL APPS/LINKS

- App for creating spreadsheets, such as Excel or Numbers, or an interactive table, such as Google Docs
- App for engaging in collaborative tasks, such as OneNote Class Notebook

EMPATHISE | DEFINE | IDEATE | PROTOTYPE | TEST

→ IDEATE

The Ideate stage of the design thinking process is all about generating lots of ideas. Students need to be flexible in their thinking and be able to move beyond obvious ideas. At this stage, ideas are not judged, just generated and gathered.

ACTIVITY 1: GENERATE BUS SHELTER IDEAS

1. Provide students with an app such as Popplet or Kidspiration to help them collate and organise their ideas, or show them how to create a concept map. If using a pen or pencil, have them use one colour for their original ideas. If using an app, have them choose one colour for their ideas.
2. As students are generating ideas about bus shelters, have them group them according to materials used, shapes in the design, interesting or unusual features (inclusions) and ways of sharing this information with the council.
3. After students have created their ideas, provide them with time to look at other groups' ideas.
4. Students return to their original collection of ideas and add further ideas, taking inspiration from other groups. Have them use a different colour to make it easy to see their thought progression.

ACTIVITY 2: CONSIDER FUN BUS SHELTERS

1. Watch a video about people interacting with bus shelters (see **Useful apps/links**).
2. Have students think about why it might be worth considering how to make bus shelters interesting and perhaps even entertaining.
3. Have students return to their original collection of ideas and add to it using a third colour.
4. Students can update **Learning journal template 3 (Ideate page)**.

PROMPTS

- What sorts of materials might you use in the bus shelter?
- Which materials will be waterproof?
- Which materials will be strong?
- Which materials would best suit the community space?
- How could bus travellers be entertained while they are waiting?

MORE VOCABULARY

- feedback – information about, for example, a person's performance or the design of a product, which can be used to make improvements
- ideate – generate many ideas without making judgements about the ideas

JOURNAL TIP

When choosing three ideas to include in the journal, try to choose three ideas that use different materials or focus on different aspects of the challenge.

USEFUL APPS/LINKS

- Information about sustainable bus shelters, such as at mea.digital/sm105
- Video showing a bus shelter prank entertaining commuters, such as at mea.digital/sm106
- App for creating semantic maps (links between different words and/or concepts), such as Popplet or Kidspiration

ASSESSMENT

At the Ideate stage, assessment could include observations about the number and diversity of student ideas, and their ability to provide feedback and create additional ideas. Reflection in the journal should provide an insight into some of the reasoning behind student choices.

→ PROTOTYPE

At this stage of the design thinking process, students are asked to create a physical prototype of a solution. It is the stage where students need to get their ideas out of their heads and presented in a way that engages other students and helps them to understand the concept. When students create, it helps them to think and solve problems and disagreements. Students can role-play, make a storyboard or use sticky notes when they prototype. The most important feature is that viewers can interact with whatever is produced.

Encourage students to photograph or film during the Prototype and Test stages. This information can be used to show the learning behind the design thinking process in action.

ACTIVITY 1: DRAW AND BUILD THE BASIC STRUCTURE

1. Have students draw their initial structure, highlighting shapes they have incorporated.
2. Students then build the first design using cardboard or construction materials.
3. Have students consider the basic structure and whether or not it will be strong.
4. Students continue prototyping the basic structure until they are happy with the result.

ACTIVITY 2: DEVELOP ADDITIONAL FEATURES

1. After students have decided on their basic structure, they develop additional features. Have students refer to the design brief to check which features are compulsory and which are optional.
2. When designing the additional features, students need to consider how the features will be incorporated into the original structure. They should also be thinking about the types of materials that would need to be used if a full-scale model was built by the council.

Ask students to fill in the Prototype part of **Learning journal template 4 (Prototype and test page)**. See the **Journal tip** for further student guidance.

PROMPTS

- Have you included all the compulsory features?
- How will you decide which optional features to include?
- Who will you ask to give feedback about your design?

MORE VOCABULARY

- feedback – information about, for example, a person's performance or the design of a product, which can be used to make improvements
- prototype – an initial version of a model of a product or process that is used to develop a final model

TOP TIP!

Students may add labels to prototypes to explain some of the main features. Photographing and annotating pictures of prototypes can be useful.

When asking for feedback, students could ask each other some of the following questions:

- What is the most important feature of your design?
- Do you think that your design could be easily built?
- What materials would be used in your design?
- What do you need to change? How might you do this?

JOURNAL TIP

Remind students to highlight the main features of their prototype, including the types of materials used for each part. If students are creating an electronic journal, they can insert a photo of their prototype and annotate it.

USEFUL APPS/LINKS

- App for taking photographs or video, such as Adobe Spark Video or iMovie

ASSESSMENT

Observe students as they make changes to their designs. Are they able to consider feedback, make modifications and move rapidly through this process, or do they have difficulties with holding on to an idea and accepting feedback?

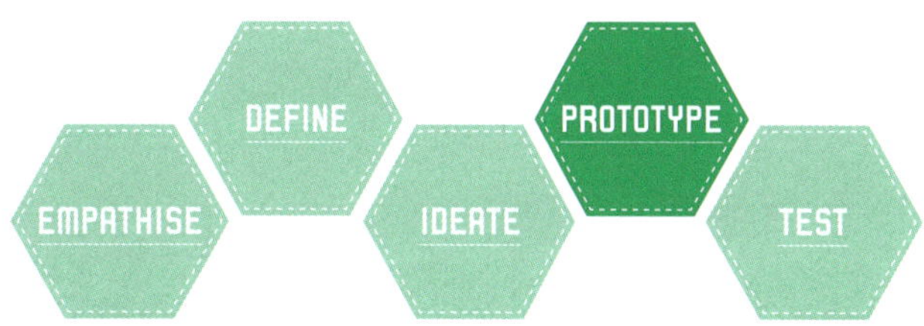

→ TEST

At this stage of the design thinking process, students test their prototype to see how it meets the criteria in the challenge.

ACTIVITY: TEST FEEDBACK

1. Have students gather feedback about the prototypes. Provide them with **Generic reproducible 12 (Prototype and test)** to record the ideas.
2. Have others consider how stable the design appears, whether the compulsory features have been included and which optional features have been added. Have them also discuss the recommended materials.
3. Students continue to cycle through the Prototype and Test stages until they have completed their design.

Ask students to fill in **Learning journal template 4 (Prototype and test page)**. See the **Journal tip** for further student guidance.

PROMPTS

- Does the prototype meet bus travellers' needs?
- Do features need to be added or removed?
- Do you need to change the types of materials?

MORE VOCABULARY

- evaluate – assess something, perhaps considering what worked and what didn't
- feature – a specific aspect of something, such as size, shape, colour, quality
- feedback – information about, for example, a person's performance or the design of a product, which can be used to make improvements
- prototype – an initial version of a model of a product or process that is used to develop a final model
- review – consider an idea, process or product and assess what works and what needs to be changed

JOURNAL TIP

Ask students to think about why it is important to test their ideas before they build their final design.

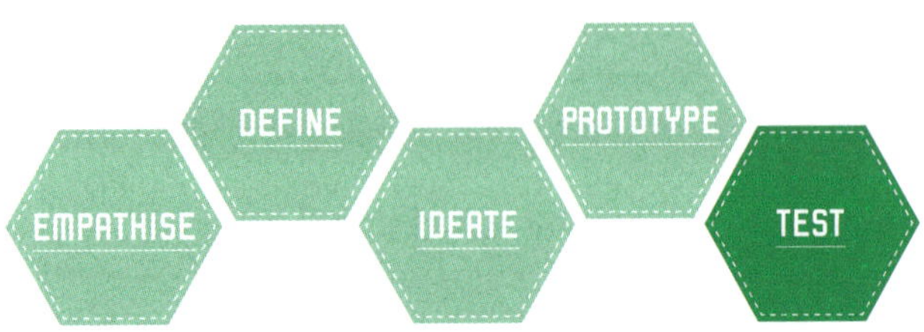

→ SHARE AND EVALUATE

At this stage of the investigation, students are provided with an opportunity to share their final design, as well as the processes involved in the investigation. Students evaluate their learning journals as well as their solutions.

ACTIVITY 1: FINALISE DESIGNS

1. Allow students to finalise their designs. They should also create a 30–60 second pitch for the council to promote their bus shelter design. A multimedia app such as Adobe Spark Video can be used by students for the pitch. Remind them to highlight the key features, materials used, ease of construction and aesthetics.
2. Set up a time for other people to see the different designs and provide feedback. This could include some experts from the local council, an architecture firm or public transport organisation.
3. Students should include their learning journals with the display so others can see the different stages of the design process.

ACTIVITY 2: EVALUATE AND GIVE FEEDBACK

1. Provide students with **Generic reproducible 2 (Self-evaluation)**.
2. Provide participants with tokens or stickers so they can vote for their favourite design or create an online survey with photos of the different designs for others to vote on.

ASSESSMENT

Ask students to again complete **Generic reproducible 1 (Key vocabulary table)** using the key vocabulary for this unit. Compare their table with the one they completed at the Tune-in stage, to demonstrate changes in understanding.

Students complete **Generic reproducible 3 (Responding to the investigation)**. Compare their responses to their responses to **Generic reproducible 2**.

Teachers complete **Generic reproducible 5 (Design thinking assessment rubric)** for each student. Students compare the feedback they are given by the teacher with their self-assessment of how they used the design thinking process to solve problems **(Generic reproducible 3)**.

TUNE IN

STEM INVESTIGATIONS

Name: ....

Date: ....

Think about the property you are testing and then complete the tables.

Use this table to plan your test.

Property being tested:
Materials you are testing:
Steps for your test:

Use this table to record your observations.

Material	**Observations**

REPRODUCIBLE 1.2 FEATURES OF BUS SHELTERS

EMPATHISE

STEM INVESTIGATIONS

Name: ....

Date: ....

Find out about bus shelters around the world. Learn about the shapes in their design and the materials they use. Find out about some of their interesting features.

Write your notes in the table.

Bus shelter description (and image)	**Location**	**Main features**	**Source of image or information**

Write one or two sentences to summarise what you found out.

STEM Investigations, MP, ISBN 978 1 4202 4319 2 © Macmillan Science and Education Australia 2018

Name: ....

Date: ....

Create a design brief for the class. Use this template to write all the things that need to be included or thought about.

The aim of this investigation is to design a bus shelter.

Your bus shelter design must include the following features:
Optional features:
Maximum size of model:

You will need to create a pitch that is 30–60 seconds long. The aim of this is to convince others that your bus shelter is the best one to build.

You may present your pitch in one of the following ways. Choose an option and write any extra details.

- ☐ Multimedia presentation
- ☐ Podcast
- ☐ Live presentation
- ☐ Other:

STEM Investigations, MP, ISBN 978 1 4202 4319 2 © Macmillan Science and Education Australia 2018

DESIGN A PLAYGROUND FOR PLAYING AND LEARNING

→ INTRODUCTION

Children experience forces and use simple machines every day. Most of the time they do not realise this because they don't have the language and scientific knowledge to identify and discuss their experiences. Playgrounds can act as a science laboratory, giving children experiences in push, pull and twist forces and simple machines as they play.

In this STEM investigation, students will learn about basic forces and simple machines. They will be challenged to apply their learning, together with the mathematical skills of measuring and mapping, to creating an exciting, engaging and instructional playground. They explore the perspectives of others and consider the range of play needs of students from Foundation to Year 6.

This investigation allows for the diverse learning needs of EAL, remedial and extension students as they relate personal experiences to the physics under investigation.

THE CHALLENGE

Your school principal has decided that the school needs a new playground, and she has announced a student competition. To win, you will need to design the most exciting playground you can imagine. There is one catch: the playground has to teach children about science.

Your challenge is to design a playground that will teach children about the forces of push and pull as they play. You will need to create simple models of your equipment and also plan the play space. As part of this investigation, you will learn all about simple machines and forces.

KEY UNDERSTANDINGS

- We can move things by applying a force such as a push or a pull.
- Push or pull forces can happen with contact or from a distance.
- Forces change the speed, direction and shape of an object.
- Simple machines are all around us.

KEY VOCABULARY

contact force – a force that acts on an object by touching it

force – a push or pull on an object that makes it move, or change direction or shape

non-contact force – a force that acts on another object without touching it

simple machine – one of six tools that make pushing or pulling an object easier

KEY SKILLS

- Identify contact forces and forces that work from a distance, including generating force diagrams to share understanding.
- Identify and create simple machines, such as levers and inclined planes, correctly identifying the load and the effort.
- Measure an area accurately, using correct measurement units and tools.
- Draw simple maps and plans by hand or using digital technologies such as SketchUp.

KEY ACTIONS

- Identify basic forces and simple machines.
- Investigate a playground and identify the best equipment.
- Survey other students.
- Design a fun and educational playground.
- Share your ideas.

OVERVIEW OF STAGES

TUNE IN:

Students learn about push and pull forces, including contact and non-contact forces. They then explore the six simple machines, and identify these concepts in their school environment.

EMPATHISE

Students will explore a new playground and apply their knowledge of forces and simple machines by creating simple sketches of the playground that illustrate these elements. They survey other students to identify popular play equipment.

DEFINE

Students create a short list of appropriate playground equipment that promote learning. With guidance, they survey and map an area of the school proposed for the location of the new playground.

IDEATE

Students brainstorm ideas for playgrounds and create brainstorm sheets showing the elements they believe will make a successful playground. They seek peer feedback on their proposals and refine their designs to reflect the feedback.

PROTOTYPE

Students create a bird's-eye view design and create a three-dimensional series of models of their play equipment. They also create a sign, to sit beside the equipment, that simply explains the forces and simple machines involved. They seek feedback from peers to assist them to improve their arrangement and final design.

TEST

Having finalised their prototype, students seek feedback initially from their peers for evaluation of their incorporation of forces and simple machines. They then seek feedback from the students surveyed during the Empathise stage for the functionality of their design.

SHARE AND EVALUATE:

Students create a final proposal, incorporating reflections on the design journey, for presentation to their peers and the school principal, leadership team, school council or student leadership team.

SUGGESTED SCHEDULE

LESSON	STAGE
1–3	**Tune in:** Learn about forces and simple machines, and identify these within the school environment
4–5	**Empathise:** Explore forces and simple machines outside the school; learn about own and others' perspectives about play equipment
6–8	**Define:** Develop an understanding of relevant play equipment; measure and map the proposed area for a new playground
9–11	**Ideate:** Develop and refine ideas for a new playground; write in journal
12–14	**Prototype** and **Test:** Conduct prototype development and evaluate designs; write in journal
15–17	**Share and evaluate:** Share and evaluate final designs; pitch ideas to key stakeholders

→ CURRICULUM LINKS

SCIENCE

YEAR	STRAND	SUB-STRAND AND CONTENT
4	Science Understanding	Physical sciences: • Forces can be exerted by one object on another through direct contact or from a distance
3 & 4	Science as a Human Endeavour	Nature and development of science: • Science involves making predictions and describing patterns and relationships

TECHNOLOGIES

YEAR	STRAND	CONTENT
3 & 4	Digital Technologies Knowledge and Understanding	• Identify and explore a range of digital systems with peripheral devices for different purposes, and transmit different types of data • Recognise different types of data and explore how the same data can be represented in different ways
	Digital Technologies Processes and Production Skills	• Collect, access and present different types of data using simple software to create information and solve problems
	Design and Technologies Knowledge and Understanding	• Recognise the role of people in design and technologies occupations and explore factors, including sustainability, that impact on the design of products, services and environments to meet community needs • Investigate how forces and the properties of materials affect the behaviour of a product or system • Investigate the suitability of materials, systems, components, tools and equipment for a range of purposes
3 & 4*	Design and Technologies Processes and Production Skills	• Critique needs or opportunities for designing and explore and test a variety of materials, components, tools and equipment and the techniques needed to produce designed solutions • Generate, develop and communicate design ideas and decisions using appropriate technical terms and graphical representation techniques • Evaluate design ideas, processes and solutions based on criteria for success developed with guidance and including care for the environment

* If students are making a model of their product.

MATHEMATICS

YEAR	STRAND	SUB-STRAND AND CONTENT
4	Measurement and Geometry	Using units of measurement: • Use scaled instruments to measure and compare lengths, masses, capacities and temperatures • Compare objects using familiar metric units of area and volume Location and transformation: • Use simple scales, legends and directions to interpret information contained in basic maps
	Statistics and Probability	Data representation and interpretation: • Select and trial methods for data collection, including survey questions and recording sheets

This investigation also links to the General Capabilities:

- Literacy
- Numeracy
- Information and Communication Technology (ICT) Capability
- Critical and Creative Thinking.

→ ASSESSMENT

The following resources are provided for assessing students at different stages of the STEM investigations:

- Generic reproducible 1 (Key vocabulary table), for assessing understanding of vocabulary
- Generic reproducible 2 (Self-evaluation), for student self-evaluation of the learning process
- Generic reproducible 3 (Responding to the investigation)
- Generic reproducible 5 (Design thinking assessment rubric), for evaluating student engagement in the design thinking stages
- Generic reproducible 10 (Group task organiser), for assessing cooperative learning strategies
- Learning journal templates 1, 2, 3 and 4, incorporating student reflection and evaluation.

GETTING READY FOR THE INVESTIGATION

You can prepare yourself and students for this STEM investigation in the following ways:

- Identify a suitable space for the students to use as their location for the new playground. This may be an existing play area or a new space to explore. Consider a space that is large enough to support some play equipment, but not so large that the final design becomes too challenging for the students to map.
- Locate a safe space to conduct the Tune-in activities.
- Watch the suggested simple machines video clip or select another and decide on the best teaching methodology for your class.
- Conduct your own treasure hunt for simple machines in your school, locating at least one example of each to share with the students.
- If you have ready access to some Hot Wheels cars or similar products, the various racetracks and other equipment can be used alongside this investigation for imaginative play. This allows for some spontaneous discussion about forces and simple machines through play and verbal interaction.
- Investigate a suitable local playground to explore in the Empathise stage. Many local council playgrounds offer different equipment for the students to observe.
- Arrange a time for the principal, school leadership team, school council or student leaders to review student design and ideas.

USEFUL APPS

- App or website for creating online surveys, such as Typeform
- App for mapping, such as SketchUp or DrawIsland
- App or program for note-taking using text, drawings, images, weblinks and audio, such as Notability or OneNote Class Notebook
- App for creating videos, such as Adobe Spark Video (via a teacher-created class account)

USEFUL LINKS

- Video clips explaining forces, simple machines and gravity, such as at mea.digital/sm1, mea.digital/sm2, mea.digital/sm3
- Local playground listings, such as at mea.digital/sm4
- Articles about the jigsaw strategy, such as at mea.digital/sm5
- Examples of push and pull forces, such as at mea.digital/sm6, mea.digital/sm7
- Simple machines explanations, such as at mea.digital/sm8, mea.digital/sm9, (for more capable readers) mea.digital/sm10
- Articles for teachers about simple machines, such as at mea.digital/sm11, mea.digital/sm12
- An additional Tune-in activity for exploring forces in a playground, such as at mea.digital/sm13

RESOURCES PROVIDED

- Generic reproducibles 1, 2, 3, 5, 10
- Reproducibles 2.1, 2.2, 2.3, 2.4, 2.5
- Learning journal templates 1, 2, 3, 4

MATERIALS NEEDED

- Drinking straw (for every student)
- Ping-pong balls (1 per pair)
- Paper straws
- Selection of soft sports balls
- Class camera
- Measuring equipment such as trundle wheels, long measuring tape
- Grid paper
- Large brainstorming paper
- Small whiteboards and markers
- Sticky notes (about half a pack per group)
- Basic modelling materials, such as straws, icypole sticks, plasticine, toothpicks and recycled modelling materials

KEY SCIENCE KNOWLEDGE

This section provides an overview of the key science concepts and vocabulary needed for this unit.

Force is the term used in science to explain the actions of pushing, pulling and twisting. Forces can be **contact forces** (such as using a door or a screwdriver) or **non-contact forces** (at a distance – such as gravity and the attraction of some metals to magnets). In this investigation, the push and pull forces will be investigated; however, some students may ask about twist force and so this is included where relevant.

IDENTIFYING FORCES

We know a force is acting if there has been an observable change in the shape, speed or direction of an object. Pressure (a push force) can change the shape of an object, such as a raw egg when it is dropped. Pulling a door towards you with more or less force will change the speed at which the door moves. A ball that collides with a wall will change direction. An object that stops another object from moving is also exerting a force.

If there is no winner in a tug-of-war match, then each team must have pulled with equal force – the forces were balanced.

Forces can be marked on a diagram, using arrows to show the direction of movement. A longer arrow is used to indicate a larger force. Forces are balanced when they are equal but from opposing directions – the object of the forces will maintain a constant state.

INERTIA

The force needed to change the movement of an object depends on the object's mass. The resistance to change is called inertia. The greater the mass of an object, the more force or effort is required to change its movement (including its direction). It is easier to roll a tennis ball than to roll a bowling ball. Conversely, the force required to stop a bowling ball is greater than the force to stop a tennis ball.

SIMPLE MACHINES

Simple machines are used to magnify force. This means that less work (effort or energy) can be done to exert a greater force. We use simple machines every day to make our lives easier and there are many examples at home and at school. The six simple machines are a lever, a wheel and axle, an inclined plane, a wedge, a pulley and a screw. Simple machines can be combined into a compound (complex) machine such as a bicycle.

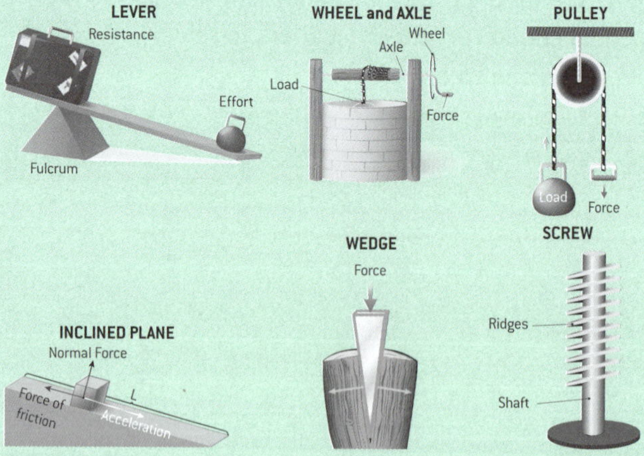

Six simple machines make our everyday lives much easier.

KEY VOCABULARY

contact force – a force that acts on an object by touching it
force – a push or pull on an object that makes it move, or change direction or shape
non-contact force – a force that acts on another object without touching it
simple machine – one of six tools that make pushing or pulling an object easier

TUNE IN

1. Ask students to complete **Generic reproducible 1 (Key vocabulary table)** using the key vocabulary for this unit. This reproducible will also be used at the end of the unit, to demonstrate changes in understanding.
2. Ask a student to step outside the classroom, close the door behind them and come back in again. Ask them how they moved the door. Elicit the words 'push' and 'pull' and discuss how they already know about the two major forces to be investigated. Explain that this is a contact force because the student touched the door to apply force.
3. Watch a video to introduce forces (see **Useful apps/links**). If it is safe to do so, have the students act out the movements of pushing, pulling and twisting. Ask, 'What are the names of the forces we learned about in the video? What were some of the forces we can see in action in a playground? Can you think of some other times we see push and pull forces in action?'

ACTIVITY 1: PUSH, PULL AND BALANCED FORCES

1. Allocate each student a straw, a partner and a ping-pong ball. Explain that they are not to share their straws.
2. Ask students to place the ping-pong balls on the floor and experiment with how they can blow (push) and suck (pull) them around individually and together. Ensure that students can correctly identify push, pull and balanced forces and distinguish between a contact and non-contact force.
3. Summarise the learning by creating a class poster showing forces, using arrows to show the direction and strength of the forces.

ACTIVITY 2: THROWING, DROPPING, ROLLING AND BOUNCING BALLS

1. In pairs or small groups, students can experiment with gently throwing, dropping, rolling and bouncing a soft ball.
2. Have them draw force diagrams in their learning journals to record their observations, using the poster from Activity 1 as a guide.
3. Ask, 'How do you know a force has been applied? How does the strength of the force change the outcome? Is this a contact or non-contact force?'

ACTIVITY 3: LEARNING ABOUT SIMPLE MACHINES

1. Watch and discuss a video to investigate simple machines (see **Useful apps/links**).

ACTIVITY 4: SIMPLE MACHINES TREASURE HUNT

1. Explain that the students will be going on a treasure hunt around the school to locate the six simple machines.
2. Distribute **Reproducible 2.1 (Simple machines treasure hunt)** and explain the activity.
3. Help students to identify at least one example of each.
4. Introduce the challenge and read the student card together. Ask students to think about the equipment they enjoy in playgrounds. Have them consider that the play equipment they identified may represent one or more type of simple machine.
5. Introduce the design thinking process by reviewing the stages on the student card. Explain that students will keep a journal about their learning at the different stages of the design.

TOP TIP! Any playground is a forces laboratory. When students understand push and pull forces and recognise simple machines, they can experiment, discuss and share their learning with rich oral language opportunities.

USEFUL APPS/LINKS

- Video clip to introduce forces, such as at mea.digital/sm1
- Video clip to introduce simple machines, such as at mea.digital/sm2

→ EMPATHISE

During the Empathise stage of the design thinking process, students focus on finding out about different points of view. To understand the play preferences of others, they need to first understand the interests of their peers and then find out more about older and younger students. This includes considering the physical needs and abilities of different age groups.

Students will take notes, sketch, identify forces and simple machines, and survey students from older and younger grades.

ACTIVITY 1: PLAYGROUND EXCURSION

1. Organise an excursion to a local community playground with equipment that is different from that of the school playgrounds (see **Useful apps/links**).
2. Give the students time to play and explore, and then have them work in pairs to identify the forces and simple machines evident in the equipment.
3. Students document their observations in **Reproducible 2.2 (Playground investigation and survey)**, filling in the first three columns.
4. Take photographs of the students playing and of the equipment, to use for Activity 2. Roughly measure and record the dimensions of any equipment likely to be included in student designs and note this for the next stages.

ACTIVITY 2: EQUIPMENT SURVEY

1. Arrange for students to survey students from other year levels to gain an understanding of the preferences of older and younger students.
2. Show the collected photographs to survey subjects and ask about their favourite piece of play equipment. Record their choice in the fourth column of the table on **Reproducible 2.2**, as well as their age and grade.
3. After all grade levels have been surveyed, help students to collate their results as a class to show the most popular to the least popular equipment and then discuss which equipment they think might be both popular and educational.

PROMPTS

- What forces do you think are involved when you play on this piece of equipment? What pushes or pulls can you identify?
- Can you name any simple machines in this equipment?
- Would this be a good piece of equipment for a school playground?
- Would this help students learn about forces and simple machines?

MORE VOCABULARY

- empathise – understand and consider another person or group's point of view
- point of view – an opinion, attitude or judgement considered in a particular way

JOURNAL TIP

Ask students to complete **Learning journal template 1 (Empathise page)** while they are doing the different tasks. Remind them to date their notes and include photos of relevant information or pictures.

USEFUL APPS/LINKS

- Local playground finder website, such as at mea.digital/sm4

ASSESSMENT

This stage of the design thinking process offers opportunities to observe students collecting information, developing questions, and recording their notes and thinking in their journal.

TOP TIP! Don't move too quickly from the play and explore stage of Activity 1 to the written task. This time to explore, discuss and reflect will allow the students to develop oral language and rich experience to guide the rest of the investigation. This is an opportunity to assist those requiring additional language support to name equipment and identify forces.

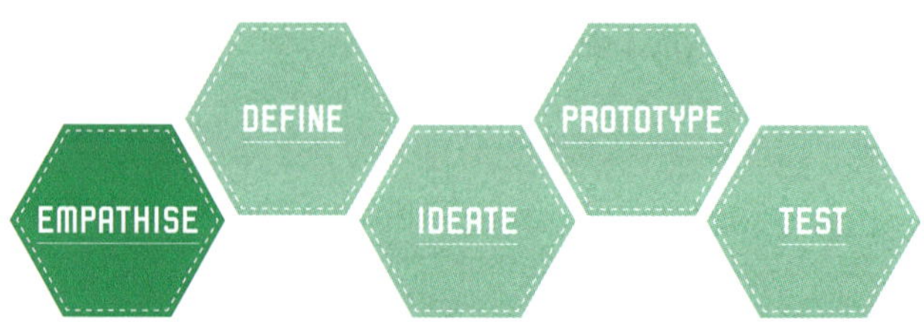

→ DEFINE

The main focus of this stage of the design thinking process is to reframe the challenge. The initial challenge is quite open, so at this stage students learn how to define what needs to be done. This includes noting insights that have been generated.

ACTIVITY 1: RANK EQUIPMENT CHOICES

1. Review the findings of the survey and discuss which equipment is likely to be most effective for teaching students about forces and simple machines, and which is most popular. Consider also any experiences at other playgrounds and on the school's existing equipment.
2. Have students complete **Reproducible 2.3 (Need, want, think about)**. Encourage them to add any other equipment they have enjoyed if they can name the forces and simple machines involved.

ACTIVITY 2: DEFINE THE PLAYGROUND SPACE

1. Explain to students that they are going to create a map (see **Useful apps/links**), using accurate measurements of the proposed playground space. Revise standard measurement units and use of the measuring equipment.
2. Distribute **Reproducible 2.4 (Measure and sketch)**. It might be useful to have this photocopied onto A3 paper if your students are less familiar with mapping and measurement.
3. Have students sketch on the reproducible the space and record the measurements of its perimeter, and any natural features or structures to be included. If appropriate, have them measure the distances relating to the natural features.
4. In the classroom, distribute **Reproducible 2.5 (Create a playground map)**. Have students use their field measurements to create a map of the playground space on it.

Students can update **Learning journal template 2 (Define page)**.

PROMPTS

- Is this equipment going to help students learn about forces and simple machines?
- Is this equipment safe and fun for Foundation to Year 6 students?
- How can we correctly measure the edges or circumference of this space and the area?
- Are there any natural features or structures we need to design the playground around?

MORE VOCABULARY

- define – state the meaning of something
- effective – likely to work in the manner expected
- insight – an accurate understanding of someone or something

JOURNAL TIP

Discuss the term 'insight' and explain that it relates to something students have learned about the people and their responses to the surveys as well as information gathered through research or excursions. You could refer to **Learning journal template 2**.

USEFUL APPS/LINKS

- Mapping software such as SketchUp could be used to create a map of the playground. This is suggested as a learning activity in the Test stage, but a teacher-generated map could help students in need of additional assistance here.

→ IDEATE

The Ideate stage of the design thinking process is all about generating lots of ideas. Students need to be flexible in their thinking and be able to move beyond obvious ideas. At this stage, ideas are not judged, just generated and gathered.

ACTIVITY 1: BRAINSTORM TOGETHER

1. Distribute sticky notes and coloured markers to all students. Follow a creative thinking routine (see **Useful apps/links**) to help generate ideas:
   - List the obvious ideas and stick these on the whiteboard or on a poster.
   - Brainstorm 'hidden' ideas (see **Prompts**).
   - Ask students to share their thinking and observations with a member of a different team.
2. Allow students to create a copy of any sticky note that sparks an idea to bring back to their team for further consideration.
3. Have the students draw or create simple models of all of the equipment in their Need and Want columns in **Reproducible 2.3**. Drawing should be done in their learning journals.

ACTIVITY 2: SYNTHESISE IDEAS

1. Give student teams a large piece of paper, small whiteboards and sticky notes, and have them gather their completed **Reproducibles 2.2** and **2.3**, learning journals and their collections of sticky notes.
2. Using all of the resources, encourage students to create some brainstorm sheets showing the elements they believe will make a successful playground, or sketch, describe, create basic maps or record their thinking another way (see **Useful apps/links**). Continue circulating and using the prompts to guide their thinking.
3. Jigsaw the groups (see **Useful apps/links**) by leaving one team member with the design and having other members move to a different group to discuss other designs and ideas. Have the team member who remains listen to the feedback without defending their ideas. They record any key observations from others.
4. Re-form the groups to discuss the feedback from others and consider new ideas.
5. Repeat the activity until each group has a bank of ideas. Encourage thinking about synthesising the equipment and experimenting with layout and equipment choices.

PROMPTS

- Which equipment did you like and which equipment was popular on your surveys?
- What is the most creative way you can reimagine that equipment?
- Can you combine or synthesise some parts of your ideas to create something new and exciting?
- How many forces and simple machines can you name in your design?
- Is this the best use of the space available?

MORE VOCABULARY

- feedback – information about, for example, a person's performance or the design of a product, which can be used to make improvements
- ideate – generate many ideas without making judgements about the ideas
- reflect – consider and evaluate
- synthesise – combine two or more ideas to create something new

USEFUL APPS/LINKS

- Creative thinking routines, such as at mea.digital/sm238
- App for recording the Ideate process, such as Notability or OneNote Class Notebook
- Article about the jigsaw technique, such as at mea.digital/sm5

ASSESSMENT

At the Ideate stage, assessment could include observations about the number and diversity of student ideas, and student ability to provide feedback and create additional ideas. Reflection in the journal should provide an insight into some of the reasoning behind student choices.

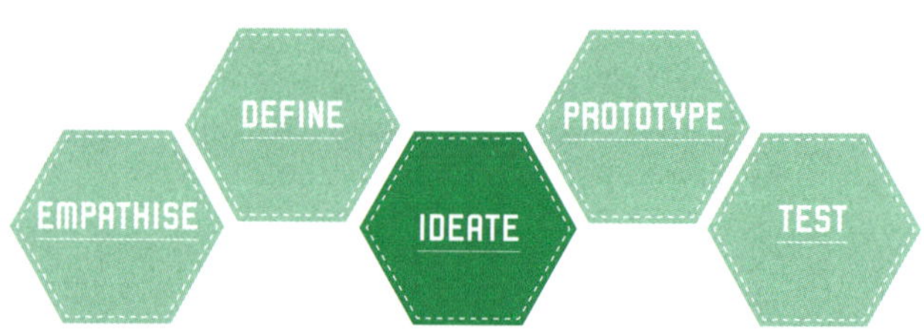

→ PROTOTYPE

At this stage, students are asked to create a physical prototype of a solution. Students need to get their ideas out of their heads and present them in a way that engages other students and helps them to understand the concept. When students create, it helps them to think and solve problems and disagreements.

Encourage students to photograph or film during the Prototype and Test stages. This information can be used to show the learning behind the design thinking process in action.

ACTIVITY 1: COMPLETE PLAYGROUND DESIGNS

1. Using all of the Ideate feedback, have students work in their teams to complete a simple map or bird's-eye view of their design. Ensure that they use grid paper to keep the map to scale, using the initial measurements of the playground equipment.
2. Use sticky notes to record the contact or non-contact forces and the simple machines in each piece of equipment. These will form the basis of a sign to go beside the equipment.

ACTIVITY 2: TRANSFORM IDEAS INTO PROTOTYPES

1. Distribute **Generic reproducible 10 (Group task organiser)** and have each group complete it.
2. Provide students with a range of materials to use to create their prototype. Remind students that a prototype should be created rapidly and it is not meant to look 'nice'.
3. Students should create a sign to go beside the equipment, explaining the forces and simple machines involved.
4. Ask students to see if their prototype works and get feedback from the group. Students could ask each other:
   - » What simple machines are you including in this prototype?
   - » How does it show forces?
   - » Which parts need changing? How might you do this?
5. Students use the feedback to prototype again.

Ask students to fill in the Prototype part of **Learning journal template 4 (Prototype and test page)**. See the **Journal tip** for further student guidance.

PROMPTS

- Does this equipment show forces and simple machines?
- Will it be a good space for many children to play?
- What else can you try to make your ideas work?

TOP TIP! Some students may find the process of creating a map challenging. It can be helpful for them to create a simple footprint outline or two-dimensional representation of the equipment to scale (see Useful apps/links). They can then move these to experiment with the playground layout and consider how the elements might fit together in a map.

MORE VOCABULARY

- feedback – information about, for example, a person's performance or the design of a product, which can be used to make improvements
- prototype – an initial version of a model of a product or process that is used to develop a final model

JOURNAL TIP

Remind students to highlight the main features of their prototype. If students are creating an electronic journal, they can insert a photo of their prototype and annotate it.

USEFUL APPS/LINKS

- App for creating a simple bird's-eye view map, such as DrawIsland, or a three-dimensional deisign, such as SketchUp
- App for recording the progress of design development, such as Adobe Spark Video
- Note-taking and collaboration apps and programs such as Notability and OneNote Class Notebook

ASSESSMENT

Observe students as they make changes to their designs. Are they able to consider feedback, make modifications and move rapidly through this process, or do they have difficulties with holding on to an idea and accepting feedback?

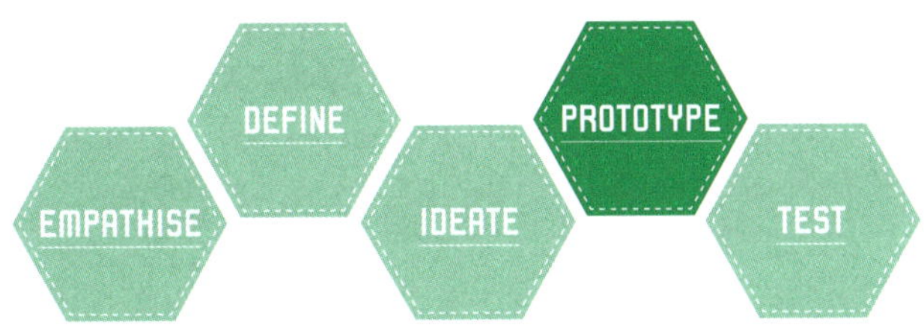

TEST

At this stage of the design thinking process, students test their prototype to see how it meets the criteria in the challenge.

ACTIVITY: TEST FEEDBACK

1. Students share their prototypes with another group from the class.
2. Ask students to evaluate whether the playground design will teach children about forces.
3. Students can consult with one of the people who completed their initial survey, or who they interviewed. Looking at the model and sign, can they identify how the playground equipment uses forces?
4. Provide the opportunity to cycle through the Prototype and Test stages for the last time.

Ask students to fill in **Learning journal template 4 (Prototype and test page)**. See the **Journal tip** for further student guidance.

PROMPTS

- Does your prototype do what you wanted it to do?
- Are there other features that need to be added?
- How can you act on the feedback?
- How has the feedback been helpful to you?

MORE VOCABULARY

- feature – a specific aspect of something, such as size, shape, colour, quality
- feedback – information about, for example, a person's performance or the design of a product, which can be used to make improvements
- prototype – an initial version of a model of a product or process that is used to develop a final model

JOURNAL TIP

Ask students to think about why it is important to test ideas before they create final designs. Have them consider how feedback helped them refine and improve.

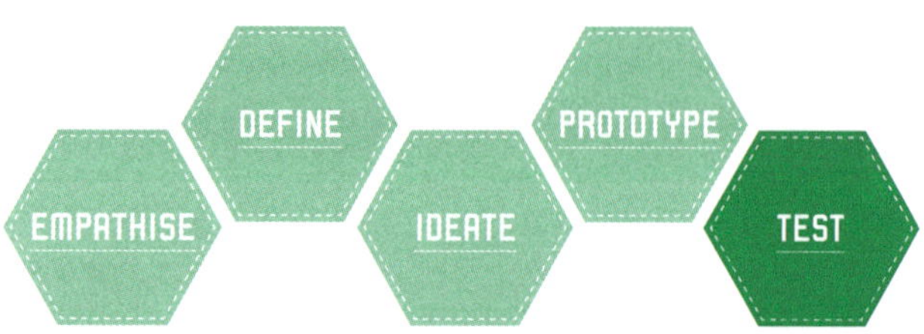

SHARE AND EVALUATE

At this stage, students are provided with an opportunity to share their final designs, as well as the processes involved in the investigation. Students evaluate their learning journals as well as their solutions.

ACTIVITY 1: FINALISE DESIGNS

1. Provide students with the time to create their final designs, as a hand-drawn design, digital bird's-eye view map or as a three-dimensional design.
2. Develop a proposal incorporating the design and their notes about the forces and simple machines. Consider an app such as Notability, Prezi, Adobe Spark Video or Aurasma.

ACTIVITY 2: EVALUATE AND GIVE FEEDBACK

1. Provide students with **Generic reproducible 2 (Self-evaluation)** to complete.
2. Ask students to provide feedback to each other about the most interesting features, the aspects that were most difficult and the changes that they would make if they repeated the task.
3. Provide students with opportunities to share their designs with a wider group, such as the school principal, leadership team, school council or student leadership team.

ASSESSMENT

Ask students to again complete **Generic reproducible 1 (Key vocabulary table)** using the key vocabulary for this unit. Compare their table with the one they completed at the Tune-in stage, to demonstrate changes in understanding.

Students complete **Generic reproducible 3 (Responding to the investigation)**. Compare their responses to their responses to **Generic reproducible 2**.

Teachers complete **Generic reproducible 5 (Design thinking assessment rubric)** for each student. Students compare the feedback they are given by the teacher with their self-assessment of how they used the design thinking process to solve problems (**Generic reproducible 3**).

Name: ....

Date: ....

Simple machine	Location	Sketch of simple machine you found
Lever 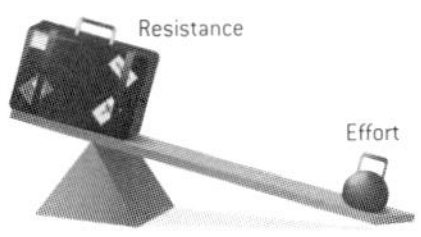		
Wheel and axle 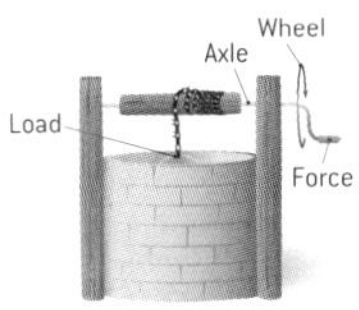		
Pulley 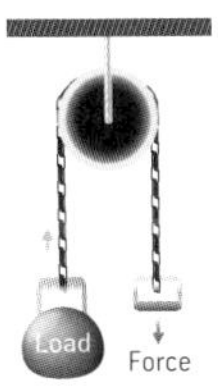		
Inclined plane 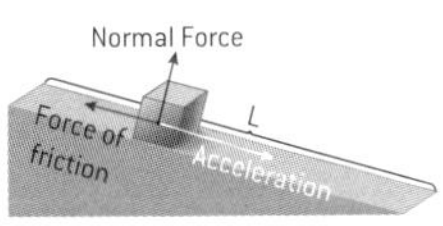		
Wedge 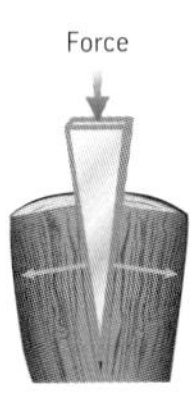		
Screw 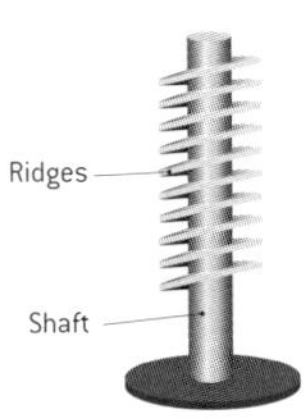		

REPRODUCIBLE 2.2

PLAYGROUND INVESTIGATION AND SURVEY

EMPATHISE

STEM INVESTIGATIONS

Name: ....

Date: ....

Name of playground equipment and simple sketch	Can you feel any push or pull forces while you are playing? Are they direct forces or from a distance? (Tick any you think are right.)	Which simple machines can you name? (Tick any you think are right.)	Number of students who chose this equipment as their favourite (Include age and grade.)
	☐ push ☐ pull ☐ twist ☐ direct ☐ from a distance	☐ lever ☐ pulley ☐ wedge ☐ inclined plane ☐ screw ☐ wheel and axle	
	☐ push ☐ pull ☐ twist ☐ direct ☐ from a distance	☐ lever ☐ pulley ☐ wedge ☐ inclined plane ☐ screw ☐ wheel and axle	

What was the most popular play equipment?

What was the least popular play equipment?

STEM Investigations, MP, ISBN 978 1 4202 4319 2 © Macmillan Science and Education Australia 2018

DEFINE

STEM INVESTIGATIONS

Name: ....

Date: ....

Record which equipment you:

- need in your design
- want in your design
- could consider including in your design.

Need:

Want:

Think about:

STEM Investigations, MP, ISBN 978 1 4202 4319 2 © Macmillan Science and Education Australia 2018

DEFINE

STEM INVESTIGATIONS

Name: ....

Date: ....

Record your measurements of the playground space in the table.

Length of playground space	Width of playground space	Natural features (such as trees) or structures (such as buildings or walls) to consider in your design

Work out the total area of the playground.

Sketch the playground space. Include your measurements, and any structures and natural features.

STEM Investigations, MP, ISBN 978 1 4202 4319 2

DEFINE

STEM INVESTIGATIONS

Name: ....

Date: ....

Create a simple map of your playground, showing the length, width and any natural features or structures to be considered.

Use your measurements and your sketch on Reproducible 2.4 to help you.

Remember to draw a scale and a north point.

BRIDGE THE GAP TO HELP A TOWN

INTRODUCTION

Floods are part of the Earth's weather systems. During a flood, large volumes of rain result in an increase in the amount of water in waterways. Flooding can have a devastating impact on communities, affecting crops and livestock, homes and infrastructure, and access to food, clean water and services. Sometimes communities become isolated due to the damage done to roads and bridges.

This investigation provides students with the opportunity to learn about the structure of bridges and the impact of flooding on infrastructure and surrounding land. They are challenged to create a simple model of a bridge. The bridge model should be part of an education campaign about the effects of flooding on communities, such as a community that has been isolated because of flood damage to its bridge. Students explore how strong structures are designed and built. They are provided with material constraints for their model and learn different techniques for connecting materials. The investigation could be diversified by changing the material constraints or test criteria.

THE CHALLENGE

A small town has experienced two big floods recently. Water levels in the local river were very high and the current was very strong, making the only bridge into the town unstable and unsafe. You want to raise awareness of the impact of floods on communities.

Your challenge is to build a model bridge as part of a campaign about the effects of flooding. Your bridge should span a 20-centimetre gap and have no middle supports. It should be made from up to three sheets of A4 paper and one metre of masking tape only. As part of your investigation, you will learn how floods can affect rivers and the land.

KEY UNDERSTANDINGS

- The Earth's surface changes over time as a result of natural processes.
- A bridge can be destroyed when fast floodwater rubs away the riverbed.
- Rising floodwater can damage a bridge's structure.
- Strong and fast floodwater and rubbish can collapse a bridge.

KEY SKILLS

- Make careful observations.
- Develop research skills.
- Investigate strong and stable shapes and solids.
- Design and create three-dimensional models.
- Design fair tests for a model.
- Transform ideas into something that can be seen – discuss, write, draw and build ideas.

KEY VOCABULARY

floodwater – water that overflows onto land that is usually dry

force – a push or pull on an object that makes it move, or change direction or shape

span – the distance across something

stability – ability not to collapse or overturn

structure – an object with different parts

KEY ACTIONS

- Explore shapes and structures of bridges.
- Learn how floods affect people and bridges.
- Create a design for a model bridge.
- Design a fair test for a model.
- Build a model using limited materials.
- Create a campaign about flooding.

OVERVIEW OF STAGES

TUNE IN:

Students find out about floods and bridges. They complete a gallery walk focusing on the impact of floods on bridges in particular. Students explore strong structures, stability and forces.

EMPATHISE

Students find out about the impact of flooding on others through engagement with different resources including video clips and articles. They consider the responses of people witnessing and living through a flood, in particular the issues that arise when floodwaters isolate an area.

DEFINE

Students consider the information gathered about the impact of flooding. They consider the main areas they need to explore further, such as the features of flooding and the design of bridges.

IDEATE

Students come up with creative ideas for how to create a bridge for an area that is prone to floods. Their bridge would be a temporary structure.

PROTOTYPE

Students choose a couple of ideas to develop further and prototype. This may include drawing and constructing. When constructing, students are provided with specific materials for the task.

TEST

Students test the design of their bridge. They create a simple test to see if their bridge is strong enough to hold a small metal car in the middle of the span.

SHARE AND EVALUATE:

Students create their final design as well as a short campaign to raise awareness of the impact of flooding on communities. They are provided with an opportunity to share their designs and evaluate both their own and others' solutions.

Students may have the opportunity to share their ideas with someone from a local water company, environmental scientist or engineer.

SUGGESTED SCHEDULE

LESSON	STAGE
1–3	**Tune in:** Find out about floods and bridge structures; explore strong shapes, stability and forces
4–7	**Empathise:** Learn about others' experiences in floods; write in journal
8–10	**Define:** Consider information gathered about the impact of flooding; consider main areas to explore further and collate information about flooding and design of bridges; write in journal
11–12	**Ideate:** Come up with creative ideas for how to create a bridge for an area that is prone to floods; write in journal
13–17	**Prototype** and **Test:** Develop a couple of ideas, including drawing and constructing designs; design a simple test to assess the strength of the bridge; write in journal
18–21	**Share and evaluate:** Provide time to complete the final design; create a short awareness campaign about the impact of flooding; share final designs; evaluate self and others

CURRICULUM LINKS

SCIENCE

YEAR	STRAND	SUB-STRAND AND CONTENT
4	Science Understanding	Earth and space sciences: • Earth's surface changes over time as a result of natural processes and human activity Physical sciences: • Forces can be exerted by one object on another through direct contact or from a distance
3 & 4	Science as a Human Endeavour	Use and influence of science: • Science knowledge helps people to understand the effect of their actions
	Science Inquiry Skills	Questioning and predicting Planning and conducting Processing and analysing data and information Evaluating

TECHNOLOGIES

YEAR	STRAND	CONTENT
3 & 4	Technologies Contexts	• Recognise the role of people in design and technologies occupations and explore factors, including sustainability, that impact on the design of solutions to meet community needs • Investigate how forces and the properties of materials affect the behaviour of a product or system • Investigate the suitability of materials, systems, components, tools and equipment for a range of purposes
	Design and Technologies Processes and Production Skills	• Select and use materials, components, tools, equipment and techniques and use safe work practices to make designed solutions • Generate, develop and communicate design ideas and decisions using appropriate technical terms and graphical representation techniques • Evaluate design ideas, processes and solutions based on criteria for success developed with guidance and including care for the environment and communities • Plan a sequence of production steps when making designed solutions

MATHEMATICS

YEAR	STRAND	SUB-STRAND AND CONTENT
3	Measurement and Geometry	Using units of measurement: • Measure, order and compare objects using familiar metric units of length, mass and capacity • Make models of three-dimensional objects and describe key features
4	Measurement and Geometry	Using units of measurement: • Use scaled instruments to measure and compare lengths, masses, capacities and temperatures

This investigation also links to the General Capabilities:

- Literacy
- Numeracy
- Information and Communication Technology (ICT) Capability
- Critical and Creative Thinking.

This investigation also links to the Cross-Curriculum Priority of Sustainability.

ASSESSMENT

The following resources are provided for assessing students at different stages of the STEM investigations:

- Generic reproducible 1 (Key vocabulary table), for assessing understanding of vocabulary
- Generic reproducible 2 (Self-evaluation), for student self-evaluation of the learning process
- Generic reproducible 3 (Responding to the investigation)
- Generic reproducible 5 (Design thinking assessment rubric), for evaluating student engagement in the design thinking stages
- Learning journal templates 1, 2, 3 and 4, incorporating student reflection and evaluation.

GETTING READY FOR THE INVESTIGATION

You can prepare yourself and students for this STEM investigation in the following ways:

- Identify groups of students who will work well together.
- Review the **Key science knowledge** that supports this investigation, and look at the **Useful links**.
- Investigate the **Useful apps**.
- Gather materials for the science activities during the Tune-in session, including materials for exploring floating and nets for shapes.
- Gather pictures of bridges damaged during floods and images of different bridge structures.
- Start collecting additional materials for prototyping (as shown on the **Materials needed** list).
- Determine where prototypes will be kept between lessons.
- Create a wall space where students can share their ideas in the Ideate stage.
- Organise the class into pairs.
- Start thinking about:
  - » sourcing information about floods and bridges
  - » inviting someone to speak about the work people do to help communities experiencing difficulties with floods, such as through Engineers Without Borders
  - » making connections with a water company or environmental engineer
  - » time and material constraints for the task
  - » finding experts to provide feedback to students
  - » other students and classes that can be involved in the survey and evaluation stages
  - » how, when and where the designs will be shared and evaluated.

USEFUL APPS

- App for sharing ideas, thoughts, questions and images, such as Padlet or Lino
- App for creating multimedia presentations, such as Adobe Spark Video (via a teacher-created class account), Prezi or iMovie
- App for engaging in collaborative tasks, such as OneNote Class Notebook or SharePoint
- App for creating spreadsheets, such as Excel or Numbers, or an interactive table, such as Google Docs

USEFUL LINKS

- Video clip of moving floodwater, such as at mea.digital/sm149
- Free, printable nets, such as at mea.digital/sm150
- Information about stable and unstable structures, such as at mea.digital/sm151
- Video clip about floods and eyewitness accounts, such as at mea.digital/sm152
- Images of bridges before and after floods, such as at mea.digital/sm153
- Article containing eyewitness accounts of floods, such as at mea.digital/sm154
- Images of interesting bridges, such as at mea.digital/sm155
- Relevant not-for-profit organisations, such as at mea.digital/sm156

RESOURCES PROVIDED

- Generic reproducibles 1, 2, 3, 4, 5, 12
- Reproducibles 3.1, 3.2, 3.3
- Learning journal templates 1, 2, 3, 4

MATERIALS NEEDED

- Paper
- Scissors
- Tape – different widths, strengths, materials
- Small toy cars
- Weights
- Hose or spray water bottles
- Small waterproof items, such as plastic toys and construction blocks
- Rigid and flexible waterproof materials
- Construction blocks, such as Lego
- Ruler
- Masking tape
- A4 paper

KEY SCIENCE KNOWLEDGE

This section provides an overview of the key science concepts and vocabulary needed for this unit.

FLOODING

The Earth's surface changes over time as a result of natural processes, including flooding. **Floods** occur when land that is usually not covered by water becomes covered by an overflow of water, often because of unusually heavy rain. Floods that happen very quickly are called flash floods. Flooding can also be caused by a tsunami – a large wave generated by an underwater earthquake.

Floods can occur anywhere. Floods often damage infrastructure, such as roads, power lines and bridges, cutting off essential services and isolating communities. They can also destroy crops and endanger lives. A bridge that has stood for hundreds of years can be destroyed when fast floodwater rubs away a riverbed, weakening the bridge's supports.

FORCES

A **force** is a push or pull on an object. A force can make an object change shape, such as the force of floodwaters slamming into a bridge. It can make something speed up, such as rubbish in a river as the speed of floodwaters increases. It can also make an object stay in its place. Forces can be marked on a diagram, using arrows to show the direction of movement.

A contact force is one that acts on an object by touching it, such as fast floodwater pushing against a bridge. A non-contact force acts on another object without touching it, such as a magnet attracting some iron filings.

STRONG AND STABLE SHAPES AND STRUCTURES

The **stability** of a **structure** is its ability to not collapse or be overturned. The stability of an object depends on the strength of its parts. Bridges need to be strong and stable enough to withstand forces from weight, wind and floodwater.

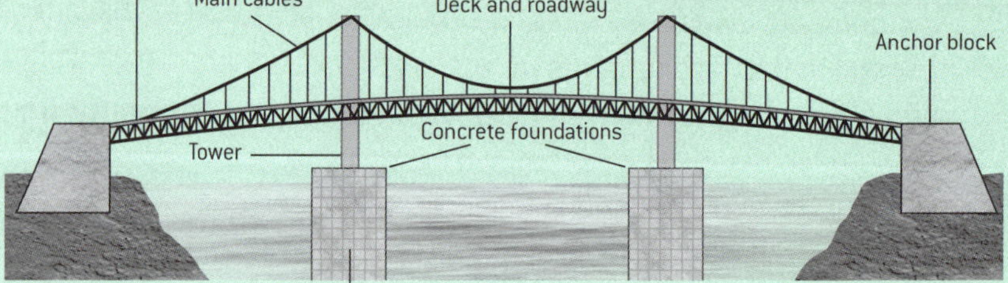

The Akashi–Kaikyo Bridge in Japan spans 3991 metres. It was designed to withstand earthquakes and extreme winds.

Triangles are the strongest geometric shape. Triangles can be seen in bridges around the world, such as the Oresund Bridge, which has a **span** across the water between Denmark and Sweden. A square or box can be made more stable by adding a triangular framework called a truss. Bridges use triangular trusses to support beams and other structural parts.

A cylinder is an example of a strong solid. Cylinders have been used in the Saltash Bridge in Bristol, England.

KEY VOCABULARY

flood – water that overflows onto land that is usually dry
force – a push or pull on an object that makes it move, or change direction or shape
span – the distance across something
stability – ability not to collapse or overturn
structure – an object with different parts

→ TUNE IN

1. Ask students to complete **Generic reproducible 1 (Key vocabulary table)** using the key vocabulary for this unit. This reproducible will also be used at the end of the unit, to demonstrate changes in understanding.
2. Create a gallery walk with pictures of places during and after a flood (see **Useful apps/links**). Include images of bridges that have been damaged and landscapes that have changed. Have students discuss some of the images and their response. What did they feel? What might be some of the problems for people living in a community that floods often?
3. Students need to understand about floods, the force of water and the effects of floods on the land, strong shapes, stability and floating before beginning the challenge.

ACTIVITY 1: FORCE OF WATER

1. Show students a short video clip of moving floodwater (see **Useful apps/links**).
2. Provide students with tubs, spray water bottles and small waterproof objects, such as plastic toys or construction blocks.
3. Have students set up the objects and spray them with the water at the base. If possible, go outside and use a hose to show impact with faster flowing water.
4. Explore the impact that water has on objects that are not attached to the ground, such as a toy, and objects that are fixed, such as a Lego tower attached to a base.
5. Discuss how this force relates to the force of floodwaters on a structure such as a bridge.
6. Have students explore different shapes as well as rigid and flexible materials, to see if there are any differences. Have students collate their information in a table.

TOP TIP!

Run a short session to experiment with different ways to connect paper using masking tape. Students should share their ideas. These will be useful skills to have when students are creating their prototypes with paper.

ACTIVITY 2: SHAPE, STRENGTH AND STABILITY

1. Provide students with different shaped containers to consider; thin cardboard boxes and cylinders are useful.
2. Have students deconstruct the containers to learn about the nets that they create. Look at the similarities and differences between the nets.
3. Provide students with some nets to cut out and then create (see **Useful apps/links**).
4. Have students come up with a simple test to determine which solid is the strongest. Discuss the importance of changing only one variable in the test, such as the type or amount of weights placed on top of a structure. Demonstrate how to create a table to record observations.
5. Have students create a test to determine which solid is the most stable, such as rolling a small ball at each.
6. Discuss students' observations for both tests and how this information may be helpful when they design a structure.

4. Introduce the STEM investigation and challenge to the students. Provide them with the student card and read the information together. Explain that their bridge prototype must be able to bear the weight of a small toy car.
5. Introduce the design thinking process by reviewing the stages on the student card. Explain that students will keep a journal about their learning at the different stages of the design.

USEFUL APPS/LINKS

- Images of bridges before and after floods, such as at mea.digital/sm153
- Video clip of moving floodwater, such as at mea.digital/sm149
- Free, printable nets, such as at mea.digital/sm150

→ EMPATHISE

During the Empathise stage of the design thinking process, students focus on finding out about different points of view. To empathise with others, they need to research some of the experiences people have had during and after floods. This includes finding out about the impact of flooding on communities and daily lives. Students will take notes, ask questions, draw diagrams and take photos where relevant.

ACTIVITY: EYEWITNESS ACCOUNTS

1. Have students watch a video clip about people's experiences of a flood (see **Useful apps/links**).
2. Have students focus on questions such as, 'What caused the flooding? What were some of the main problems for home owners? How did some of the people feel? What were some of the unusual things people reported seeing?'
3. Provide students with **Reproducible 3.1 (Flood experiences)** to make notes about people's experiences.
4. Provide students with a link or hard copy to an article with eyewitness accounts of flooding (see **Useful apps/links**) or read some quotes from eyewitnesses, to be selective about what students read. Have students complete the second part of **Reproducible 3.1** by adding notes about the article.
5. Discuss any differences between watching a video clip about floods and reading eyewitness accounts. Ask, 'How did you feel when you saw and heard people talking about the floods? How did you feel when you read about people's experiences in a flood? Which type of account did you find more powerful?'

PROMPTS

- What were some of the issues for people caught up in the floods?
- What were some of the words people used to describe their experiences?
- How did people manage to escape the floods?
- What was something surprising that you found out?
- What was one interesting insight you found out?

MORE VOCABULARY

- empathise – understand and consider another person or group's point of view
- point of view – an opinion, attitude or judgement considered in a particular way

JOURNAL TIP

Ask students to complete **Learning journal template 1 (Empathise page)** while they are doing the different tasks. Remind them to date their notes and include photos of relevant information or pictures.

USEFUL APPS/LINKS

- Video clip about floods and eyewitness accounts, such as at mea.digital/sm152
- Images of bridges before and after floods, such as at mea.digital/sm153
- Article containing eyewitness accounts of floods, such as at mea.digital/sm154
- App for creating shared documents, such as OneNote Class Notebook or SharePoint

ASSESSMENT

This stage of the design thinking process offers opportunities to observe students collecting information, developing questions, and recording their notes and thinking in their journal.

TOP TIP! Before sharing images or videos of flooding, check that the content is suitable. Alert students to the type of content that they might find. It may be helpful to create a list of useful websites for students to access before students begin their research.

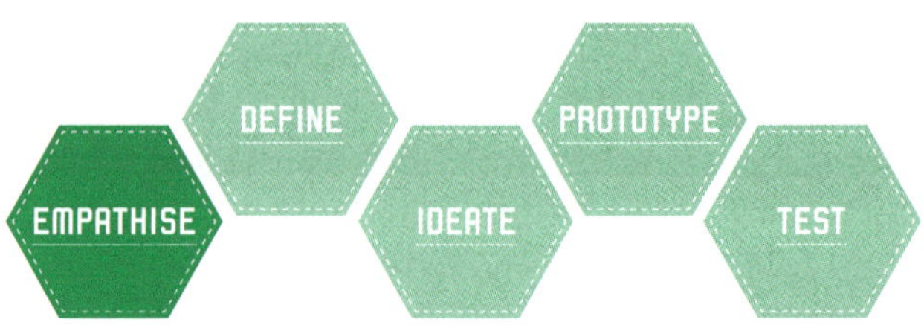

→ DEFINE

The main focus of this stage of the design thinking process is to reframe the challenge. At this stage, students learn how to define what needs to be done. This includes noting insights that have been generated.

ACTIVITY 1: CONSIDER INFORMATION ABOUT FLOODING

1. Have students consider the information collected from eyewitnesses.
2. Ask students to create a list of specific reasons why people might use a bridge, such as 'drive to work', 'deliver petrol to a petrol station'.
3. Have students respond to 'what if' questions relating to when a bridge has been damaged, such as, 'What if tankers couldn't deliver petrol to petrol stations/school children couldn't take the bus to school/delivery vans couldn't deliver fresh food to the supermarket/the pharmacy was on the other side of the bridge and you needed some medicine?'

ACTIVITY 2: DISCUSS BRIDGE STRUCTURES

1. Review the main shapes used for strength and stability when building bridges.
2. View pictures of different bridges (see **Useful apps/links**), pointing out shapes and solids such as triangles and cylinders.
3. Provide students with **Generic reproducible 4 (Key question table)** to record their research questions and notes.
4. Discuss the information collected and any additional information that is still required.

Students can update **Learning journal template 2 (Define page)**.

PROMPTS

- Will the type of shape used affect your design?
- Which bridges might provide useful design ideas?
- What other information do you need?

ACTIVITY 3: CREATE A BRIDGE PLAN

1. Have students create a bridge plan to help them focus their investigation.
2. Have students add information to their plan during the investigation, including how they will test the bridge for strength and stability.
3. Remind students about the short campaign they need to create at the end of the investigation to raise awareness of the impact of flooding.

MORE VOCABULARY

- define – state the meaning of something
- insight – an accurate understanding of someone or something
- point of view – an opinion, attitude or judgement considered in a particular way

JOURNAL TIP

Discuss the term 'insight' and explain that it relates to something students have learned about the people and their responses to the surveys as well as information gathered through research or excursions. You could refer to **Learning journal template 2**.

USEFUL APPS/LINKS

- Images of interesting bridges, such as at mea.digital/sm155

EMPATHISE DEFINE IDEATE PROTOTYPE TEST

→ IDEATE

The Ideate stage of the design thinking process is all about generating lots of ideas. Students need to be flexible in their thinking and be able to move beyond obvious ideas. At this stage, ideas are not judged, just generated and gathered.

ACTIVITY 1: GENERATE BRIDGE STRUCTURE IDEAS

1. Have students generate ideas for their bridge structure. They may find it useful to use a small whiteboard or paper to draw their ideas as well as write them. If using a whiteboard, have students take photographs of their ideas and collate them in a share document, such as Padlet or Lino.
2. Provide students with time to look at other students' ideas. Viewing other ideas may provide students with prompts to develop their own ideas further.

ACTIVITY 2: GENERATE AWARENESS-RAISING IDEAS

1. Provide students with time to think about the different ways that they could create an awareness campaign about the impact of floods.
2. Encourage students to think about the following aspects:
   - type of campaign, such as community newsletter, guest speaker, fundraiser, posters, gallery walk
   - key information to include, such as causes of floods, impact on communities, eyewitness statements
   - purpose of campaign: raise awareness about the impact of floods on communities
   - how the bridge will be used in the campaign, such as with photos or as part of a presentation.
3. Provide students with **Reproducible 3.2 (Flood campaign)** to help them plan their campaign.

PROMPTS

- How might you use your materials best to create your bridge design?
- What do you think should be the key focus of the campaign? Why?
- How could you find out about organisations who assist people affected by floods?

MORE VOCABULARY

- feedback – information about, for example, a person's performance or the design of a product, which can be used to make improvements
- ideate – generate many ideas without making judgements about the ideas

JOURNAL TIP

Have students fill in **Learning journal template 3 (Ideate page)** as they complete the activities. When choosing three ideas to include in the journal, try to choose three ideas that use different materials or focus on different aspects of the challenge.

USEFUL APPS/LINKS

- App for sharing ideas, thoughts, questions and images, such as Padlet or Lino

ASSESSMENT

At the Ideate stage, assessment could include observations about the number and diversity of student ideas, and their ability to provide feedback and create additional ideas. Reflection in the journal should provide an insight into some of the reasoning behind student choices.

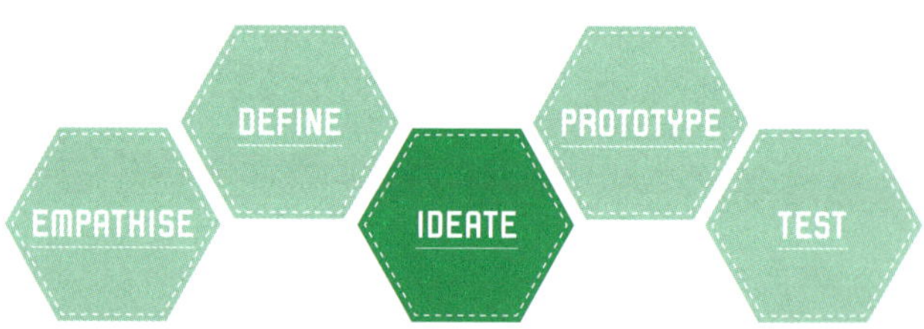

→ PROTOTYPE

At this stage of the design thinking process, students are asked to create a physical prototype of a solution. It is the stage where students need to get their ideas out of their heads and presented in a way that engages other students and helps them to understand the concept. When students create, it helps them to think and solve problems and disagreements. Students can role-play, make a storyboard or use sticky notes when they prototype. The most important feature is that viewers can interact with whatever is produced.

Encourage students to photograph or film during the Prototype and Test stages. This information can be used to show the learning behind the design thinking process in action.

ACTIVITY 1: CHOOSE AND EXPLORE STRUCTURES

1. Students choose one of the key shapes/solids they are incorporating into their bridge.
2. Students make different versions of the structure they are creating, to work out which is the strongest and most stable.
3. Students choose another shape/solid to explore, and repeat step 2.

ACTIVITY 2: TRANSFORM IDEAS INTO PROTOTYPES

1. Students prototype their complete bridge design using paper and tape only.
2. Students need to consider how the bridge will support a toy car in the middle of the span and how it will be connected to the land at each side of the river.
3. It may be helpful for students to photograph their prototypes at different stages so they can identify which aspects of the design work best.
4. Students test their designs and continue to cycle through the construction phase of prototyping.

Ask students to fill in the Prototype part of **Learning journal template 4 (Prototype and test page)**. See the **Journal tip** for further student guidance.

PROMPTS

- Have you made sure your bridge meets all of the design criteria?
- How will you test the design of your bridge?
- Who will provide feedback about your design?

TOP TIP!

When asking for feedback, students could ask:

- Which part of your design provides strength to your bridge?
- Do you think that your bridge could be built using different materials?
- What do you need to change?

MORE VOCABULARY

- feedback – information about, for example, a person's performance or the design of a product, which can be used to make improvements
- prototype – an initial version of a model of a product or process that is used to develop a final model

JOURNAL TIP

Remind students to highlight the main features of their prototype. If students are creating an electronic journal, they can insert a photo of their prototype and annotate it.

USEFUL APPS/LINKS

- App for taking photographs or video, such as Adobe Spark Video or iMovie

ASSESSMENT

Observe students as they make changes to their designs. Are they able to consider feedback, make modifications and move rapidly through this process, or do they have difficulties with holding on to an idea and accepting feedback?

EMPATHISE DEFINE IDEATE **PROTOTYPE** TEST

TEST

At this stage of the design thinking process, students test their prototype to see how it meets the criteria in the challenge.

ACTIVITY 1: GET TEST FEEDBACK

1. Provide students with **Generic reproducible 12 (Prototype and test)** to record feedback about the prototypes.
2. Have others consider the effectiveness of the design and how easy it is to use.
3. Students continue to cycle through the Prototype and Test stages.

ACTIVITY 2: TEST DESIGNS

1. Students design a simple test to check which of their prototypes is the strongest and which is the most stable. Strength can be measured by the ability to support a small toy car in the middle of the span. Stability can be tested using a small fan or water.
2. Provide students with **Reproducible 3.3 (Bridge test)** to plan and record.
3. Students use the information gathered from the tests to change their designs. They should test each new design and add their observations to **Reproducible 3.3**.

Ask students to fill in **Learning journal template 4 (Prototype and test page)**. See the **Journal tip** for further student guidance.

PROMPTS

- Does your prototype do what you wanted it to do?
- Are there features that need to be added or removed?

MORE VOCABULARY

- feedback – information about, for example, a person's performance or the design of a product, which can be used to make improvements
- prototype – an initial version of a model of a product or process that is used to develop a final model

JOURNAL TIP

Ask students to think about why it is important to test their ideas before they build their final design.

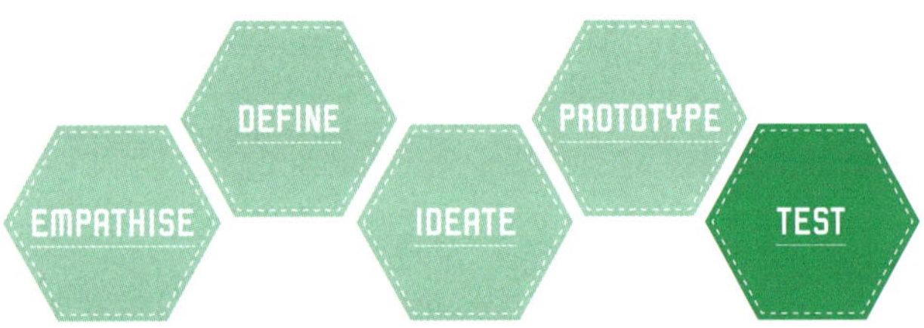

SHARE AND EVALUATE

At this stage of the investigation, students are provided with an opportunity to share their final design, as well as the processes involved in the investigation. Students evaluate their learning journals as well as their solutions.

ACTIVITY 1: FINALISE DESIGNS

1. Allow students to finalise their designs and create a short campaign to raise awareness of the impact of floods.
2. Arrange for other people to see the different designs and provide feedback. This could include experts from the local water company, environmental scientists or engineers.
3. Students should include their learning journals with the display so others can see the different stages of the design process.

ACTIVITY 2: EVALUATE AND GIVE FEEDBACK

1. Provide students with **Generic reproducible 2 (Self-evaluation)**.
2. During the sharing session, provide participants with tokens or stickers so they can vote for their favourite design or create an online survey with photos of the different designs for others to vote.

ASSESSMENT

Ask students to again complete **Generic reproducible 1 (Key vocabulary table)** using the key vocabulary for this unit. Compare their table with the one they completed at the Tune-in stage, to demonstrate changes in understanding.

Students complete **Generic reproducible 3 (Responding to the investigation)**. Compare their responses to their responses to **Generic reproducible 2**.

Teachers complete **Generic reproducible 5 (Design thinking assessment rubric)** for each student. Students compare the feedback they are given by the teacher with their self-assessment of how they used the design thinking process to solve problems (**Generic reproducible 3**).

EMPATHISE

STEM INVESTIGATIONS

Name: ....

Date: ....

Watch a video clip and read an article with eyewitness accounts of floods. Write the information you collect in the table.

Question/ information	**Video clip**	**Article**
Where was the flood?		
What caused the flood?		
What problems were people experiencing?		
What were some words used to describe the experience?		
What were people doing to cope?		
Other information		

STEM Investigations, MP, ISBN 978 1 4202 4319 2

IDEATE

STEM INVESTIGATIONS

Name: ....

Date: ....

Use this table to help plan your campaign about the impact of floods.

Purpose of the campaign: The purpose is to raise awareness about the impact of floods on communities.
Key information to include: (Tick three pieces of key information that you will include.) ☐ causes of floods ☐ impact of floods on communities ☐ how floods affect bridges ☐ how people can help flood victims ☐ advice for people in areas that might flood ☐ other:
Type of campaign: (Tick one of the boxes or write your own idea.) ☐ newsletter ☐ guest speaker ☐ poster ☐ other:
How my bridge design will be used in the campaign:
Other important things to think about or organise:

STEM Investigations, MP, ISBN 978 1 4202 4319 2 © Macmillan Science and Education Australia 2018

Name: ....

Date: ....

As you prototype your different bridge designs, you will need to test them for strength (ability to support a car in the middle of the bridge span) and stability (ability to stay upright against a force).

Plan how you might do this, and record your ideas and observations in the tables.

Steps for testing strength:	Steps for testing stability:
Materials needed:	Materials needed:

Observations

Prototype number	Strength (ability to support weight of car)	Stability (ability to stay upright against a force)
1		
2		
3		

DESIGN AN AMAZING MAZE FOR YOUR SCHOOL FAIR

INTRODUCTION

Mazes have been a part of human culture for thousands of years. In the Middle Ages, many famous hedge mazes were created for royal entertainment. In the UK there are more than 100 hedge mazes. Humans have always been fascinated with the twists and turns of mazes. As well as physical mazes, there are plenty of digital mazes to explore.

This investigation provides students with the opportunity to learn about the different features of mazes. They explore mazes and observe others attempting them. They are challenged to create a design for a maze and use computer software to create it. They also consider materials that could be used to create a full-scale model and how the materials could be reused.

This investigation could be expanded to include programming of robots to complete a maze.

THE CHALLENGE

Your school fair will be happening soon and the school principal wants to have a maze. You think you can make a maze that will keep everyone busy. What materials could you make it from?

Your challenge is to design a maze using a coding program. It will have at least one correct pathway, and dead ends. Make a presentation including your design, how you would build it and what you would do with the materials afterwards. As part of your investigation, you will learn about coding programs and the physical properties of materials.

KEY UNDERSTANDINGS

- Coding is the method for telling a computer, app or phone what to do.
- Algorithms are a set of rules or steps needed to perform a task.
- Different materials have different properties, which affect their use.
- Properties of materials include strength and stability.
- The properties of materials affect their use.

KEY VOCABULARY

algorithm – a set of instructions or rules for performing a task

logic – a way of thinking that helps in checking facts and making predictions

property – feature of a material, such as strength or ability to retain heat

stability – ability of something to not move or change

KEY SKILLS

- Make careful observations.
- Give accurate directions.
- Provide a sequence of commands or steps.
- Code using coding software.
- Transform ideas into something that can be seen.

KEY ACTIONS

- Find out information about mazes.
- Observe and interview others.
- Explore different materials.
- Create steps for following instructions.
- Draw a design for a maze.
- Create a maze using coding software.

OVERVIEW OF STAGES

TUNE IN:

Students find out about the history of mazes as well as about different types. They have the opportunity to complete different mazes. Students explore the strength and stability of different materials, how to create simple algorithms and simple maze theory.

EMPATHISE

Students find out about the features of mazes, including circular paths and shortcuts. They observe others attempting different types of mazes and interview them about their experiences to learn what makes a challenging and enjoyable maze.

DEFINE

Students analyse the results of their observations and interviews. They consider different options for software coding and robotics. They also think about the materials available for creating a full-scale maze as well as the size constraints.

IDEATE

Students come up with creative ideas for using different materials, shapes and features in a maze.

PROTOTYPE

Students choose a couple of ideas to develop further and prototype. This may include drawing, constructing or programming with code.

TEST

Students test the design of their maze, checking that it is possible to enter and exit the maze at different points. They consider the best materials to use for the construction of the maze.

SHARE AND EVALUATE:

Students create their final design and demonstrate their computer-generated maze to other students. Students may be able to share ideas with a mathematician or games enthusiast.

SUGGESTED SCHEDULE

LESSON	STAGE
1–4	**Tune in:** Find out about the history of mazes as well as different types; complete different mazes; explore the strength and stability of different materials, how to create simple algorithms and simple maze theory
5–7	**Empathise:** Find out about the features of mazes, including circular paths and shortcuts; observe others attempting different types of mazes and interview them about their experiences; write in journal
8–9	**Define:** Analyse results of observations and interviews; consider different options for software coding and robotics, available materials, size constraints and any possible issues; write in journal
10–11	**Ideate:** Come up with creative ideas for using different materials, shapes and features in a maze; write in journal
12–17	**Prototype** and **Test:** Develop a couple of ideas, including drawing and constructing designs; write code for the maze; write in journal
18–21	**Share and evaluate:** Provide time to complete the final design; share final designs; evaluate self and others

→ CURRICULUM LINKS

SCIENCE

YEAR	STRAND	SUB-STRAND AND CONTENT
4	Science Understanding	Chemical sciences: • Natural and processed materials have a range of physical properties that can influence their use
3 & 4	Science as a Human Endeavour	Nature and development of science: • Science involves making predictions and describing patterns and relationships
	Science Inquiry Skills	Questioning and predicting Processing and analysing data and information Communicating

TECHNOLOGIES

YEAR	STRAND	CONTENT
3 & 4	Design and Technologies Knowledge and Understanding	• Investigate the suitability of materials, systems, components, tools and equipment for a range of purposes
	Digital Technologies Processes and Production Skills	• Define simple problems, and describe and follow a sequence of steps and decisions (algorithms) needed to solve them

MATHEMATICS

YEAR	STRAND	SUB-STRAND AND CONTENT
3	Measurement and Geometry	Location and transformation: • Create and interpret simple grid maps to show position and pathways
4	Measurement and Geometry	Location and transformation: • Create symmetrical patterns, pictures and shapes with and without digital technologies

This investigation also links to the General Capabilities:

AC

- Literacy
- Numeracy
- Information and Communication Technology (ICT) Capability
- Critical and Creative Thinking.

→ ASSESSMENT

The following resources are provided for assessing students at different stages of the STEM investigations:

- Generic reproducible 1 (Key vocabulary table), for assessing understanding of vocabulary
- Generic reproducible 2 (Self-evaluation), for student self-evaluation of the learning process
- Generic reproducible 3 (Responding to the investigation)
- Generic reproducible 5 (Design thinking assessment rubric), for evaluating student engagement in the design thinking stages
- Learning journal templates 1, 2, 3 and 4, incorporating student reflection and evaluation.

GETTING READY FOR THE INVESTIGATION

You can prepare yourself and students for this STEM investigation in the following ways:

- Identify groups of students who will work well together. Organise the class into pairs.
- Review the **Key science knowledge** that supports this investigation, and look at the **Useful links**.
- Investigate the **Useful apps**.
- Gather materials for the science activities about properties of materials and algorithms during the Tune-in session, including different materials and a range of mazes to solve.
- Start collecting additional materials for prototyping (as shown on the **Materials needed** list).
- Determine where prototypes will be kept between lessons.
- Create a wall space where students can share their ideas in the Ideate stage.
- Decide on the materials that will be available for creating the mazes and whether or not a full-scale model will be built.
- Decide whether robots such as Bee-Bots or Spheros can be incorporated into the investigation.
- Investigate the coding apps suggested (see **Useful links**) and create accounts where necessary.
- Run some introductory sessions for the coding software students will use.
- Start thinking about:
  - » sourcing information about mazes
  - » making connections with a game developer
  - » time constraints for the task
  - » other students and classes that can be involved in the survey and evaluation stages
  - » how, when and where the designs will be shared and evaluated.

USEFUL APPS

- App for sharing ideas, thoughts, questions and images, such as Padlet or Lino
- App for creating shared documents, such as OneNote Class Notebook or SharePoint
- App for creating multimedia presentations, such as Adobe Spark Video (via a teacher-created class account), Prezi or iMovie
- App for engaging in collaborative tasks, such as OneNote Class Notebook or SharePoint
- App for coding, such as Scratch

USEFUL LINKS

- Information about mazes, including historical information, such as at mea.digital/sm108
- Information for teachers about explaining algorithms, such as at mea.digital/sm109
- Links to free, printable mazes, such as at mea.digital/sm110
- Links to free, interactive mazes, such as at mea.digital/sm111
- The world's top mazes, such as at mea.digital/sm112, mea.digital/sm113

RESOURCES PROVIDED

- Generic reproducibles 1, 2, 3, 5, 12
- Reproducibles 4.1, 4.2, 4.3
- Learning journal templates 1, 2, 3, 4

MATERIALS NEEDED

- Recycled materials, such as assorted cardboard boxes, cardboard offcuts, tubes, string, ribbon
- Scissors
- Tape – different widths, strengths, materials
- PVA glue
- Hot glue guns and glue (optional)
- Staplers and staples
- Cardboard
- Coloured paper
- Foil
- Bubble wrap
- Cotton, felt and other materials
- Construction blocks, such as Lego
- Small balls for testing stability

Hot glue guns can be dangerous. Make sure students are supervised at all times.

KEY SCIENCE KNOWLEDGE

This section provides an overview of the key science concepts and vocabulary needed for this unit.

MAZES AND MAZE THEORY

There are many different types of mazes, and different theories for solving them.

Simple mazes do not have circular paths (passage loops) leading back to where you started or any shortcuts via bridges. You can use 'wall following' to move from the entry to the exit of a simple maze. If the simple maze is three-dimensional, place a hand on either of the walls. Maintain contact with the same side of the wall while walking, until you reach the exit. The same method can be used to solve a paper maze.

Methods to solve other types of mazes include Trémaux's **algorithm**, which can be applied to all mazes.

COMPUTATIONAL THINKING

Computational thinking is the thought process related to problems and their solutions. It is most commonly associated with computer applications, but it can be used for other types of problem solving. Some terms related to computational thinking are:

- algorithm – a set of rules or steps for performing a task
- **logic** – thinking that allows analysis and prediction
- patterns – repeating elements, for example in a design
- evaluation – the act of making judgements, which may include design criteria
- creating – designing and making different things as well as evaluating
- debugging – finding and fixing what is wrong.

Simple maze theory can be used to escape this maze.

BUILDING WITH DIFFERENT MATERIALS

Materials have different **properties**, which affect how the materials can be used. Some of the properties of materials include strength, hardness and flexibility.

Materials can be natural (made from plants or animals, such as silk, cotton) or synthetic (made from chemicals, such as polythene). Common materials include metals, plastics, glass, wood and fabrics. The properties of these materials determine how they can be best used.

The **stability** of a structure relates to its ability to not move or change. The shape of a structure affects its stability. Triangles are the strongest shape. Cylinders are also very strong and stable. Other shapes, such as squares, sometimes incorporate triangular trusses to increase strength and stability.

KEY VOCABULARY

algorithm – a set of instructions or rules for performing a task
logic – a way of thinking that helps in checking facts and making predictions
property – a feature of a material, such as strength or ability to retain heat
stability – ability of something to not move or change

TUNE IN

1. Ask students to complete **Generic reproducible 1 (Key vocabulary table)** using the key vocabulary for this unit. This reproducible will also be used at the end of the unit, to demonstrate changes in understanding.
2. Provide students with some different mazes to try.
3. Have students discuss the mazes: 'Which mazes were easy/difficult to finish? Why? Which mazes did/didn't you like? Why?'
4. Students need to understand about algorithms, properties of materials and stability before beginning the challenge. Complete the following activities or similar.

ACTIVITY 1: EXPLORING ALGORITHMS

1. Demonstrate a simple task to students, such as making a jam sandwich. Write down each of the steps as they are performed. Introduce the term 'algorithm'. Explain that an algorithm is a series of steps or rules that need to be followed to complete a task.
2. Provide students with two copies of **Reproducible 4.1 (Treasure map)**. Have students work in pairs. Each student chooses a starting point on their treasure map and a location for the treasure. They draw the path and some landmarks (such as trees, lake, rocks) and then create a series of written instructions for their partner. A grid reference (such as B2) should be provided to indicate the start of the instructions.
3. Explain that each step represents one block on the grid. Instructions should include 'left, right, straight ahead, number of steps' and could also include terms such as 'until you arrive at ...'
4. Students swap their instructions and use a blank treasure map to show the path to the treasure. Provide time to discuss which instructions were helpful, any issues with creating or following instructions and what students could do to create a better algorithm.

ACTIVITY 2: TESTING MATERIALS

1. Provide students with a range of materials. Have them design a simple test to explore the relative strength of the materials. This could include how much weight a material can hold when suspended between two blocks.
2. Have students record their findings and share their responses.

ACTIVITY 3: TESTING STABILITY

1. Provide students with cardboard, tape and scissors. Have them create different three-dimensional objects, such as a cube, cylinder and triangle, then roll a ball at each of them. Give students a copy of **Reproducible 4.2 (Stable shapes)** to record their observations.
2. Provide students with time to create their own shapes and test their stability.

5. Introduce the STEM investigation and challenge to the students. Provide them with the student card and read the information together.
6. Introduce the design thinking process by reviewing the stages on the student card. Explain that students will keep a journal about their learning at the different stages of the design.

TOP TIP! When designing stability and materials tests, make sure students have only one variable. For example, when rolling the ball at the different structures, consider the distance and the speed of the ball.

USEFUL APPS/LINKS

- Links to free, printable mazes, such as at mea.digital/sm110
- Links to free, interactive mazes, such as at mea.digital/sm111

→ EMPATHISE

During the Empathise stage of the design thinking process, students focus on finding out about different points of view. To empathise with others, they need to research different types of mazes. This includes observing and finding out about how others interact with mazes. Students will take notes, ask questions, draw diagrams and take photos where relevant.

ACTIVITY 1: MAZE FEATURES

1. Have students create a collection of images, information and links about mazes.
2. Provide students with some background about mazes, which could be shared and discussed with students.
3. Create a collaborative work document using an app such as Padlet or OneNote Class Notebook.
4. Provide students with time to collect images of mazes and information about different types of mazes.
5. Encourage students to add to the collaborative space throughout the investigation.

ACTIVITY 2: OBSERVE MAZE SOLVING

1. Organise for students to work with students from another class or year level.
2. Provide students with a simple maze and a more complex maze, or have the class choose mazes to use.
3. Students from another class or year level attempt the different mazes while students involved in the investigation make observations about how the person approaches the maze, whether or not it appears difficult, if they have to go back to the start at any point and whether or not they persevere or give up.
4. Students then interview others to find out about their experiences and opinions. Provide students with **Reproducible 4.3 (Maze observations)** for recording observations as well as other notes during the interview.

PROMPTS

- Which types of maze did people like best, the simple maze or more complex maze?
- What were some of the issues with the mazes?
- How did you know if someone was enjoying or not enjoying completing a maze?
- What was one interesting thing you found out?

MORE VOCABULARY

- empathise – understand and consider another person or group's point of view

JOURNAL TIP

Ask students to complete **Learning journal template 1 (Empathise page)** while they are doing the different tasks. Remind them to date their notes and include photos of relevant information or pictures.

USEFUL APPS/LINKS

- Information about mazes, including historical information, such as at mea.digital/sm108
- Links to websites with free, printable mazes, such as at mea.digital/sm110
- App for sharing ideas, thoughts, questions and images, such as Padlet or Lino
- App for creating shared documents, such as OneNote Class Notebook or SharePoint

ASSESSMENT

This stage of the design thinking process offers opportunities to observe students collecting information, developing questions, and recording their notes and thinking in their journal.

TOP TIP! Before starting the observation session, discuss what students might be focusing on, for example facial expression, comments and body language.

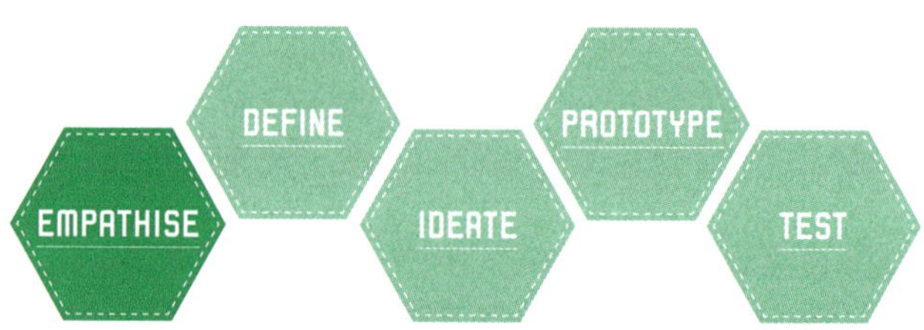

DEFINE

The main focus of this stage of the design thinking process is to reframe the challenge. The initial challenge is quite open, so at this stage students learn how to define what needs to be done. This includes noting insights that have been generated.

ACTIVITY 1: CONSIDER OBSERVATIONS OF MAZE ENGAGEMENT

1. Have students consider the information collected about how people interacted with mazes.
2. Discuss the different kinds of information collected, such as facial expression, body language and tone of voice. Create a large table, on a whiteboard or an interactive document such as OneNote Class Notebook. Create headings for the key types of observations, such as facial expression. Have groups of students write examples of what they observed onto sticky notes. Students then stick the note in the relevant section of the table.
3. Discuss which observations showed that someone was enjoying the activity and which showed that someone was not enjoying the activity.

ACTIVITY 2: CONSIDER INTERVIEW RESULTS

1. Review the interview results as a class.
2. Discuss the following questions:
   » Which mazes did people like best? Why did they like them?
   » Which mazes did people find difficult? Why?
   » Which features of the mazes did people find engaging?
   » Which features of the mazes did people find frustrating?
   » What were some of the words people used to describe how they felt about completing the maze task?
3. When thinking about the words used to describe people's response to the task, have students group the words into 'positive' and 'negative' responses.
4. Having considered the information gathered through observing, interviewing and researching mazes, provide students with any constraints, such as size of maze, materials available, inclusion of ideas for reusing materials and computer software to be used.

Students can update **Learning journal template 2 (Define page)**.

PROMPTS

- How will you use the information you gathered in the observation and interviews to help you design an interesting maze?
- Will it make a difference if you create a simple maze or a complex maze?
- How will you check that your design will be enjoyable?
- What other information do you need?

MORE VOCABULARY

- define – state the meaning of something
- insight – an accurate understanding of someone or something
- point of view – an opinion, attitude or judgement considered in a particular way

JOURNAL TIP

Discuss the term 'insight' and explain that it relates to something students have learned from the information gathered through research or excursions. You could refer to **Learning journal template 2**.

USEFUL APPS/LINKS

- App for engaging in collaborative tasks, such as OneNote Class Notebook

EMPATHISE DEFINE IDEATE PROTOTYPE TEST

→ IDEATE

The Ideate stage of the design thinking process is all about generating lots of ideas. Students need to be flexible in their thinking and be able to move beyond obvious ideas. At this stage, ideas are not judged, just generated and gathered.

ACTIVITY 1: CONSIDER SHAPES

1. Provide students with time to think of some ideas for the shape or shapes they might use when designing their maze.
2. Let students review pictures of different mazes before beginning the ideation process.
3. Encourage them to use their imagination.

ACTIVITY 2: CONSIDER MATERIALS AND REUSE

1. Have students consider the types of materials that they might use if they were building a full-scale model of their maze.
2. Have students choose two different materials (such as cardboard boxes and hay bales) and then come up with some ideas for each material.
3. When they have generated some ideas for each material, have students consider how the materials could be reused after the maze was no longer needed.
4. Students should create a simple matrix to gather their ideas, using the headings 'Material 1', 'Ways to use material 1', 'Material 2' and 'Ways to use material 2'.
5. Update **Learning journal template 3 (Ideate page)**.

PROMPTS

- What sorts of materials might you use?
- How can you make the maze easy to build?
- How can you make it more interesting?
- What if you had to use different materials?

MORE VOCABULARY

- feedback – information about, for example, a person's performance or the design of a product, which can be used to make improvements
- ideate – generate many ideas without making judgements about the ideas

JOURNAL TIP

When choosing three ideas to include in the journal, try to choose three ideas that use different materials or focus on different aspects of the challenge.

USEFUL APPS/LINKS

- The world's top mazes, such as at mea.digital/sm112, mea.digital/sm113

ASSESSMENT

At the Ideate stage, assessment could include observations about the number and diversity of student ideas, and their ability to provide feedback and create additional ideas. Reflection in the journal should provide an insight into some of the reasoning behind student choices.

EMPATHISE DEFINE IDEATE PROTOTYPE TEST

PROTOTYPE

At this stage of the design thinking process, students are asked to create a physical prototype of a solution. It is the stage where students need to get their ideas out of their heads and presented in a way that engages other students and helps them to understand the concept. When students create, it helps them to think and solve problems and disagreements. Students can role-play, make a storyboard or use sticky notes when they prototype. The most important feature is that viewers can interact with whatever is produced.

Encourage students to photograph or film during the Prototype and Test stages. This information can be used to show the learning behind the design thinking process in action.

ACTIVITY 1: CHOOSE IDEAS

1. Have students choose one of their top ideas to explore further.
2. Have them draw their maze design using a small whiteboard or pencil and paper.
3. After students have created their first design, have them review it and ask others for feedback. They should then make changes according to the feedback.
4. Have students choose another of their top design ideas and repeat the process.

ACTIVITY 2: PROGRAM THE MAZE

1. After students have selected their final idea, have them start creating their maze using a coding app such as Scratch.
2. They will need to consider the set of instructions needed to create their maze.
3. Students will need to check that their instructions are creating the correct design.

ACTIVITY 3: CONSTRUCT THE MAZE

1. Provide students with simple materials, such as cardboard, tape and scissors, or construction blocks, and have them create the maze that they have designed.
2. Remind students to check that the constructed maze is a scale model of the drawn or programmed maze.

Ask students to fill in the Prototype part of **Learning journal template 4 (Prototype and test page)**. See the **Journal tip** for further student guidance.

PROMPTS

- What is the main feature of your prototype?
- Where do you start and end in the maze?
- Is the maze a simple maze or a complex maze?
- Who will provide feedback about your design?

MORE VOCABULARY

- feedback – information about, for example, a person's performance or the design of a product, which can be used to make improvements
- prototype – an initial version of a model of a product or process that is used to develop a final model

JOURNAL TIP

Remind students to highlight the features of their prototype. If students are creating an electronic journal, they can insert a photo of their prototype and annotate it or include coding screengrabs.

TOP TIP! When asking for feedback, students could ask each other some of the following questions:

- What is the most important part?
- How does someone get out of the full-scale maze if they become stuck?
- What do you need to change?
- Will you need help with the coding program?

USEFUL APPS/LINKS

- App for taking photographs or video, such as Adobe Spark Video or iMovie

ASSESSMENT

Observe students as they make changes to their designs. Are they able to consider feedback, make modifications and move rapidly through this process, or do they have difficulties with holding on to an idea and accepting feedback?

EMPATHISE · DEFINE · IDEATE · **PROTOTYPE** · TEST

→ TEST

At this stage of the design thinking process, students test their prototype to see how it meets the criteria in the challenge.

ACTIVITY: TEST FEEDBACK

1. Have students gather feedback about the prototypes. This may include asking others to try their maze. Provide them with **Generic reproducible 12 (Prototype and test)** to record the ideas.
2. When providing feedback, have others consider the effectiveness of the design and how interesting and challenging it is.
3. Students continue to cycle through the Prototype and Test stages until they have completed their design.

Ask students to fill in **Learning journal template 4 (Prototype and test page)**. See the **Journal tip** for further student guidance.

PROMPTS

- Does your prototype do what you wanted it to do?
- Are there features that need to be added or removed?

MORE VOCABULARY

- evaluate – assess something, perhaps considering what worked and what didn't
- feature – a specific aspect of something, such as size, shape, colour, quality
- feedback – information about, for example, a person's performance or the design of a product, which can be used to make improvements
- prototype – an initial version of a model of a product or process that is used to develop a final model
- review – consider an idea, process or product and assess what works and what needs to be changed

JOURNAL TIP

Ask students to think about why it is important to test their ideas before finalising their design.

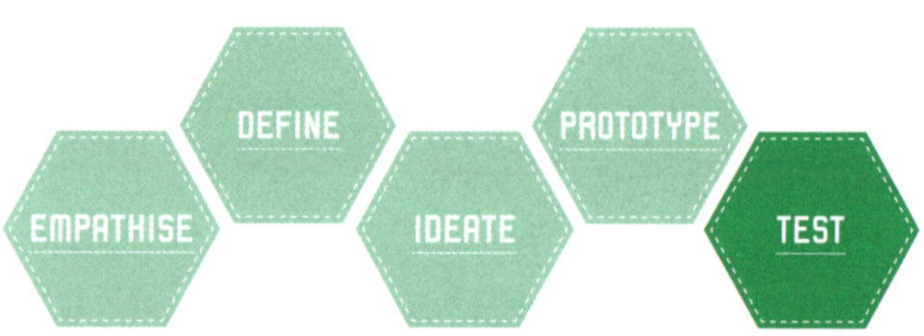

→ SHARE AND EVALUATE

At this stage of the investigation, students are provided with an opportunity to share their final design, as well as the processes involved in the investigation. Students evaluate their learning journals as well as their solutions.

ACTIVITY 1: FINALISE DESIGNS

1. Allow students to finalise their designs and put together a short presentation. They should also create a short piece of writing or infographic to show how the materials in the full-scale model could be reused. They may need a little extra time to investigate useful ways to recycle or reuse materials.
2. Set up a time for other people to see the different designs and provide feedback. People could include mathematicians or games enthusiasts.
3. Students should include their learning journals with the display so others can see the different stages of the design process.

ACTIVITY 2: EVALUATE AND GIVE FEEDBACK

1. Provide students with **Generic reproducible 2 (Self-evaluation)**.
2. During the sharing session, provide participants with tokens or stickers so they can vote for their favourite design or create an online survey with photos of the different designs for others to vote on.

ASSESSMENT

Ask students to again complete **Generic reproducible 1 (Key vocabulary table)** using the key vocabulary for this unit. Compare their table with the one they completed at the Tune-in stage, to demonstrate changes in understanding.

Students complete **Generic reproducible 3 (Responding to the investigation)**. Compare their responses to their responses to **Generic reproducible 2**.

Teachers complete **Generic reproducible 5 (Design thinking assessment rubric)** for each student. Students compare the feedback they are given by the teacher with their self-assessment of how they used the design thinking process to solve problems **(Generic reproducible 3)**.

Name: ....

Date: ....

1. Draw your treasure map on one copy of this page.
2. Write some instructions for your partner to find the hidden treasure. Here are some useful words to use:

   left right straight ahead until you reach ... stop

3. Give your partner a clean copy of this page. Now give them your instructions to find the treasure!

	1	2	3	4	5	6
A						
B						
C						
D						
E						
F						

STEM Investigations, MP, ISBN 978 1 4202 4319 2 © Macmillan Science and Education Australia 2018

TUNE IN

Name: ....

Date: ....

1. Create the shapes and objects listed in the table. Test how stable they are by rolling a ball at them. Write your observations.
2. Create your own shapes or objects. Write them in the table and test how stable they are. Record your observations.

   Which shapes and objects were the most stable? Why do you think so?

   Which shapes and objects were the least stable? Why do you think so?

Shape or object	Observations
Triangle 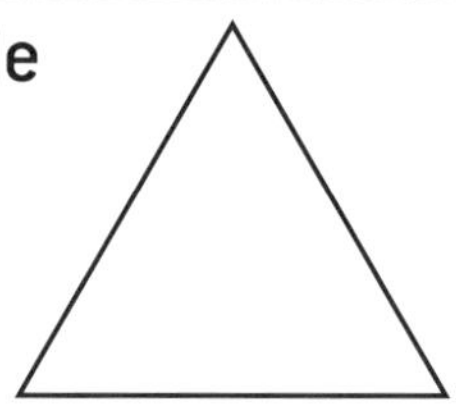	
Cylinder 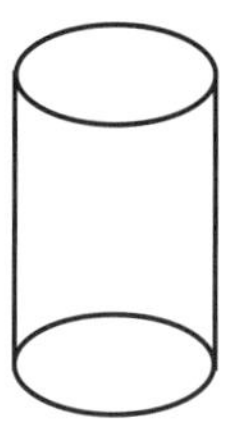	
Cube 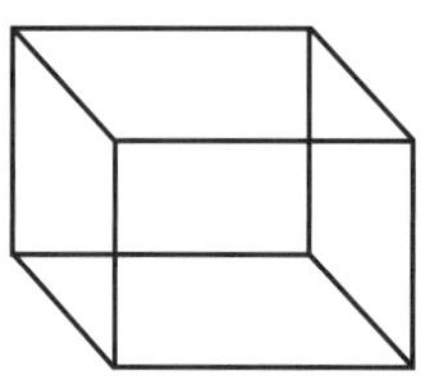	

STEM Investigations, MP, ISBN 978 1 4202 4319 2

EMPATHISE

STEM INVESTIGATIONS

Name: ....

Date: ....

1. Observe people working on two different types of maze – a simple maze and a complex maze. Write in the table what you **see** and **hear** (for example, facial expressions, comments or body language such as tapping fingers). Are people excited, frustrated, competitive or bored?
2. Ask people how they felt about doing the maze tasks. Write your notes in the table.

1. Observation	
Facial expression (e.g. eyebrows, lips moving)	
Body language (e.g. hunched, tapping fingers, looking around)	
Comments (e.g. talking to self, asking questions)	
2. Interview	
What did you like best about the mazes?	
What did you like least about the mazes?	
Which maze did you like the best? Why?	
What are some words you would use to describe how you felt about doing this activity?	

SAVE THE DAY WITH ICE CREAM!

MANAGED WORLD 5

INTRODUCTION

This investigation uses a common classroom activity, making ice cream in a bag, as part of a deeper investigation. Students learn about states of matter and how heating and cooling can change the state of matter. They manipulate freezing point to create their own ice cream. Students apply this knowledge to a real-life situation, where they need to change liquid ingredients into solid ice cream.

This engaging hands-on activity gives rich language opportunities outside of the science vocabulary, allowing teachers to support students to develop greater precision in their use of descriptions and observations. There are many opportunities for peer discussion and collaboration.

THE CHALLENGE

Your school is having a fundraising evening with an outdoor cinema. Your class is running an ice-cream stall to raise money. The donated ice-cream machine has broken, leaving you with only the ingredients. Can your class work together to save the day?

Your challenge is to design a machine that will help you use ice and the donated ingredients to churn one serve of ice cream at a time. As part of your investigation, you will learn how things change state between solids, liquids and gases, and how heat moves from one object to another.

KEY UNDERSTANDINGS

- A solid melts to become a liquid.
- A liquid freezes to become a solid.
- A liquid evaporates to become a gas.
- Solids, liquids and gases change states when heated or cooled.
- Different substances change states at different temperatures.

KEY SKILLS

- Use the words 'solid', 'liquid', 'gas' and 'conduction' correctly, with explanations.
- Explain how temperature affects the state of a substance, correctly using terms such as 'melting' and 'freezing' and relating these to the addition or removal of heat.
- Make careful observations, sharing ideas and hypotheses with peers and teachers.
- Measure and compare temperatures accurately using a thermometer, using comparative language to explain differences in state.

KEY VOCABULARY

conduction – the movement of heat energy from one object to another

freezing point – the temperature at which a liquid changes to a solid

state of matter – one of the forms in which physical things can exist, such as solid, liquid and gas

KEY ACTIONS

- Explore solids, liquids and gases and how they change state.
- Interview an adult about their experiences of dealing with a challenging situation.
- Come up with ways to make ice cream.
- Make a prototype of an ice-cream machine.

→ OVERVIEW OF STAGES

TUNE IN:

Students learn about the basic states of matter (solid, liquid, gas) and investigate how adding or removing heat creates a change in the state. They learn about freezing point by creating ice cream.

EMPATHISE

Students interview a parent or other adult and learn about a time when they had to overcome an unexpected obstacle. They reflect on the personal qualities that help people overcome last-minute challenges.

DEFINE

Students identify the necessary conditions for changing a liquid to a solid. They consider the key features needed to successfully create a machine to churn and freeze ice cream.

IDEATE

Students generate design ideas for an ice-cream machine. They collaborate with peers to evaluate, synthesise and refine their ideas before selecting one idea to prototype.

PROTOTYPE

Students cycle through the process of creating, gaining feedback, evaluating and prototyping until they achieve a prototype that meets the design brief.

TEST

Students evaluate their final prototype against the criteria they identified during the Define stage. They will make changes based on their testing results.

SHARE AND EVALUATE:

Students finalise their design and prepare to share their ideas with a defined audience, receiving feedback about their final product. Guests such as qualified parents or friends could be invited to provide feedback.

→ SUGGESTED SCHEDULE

LESSON	STAGE
1–3	**Tune in:** Learn about states of matter and the effect of temperature change
4–5	**Empathise:** Interview a significant adult and learn about overcoming adversity; write in journal
6–7	**Define:** Identify the key elements needed for successful prototype design; write in journal
8–9	**Ideate:** Develop a series of ideas and select one for prototyping; write in journal
10–14	**Prototype** and **Test:** Create and evaluate a prototype according to criteria; write in journal
15–16	**Share and evaluate:** Share finished products and receive peer and teacher evaluation; write in journal

CURRICULUM LINKS

SCIENCE

YEAR	STRAND	SUB-STRAND AND CONTENT
3	Science Understanding	Chemical sciences: • A change of state between solid and liquid can be caused by adding or removing heat Physical sciences: • Heat can be produced in many ways and can move from one object to another
4	Science Understanding	Chemical sciences: • Natural and processed materials have a range of physical properties that can influence their use
3 & 4	Science as a Human Endeavour	Use and influence of science: • Science knowledge helps people to understand the effect of their actions

TECHNOLOGIES

YEAR	STRAND	CONTENT
3 & 4	Design and Technologies Knowledge and Understanding	• Investigate how forces and the properties of materials affect the behaviour of a product or system • Investigate the suitability of materials, systems, components, tools and equipment for a range of purposes
	Design and Technologies Processes and Production Skills	• Critique needs or opportunities for designing and explore and test a variety of materials, components, tools and equipment and the techniques needed to produce designed solutions • Generate, develop and communicate design ideas and decisions using appropriate technical terms and graphical representation techniques • Evaluate design ideas, processes and solutions based on criteria for success developed with guidance and including care for the environment
	Digital Technologies Knowledge and Understanding	• Recognise different types of data and explore how the same data can be represented in different ways
	Digital Technologies Processes and Production Skills	• Collect, access and present different types of data using simple software to create information and solve problems • Plan, create and communicate ideas and information independently and with others, applying agreed ethical and social protocols

MATHEMATICS

YEAR	STRAND	SUB-STRAND AND CONTENT
3	Measurement and Geometry	Using units of measurement: • Measure, order and compare objects using familiar metric units of length, mass and capacity
4	Measurement and Geometry	Using units of measurement: • Use scaled instruments to measure and compare lengths, masses, capacities and temperatures

This investigation also links to the General Capabilities:

- Literacy
- Numeracy
- Information and Communication Technology (ICT) Capability
- Critical and Creative Thinking.

ASSESSMENT

The following resources are provided for assessing students at different stages of the STEM investigations:

- Generic reproducible 1 (Key vocabulary table), for assessing understanding of vocabulary
- Generic reproducible 2 (Self-evaluation), for student self-evaluation of the learning process
- Generic reproducible 3 (Responding to the investigation)
- Generic reproducible 5 (Design thinking assessment rubric), for evaluating student engagement in the design thinking stages
- Learning journal templates 1, 2, 3 and 4, incorporating student reflection and evaluation.

GETTING READY FOR THE INVESTIGATION

You can prepare yourself and students for this STEM investigation in the following ways:

- Familiarise yourself with making ice cream in a bag (see **Useful links**). Be sure you can discuss and guide students through the process.
- Consider the best teaching approach for your students to reflect on their personal strengths during the Empathise stage.
- Gather a variety of resources to assist students to create their prototypes from recycling centres and other sources.
- Contact parents to try to make connections with a scientist or engineer as a possible audience member for the Share stage or to agree to be interviewed for the Empathise stage.

USEFUL APPS

- Apps for online surveys, such as Typeform or Excel Survey
- App for collating notes, such as Notability or OneNote Class Notebook
- App for creating sematic maps, such as Popplet
- App for recording the progress of their design development, such as Adobe Spark (via a teacher-created class account)
- App for creating interactive links (for example, between descriptions, videos, images and websites and a main image), such as ThingLink

USEFUL LINKS

- Video clip introducing matter, such as at mea.digital/sm37
- Video clip and article about making ice cream in a bag, such as at mea.digital/sm38
- The science behind ice cream in a bag, such as at mea.digital/sm39
- Articles for teachers about states of matter, such as at mea.digital/sm40, mea.digital/sm41
- Activity about changes of state, such as at mea.digital/sm42

RESOURCES PROVIDED

- Generic reproducibles 1, 2, 3, 5, 6, 9, 11
- Reproducibles 5.1, 5.2, 5.3
- Learning journal templates 1, 2, 3, 4

MATERIALS NEEDED

- Thermometers
- Warm and cold water
- Bags of ice
- Jugs and disposable cups and spoons
- Kettle (under teacher supervision)
- Sealable bags (medium and large)
- Tea towels
- Cream or lactose-free alternatives, caster sugar, maple syrup, vanilla essence, table salt (less likely to pierce bags than rock salt)
- Brainstorming paper
- Markers and highlighters
- Sticky notes and index cards
- Variety of new and recycled construction materials
- Tape, glue and glue guns

Hot glue guns can be dangerous. Make sure students are supervised at all times.

Ice cream in a bag works well with equal volume substitution of lactose-free cream or coconut cream for the regular cream, and maple syrup for the sugar. Beware of honey as a sweetener as this can be an issue for some types of food intolerance.

KEY SCIENCE KNOWLEDGE

This section provides an overview of the key science concepts and vocabulary needed for this unit.

STATES OF MATTER

There are three main **states of matter**, each with distinctive, observable features:

- In the solid state, particles are tightly packed and rigid, forming a fixed shape. Particles in a solid state vibrate in place, but don't move around.
- In the liquid state, particles are less tightly packed, can flow between containers and take the shape of any container. Particles in liquid flow past and around each other but remain connected.
- In the gas state, particles move far apart and move quickly, filling the available space in a container. Particles in gas move independently from each other.

CONDUCTION AND CHANGES OF STATE

Heat **conduction** occurs when energy flows between or away from objects. This flow of energy depends on the temperature difference between an object and its surroundings. Consider chocolate: you can heat solid chocolate to create a liquid, or you can cool liquid chocolate to create a solid. The process of heating or cooling is the conduction of heat and it changes the state of the substance:

- When heat is added, solids become liquids and liquids become gases.
- When heat is removed (cooling), gases become liquids and liquids become solids.

SOLID

Solids have atoms or molecules that sit tightly together. They have a definite shape and size. They are very difficult to compress.

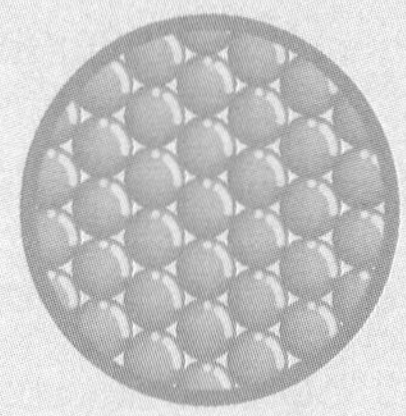

LIQUID

Liquids contain atoms or molecules that can move more than solids. They have a fixed volume, will flow and take on the shape of their container. They can be slightly compressed.

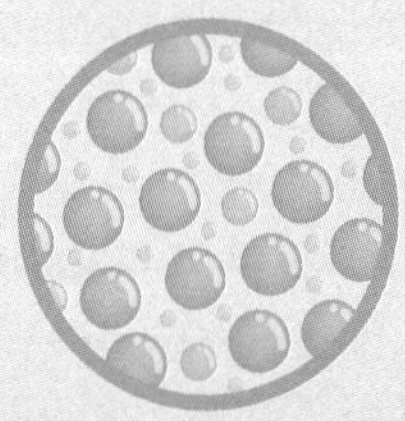

GAS

Gases have no fixed shape or volume. The atoms are moving rapidly and can spread out. They can be compressed.

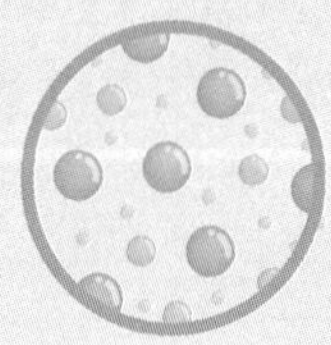

FREEZING POINTS

The temperature at which these changes occur varies depending on the substance. The **freezing point** for pure water is 0 degrees Celsius; however, for nitrogen it is –210 degrees Celsius. Freezing point can be changed by adding other substances such as salt. In this investigation, salt is added to decrease the freezing point of ice. The salty mix of ice and water can reach a temperature as low as –6 degrees Celsius. This helps speed up the process of conducting heat away from the liquid ingredients and so the ingredients freeze to become ice cream.

KEY VOCABULARY

conduction – the movement of heat energy from one object to another

freezing point – the temperature at which a liquid changes to a solid

state of matter – one of the forms in which physical things can exist, such as solid, liquid and gas

→ TUNE IN

1. Ask students to complete **Generic reproducible 1 (Key vocabulary table)** using the key vocabulary for this unit. This reproducible will also be used at the end of the unit, to demonstrate changes in understanding.
2. Introduce the general challenge and create a table on the whiteboard comparing favourite ice-cream flavours.
3. Listen to a song about states of matter (see **Useful apps/links**), making up actions for each of solid (such as a fist), liquid (such as rubbing hands) and gas (such as waving hands in the air). Ask, 'Was the energy in the music and your hand gestures different for each state of matter? Can you give the examples of each state of matter in the song?'

ACTIVITY 1: STATES OF MATTER

1. Watch a short video clip about states of matter (see **Useful apps/links**).
2. Distribute **Reproducible 5.1 (States of matter)**, pausing the video where necessary to complete the reproducible together. Add vocabulary clarifications, explanations and more detail in response to questions and discussion.
3. Play an interactive sorting game (see **Useful apps/links**).

ACTIVITY 2: HEAT AND COLD CAN REALLY MOVE!

1. Set up a series of experiment stations prior to the lesson.
2. Distribute **Reproducible 5.2 (Changes in states of matter)** and explain the rotations. Demonstrate how to read a thermometer and explain that the boiling water station cannot be used without a teacher present.
3. Encourage students to move around the stations, following the instructions on **Reproducible 5.2** and recording their observations.
4. Explain that conduction is the way that heat moves through materials, and that hotter objects will always lose energy and become cooler.

ACTIVITY 3: MAKING ICE CREAM IN A BAG

1. Read some information or watch a video clip about making ice cream in a bag (see **Useful apps/links**). Distribute **Reproducible 5.3 (Ice cream in a bag)**.
2. Share some hints, such as being careful to seal the bags and to wrap the larger bag in a tea towel and knead it like dough.
3. Students can complete the activity in pairs, taking turns to check the consistency of the ice-cream mix and recording observations while mixing or kneading.
4. Share the finished ice cream between student pairs in disposable cups and explain the role of ice in decreasing freezing point.
5. Complete **Reproducible 5.3**.

4. Introduce the STEM investigation and challenge. Provide students with the student card and read it together.
5. Introduce the design thinking process. Explain that students will keep a journal about their learning at the different stages of the design.

TOP TIP! Always be very careful to allow for food allergies and intolerances. It is best to contact parents directly prior to making ice cream in a bag and clarify any safety concerns. Also, remind students that ice cream and similar foods are fun to eat occasionally, but they are not something to eat every day.

USEFUL APPS/LINKS

- Song about states of matter, such as at mea.digital/sm43
- Video clips about states of matter, such as at mea.digital/sm44, mea.digital/sm45, mea.digital/sm46
- Game to sort solids, liquids and gases, such as at mea.digital/sm47
- Video and article about making ice cream in a bag, such as at mea.digital/sm38

EMPATHISE

During the Empathise stage of the design thinking process, students focus on finding out about different points of view. To empathise with others, they need to understand how others have felt when confronted by challenges, how they have overcome them and the skills they called upon. This includes reflecting on their own strengths and limitations. Students will take notes, ask questions, reflect on their own and others' strengths and create displays.

ACTIVITY 1: INTERVIEW A PARENT OR OTHER ADULT

1. Share with students a time when you had a last-minute problem and how you overcame it. Emphasise the initial feelings of frustration and the importance of persevering when things don't go as planned.
2. Distribute **Generic reproducible 11 (Student interview)** and agree as a class about the questions to ask a significant person.
3. Allow time for students to conduct the interview.
4. Share responses and explore the ways in which these adults overcame last-minute problems.

ACTIVITY 2: COMPLETE A PERSONAL STRENGTH INVENTORY

1. Ask students to identify some qualities they like about others in the grade. You might like to share this orally or in written form.
2. Create a personal strength chain using classmates' comments or use a proforma (see **Useful apps/links**).
3. Explain to a partner how one of their personal strengths would help them in this STEM Investigation scenario.

PROMPTS

- How do the adults we know deal with things going wrong?
- What qualities and behaviours did these adults show?
- What qualities and behaviours can you show if your STEM investigation doesn't go as you planned?

MORE VOCABULARY

- empathise – understand and consider another person or group's point of view
- personal strengths – the special things about you that help you do well
- point of view – an opinion, attitude or judgement considered in a particular way
- qualities – attitudes, thoughts and behaviours that make us special and unique

JOURNAL TIP

Ask students to complete **Learning journal template 1 (Empathise page)** while they are doing the different tasks. Remind them to date their notes and include photos of relevant information or pictures.

USEFUL APPS/LINKS

- Article and activity about appreciating personal qualities, such as at mea.digital/sm48
- App for online surveys, such as Typeform or Excel Survey

ASSESSMENT

This stage of the design thinking process offers opportunities to observe students collecting information, developing questions, and recording their notes and thinking in their journal.

TOP TIP!

These activities are rich in oral language opportunities. Often, students of this age need the adults around them to act as synonym and antonym finders, assisting them to broaden and deepen their oral and written vocabulary. Opportunities to discuss the qualities and behaviours of others allows students to identify role-models and develop the language and cognition for personal reflection that enables them to successfully engage in metacognition.

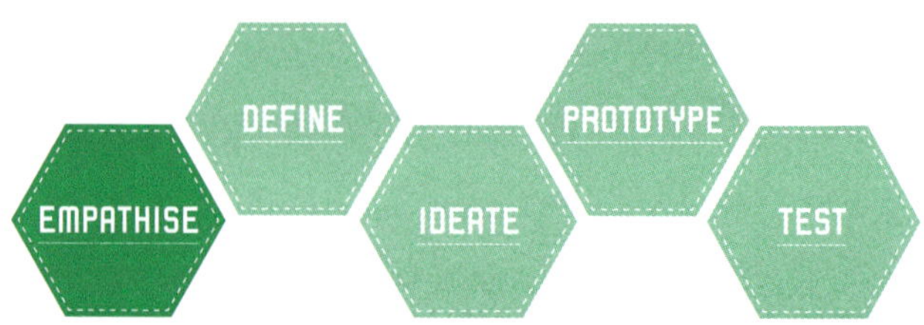

→ DEFINE

The main focus of this stage of the design thinking process is to reframe the challenge. The initial challenge is quite open, so at this stage students learn how to define what needs to be done. This includes noting insights that have been generated.

ACTIVITY 1: CONSIDER OBSERVATIONS

1. Allocate students to investigation groups and distribute **Generic reproducible 9 (See, think, wonder)** and **Generic reproducible 6 (In the frame)**.
2. Ask students to reflect on the activities from the Tune-in session and the information on the task card. Complete **Generic reproducible 9** as a group.
3. Have students share their completed sheets with another group and discuss their insights on the task.
4. Ask students to add further details if they gained insights through their discussion with another group.

ACTIVITY 2: CONSIDER INSIGHTS

1. Using the completed **Generic reproducible 6 (In the frame)** and **Reproducibles 5.1, 5.2 and 5.3**, have groups arrange sticky notes to identify the key ingredients, materials and processes that they will need to include in their plans for their ice-cream machines.
2. Encourage students to rank or order their sticky notes to reflect the importance of each ingredient, material and process.
3. Conduct a silent gallery walk where students walk silently to observe the ideas of others. At this stage there should be no discussion – students consider the ideas and perspectives of others without defence or questioning.
4. Have groups review their own priorities and make any revisions.

Students can update **Learning journal template 2 (Define page)**.

PROMPTS

- What is the process that will change a liquid to a solid in your machine?
- What are the essential elements of an effective ice-cream machine?
- What would be helpful to include?
- What ideas can you ignore as unhelpful or not essential?

MORE VOCABULARY

- define – state the meaning of something
- effective – likely to work in the manner expected
- insight – an accurate understanding of someone or something
- point of view – an opinion, attitude or judgement considered in a particular way

JOURNAL TIP

Discuss the term 'insight' and explain that it relates to something students have learned about the people and their responses to the surveys as well as information gathered through learning activities. Ask students to identify how they can use their personal strengths to assist them to succeed in this challenge.

USEFUL APPS/LINKS

- App for collating notes, such as Notability or OneNote Class Notebook
- App for creating sematic maps, such as Popplet

EMPATHISE DEFINE IDEATE PROTOTYPE TEST

IDEATE

The Ideate stage of the design thinking process is all about generating lots of ideas. Students need to be flexible in their thinking and be able to move beyond obvious ideas. At this stage, ideas are not judged, just generated and gathered.

ACTIVITY: GENERATE IDEAS

1. Allow students time to review their notes from previous lessons and their priorities for materials and processes in their ice-cream machines.
2. Review key vocabulary and discuss how students need to change a liquid to a solid by using the freezing point.
3. Have each student create a series of four brief, annotated sketches of their idea for an ice-cream machine, with one idea per sticky note or card.
4. One at a time, have students place a sticky note or a card on a display board or whiteboard. The next student can add their idea to an existing image or create a new section of the display.
5. Continue to silently place ideas on display until all ideas have been shared.
6. Invite students to look at the different ideas and groupings and share feedback with each other about commonalities and differences in the designs.
7. Allow students to add new designs, move ideas to new groupings and share their observations and ideas with others.
8. Encourage students to continue generating and revising their ideas to reflect their own insights and the feedback from others.
9. Ask students to record three of their previous or revised ideas in **Learning journal template 3 (Ideate page)**, identifying and explaining which idea they would like to explore further.

PROMPTS

- How do these ideas relate to the task of making an ice-cream machine?
- What ideas, structures, methods and materials seem to be popular?
- How could you test your ideas?
- How could you synthesise your ideas or change them completely?

MORE VOCABULARY

- feedback – information about, for example, a person's performance or the design of a product, which can be used to make improvements
- ideate – generate many ideas without making judgements about the ideas
- reflect – consider and evaluate
- synthesise – combine two or more ideas to create something new

JOURNAL TIP

When choosing ideas to include in the journal, try to choose three ideas that aren't related.

USEFUL APPS/LINKS

- App for collating notes, such as Notability or OneNote Class Notebook
- App for creating sematic maps, such as Popplet
- App for sharing and grouping ideas, such as Padlet
- Article about creative thinking tools, such as mea.digital/sm49

ASSESSMENT

At the Ideate stage, assessment could include observations about the number and diversity of student ideas, and their ability to provide feedback and create additional ideas. Reflection in the journal should provide an insight into some of the reasoning behind student choices.

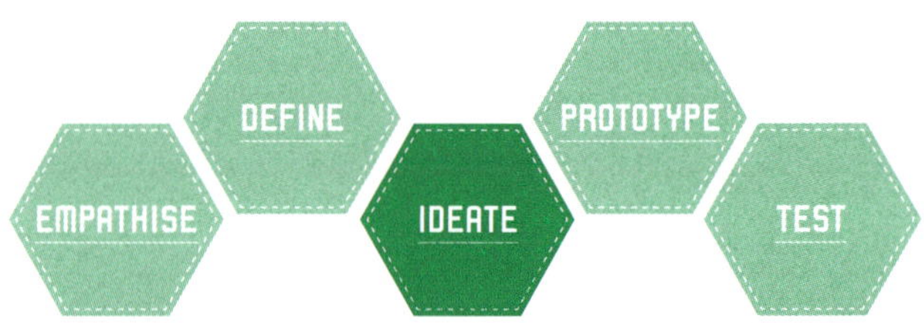

→ PROTOTYPE

At this stage, students are asked to create a physical prototype of a solution. Students need to get their ideas out of their heads and present them in a way that engages other students and helps them to understand the concept. When students create, it helps them to think and solve problems and disagreements.

Encourage students to photograph or film during the Prototype and Test stages. This information can be used to show the learning behind the design thinking process in action.

ACTIVITY: TRANSFORM IDEAS INTO PROTOTYPES

1. Ask students to review their science knowledge from the Tune-in session and their ideas from the Ideate stage. They can discuss with a partner an idea that they take pride in.
2. Distribute a new copy of **Generic reproducible 6 (In the frame)** and ask students to organise their ideas into least relevant and most relevant. Provide them with prompt questions to help them identify and colour code essential and preferred design elements of their designs:
   - » Will this element help to freeze or mix your ice-cream ingredients?
   - » Will this element help to make your machine easy to use?
   - » Can you see any elements to change?
   - » How else could you achieve your goal?

   Students continue to reflect and refine their ideas until they are ready to create a prototype.
3. Provide students with materials for their prototype. Remind them that it should be created rapidly, and can be labelled.
4. Encourage students to evaluate their prototype using the suggested prompts and seek feedback from their peers. When asking for feedback, students could ask each other some of the following questions:
   - » What is the main feature of your prototype?
   - » How does it work?
   - » Which aspects work best? Which aspects need changing? How might you do this?
   - » What other materials might you need?
   - » Considering what you learned about personal strengths in the Empathise stage, who is best suited to which tasks?
5. Support students to use the feedback to refine their prototypes.

Ask students to fill in the Prototype part of **Learning journal template 4 (Prototype and test page)**. See the **Journal tip** for further student guidance.

TOP TIP! The Prototype stage is often very messy. It is important that students are focusing on their ideas, rather than the end product. Provide them with lots of materials – recycling depots can be a useful source of resources. Student may add labels to prototypes to explain some of the main features. Photographing and annotating pictures of prototypes can be useful.

MORE VOCABULARY

- feedback – information about, for example, a person's performance or the design of a product, which can be used to make improvements
- prototype – an initial version of a model of a product or process that is used to develop a final model

JOURNAL TIP

Remind students to highlight the main features of their prototype. If students are creating an electronic journal, they can insert a photo of their prototype and annotate it.

USEFUL APPS/LINKS

- App for recording the progress of design development, such as Adobe Spark Video
- App for notetaking and collaboration, such as Notability or OneNote Class Notebook
- App for creating interactive links (for example, between descriptions, videos, images and websites and a main image), such as ThingLink

ASSESSMENT

Observe students as they make changes to their designs. Are they able to consider feedback, make modifications and move rapidly through this process, or do they have difficulties with holding on to an idea and accepting feedback?

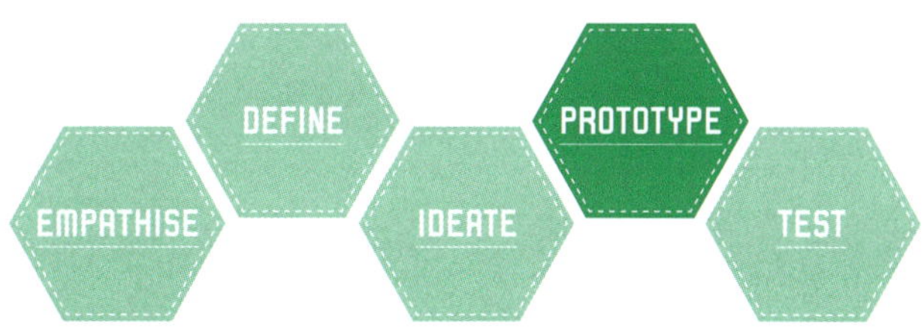

→ TEST

At this stage of the design thinking process, students test their prototype to see how it meets the criteria in the challenge.

ACTIVITY: TEST FEEDBACK

1. Ask students to share their prototype with a peer, seeking feedback about the effectiveness of their design.
2. Ask students to reflect on how well their design meets the initial challenge. Could they make a single serve of ice cream with their design? Consider any improvements to be made.
3. Provide the opportunity to cycle through the Prototype and Test stages again.

Ask students to fill in **Learning journal template 4 (Prototype and test page)**. See the **Journal tip** for further student guidance.

PROMPTS

- Does your prototype do what you wanted it to do?
- Are there other features that need to be added?
- Are there any notes or additional information you need to add to your prototype?

MORE VOCABULARY

- effective – likely to work in the manner expected
- evaluate – assess something, perhaps considering what worked and what didn't
- feature – a specific aspect of something, such as size, shape, colour or quality
- feedback – information about, for example, a person's performance or the design of a product, which can be used to make improvements
- prototype – an initial version of a model of a product or process that is used to develop a final model
- review – consider an idea, process or product and assess what works and what needs to be changed

JOURNAL TIP

Ask students to think about why it is important to test their ideas before they build their final design.

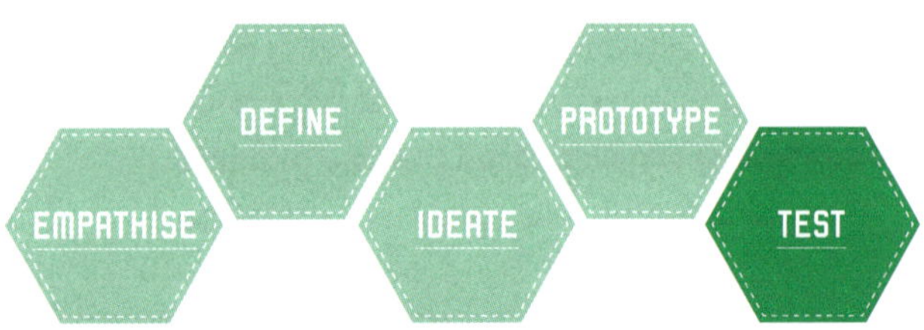

→ SHARE AND EVALUATE

At this stage of the investigation, students are provided with an opportunity to share their final design, as well as the processes involved in the investigation. Students evaluate their learning journals as well as their solutions.

ACTIVITY: FINALISE DESIGNS

1. Allow students time to create a final design.
2. Provide the time for students to use annotations, video, interactive apps or other creative technologies to explain and expand on their ideas and their learning through this investigation.

ASSESSMENT

Ask students to again complete **Generic reproducible 1 (Key vocabulary table)** using the key vocabulary for this unit. Compare their table with the one they completed at the Tune-in stage, to demonstrate changes in understanding.

Students complete **Generic reproducible 3 (Responding to the investigation)**. Compare their responses to their responses to **Generic reproducible 2 (Self-evaluation)**.

Teachers complete **Generic reproducible 5 (Design thinking assessment rubric)** for each student. Students compare the feedback they are given by the teacher with their self-assessment of how they used the design thinking process to solve problems **(Generic reproducible 3)**.

TUNE IN

STEM INVESTIGATIONS

Name: ....

Date: ....

Draw a line to match each state of matter to a description of its properties.

Solid	Particles connected with space between them Takes the shape of a container You can push things into it or move through it slowly
Liquid	Particles moving away from each other Spreads out to fill the space available You can move freely through it
Gas	Particles packed tightly Doesn't need a container You can't move through it

What do we call the changes of states? Draw a line from each description to its matching word.

solid → liquid	evaporate
liquid → gas	freeze
liquid → solid	condense
gas → liquid	melt

Move around the room and observe the changes in states of matter and the temperature of the substance at each station.

TUNE IN

STEM INVESTIGATIONS

Name: ....

Date: ....

Station	What to do	Observations and answers
Lots of ice and lots of water	Look at the two cups: • ice slurry of crushed ice and a little water • ice cubes floating in water. What are the two different states of matter?	
Hot and cold	Pour some warm water from the jug or the tap into one cup. Pour cold water into another cup. Measure the temperature of the water and add three cubes of ice to each cup. After two minutes, measure the temperatures again. Compare your results.	
Hot water and more heat	Your teacher will add heat to warm water by boiling the kettle. What can you observe about hot water when more heat is added?	

Name: ....

Date: ....

Mix your ice cream in a bag. Stop mixing every couple of minutes. Can you observe when the liquid ingredients become solid?

Stage	Observations
Before adding the mixture to the ice	
After 2 minutes in the ice	
After 4 minutes in the ice	
After 6 minutes in the ice	
After 8 minutes in the ice	
After 10 minutes in the ice	

Listen to your teacher's explanation about salt in the ice. Use your own words to explain how the salt in the ice helped you to make your ice cream.

....

....

....

....

....

....

STEM Investigations, MP, ISBN 978 1 4202 4319 2 © Macmillan Science and Education Australia 2018

KEEP THE WATER TAPS COOL

INTRODUCTION

Access to clean water is considered a basic human right. In developed countries, most people are fortunate to access water that is clean and delivered to taps in their homes, workplaces and community facilities. In warmer months in countries with warm or hot climates, water taps, including taps at schools, often deliver warm water, and so people are often less likely to drink the amount of water they need to maintain good health.

This investigation provides students with the opportunity to learn about the importance of water for humans. They are challenged to create a solution for warmer months when drinking water is often warm and less palatable, and they should encourage other students to drink cool water. They explore heat transfer and materials that are good conductors. Students also consider creating accessories to make access to cool water easy and effective. They explore some simple machines to help with their designs.

THE CHALLENGE

During summer, the drinking taps in your schoolyard can get too hot to touch. The water is warm as it comes out. The teachers want to come up with a quick solution to fix this, without replacing the taps.

Your challenge is to stop these water taps getting hot or to cool the water. Think about materials the taps could be covered in. Perhaps something could be added? You also need to encourage students to use the taps and drink more water. As part of your investigation, you will test materials and discover how they conduct heat.

KEY UNDERSTANDINGS

- Heat is a type of energy.
- Heat can move from one object to another.
- Some materials conduct heat more easily than others.
- Materials that do not conduct heat well are called insulators.
- Simple machines can be used to make work easier.

KEY VOCABULARY

conductor – a material that is good at allowing heat and sound to go in and out

heat – a form of energy

insulator – a material that helps to stop heat or sound from going in or out

property – feature of a material

temperature – a measure of how hot something is and the heat movement between objects

KEY SKILLS

- Make careful observations.
- Learn about heat and heat movement, especially conduction of heat.
- Conduct fair experiments, including considering variables.
- Find out about the importance of drinking water for health.
- Transform ideas into something that can be seen – discuss, write, draw and build ideas.

KEY ACTIONS

- Find out about the importance of drinking water.
- Explore how heat moves.
- Learn about materials used for insulation.
- Create a design to keep water cool.
- Raise awareness of the importance of drinking water for good health.

OVERVIEW OF STAGES

TUNE IN:

Students find out about the importance of water for good health. They consider their own responses to different water temperatures. Students explore heat transfer, insulation and simple machines.

EMPATHISE

Students find out about other students' water drinking habits through the creation of a survey. They observe the use of the school's drinking water taps and gather information to help find out which taps are used most often by students.

DEFINE

Students analyse the results of their surveys and observations. They gather information about the temperature of different taps and discuss why there might be issues with them.

IDEATE

Students come up with creative ideas for insulating the water pipes and/or taps so that water can remain cool. They are also challenged to create an accessory that is easily used and helps to keep water at a pleasant drinking temperature.

PROTOTYPE

Students choose a couple of ideas to develop further and prototype. This may include drawing and constructing.

TEST

Students test the design of their drinking tap insulation or accessory and get student feedback. They consider different ways to work out the effectiveness of the design as well as its ease of use.

SHARE AND EVALUATE:

Students create their final design as well as a short campaign to raise awareness of the importance of water for good health. They share their designs and evaluate their own and others' solutions. Students may be able to share their ideas with a local water company, school council or engineer.

SUGGESTED SCHEDULE

LESSON	STAGE
1–3	**Tune in:** Find out the importance of water for good health; consider individual water temperature preferences; explore heat transfer, insulation and simple machines
4–7	**Empathise:** Survey others to find out about their water drinking habits; observe use of the school's drinking water taps; write in journal
8–10	**Define:** Analyse results of survey and observation; gather information about the temperature of different taps; consider issues; write in journal
11–12	**Ideate:** Come up with creative ideas for insulating water pipes and taps so water can remain cool; create an accessory for a tap that is easy to use and effective; write in journal
13–17	**Prototype** and **Test:** Develop a couple of ideas, including drawing and constructing designs; write in journal
18–21	**Share and evaluate:** Provide time to complete the final design; create a short water awareness campaign; share final designs; evaluate self and others

CURRICULUM LINKS

SCIENCE

YEAR	STRAND	SUB-STRAND AND CONTENT
3	Science Understanding	Physical sciences: • Heat can be produced in many ways and can move from one object to another
4	Science Understanding	Chemical sciences: • Natural and processed materials have a range of physical properties that can influence their use
3 & 4	Science as a Human Endeavour	Nature and development of science: • Science involves making predictions and describing patterns and relationships Use and influence of science: • Science knowledge helps people to understand the effect of their actions
	Science Inquiry Skills	Questioning and predicting Planning and conducting Processing and analysing data and information Communicating

TECHNOLOGIES

YEAR	STRAND	CONTENT
3 & 4	Design and Technologies Knowledge and Understanding	• Investigate the suitability of materials, systems, components, tools and equipment for a range of purposes • Recognise the role of people in design and technologies occupations and explore factors, including sustainability, that impact on the design of solutions to meet community needs
	Design and Technologies Processes and Production Skills	• Select and use materials, components, tools, equipment and techniques and use safe work practices to make designed solutions • Generate, develop and communicate design ideas and decisions using appropriate technical terms and graphical representation techniques

MATHEMATICS

YEAR	STRAND	SUB-STRAND AND CONTENT
3	Measurement and Geometry	Using units of measurement: • Measure, order and compare objects using familiar metric units of length, mass and capacity
4	Measurement and Geometry	Using units of measurement: • Use scaled instruments to measure and compare lengths, masses, capacities and temperatures

This investigation also links to the General Capabilities:

- Literacy
- Numeracy
- Information and Communication Technology (ICT) Capability
- Critical and Creative Thinking.

ASSESSMENT

The following resources are provided for assessing students at different stages of the STEM investigations:

- Generic reproducible 1 (Key vocabulary table), for assessing understanding of vocabulary
- Generic reproducible 2 (Self-evaluation), for student self-evaluation of the learning process
- Generic reproducible 3 (Responding to the investigation)
- Generic reproducible 5 (Design thinking assessment rubric), for evaluating student engagement in the design thinking stages
- Learning journal templates 1, 2, 3 and 4, incorporating student reflection and evaluation.

GETTING READY FOR THE INVESTIGATION

You can prepare yourself and students for this STEM investigation in the following ways:

- Identify groups of students who will work well together.
- Review the **Key science knowledge** that supports this investigation, and look at the **Useful links**.
- Investigate the **Useful apps**.
- Gather materials for the science activities about heat transfer and insulation during the Tune-in session, including small plastic shot glasses and spoons made from different materials.
- Start collecting additional materials for prototyping (as shown on the **Materials needed** list).
- Determine where prototypes will be kept between lessons.
- Create a wall space where students can share their ideas in the Ideate stage.
- Organise the class into pairs.
- Start thinking about:
  - » sourcing information about insulation materials and the importance of water intake for humans
  - » inviting someone to speak about the importance of water, how it is collected, stored and distributed
  - » making connections with a water company or environmental engineer
  - » time constraints for the task
  - » which drinking taps are available to be monitored
  - » other students and classes that can be involved in the survey and evaluation stages
  - » how, when and where the designs will be shared and evaluated.

USEFUL APPS

- App for creating interactive links (for example, between descriptions, videos, images and websites and a main image), such as ThingLink
- App for creating multimedia presentations, such as Adobe Spark Video (via a teacher-created class account), Prezi or iMovie
- Survey app, such as SurveyMonkey or Typeform
- App for engaging in collaborative tasks, such as OneNote Class Notebook or SharePoint
- Three-dimensional modelling app, such as SketchUp
- App for creating spreadsheets, such as Excel or Numbers, or an interactive table, such as Google Docs

USEFUL LINKS

- Video clip about why it is important to drink water, such as at mea.digital/sm114
- Interactive activity about insulators, such as at mea.digital/sm115
- Video clip of a Rube Goldberg machine, such as at mea.digital/sm116
- Information about heat transfer, such as at mea.digital/sm117
- Information for teachers about the properties of materials, such as at mea.digital/sm118
- Information for teachers about simple machines, such as at mea.digital/sm119

RESOURCES PROVIDED

- Generic reproducibles 1, 2, 3, 5, 12
- Reproducibles 6.1, 6.2, 6.3
- Learning journal templates 1, 2, 3, 4

MATERIALS NEEDED

- Recycled materials, such as assorted cardboard boxes, cardboard offcuts, tubes, string, ribbon
- Scissors
- Tape – different widths, strengths, materials
- PVA glue
- Hot glue guns and glue (optional)
- Staplers and staples
- Split pins
- Rulers, erasers, plank of wood, can, books for lever exploration
- Drinking glasses – same size (could be small plastic shot glasses)
- Jugs for very cold water, room-temperature water and warm water
- Kettle
- Metal, wooden, ceramic and plastic spoons
- Coffee cups
- Tea bags
- Thermometers
- Cardboard
- Coloured paper
- Foil
- Bubble wrap
- Cotton, felt and other materials
- Infrared thermometer (optional)

Hot glue guns can be dangerous. Make sure students are supervised at all times.

KEY SCIENCE KNOWLEDGE

This section provides an overview of the key science concepts and vocabulary needed for this unit.

ENERGY AND HEAT

Energy is the ability of an object to do work or to cause movement. It is *not* a mass or a force. It is measured in joules or calories. We experience energy in forms such as light, heat and sound, and as electrical and chemical energy. **Heat** energy is also known as thermal energy.

TEMPERATURE AND MOVEMENT OF ENERGY

Temperature and heat are related but are not the same thing. Temperature is a measure of how hot something is – heat energy will move from a hotter object that is next to a cooler object. For example, ice in a drink will melt as heat moves from the liquid to the ice. The drink becomes cooler as the ice melts. Common measurements of temperature include degrees Celsius and degrees Fahrenheit. The movement of heat from one object to another is called conduction.

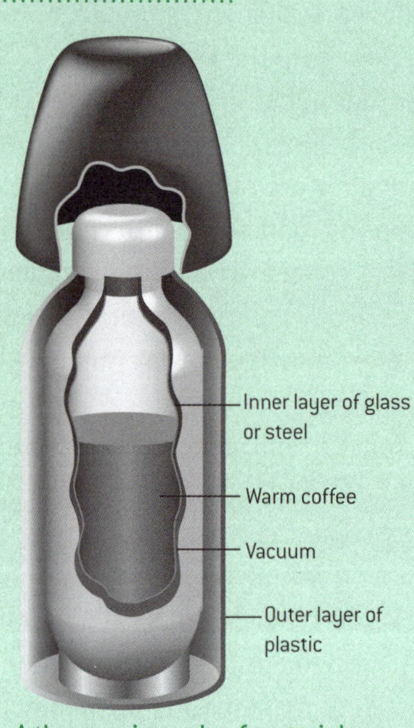

A thermos is made of materials that are good insulators.

CONDUCTORS AND INSULATORS

Some materials have **properties** that make them better than others at conducting heat. Copper is a good **conductor**, and it is often used on the bottom of saucepans to help transfer heat from the stovetop to the food being heated.

Materials such as plastic don't conduct heat energy very well – they are good **insulators**. Good insulators trap air, which forms an additional layer. A polystyrene cup and double-glazed windows are good examples of this. Insulation reduces the amount of heat movement from one place to another.

SIMPLE MACHINES

A machine is something that does work and makes work easier. We are surrounded by machines. Scissors, can openers and egg beaters are all examples of common machines.

The six types of simple machine are shown in the table. Simple machines can be combined into a compound (complex) machine such as a bicycle.

MACHINE	USE	EXAMPLE
Lever	lifting and opening things	seesaw
Ramp	getting from a higher point to a lower point or the reverse	wheelchair ramp
Wedge	separating an object (such as an axe blade splitting a piece of wood) or keeping things together	doorstop
Wheel and axle (rod that passes through the centre of a wheel)	allows wheel to turn	steering wheel
Pulley (wheel combined with a rope, cord or chain)	allows something to be moved up or down	window blind pulley
Screw (twisted inclined ramp)	moves in a circle and allows something to move up or down	metal screw

KEY VOCABULARY

conductor – a material that is good at allowing heat and sound to go in and out
heat – a form of energy
insulator – a material that helps to stop heat or sound from going in or out
property – feature of a material
temperature – a measure of how hot something is and the heat movement between objects

→ TUNE IN

1. Ask students to complete **Generic reproducible 1 (Key vocabulary table)** using the key vocabulary for this unit. This reproducible will also be used at the end of the unit, to demonstrate changes in understanding.
2. Provide each student with three small glasses.
3. Pour very cold water into one glass. Have students drink the water and write words that describe their response. List useful words for students to use.
4. Repeat the process with room-temperature water and warm (not hot) water.
5. Discuss the responses: 'Which water did you like drinking best? Why? Which water did you like the least? Why?'
6. Have students watch a video that explains the importance of water for good health (see **Useful apps/links**).
7. Students need to understand about conduction, insulation and using simple machines (for creating accessories) before beginning the challenge.

ACTIVITY 1: HEAT CONDUCTION

1. This activity needs close adult supervision as it involves boiling water. It may need to be a demonstration activity.
2. Pour boiling water into a coffee cup and place metal, wooden, ceramic and plastic spoons into the cup, with the handles sticking out. Have students feel the difference in temperature between the different materials.
3. Discuss how the heat moved from the water to the spoons. Explain that metals are good conductors and that other materials, such as plastic, are good insulators.

ACTIVITY 2: INSULATION

1. Place some warm tea in a ceramic cup and in a cup made of another material, such as polystyrene. Measure the temperature of the tea.
2. Provide student with **Reproducible 6.1 (Tea temperature)**. Measure the temperature of the tea in each cup every three minutes and discuss what is happening. Are there any differences between the ceramic and polystyrene cups?
3. Provide students with a link to an interactive activity about insulation to explore more materials (see **Useful apps/links**).

ACTIVITY 3: WORKING WITH LEVERS

1. Explain that the following activity focuses on one of the six simple machines: the lever.
2. Have students place a ruler under a heavy book and a small block under the ruler at the end closest to the book. Now have them try to lift the book.
3. Have students move the small block to different positions and observe where it is easier to lift the book. Explain that the ruler is acting as a lever (a simple machine) and the block is acting as a pivot, the position of which changes the amount of work the person using the lever has to do.

8. Introduce the STEM investigation and challenge to the students. Provide them with the student card and read the information together.
9. Introduce the design thinking process by reviewing the stages on the student card. Explain that students will keep a journal about their learning at the different stages of the design.

TOP TIP! Find out if the colour of a material has an impact on heat movement. Wrap different coloured pieces of paper around a series of jars filled with warm water and measure the change in temperature over time.

USEFUL APPS/LINKS

- Video about why it is important to drink water, such as at mea.digital/sm114
- Interactive activity about insulators, such as at mea.digital/sm115

→ EMPATHISE

During the Empathise stage of the design thinking process, students focus on finding out about different points of view. To empathise with others, they need to research some of the points of view associated with drinking water. This includes finding out about water drinking habits. Students will take notes, ask questions, draw diagrams and take photos where relevant.

ACTIVITY 1: SURVEY WATER DRINKING HABITS

1. Have students create a survey to find out about other students' water drinking habits. Make sure students include questions to find out about:
   - use of the school taps
   - water bottle use
   - refilling of water bottles
   - the ideal temperature of drinking water
   - the amount of water students drink while at school
   - issues to do with drinking water.
2. Model how to create questions and have groups of students generate questions for each area of investigation.
3. Decide whether a class survey will be created or each group will create their own survey. Create a paper survey or use a survey app (see **Useful apps/links**).

ACTIVITY 2: OBSERVE USE OF WATER TAPS

1. Provide students with a map of the school and locate all the different taps that provide drinking water for students.
2. Organise students into teams and roster them on over two or three lunchtimes, so they can observe the number of times that each tap is used during the week, and by which year levels.
3. Have students keep a tally of the usage of each tap and keep a record, either for each tap, or within a shared spreadsheet or table.

PROMPTS

- What were some of the places around the school that had drinking water?
- Which year levels used the drinking taps the most?
- Did anyone use the drinking taps to refill their water bottle?
- Were all the taps working?
- What was one interesting thing you found out?

MORE VOCABULARY

- empathise – understand and consider another person or group's point of view
- point of view – an opinion, attitude or judgement considered in a particular way

JOURNAL TIP

Ask students to complete **Learning journal template 1 (Empathise page)** while they are completing the different tasks. Remind them to date their notes and include photos of relevant information or pictures.

USEFUL APPS/LINKS

- App for creating surveys, such as SurveyMonkey or Typeform
- App for creating shared documents, such as OneNote Class Notebook or SharePoint

ASSESSMENT

This stage of the design thinking process offers opportunities to observe students collecting information, developing questions, and recording their notes and thinking in their journal.

TOP TIP! Keep the same groups of students tallying the same taps during the week, for consistency.

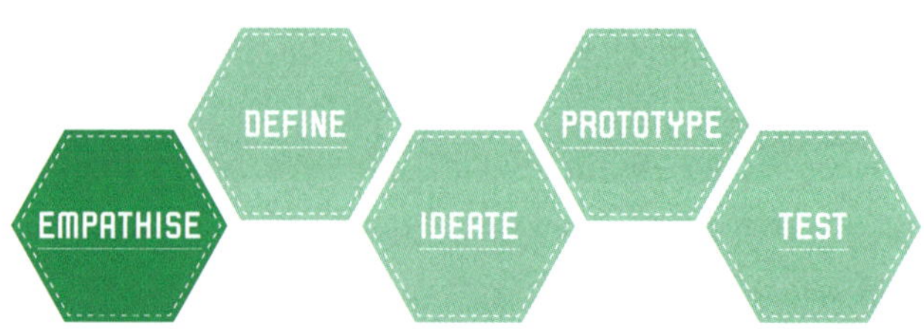

DEFINE

The main focus of this stage of the design thinking process is to reframe the challenge. The initial challenge is quite open, so at this stage students learn how to define what needs to be done. This includes noting insights that have been generated.

ACTIVITY 1: CONSIDER COLLECTED DATA

1. Have students consider the information collected about the usage of the different water taps around the school.
2. Show students how to enter the data into a spreadsheet and then tally the usage of the taps across the week. Use the data to hand-draw graphs or use the graph tool in the spreadsheet app.
3. Students could use an interactive app, such as ThingLink, to create an interactive map that provides information about the usage for each tap in the school. Students do this by creating a link to the relevant data at each place on the map.
4. If students are not using digital technologies, they could create a map with a key, highlighting the taps with the most and least usage.

ACTIVITY 2: CONSIDER SURVEY RESULTS

1. Review the survey results as a class. If using a digital survey tool, show students how to interpret the different types of data provided, including percentages, graphs and ranks.
2. Have students compare the information from the tap usage with the survey tool about water use.
3. Have students consider the key information that they have found out from the survey, such as, 'Do most students use their own water bottles? What is the average amount of water students drink at school? What were some of the issues raised to do with drinking water at school?'

ACTIVITY 3: TEST TAPS

1. Have students design a simple test to find out about the water temperature of different taps during the day.
2. Provide them with **Reproducible 6.2 (Water temperature)** to help them design their test and record the data.
3. Provide them with the equipment and time to collect this information before moving on to the Ideate stage.

Students can update **Learning journal template 2 (Define page)**.

PROMPTS

- How will you measure the temperature of the water in the taps?
- Will time of day make a difference to your results?
- How often do you think the temperature should be taken?
- What other information do you need?

MORE VOCABULARY

- define – state the meaning of something
- insight – an accurate understanding of someone or something
- point of view – an opinion, attitude or judgement considered in a particular way

JOURNAL TIP

Discuss the term 'insight' and explain that it relates to something students have learned about the people and their responses to the surveys as well as information gathered through research or excursions. You could refer to **Learning journal template 2**.

USEFUL APPS/LINKS

- App for creating interactive links (for example, between descriptions, videos, images and websites and a main image), such as ThingLink
- App for creating spreadsheets such as Excel or Numbers, or an interactive table, such as Google Docs
- App for engaging in collaborative tasks, such as OneNote Class Notebook

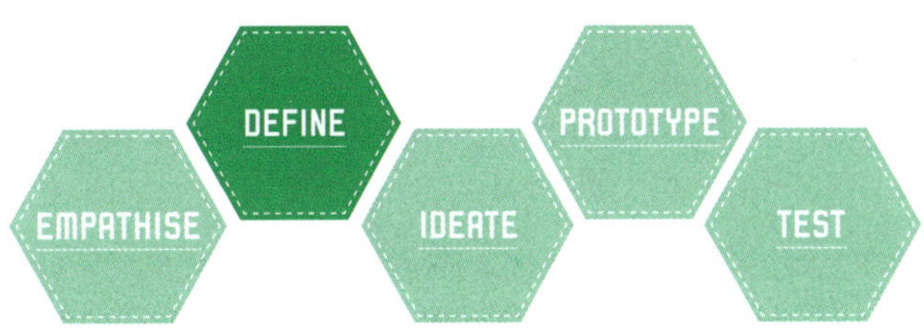

→ IDEATE

The Ideate stage of the design thinking process is all about generating lots of ideas. Students need to be flexible in their thinking and be able to move beyond obvious ideas. At this stage, ideas are not judged, just generated and gathered.

ACTIVITY 1: THINK ABOUT INSULATION

1. Provide students with time to think of some ideas for insulating the pipes and taps so that the drinking water stays cool. Get them to note their ideas in **Reproducible 6.3 (Tap ideas)**.
2. Let students look at some of the drinking water taps around the school to find out how much of the piping is external. It might be helpful if they take some photos of the different taps.
3. Have students think of materials, structures and processes that they might use. Encourage them to use their imagination with their ideas.

ACTIVITY 2: THINK ABOUT ACCESSORIES

1. After students have written some ideas for the pipes and taps, have them consider some ideas for creating an accessory for the part of the tap that dispenses the water. The accessory should be effective and easy to use. Get them to note their ideas in **Reproducible 6.3**.
2. Encourage students to consider incorporating levers or other simple machines. Provide them with some time to explore the other simple machines, if needed. They might get some inspiration from a video clip of a Rube Goldberg machine (see **Useful apps/links**).

ACTIVITY 3: THINK ABOUT PROMOTING WATER

1. Have students come up with ideas for addressing issues regarding how much water students at their school drink. They will need to refer to their water drinking habits survey results.
2. Get students to think of other barriers to people drinking water, other than warmth.
3. Have students brainstorm solutions to some of these issues. Get them to note their ideas in **Reproducible 6.3**.

PROMPTS

- What sorts of materials might you use?
- Which ideas would be easy to use?
- Could you use some simple machines in your idea?

MORE VOCABULARY

- feedback – information about, for example, a person's performance or the design of a product, which can be used to make improvements
- ideate – generate many ideas without making judgements about the ideas

JOURNAL TIP

Have students make notes on **Learning journal template 3 (Ideate page)**. When choosing three ideas to include in the journal, try to choose three ideas that use different materials or focus on different aspects of the challenge.

USEFUL APPS/LINKS

- Video of a Rube Goldberg machine, such as at mea.digital/sm116

ASSESSMENT

At the Ideate stage, assessment could include observations about the number and diversity of student ideas, and their ability to provide feedback and create additional ideas. Reflection in the journal should provide an insight into some of the reasoning behind student choices.

EMPATHISE DEFINE IDEATE PROTOTYPE TEST

PROTOTYPE

At this stage of the design thinking process, students are asked to create a physical prototype of a solution. It is the stage where students need to get their ideas out of their heads and presented in a way that engages other students and helps them to understand the concept. When students create, it helps them to think and solve problems and disagreements. Students can role-play, make a storyboard or use sticky notes when they prototype. The most important feature is that viewers can interact with whatever is produced.

Encourage students to photograph or film during the Prototype and Test stages. This information can be used to show the learning behind the design thinking process in action.

ACTIVITY 1: CHOOSE IDEAS

1. Have students choose one idea to explore further.
2. Have them expand on the idea by recording connected ideas.
3. Ask students to choose a different idea to expand. Repeat the steps for the first idea.
4. Have students choose one idea to focus on. It may be a combination of the two original ideas.

ACTIVITY 2: TRANSFORM IDEAS INTO PROTOTYPES

1. After students have selected their final idea, have them start prototyping with different materials.
2. When focusing on the insulation aspect of the task, students will need to consider how the water can be kept cool. When focusing on the creation of an accessory, they will need to consider ease of attachment and use.

Ask students to fill in the Prototype part of **Learning journal template 4 (Prototype and test page)**. See the **Journal tip** for further student guidance.

PROMPTS

- Have you been clear about which tap in the school your design is for?
- How will you test whether the materials you have chosen will work?
- Who will you ask to provide feedback about your design?

TOP TIP! It is important that students are focusing on their ideas, rather than the end product. Students may add labels to prototypes to explain some of the main features. Photographing and annotating pictures of prototypes can be useful.

When asking for feedback, students could ask each other some of the following questions:

- What is the most important part of your design?
- Can your design be easily used?
- Are there any safety issues associated with your design?
- What do you need to change? How might you do this?
- Will you need some help from adults to use your design with a drinking tap?

MORE VOCABULARY

- feedback – information about, for example, a person's performance or the design of a product, which can be used to make improvements
- prototype – an initial version of a model of a product or process that is used to develop a final model

JOURNAL TIP

Remind students to highlight the main features of their prototype. If students are creating an electronic journal, they can insert a photo of their prototype and annotate it.

USEFUL APPS/LINKS

- App for taking photographs or video, such as Adobe Spark Video or iMovie

ASSESSMENT

Observe students as they make changes to their designs. Are they able to consider feedback, make modifications and move rapidly through this process, or do they have difficulties with holding on to an idea and accepting feedback?

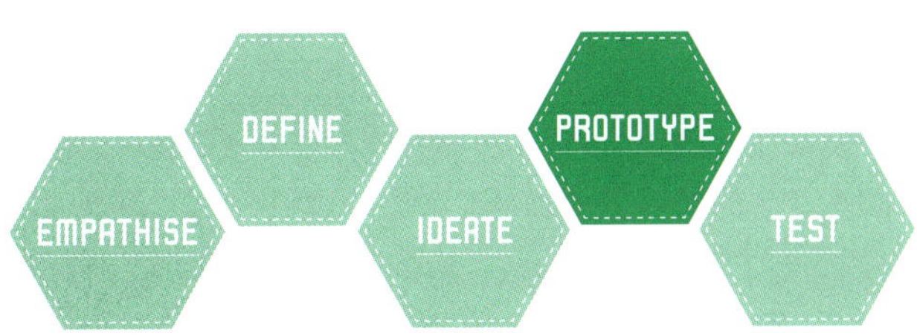

→ TEST

At this stage of the design thinking process, students test their prototype to see how it meets the criteria in the challenge.

ACTIVITY: TEST FEEDBACK

1. Have students gather feedback about the prototypes. Provide them with **Generic reproducible 12 (Prototype and test)** to record the ideas.
2. When providing feedback, have others consider the effectiveness of the design and how easy it is to use or implement.
3. Students continue to cycle through the Prototype and Test stages until they have completed their design.

Ask students to fill in **Learning journal template 4 (Prototype and test page)**. See the **Journal tip** for further student guidance.

PROMPTS

- Does your prototype do what you wanted it to do?
- Are there features that need to be added or removed?

MORE VOCABULARY

- evaluate – assess something, perhaps considering what worked and what didn't
- feature – a specific aspect of something, such as size, shape, colour or quality
- feedback – information about, for example, a person's performance or the design of a product, which can be used to make improvements
- prototype – an initial version of a model of a product or process that is used to develop a final model
- review – consider an idea, process or product and assess what works and what needs to be changed

JOURNAL TIP

Ask students to think about why it is important to test their ideas before they build their final design.

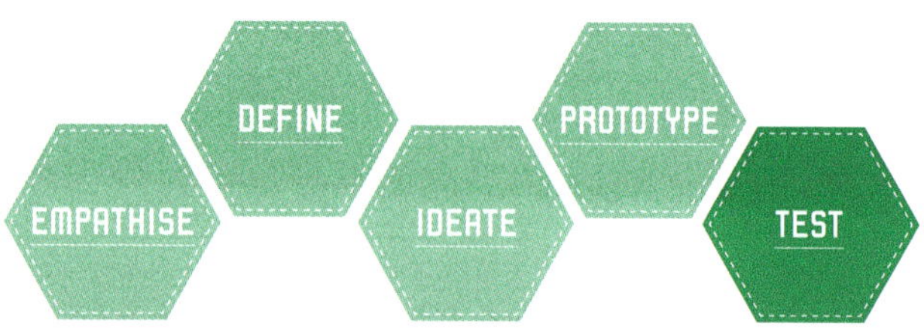

→ SHARE AND EVALUATE

At this stage of the investigation, students are provided with an opportunity to share their final design, as well as the processes involved in the investigation. Students evaluate their learning journals as well as their solutions.

ACTIVITY 1: BRING THE DESIGNS TOGETHER

1. Allow students to finalise their designs and create a short campaign about the importance of water for good health. This may be a short video clip using an app such as Adobe Spark Video or an interactive poster using an app such as ThingLink.
2. Arrange for other people to see the different designs and provide feedback. They could be from a local water company or school council.
3. Students should include their learning journals with the display so others can see the different stages of the design process.

ACTIVITY 2: EVALUATE AND GIVE FEEDBACK

1. Provide students with **Generic reproducible 2 (Self-evaluation)**.
2. Provide participants with tokens or stickers so they can vote for their favourite design, or create an online survey with photos of the different designs for others to vote on.

ASSESSMENT

Ask students to again complete **Generic reproducible 1 (Key vocabulary table)** using the key vocabulary for this unit. Compare their table with the one they completed at the Tune-in stage, to demonstrate changes in understanding.

Provide students with the original hexagons and ask them to add words they have learned (in a different colour). Have them arrange and photograph the words. Compare the final and original photos and discuss.

Students complete **Generic reproducible 3 (Responding to the investigation)**. Compare their responses to their responses to **Generic reproducible 2**.

Teachers complete **Generic reproducible 5 (Design thinking assessment rubric)** for each student. Students compare the feedback they are given by the teacher with their self-assessment of how they used the design thinking process to solve problems (**Generic reproducible 3**).

TUNE IN

STEM INVESTIGATIONS

Name: ....

Date: ....

Compare the temperature of a cup of tea in two different cups. Measure the temperature every three minutes and discuss your observations.

	Cup 1 (ceramic)	Cup 2 (polystyrene)
Time	**Temperature and observations**	**Temperature and observations**
Start		
3 minutes		
6 minutes		
9 minutes		
12 minutes		
15 minutes		

REPRODUCIBLE 6.2 WATER TEMPERATURE

DEFINE

STEM INVESTIGATIONS

Name: ....

Date: ....

Use this table to record the temperature of the water in different taps around the school.

Tap location and description	First measurement		Second measurement		Third measurement	
	Time	Temp.	Time	Temp.	Time	Temp.

STEM Investigations, MP, ISBN 978 1 4202 4319 2

Name: ....

Date: ....

Write your ideas in bullet points, then circle the ideas that you like best.

Ideas for insulating the tap and pipes

Ideas for a tap accessory

Ideas to encourage students to drink water

DESIGN AN ENERGY-EFFICIENT PET HOUSE

INTRODUCTION

Most countries have a range of temperatures during each year. Different designs and technologies have been developed to keep houses for humans cool in summer and warm in winter. Shelters for animals need to do this too.

This investigation provides students with the opportunity to explore concepts relating to heat and heat transfer. Students are challenged to design a pet house that could be used to look after a small animal for a short-term stay in the student's backyard. They explore different materials and ways to insulate their design.

This investigation could be extended by asking students to add an exercise area, designed to keep animals active and stimulated.

THE CHALLENGE

Houses for humans need to keep us cool during summer and warm in winter. Pet houses are the same. You have a small pet coming to stay for three days, and you want it to stay in a comfortable holiday home in your backyard.

Your challenge is to design a pet house, basing it on a cardboard box. You will need to find ways to keep the house at a comfortable temperature. In this investigation, you will learn about how heat moves from one object to another, and which materials are good for insulation.

KEY UNDERSTANDINGS

- Heat is a form of energy.
- Heat can move through some materials better than others.
- Animals depend on their environment to survive.
- Animals need food, water and shelter to survive.

KEY SKILLS

- Find and collate information through reading, interviewing others and internet searches.
- Describe how heat is transferred through engagement in heat transfer activities.
- Identify important needs for animals to survive, including food, water, shelter and exercise.
- Measure lengths and create three-dimensional models of pet houses.
- Transform ideas into something that can be seen – discuss, write, draw and build ideas.

KEY VOCABULARY

energy – the ability to cause movement or do work

heat – a form of energy

temperature – a measure of hotness and the heat movement between objects

KEY ACTIONS

- Gather information about the needs of small animals.
- Measure temperature.
- Test properties of different materials.
- Create and sort ideas.
- Create an energy-efficient pet house.

→ OVERVIEW OF STAGES

TUNE IN:

Students participate in a gallery walk of different animal houses. They will identify key features and types of animal that inhabit each house. Students also explore heat transfer, insulation and the basic needs of animals.

EMPATHISE

Students question others, including experts, to find out how to care for small pets, such as guinea pigs and mice. They research different small animals that can be pets, and the needs of these animals.

DEFINE

Students make a list of important features to include in a pet house. They investigate different materials and designs. They create a class criteria sheet to refer to when building their pet house.

IDEATE

Students come up with creative ideas for an energy-efficient pet house for a small animal for temporary use. They sort the ideas into different categories.

PROTOTYPE

Students draw, label and present their design for their pet house before building a model. Initial prototypes may develop one or two components of the game before completion of the final model. A cardboard box is used as a base for the design.

TEST

Students test the prototype and ask for feedback about different aspects of the design. They refer to the criteria sheet to ensure they have included all the necessary features.

SHARE AND EVALUATE:

Students share their designs with others. Their designs may be evaluated by pet owners or experts in the community and they consider the original criteria.

→ SUGGESTED SCHEDULE

LESSON	STAGE
1–4	**Tune in:** Participate in a gallery walk of animal houses, identifying the key features and the types of animals the houses have been created for; explore heat transfer, insulation and basic needs of animals
5–7	**Empathise:** Find out about how to look after a small animal; research the needs of different small animals; write in journal
8–9	**Define:** List features to include in an energy-efficient pet house; create a class criteria sheet for the design; write in journal
10–11	**Ideate:** Choose an animal and generate ideas for a pet house for this animal; write in journal
12–17	**Prototype** and **Test:** Draw, label and present a design for the pet house; build a model using a cardboard box and other materials; test the design by gathering feedback from others; write in journal
18–21	**Share and evaluate:** Present pet designs to pet owners for feedback and evaluation; evaluate self and others

CURRICULUM LINKS

SCIENCE

YEAR	STRAND	SUB-STRAND AND CONTENT
3	Science Understanding	Physical sciences: • Heat can be produced in many ways and can move from one object to another
4	Science Understanding	Biological sciences: • Living things depend on each other and the environment to survive
3 & 4	Science as a Human Endeavour	Nature and development of science: • Science involves making predictions and describing patterns and relationships Use and influence of science: • Science knowledge helps people to understand the effect of their actions
	Science Inquiry Skills	Questioning and predicting Processing and analysing data and information Communicating

TECHNOLOGIES

YEAR	STRAND	CONTENT
3 & 4	Technologies and Contexts	• Recognise the role of people in design and technologies occupations and explore factors, including sustainability, that impact on the design of solutions to meet community needs
	Materials and Technologies Specialisations	• Investigate the suitability of materials, systems, components, tools and equipment for a range of purposes
	Design and Technologies Processes and Production Skills	• Critique needs or opportunities for designing and explore and test a variety of materials, components, tools and equipment and the techniques needed to create designed solutions • Select and use materials, components, tools, equipment and techniques and use safe work practices to make designed solutions • Generate, develop and communicate design ideas and decisions using appropriate technical terms and graphical representation techniques

MATHEMATICS

YEAR	STRAND	SUB-STRAND AND CONTENT
3	Measurement and Geometry	Shape: • Make models of three-dimensional objects and describe key features Using units of measurement: • Measure, order and compare objects using familiar metric units of length, area, mass and capacity
4	Measurement and Geometry	Using units of measurement: • Use scaled instruments to measure and compare lengths, masses, capacities and temperatures

This investigation also links to the General Capabilities:

- Literacy
- Numeracy
- Information and Communication Technology (ICT) Capability
- Critical and Creative Thinking.

This investigation links to the Cross-Curriculum Priority of Sustainability.

ASSESSMENT

The following resources are provided for assessing students at different stages of the STEM investigations:

- Generic reproducible 1 (Key vocabulary table), for assessing understanding of vocabulary
- Generic reproducible 2 (Self-evaluation), for student self-evaluation of the learning process
- Generic reproducible 3 (Responding to the investigation)
- Generic reproducible 5 (Design thinking assessment rubric), for evaluating student engagement in the design thinking stages
- Learning journal templates 1, 2, 3 and 4, incorporating student reflection and evaluation.

→ GETTING READY FOR THE INVESTIGATION

You can prepare yourself and students for this STEM investigation in the following ways:

- Identify groups of students who will work well together.
- Review the **Key science knowledge** that supports this investigation, and look at the **Useful links**.
- Investigate the **Useful apps**.
- Gather materials for the heat and insulation science activities during the Tune-in session.
- Start collecting additional materials for prototyping (as shown on the **Materials needed** list).
- Determine where prototypes will be kept between lessons.
- Create a wall space where students can share their ideas in the Ideate stage.
- Organise the class into pairs.
- Make copies of **Generic reproducible 8 (Hexagons)**.
- Start thinking about:
  - » sourcing information for the gallery walk
  - » inviting people to speak about looking after pets
  - » making connections with a vet or animal welfare organisation
  - » time constraints for the task
  - » finding an expert such as a vet, veterinary nurse or pet shop owner to provide feedback to students during the design thinking process and at the conclusion of the investigation
  - » how, when and where the designs will be shared and evaluated
  - » whether or not a budget will be provided for non-recycled materials, such as tape and glue.

USEFUL APPS

- App for creating semantic maps (links between different words and/or concepts), such as Popplet or Kidspiration
- App for creating interactive links (for example, between descriptions, videos, images and websites and a main image), such as ThingLink
- App for making podcasts, such as Podbean
- App for sharing ideas, thoughts, questions and images, such as Padlet or Lino
- App for engaging in collaborative tasks, such as OneNote Class Notebook
- App for creating a digital portfolio, using photos, videos, drawings, text notes, links to show what you know, such as Seesaw
- App for teachers so they can expand their classroom and have online conversations with the class
- App for three-dimensional modelling, such as SketchUp

USEFUL LINKS

- Heat movement experiments, such as at mea.digital/sm14, mea.digital/sm15
- Information about heat and heat movement, such as at mea.digital/sm16
- Information about the needs of pets, such as at mea.digital/sm17

RESOURCES PROVIDED

- Generic reproducibles 1, 2, 3, 4, 5, 6, 8, 10, 12
- Reproducibles 7.1, 7.2, 7.3
- Learning journal templates 1, 2, 3, 4

MATERIALS NEEDED

- Cardboard boxes
- Scissors
- Tape – different widths, strengths, materials
- PVA glue
- Hot glue guns and glue (optional)
- Cardboard tubes
- Staplers and staples
- Variety of fabrics
- Variety of materials, such as foil, cling film, bubble wrap, aluminium foil
- Plastic cups and glass jars
- Thermometers suitable for use in water
- White paper
- Coloured card
- Pens/pencils
- Sticky notes

Hot glue guns can be dangerous. Make sure students are supervised at all times.

KEY SCIENCE KNOWLEDGE

This section provides an overview of the key science concepts and vocabulary needed for this unit.

ENERGY AND HEAT

Energy is the ability for an object to do work or to cause movement. It is *not* a mass or a force. It is measured in joules. We experience energy in forms such as light, heat and sound, and as electrical and chemical energy. **Heat** energy is also known as thermal energy.

TEMPERATURE AND MOVEMENT OF ENERGY

Temperature and heat are related but are not the same thing. Temperature is a measure of hotness – heat energy will move from a hotter object that is next to a cooler object. For example, ice in a drink will melt as heat flows from the liquid to the ice. The drink becomes cooler as the ice melts. Common measurements of temperature include degrees Celsius and degrees Fahrenheit.

Metals are often used for cookware because they are good heat conductors.

Heat energy moves better through some materials than others. For example, heat moves through metal more easily than it does through wool. Materials such as wool are good for insulation (which stops heat or sound from going in or out). Many animals have their own insulation, such as fur, fat or oily feathers, to help keep them warm when the weather is cool.

ANIMALS AND THEIR ENVIRONMENT

An animal's environment is the place where it lives. An animal needs certain things in its environment to survive, including:

- access to the right amount and kind of food for energy
- access to fresh water – this helps control body temperature
- shelter from the rain, sun and wind
- enough space to exercise.

Fur and fat are essential insulation for seals.

Domestic animals usually need to be able to socialise with other animals. They should live in conditions that keep them happy. The best homes for animals are designed using materials with properties that keep them sheltered and safe.

KEY VOCABULARY

energy – the ability to cause movement or do work
heat – a form of energy
temperature – a measure of hotness and the heat movement between objects

→ TUNE IN

1. Ask students to complete **Generic reproducible 1 (Key vocabulary table)** using the key vocabulary for this unit. This reproducible will also be used at the end of the unit, to demonstrate changes in understanding.
2. Set up a gallery walk with pictures of different domestic animals' homes, such as hutches and kennels. Make sure there are no animals in the pictures. Have students guess what type of animal would live in each enclosure. This could be done using sticky notes, a survey tool such as Kahoot or a general discussion. Have students choose their favourite and explain their choice to a partner.
3. Students need to understand heat movement, insulation and key needs for animals. Set up the following activities or similar for students.

ACTIVITY 1: ANIMAL NEEDS

1. Provide groups with **Generic reproducible 8 (Vocabulary hexagons)** and ask them to write a word relating to animal needs on each hexagon.
2. Ask students to cut out the hexagons and place them so related words touch each other. If a hexagon is touching two other hexagons, its meaning must connect with both words. This task will highlight students' understanding of different words and their relationships. It also provides an opportunity for students to discuss their understandings and negotiate connections between words.
3. Take a photo of the hexagons as a record and to compare with a repeat of the activity at the end of the investigation.

ACTIVITY 2: HEAT MOVEMENT

1. Have groups of students wrap one glass jar in black paper and another glass jar in white paper. Have students seated, for safety.
2. Fill both jars with cold water and measure the temperature with a thermometer. Provide students with **Reproducible 7.1 (Heat movement)** to record results and graph data.
3. Place the jars in a warm place. Measure and record the water temperatures at regular intervals (about every hour).
4. Have students graph the data. Discuss the results and things students will need to consider when designing their pet houses.

ACTIVITY 3: INSULATION

1. Provide pairs of students with plastic cups, A4 paper and a variety of materials and fabrics.
2. Students attach different materials to sheets of paper and wrap them around the cups, with paper facing in. For example, one cup could be wrapped in foil attached to paper.
3. Provide students with **Reproducible 7.2 (Testing insulation)**. Place cups containing water in a warm place. Have students measure the temperature inside each of the cups and record observations. Have them measure the temperature at regular intervals.
4. Ask students to make a graph to show the change in temperature for the different materials. They could use a spreadsheet with graphing tools or hand-draw a graph.
5. Discuss the observations and the possible reasons for any differences.

4. Introduce the STEM investigation and challenge to the students. Provide them with the student card and read the information together.
5. Introduce the design thinking process by reviewing the stages on the student card. Explain that students will keep a journal about their learning at the different stages of the design.

TOP TIP! Explain what a fair test is (changing one variable at a time). Provide students with opportunities to repeat their experiments if there is time. Discuss how this makes the results more useful if they can be replicated.

USEFUL APPS/LINKS

- Needs of pets, such as at mea.digital/sm17
- Hot and cold water experiment, such as at mea.digital/sm14
- Heat and heat movement, such as at mea.digital/sm16

→ EMPATHISE

During the Empathise stage of the design thinking process, students focus on finding out about different points of view. To empathise with others, they need to research some of the points of view associated with looking after pets. This includes finding out about key needs. Students will take notes, ask questions, draw diagrams and take photos where relevant.

ACTIVITY 1: PET CARE

1. Organise for some pet owners or a vet to visit the class to talk about how to look after small animals as pets. If it isn't possible to have someone visit, try to arrange an online chat, using an app such as Google Hangouts or TodaysMeet.
2. Prior to the discussion, have groups of students create questions to ask the experts. Ask them to create a table to record the responses to questions. Provide students with some general questions to consider, then develop some more specific questions. A big question might be, 'Why is it important for animals to have water?' A more specific related question might be, 'How much water does a guinea pig drink each day?'
3. If it is not possible to arrange a real-time conversation, consider using a collaborative tool such as Google Docs to ask questions. The expert can respond to the students' questions by typing answers in the shared document.

ACTIVITY 2: NEEDS OF SMALL ANIMALS

1. Create a class list of small animals that are popular as pets.
2. Provide students with **Reproducible 7.3 (Pet profile)** and ask them to find out important information about the animal's needs, especially as a pet.
3. Share the information gathered through a wall display or online collaborative tool, such as Padlet.
4. Have students consider some of the common needs and some of the needs specific to particular domestic animals.

PROMPTS

- What were some of the things that all animals need?
- What do you need to think about when you have a pet?
- Which types of animals are often kept as pets?
- What was one interesting thing you found out?

MORE VOCABULARY

- empathise – understand and consider another person or group's point of view
- point of view – an opinion, attitude or judgement considered in a particular way

JOURNAL TIP

Ask students to complete **Learning journal template 1 (Empathise page)** while they are completing the different tasks. Remind them to date their notes and include photos of relevant information or pictures.

USEFUL APPS/LINKS

- App for creating surveys, such as SurveyMonkey or Typeform
- App for having conversations, such as TodaysMeet or Google Hangouts
- App for sharing ideas, thoughts, questions and images, such as Padlet or Lino

ASSESSMENT

This stage of the design thinking process offers opportunities to observe students collecting information, developing questions, and recording their notes and thinking in their journal.

TOP TIP! If using a collaborative tool with the wider community, ensure that students use only their first names, to ensure privacy. If connecting with an organisation, find out if they are able to use collaborative tools such as Google Docs.

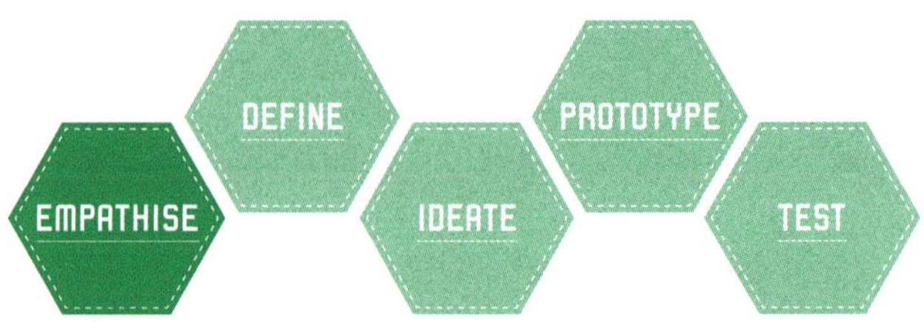

DEFINE

The main focus of this stage of the design thinking process is to reframe the challenge. The initial challenge is quite open, so at this stage students learn how to define what needs to be done. This includes noting insights that have been generated.

ACTIVITY 1: CONSIDER OBSERVATIONS

1. Discuss the information gathered from the pet experts. Provide pairs of students with two or three strips of coloured card and have them write a key piece of information or pattern that they learned.
2. Collate the information and organise into categories. Label each category and display.
3. Have students consider additional information they need to find out. Have students complete a What, Why, Where, Which and How activity:
   - What else do you need to find out about looking after pets?
   - Why do you need to know this?
   - Where might you find this information?
   - Which words will help you search for this information?
   - How will this information help you with your design challenge?
4. Provide students with time to gather the additional information they need.

Students can update **Learning journal template 2 (Define page)**.

PROMPTS

- What are the main features that need to be included in the pet house design?
- What small animals could this design challenge be for?
- What was something new that you learned from your observations?
- What other information do you need about constructing pet houses?

MORE VOCABULARY

- define – state the meaning of something
- insight – an accurate understanding of someone or something
- point of view – an opinion, attitude or judgement considered in a particular way

ACTIVITY 2: CREATE A CRITERIA SHEET

1. Guide students as they create a criteria sheet for the design challenge.
2. Define the parameters of the challenge, such as the timeframe, and how and when the designs will be shared and evaluated. Decide whether or not students will be given a budget for non-recyclable materials such as glue and tape.
3. Ask small groups of students to generate criteria that include the following areas, as well as others agreed on by the class:
   - size of pet house
   - types of pets
   - materials available
   - budget constraints (if relevant)
   - key features to be included in the pet house, such as food, water, exercise options
   - minimum and maximum temperature indoors and/or outdoors.
4. Collate the information and discuss the different suggestions. Decide which criteria to keep and which not to use for this challenge.
5. Create a final criteria sheet and share it with each student.

JOURNAL TIP

Discuss the term 'insight' and explain that it relates to something students have learned about the people and their responses to the surveys as well as information gathered through research or excursions. You could refer to **Learning journal template 2**.

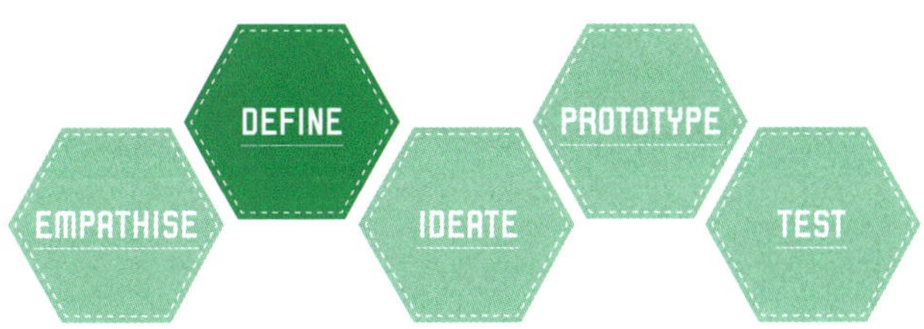

IDEATE

The Ideate stage of the design thinking process is all about generating lots of ideas. Students need to be flexible in their thinking and be able to move beyond obvious ideas. At this stage, ideas are not judged, just generated and gathered.

ACTIVITY 1: GENERATE IDEAS

1. Have students look at the different pet profiles created earlier in the investigation.
2. Have pairs or small groups of students choose two animals to consider initially.
3. Find a picture of one of the animals (such as a mouse). Use a small whiteboard, Padlet, sticky notes or pieces of paper to generate ideas about a pet house for this animal. Have students use one colour pencil/marker for their ideas.
4. Ask students to arrange their ideas into categories, such as 'food', 'shelter', 'entertainment', 'cleaning', 'bedding'.
5. Students then use a pencil/marker of a different colour to generate more ideas about a pet house for this animal.
6. Have students categorise these new ideas and combine them with the original ideas. The two different colours will demonstrate the changes in their thinking.
7. After this is complete, have students choose a different animal and repeat steps 3–6.

ACTIVITY 2: SWAP IDEAS

1. Have students look at another group's ideas for the two pets they chose.
2. Students return to their own ideas and, using a third colour, add some other ideas to their collection.

PROMPTS

- How could you insulate the house for the pet? What materials might you use?
- How might you make the house more comfortable for the pet?
- Have you thought about how the pet will get in and out of the house?
- What types of materials might be good to use in the design?

MORE VOCABULARY

- feedback – information about, for example, a person's performance or the design of a product, which can be used to make improvements
- ideate – generate many ideas without making judgements about the ideas

USEFUL APPS/LINKS

- App for sharing ideas, thoughts, questions and images, such as Padlet or Lino

ASSESSMENT

At the Ideate stage, assessment could include observations about the number and diversity of student ideas, and student ability to provide feedback and create additional ideas.

There is also the opportunity for students to learn about using other people's ideas to develop their own ideas further. It is important for them to understand the difference between copying others' ideas and using ideas for inspiration. Encourage students to take notes and reflect in their learning journal, as needed.

Reflection in the journal should provide an insight into some of the reasoning behind student choices.

EMPATHISE DEFINE IDEATE PROTOTYPE TEST

→ PROTOTYPE

At this stage, students are asked to create a physical prototype of a solution. Students need to get their ideas out of their heads and present them in a way that that engages other students and helps them to understand the concept. When students create, it helps them to think and solve problems and disagreements. Students can role-play, make a storyboard or use sticky notes when they prototype. The most important feature is that viewers can interact with whatever is produced.

Encourage students to photograph or film during the Prototype and Test stages. This information can be used to show the learning behind the design thinking process in action.

ACTIVITY: TRANSFORM IDEAS INTO PROTOTYPES

1. Have students choose a small animal. Provide them with **Generic reproducible 6 (In the frame)** to help them sort their different ideas by placing the most relevant ideas inside the frame, and the least relevant on the frame. Encourage students to justify their choices.
2. Have students remove the ideas on the frame and re-sort the ideas that are inside the frame. The most relevant ones stay inside the frame and the least relevant ones are moved onto the frame.
3. Ask students to take the ideas inside the frame and begin to sketch or model. They could use a drawing app such as SketchUp or construction blocks.
4. After students have decided on a design, provide them with **Generic reproducible 10 (Group task organiser)** to help them plan the construction of the pet house.

Ask students to fill in the Prototype part of **Learning journal template 4 (Prototype and test page)**. See the **Journal tip** for further student guidance.

PROMPTS

- What is the most important feature of your pet house?
- What parts need to be made first?
- How are the different parts attached?
- Could you use some different materials?

TOP TIP! The Prototype stage is often very messy. It is important that students are focusing on their ideas, rather than the end product. Provide them with lots of materials – recycling depots can be a useful source of resources. Students may add labels to prototypes to explain some of the main features. Photographing and annotating pictures of prototypes can be useful.

When asking for feedback, students could ask each other some of the following questions:

- How is it insulated? Does it need to keep the pet warm or cool?
- Which aspects work best? What will you keep?
- Which aspects need changing? How might you do this?

MORE VOCABULARY

- feedback – information about, for example, a person's performance or the design of a product, which can be used to make improvements
- prototype – an initial version of a model of a product or process that is used to develop a final model

JOURNAL TIP

Remind students to highlight the main features of their prototype. If students are creating an electronic journal, they can insert a photo of their prototype and annotate it.

USEFUL APPS/LINKS

- App for creating three-dimensional drawings, such as SketchUp

ASSESSMENT

Observe students as they make changes to their designs. Are they able to consider feedback, make modifications and move rapidly through this process, or do they have difficulties with holding on to an idea and accepting feedback?

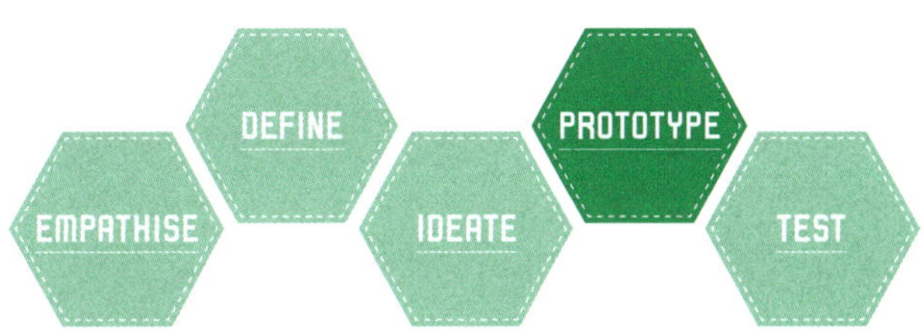

→ TEST

At this stage of the design thinking process, students test their prototype to see how it meets the criteria in the challenge.

ACTIVITY 1: TEST FEEDBACK

1. Have students gather feedback about the prototypes. Provide them with **Generic reproducible 12 (Prototype and test)** to record the ideas.
2. When providing feedback, students should consider whether or not all the criteria have been met. Remind students to test the temperature inside the pet house under different conditions, such as inside the classroom, outside in the shade and outside in the direct sunlight.
3. Students continue to cycle through the Prototype and Test stages until they have completed their design.

Ask students to fill in the rest of **Learning journal template 4 (Prototype and test page)**. See the **Journal tip** for further student guidance.

PROMPTS

- Does your prototype do what you wanted it to do?
- Are there features that need to be added or removed?

MORE VOCABULARY

- evaluate – assess something, perhaps considering what worked and what didn't
- feature – a specific aspect of something, such as size, shape, colour, quality
- feedback – information about, for example, a person's performance or the design of a product, which can be used to make improvements
- prototype – an initial version of a model of a product or process that is used to develop a final model
- review – consider an idea, process or product and assess what works and what needs to be changed

JOURNAL TIP

Ask students to think about why it is important to test their ideas before they build their final design.

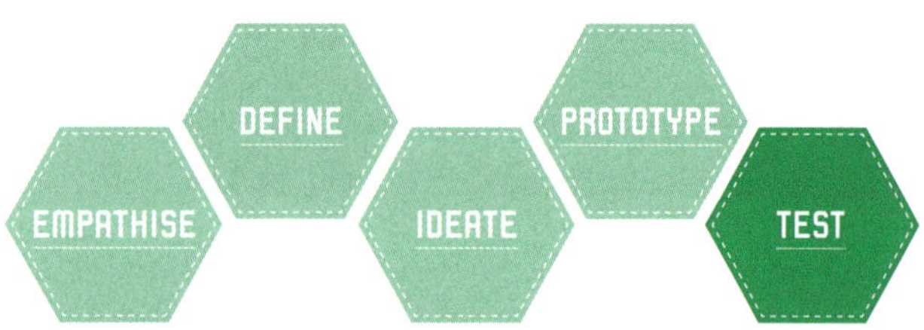

→ SHARE AND EVALUATE

At this stage, students are provided with an opportunity to share their final design, as well as the processes involved in the investigation. Students evaluate their learning journals as well as their solutions.

ACTIVITY 1: BRING THE DESIGNS TOGETHER

1. Allow students to finalise their designs.
2. If the designs are being shared electronically, provide students with time to create an annotated image, using an app such as ThingLink or a video using an app such as Adobe Spark Video (via a teacher-created account).
3. If creating a display, students should include their learning journals with the display so others can see the different stages of the design process.

ACTIVITY 2: EVALUATE AND GIVE FEEDBACK

1. Provide students with **Generic reproducible 2 (Self-evaluation)**.
2. Allow time for students to consider the feedback provided by evaluators.

ASSESSMENT

Ask students to again complete **Generic reproducible 1 (Key vocabulary table)** using the key vocabulary for this unit. Compare their table with the one they completed at the Tune-in stage, to demonstrate changes in understanding.

Provide students with their original hexagons and ask them to add words that they have learned (using a different colour). Have them arrange the words and photograph their final connections. Compare the final photo with the original photo and discuss.

Students complete **Generic reproducible 3 (Responding to the investigation)**. Compare their responses to their responses to **Generic reproducible 2**.

Teachers complete **Generic reproducible 5 (Design thinking assessment rubric)** for each student. Students compare the feedback they are given by the teacher with their self-assessment of how they used the design thinking process to solve problems **(Generic reproducible 3)**.

TUNE IN

STEM INVESTIGATIONS

Name: ....

Date: ....

Wrap one glass jar in black paper and another glass jar in white paper. Fill both jars with cold water. Place them in a warm place and measure the temperature every hour. Record your results in the table and then make a graph on a separate sheet.

Cup		Temperature (in degrees Celsius)					
		Start time:	Time:	Time:	Time:	Time:	End time:
1	Wrapped in black paper						
2	Wrapped in white paper						

TUNE IN

STEM INVESTIGATIONS

Name: ....

Date: ....

Wrap some plastic cups with different materials and fill them with cold water. Place them in a warm place and measure the temperature at different times. Record your information here.

Cup		Temperature (in degrees Celsius)					
		Start time:	Time:	Time:	Time:	Time:	End time:
1	Material:						
2	Material:						
3	Material:						
4	Material:						

STEM Investigations, MP, ISBN 978 1 4202 4319 2

EMPATHISE

STEM INVESTIGATIONS

Name: ....

Date: ....

Choose a small animal that can be kept as a pet. Find out important information about this animal that will help someone design a pet house for it.

Name of animal:	Estimated size:
Type of animal: ☐ bird ☐ reptile ☐ mammal ☐ amphibian (e.g. frog) ☐ fish	Amount of water needed each day:
Types of food eaten:	Sleep habits: ☐ Awake during the day ☐ Awake at night
Favourite activities:	Key features: ☐ skin ☐ fur ☐ feathers ☐ scales ☐ warm blooded ☐ needs heat energy
Other useful information:	

SORT THINGS WITH A COMPOST SYSTEM

INTRODUCTION

Much of the waste we make at home comes from the garden and the kitchen – this natural waste can be composted and used at home to grow more plants and food. Throwing away garden and kitchen waste means energy must be used to transport the waste to landfill. Because of the way the waste is stored in landfill, the rotting waste contributes more to global warming. So composting is better for the environment.

In this STEM investigation, students are asked to design a simple compost system to fit a tall, narrow space. The system will need to group different ingredients. Students then design signs to show how to separate the compost. They also design a poster of how the system works using symbols and pictures, so that everybody in their community can compost natural waste.

This STEM challenge is easily differentiated for students by encouraging different groups to use different degrees of complexity when creating their buildings.

KEY UNDERSTANDINGS

- Things can be living, non-living or once-living.
- Things can be grouped by what they have in common.
- Compost is a mixture of decaying organic things.
- Compost is full of nutrients that help plants grow.

KEY SKILLS

- Make careful observations and predictions about the decomposition of different things.
- Develop research skills, including using key words for searches, locating reliable sources and recording important information.
- Consider different points of view and develop empathy.
- Develop flexible thinking skills by considering feedback and evaluating ideas.

THE CHALLENGE

You are part of a community garden group. The people in the group are from many different backgrounds and speak many different languages. You want to start a composting system that everyone can use.

Your first challenge is to design a simple compost system to fit a tall, narrow space (one metre wide and three metres tall). You will need to design signs that show how to sort the waste and a poster of how the system works. Use symbols and pictures, not words. As part of your investigation, you will learn about grouping living things, non-living things and once-living things.

KEY VOCABULARY

compost – a mixture of decomposing things

decompose – break down into smaller parts, with the help of bacteria and fungi

greenhouse gas – a gas that warms the Earth's atmosphere

nutrient – something that is needed for life and growth

organic – from living or once-living things

KEY ACTIONS

- Find out about living, non-living and once-living things.
- Explore composting and who can benefit.
- Consider examples of compost systems.
- Design a compost system to group ingredients.

→ OVERVIEW OF STAGES

TUNE IN:

Find out about living, non-living and once-living things and how they can be grouped. Explore composting and different compost systems.

EMPATHISE

Students find out about who benefits from composting and how to cater for the needs of the whole community when considering compost system designs.

DEFINE

Students consider the main issues with designing compost systems that can be used by the whole community, including those who speak very little English. The parameters of the challenge are defined.

IDEATE

Students generate creative ideas for compost system designs with labels and posters to explain how they work.

PROTOTYPE

Students transform some of their ideas into physical representations. These are created rapidly, using simple materials. Students can role-play, make storyboards or use sticky notes when they prototype.

TEST

Students share their prototypes and provide feedback to each other. They are given the opportunity to cycle through the Prototype and Test stages again.

SHARE AND EVALUATE:

Final prototypes are shared and evaluated, with opportunities for feedback from the community.

→ SUGGESTED SCHEDULE

LESSON	STAGE
1–3	**Tune in:** Explore living, non-living and once-living things and how they can be grouped; find out about effective compost systems
4–7	**Empathise:** Consider who benefits from composting and how a compost system can be used by all community members; write in journal
8–9	**Define:** Consider observations and insights; define main issues; write in journal
10–11	**Ideate:** Develop ideas and write/record in journal
12–15	**Prototype** and **Test:** Conduct prototyping and testing cycles; write in journal
16–17	**Share and evaluate:** Share and evaluate designs and prototypes

CURRICULUM LINKS

SCIENCE

YEAR	STRAND	SUB-STRAND AND CONTENT
3	Science Understanding	Biological sciences: • Living things can be grouped on the basis of observable features and can be distinguished from non-living things
3 & 4	Science as a Human Endeavour	Use and influence of science: • Science knowledge helps people to understand the effect of their actions

TECHNOLOGIES

YEAR	STRAND	CONTENT
3 & 4	Design and Technologies Processes and Production Skills	• Critique needs or opportunities for designing, and explore and test a variety of materials, components, tools and equipment and the techniques needed to produce designed solutions • Generate, develop and communicate design ideas and decisions for audiences using appropriate technical terms and graphical representation techniques • Evaluate design ideas, processes and solutions based on criteria for success developed with guidance and including care for the environment • Plan a sequence of production steps when making designed solutions individually and collaboratively

MATHEMATICS

YEAR	STRAND	SUB-STRAND AND CONTENT
3 & 4	Measurement and Geometry	Using units of measurement: • Compare objects using familiar metric units of area and volume Shape: • Compare the areas of regular and irregular shapes by informal means

This investigation also links to the General Capabilities:

- Literacy
- Numeracy
- Information and Communication Technology (ICT) Capability
- Critical and Creative Thinking.

This investigation also links to the Cross-Curriculum Priority of Sustainability.

ASSESSMENT

The following resources are provided for assessing students at different stages of the STEM investigations:

- Generic reproducible 1 (Key vocabulary table), for assessing understanding of vocabulary
- Generic reproducible 2 (Self-evaluation), for student self-evaluation of the learning process
- Generic reproducible 3 (Responding to the investigation)
- Generic reproducible 5 (Design thinking assessment rubric), for evaluating student engagement in the design thinking stages
- Learning journal templates 1, 2, 3 and 4, incorporating student reflection and evaluation.

→ GETTING READY FOR THE INVESTIGATION

You can prepare yourself and students for this STEM investigation in the following ways:

- Identify groups of students who will work well together.
- Review the **Key science knowledge** that supports this investigation, and look at the **Useful apps** and **Useful links**.
- Start collecting useful materials for designing devices or processes to help stop habitat destruction (as shown in the **Materials needed** list).
- Determine where prototypes will be kept between lessons.
- Create a vocabulary wall.
- Create a wall space where students can share their ideas during the Ideate stage.
- Organise the class into pairs or small groups.
- Start thinking about:
  - » reviewing information about compost systems and the compost cycle
  - » how the posters and designs will be evaluated
  - » who will view the designs
  - » who will provide expert feedback about the designs, and whether it will be provided in person or in digital form.

USEFUL APPS

- App for creating and organising ideas, such as Popplet, Inspiration, Padlet or Ideament
- App for sharing ideas, such as Air Sketch
- App for creating symbols, such as Logo Maker
- App for creating multimedia presentations, such as iMovie or Adobe Spark Video (via a teacher-created class account)

USEFUL LINKS

- Compost time-lapse video, such as at mea.digital/sm157
- 'Compost in a bottle' experiment, such as at mea.digital/sm158
- Information about compost and how to compost, such as at mea.digital/sm159, mea.digital/sm160, mea.digital/sm161
- Compost cycle diagrams, such as at mea.digital/sm162
- Video clip about composting and the environment, such as at mea.digital/sm163

RESOURCES PROVIDED

- Generic reproducibles 1, 2, 3, 4, 5, 6
- Reproducibles 8.1, 8.2, 8.3, 8.4, 8.5
- Learning journal templates 1, 2, 3, 4

MATERIALS NEEDED

- Sticky notes
- Paper
- Cardboard
- Sticky tape
- Other building materials, such as recyclable packaging, boxes, tubes, plastic bottles
- Rubber bands
- Scissors
- Glue
- Paint
- Garden soil, natural materials such as leaves and fruit, icypole sticks
- Materials for 'compost in a bottle' experiment, such as 2-litre plastic bottles, fruit and vegetable scraps, dried grass clippings and leaves, garden soil, shredded newspaper, spray bottle, fertiliser (such as blood and bone), clear tape, scissors, permanent marker, gloves

Be mindful of the potential hazards associated with organic waste and any precautions that may need to be taken if students are collecting or handling it.

KEY SCIENCE KNOWLEDGE

This section provides an overview of the key science concepts and vocabulary needed for this unit.

LIVING THINGS

Living things have features that distinguish them from non-living things. For something to be considered living, it must show all of the following seven characteristics:

- *feeding* – All living things need to take substances from the environment to get the energy they need to grow and stay healthy.
- *movement* – Living organisms have internal movement. This means they can move substances from one part of their body to another. Some living things also have external movement, such as walking, flying or swimming.
- *respiration (breathing)* – All living things exchange gases with their environment. For example, plants take in carbon dioxide and produce oxygen.
- *excretion* – This is the removal of waste from the body. All living things excrete waste.
- *growth* – Some of the energy gained by feeding is used to help living things grow. As living things grow, they become bigger and more complex.
- *sensitivity* – Living things react to changes around them, such as light, heat and cold.

COMPOSTING

Compost is natural waste that has broken down and is used to improve soil. Composting is usually done in a bin or pile, where the waste can mix and **decompose** with the help of bacteria, fungi and oxygen.

Composting adds important **nutrients** and minerals to soil. The enriched soil can then be added to gardens, and the nutrients and minerals can be taken up by plants through their root structures.

Because of the way that natural waste is stored in landfill, it produces more powerful **greenhouse gases** than it does when it is composted.

COMPOST INGREDIENTS

Many **organic** materials can be composted, such as grass cuttings, leaves, flowers, vegetable scraps and eggshells. Microorganisms such as bacteria and fungi, as well as worms and insects, feed on these ingredients and produce compost. They need to feed on the right mix of ingredients, some of which are 'green' materials (high levels of nitrogen) and some of which are 'brown' materials (high levels of carbon).

Examples of 'brown' materials include shredded paper, dry leaves, woodchips and cardboard.

Examples of 'green' materials include fruit and vegetable scraps, grass clippings, teabags and eggshells.

KEY VOCABULARY

compost – a mixture of decomposing things
decompose – break down into smaller parts, with the help of bacteria and fungi
greenhouse gas – a gas that warms the Earth's atmosphere
nutrient – something that is needed for life and growth
organic – from living or once-living things

TUNE IN

1. Ask students to complete **Generic reproducible 1 (Key vocabulary table)** using the key vocabulary for this unit. This reproducible will also be used at the end of the unit to demonstrate changes in understanding.
2. Provide students with links to information about living, non-living and once-living things and the features that allow them to be grouped. Explore composting and effective compost systems.
3. Discuss new learning. Provide space for students to record and display key information.
4. Before engaging in the challenge, students need an understanding of how living, non-living and once-living things are grouped.

ACTIVITY 1: LIVING, NON-LIVING OR ONCE-LIVING?

1. Provide students with links to information on living, non-living and once-living things (see **Useful apps/links**).
2. Students read through information and record any questions that may arise.
3. Place students in small groups and have them create semantic maps to show different classifications of living, non-living and once-living things. Add information about the products of living things.
4. Each group can share information with the class. Display posters.

ACTIVITY 2: WHAT IS COMPOST?

1. Provoke curiosity about composting by setting up an experiment that creates compost in a bottle (over three to four weeks; see **Useful apps/links**). To see results more quickly, view a compost time-lapse video clip (see **Useful apps/links**).
2. Provide links to information about composting (see **Useful apps/links**).
3. Encourage students to find out all they can about composting. Use **Reproducible 8.1 (All about compost)** to provide question prompts and a place to record information.
4. Students form small groups and share information.

ACTIVITY 3: HOW TO MAKE A COMPOST SYSTEM

1. Explain to students that they are going to find out about making a compost system.
2. Provide students with **Reproducible 8.2 (How to make a compost system)** and with links to information on how to make compost. Students research ways to make a compost system, materials and ingredients needed, and grouping ingredients. Explain the difference between green and brown ingredients.
3. Ensure students understand the importance of adding only compostable material.
4. Have students consider examples of the compost cycle diagrams. Provide them with **Reproducible 8.3 (Composting dos and don'ts)** and challenge them to consider dos and don'ts of composting and symbols they could use to convey information.

5. Introduce the STEM investigation and challenge to the students. Provide them with the student card and read the information together.
6. Introduce the design thinking process by reviewing the stages on the student card. Explain that students will keep a journal about their learning at the different stages of the design.

USEFUL APPS/LINKS

- App for creating and organising ideas, such as Popplet, Inspiration, Padlet or Ideament
- App for sharing ideas, such as Air Sketch
- Compost time-lapse video, such as at mea.digital/sm157
- 'Compost in a bottle' experiment, such as at mea.digital/sm158
- Information about compost and how to compost, such as at mea.digital/sm159, mea.digital/sm160, mea.digital/sm161
- Compost cycle diagrams, such as at mea.digital/sm162
- Composting signs and symbols, such as at mea.digital/sm164

→ EMPATHISE

During the Empathise stage of the design thinking process, students focus on finding out about different points of view. To empathise with others, they need to research some of the challenges associated with composting.

Students will take notes, ask questions, draw diagrams and take photos where relevant.

ACTIVITY 1: COMPOST AND THE ENVIRONMENT

1. View a video clip about compost and the environment (see **Useful apps/links**) with students. Students complete **Reproducible 8.4 (Compost and the environment)**. This may need to be done as a class, with some of the concepts and vocabulary explained during the viewing.
2. Students share their responses to the video clip.
3. Make time available for students to share thoughts and feelings about the video clip. By this time, students should have enough knowledge to realise the importance of composting, and want to take action.

ACTIVITY 2: COMPOSTING IN THE COMMUNITY

1. Discuss composting with students. Find out if any students have a compost system at home and how it works.
2. Discuss urban areas and brainstorm the problems that people living in cities may face if they want their own compost systems.
3. Provide students with **Reproducible 8.5 (Composting survey)**. Explain to students that they need to find someone either in the community (if it is a city) or who lives in a city who is willing to answer the survey questions. This can be done by phone or by email.
4. Students share results and look for common concerns or thought patterns and points of view.

PROMPTS

- What information about composting had the most impact on you?
- How did people react when you proposed a community compost system?
- What are community members most concerned about?

ACTIVITY 3: GETTING THE MESSAGE ACROSS

1. Have students recall the dos and don'ts of composting and responses to surveys.
2. Explain that some community members may be unsure of how to compost correctly. Ask, 'How can we show all community members how to use a compost system correctly?'
3. Students brainstorm ideas. Refer back to composting cycle images and show related symbols (see **Useful apps/links**).
4. Provide students with paper to share more ideas of pictures/symbols that can communicate messages about composting.

MORE VOCABULARY

- empathise – understand and consider another person or group's point of view
- point of view – an opinion, attitude or judgement considered in a particular way

JOURNAL TIP

Ask students to complete **Learning journal template 1 (Empathise page)** while doing the different tasks.

USEFUL APPS/LINKS

- Video clip about composting and the environment, such as at mea.digital/sm163
- Information for teachers about how composting helps the natural environment, such as at mea.digital/sm166
- Composting signs and symbols, such as at mea.digital/sm164
- App for creating and organising ideas, such as Popplet, Inspiration, Padlet or Ideament
- App for sharing ideas, such as Air Sketch
- App for creating symbols, such as Logo Maker – Logo Creator

ASSESSMENT

This stage of the design thinking process offers opportunities to observe students collecting information, developing questions, and recording their notes and thinking in their journal.

EMPATHISE · DEFINE · IDEATE · PROTOTYPE · TEST

DEFINE

The main focus of this stage of the design thinking process is to reframe the challenge. The initial challenge is quite open, so at this stage students learn how to define what needs to be done. This includes noting insights that have been generated.

ACTIVITY 1: CONSIDER OBSERVATIONS

1. Students consider the information they gathered in the Tune-in and Empathise stages. They may work in pairs or small groups. Provide them with a whiteboard, large sheet of paper and/or sticky notes to collate some of their key information. They should refer to their information on **Reproducible 8.2 (How to make a compost system), Reproducible 8.3 (Composting dos and don'ts), Reproducible 8.4 (Compost and the environment)** and survey results. Students should transfer their main findings to **Learning journal template 2 (Define page)**.
2. Students should discuss one section of **Learning journal template 2** at a time, write their responses and then continue discussing their ideas for the next section, until the task is complete. This provides students with opportunities to hear others' responses and it provides the teacher with input points.
3. Provide students with the opportunity to research further. Ask them to write other information they would like to know. Provide them with **Generic reproducible 4 (Key question table)** to assist them to record their questions, findings and sources.

ACTIVITY 2: CONSIDER INSIGHTS

Students should think of at least one insight they have gained from the process; for example, composting can help slow global warming. Students should add this insight to **Learning journal template 2**. They should then explain how this will affect the design of a simple compost system and poster.

When considering insights, students could think about the following:

» What was something unexpected that you observed or found out? How was it unexpected?

» How will you decide on the most important aspect of your invention?

» Is there any other information that you need or would like to know? How will you find out?

ACTIVITY 3: CONSIDER CONSTRAINTS

At this stage, let students know the constraints of the challenge by describing the types of materials that will be available and how students will test their devices or processes.

PROMPTS

- What did you discover?
- What were the most important pieces of information that you gathered?
- What was something new that you learned?
- What other information do you need?

MORE VOCABULARY

- define – state the meaning of something
- insight – an accurate understanding of someone or something
- point of view – an opinion, attitude or judgement considered in a particular way

JOURNAL TIP

Discuss the term 'insight' and explain that it relates to something students have learned about the people and their responses to the surveys as well as information gathered through research or excursions. You could refer to **Learning journal template 2**.

USEFUL APPS/LINKS

- App for creating and organising ideas, such as Popplet, Inspiration, Padlet or Ideament
- App for sharing ideas, such as Air Sketch
- App for creating symbols, such as Logo Maker

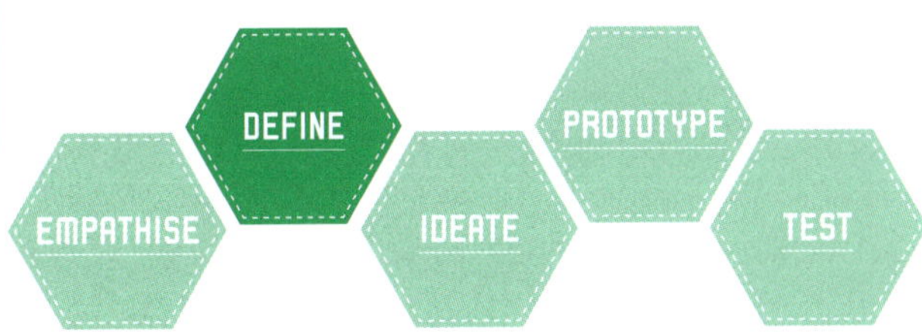

→ IDEATE

The Ideate stage of the design thinking process is all about generating lots of ideas. Students need to be flexible in their thinking and be able to move beyond obvious ideas. At this stage, ideas are not judged, just generated and gathered.

ACTIVITY: GENERATE IDEAS

1. Ask groups of students to draw or write ideas for their compost system designs.
2. Each new idea should be drawn or written on a separate piece of paper or sticky note.
3. Ask students to group ideas on a wall or board.
4. Ask students to look at the different ideas and provide feedback to each other. It is important that students don't defend their ideas at this stage. They should just be listening to the feedback.
5. After the initial feedback, ask students to come up with more ideas. Encourage them to be creative and even radical.
6. Ask students to choose three of their ideas for a design for a compost system and poster explaining how it works. Students use **Learning journal template 3 (Ideate page)** to do this.

TOP TIP!

At this stage, students may have produced a series of drawings that are annotated. They may have a collection of sticky notes, which they can organise into related ideas.

Encourage students to view and read others' ideas before giving feedback. Feedback could be within small groups or between partners. Considering others' ideas is an important part of this process, so students can build on their own ideas as they continue to ideate.

At each stage of this activity, ask students to discuss their thoughts before writing their responses. This will help them think through their ideas and select their final ideas to develop.

PROMPTS

- How do your chosen ideas meet the needs of the whole community?
- How might you test your design?
- How can you make it work for other communities?
- What if you had different materials to use?

MORE VOCABULARY

- feedback – information about, for example, a person's performance or the design of a product, which can be used to make improvements
- ideate – generate many ideas without making judgements about the ideas

JOURNAL TIP

When choosing three ideas to include in the journal, try to choose three ideas that aren't related.

USEFUL APPS/LINKS

- App for creating and organising ideas, such as Popplet, Inspiration, Padlet or Ideament
- App for sharing ideas, such as Air Sketch

ASSESSMENT

At the Ideate stage, assessment could include observations about the number and diversity of student ideas, and their ability to provide feedback and create additional ideas. Reflection in the journal should provide an insight into some of the reasoning behind student choices.

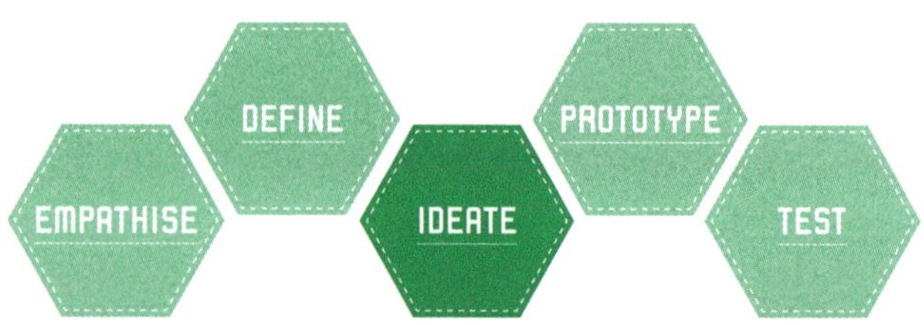

→ PROTOTYPE

At this stage of the design thinking process, students are asked to create a physical prototype of a solution. It is the stage where students need to get their ideas out of their heads and presented in a way that engages other students and helps them to understand the concept. When students create, it helps them to think and solve problems and disagreements. Students can role-play, make a storyboard or use sticky notes when they prototype. The most important feature is that viewers can interact with whatever is produced.

Encourage students to photograph or film during the Prototype and Test stages. This information can be used to show the learning behind the design thinking process in action.

ACTIVITY: TRANSFORM IDEAS INTO PROTOTYPES

1. Students review the ideas generated at the Ideate stage. Provide them with an A3 copy of **Generic reproducible 6 (In the frame)** so they can organise their ideas into two sections: least relevant and most relevant. Provide students with some question prompts to help support discussion of the ideas; for example:
   - » Why do you think this idea could be used?
   - » What parts of this idea could be improved?
   - » What would need to be changed for this idea to be used?
   - » Why do you think this idea is not so relevant to the challenge?
2. Provide students with a range of materials to use to create their prototype. Remind students that a prototype should be created rapidly and is not meant to look 'nice'.
3. After prototypes have been created, ask students to see if they work in the way they had planned and if they could be effective in getting people to compost. Feedback should be given by writing one thing that worked well and one thing that could be improved on sticky notes.
4. Students then use feedback to prototype again.

Ask students to fill in the Prototype part of **Learning journal template 4 (Prototype and test page)**. See the **Journal tip** for further student guidance.

TOP TIP!

When asking for feedback, students could ask each other some of the following questions:

- What is the main feature of your prototype?
- How does it work?
- Which parts work best? What will you keep?
- Which parts need changing? How might you do this?
- What other materials might you need?

PROMPTS

- What worked?
- How could it be improved?
- What else do you need to know, do or have?
- What other suggestions do you have?

MORE VOCABULARY

- feedback – information about, for example, a person's performance or the design of a product, which can be used to make improvements
- prototype – an initial version of a model of a product or process that is used to develop a final model

JOURNAL TIP

Remind students to highlight the main features of their prototype. If students are creating an electronic journal, they can insert a photo of their prototype and annotate it.

USEFUL APPS/LINKS

- App that can be used to create an interactive annotation of the prototype, such as ThingLink
- App for sharing ideas, such as Air Sketch

ASSESSMENT

Observe students as they make changes to their designs. Are they able to consider feedback, make modifications and move rapidly through this process, or do they have difficulties with holding on to an idea and accepting feedback?

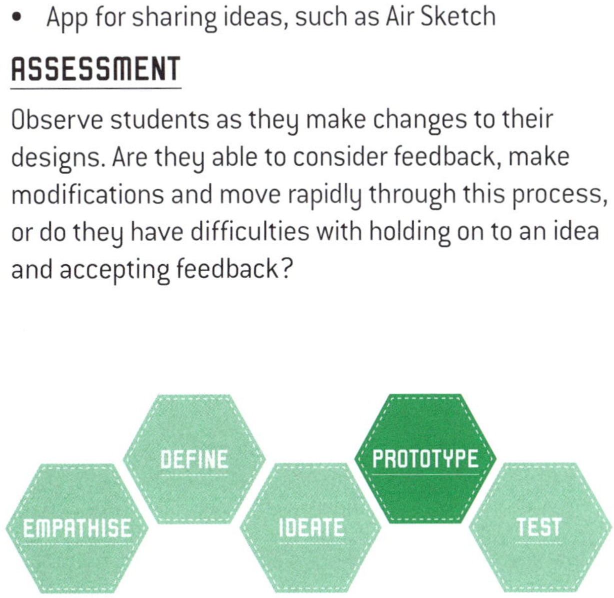

→ TEST

At this stage of the design thinking process, students test their prototype to see how it meets the criteria in the challenge. Students check to see if their prototype meets the criteria set at the start of the design process.

ACTIVITY: TEST FEEDBACK

1. Students take their last prototype and consider the original design challenge.
2. Invite the school community to view prototypes. Have them offer feedback about what works well and what could be improved, and any suggestions they may have.
3. Ask students to consider feedback to determine if their invention works. If not, what do they need to do to make it work?
4. Provide the opportunity to cycle through the Prototype and Test stages again.

Ask students to fill in **Learning journal template 4 (Prototype and test page)**. See the **Journal tip** for further student guidance.

PROMPTS

- Does your prototype do what you wanted it to do?
- Are there other features that need to be added?

MORE VOCABULARY

- evaluate – assess something, perhaps considering what worked and what didn't
- feature – a specific aspect of something, such as size, shape, colour, quality
- feedback – information about, for example, a person's performance or the design of a product, which can be used to make improvements
- prototype – an initial version of a model of a product or process that is used to develop a final model
- review – consider an idea, process or product and assess what works and what needs to be changed

JOURNAL TIP

Ask students to think about why it is important to test their ideas before they build their final design.

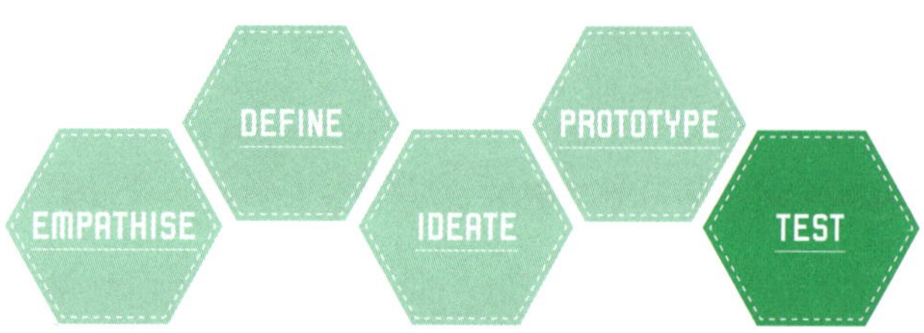

→ SHARE AND EVALUATE

At this stage of the investigation, students are provided with an opportunity to share their final design, as well as the processes involved in the investigation. Students evaluate their learning journals as well as their solutions.

ACTIVITY 1: BRING THE DESIGNS TOGETHER

1. Provide students with time to create their final designs.
2. Encourage them to film the process during prototyping and testing.
3. Students can create an iMovie or use Adobe Spark Video to demonstrate the process and thinking behind designs if technology is available.
4. Students should include their learning journals with the display so others can see the different stages of the design process.

ACTIVITY 2: EVALUATE AND GIVE FEEDBACK

1. Provide students with **Generic reproducible 2 (Self-evaluation)** to complete.
2. Ask students to provide feedback to each other about the most interesting features, the aspects that were most difficult and the changes that they would make if they repeated the task.
3. Provide students with opportunities to share their designs with the wider community. This could include inviting local community members or representatives from a community garden.

ASSESSMENT

Ask students to again complete **Generic reproducible 1 (Key vocabulary table)** using the key vocabulary for this unit. Compare their table with the one they completed at the Tune-in stage, to demonstrate changes in understanding.

Students complete **Generic reproducible 3 (Responding to the investigation)**. Compare their responses to their responses to **Generic reproducible 2**.

Teachers complete **Generic reproducible 5 (Design thinking assessment rubric)** for each student. Students compare the feedback they are given by the teacher with their self-assessment of how they used the design thinking process to solve problems **(Generic reproducible 3)**.

TUNE IN

STEM INVESTIGATIONS

Name: ....

Date: ....

Use these questions to help you to research composting.

What is compost?	How can humans make compost?
How does composting work?	**What materials can be composted?**

TUNE IN

STEM INVESTIGATIONS

Name: ....

Date: ....

Research how to make a compost system and add information to the boxes.

What do you need?	What kinds of waste do you put in a compost system?
What are 'brown' ingredients?	What are 'green' ingredients?
Why do you need both 'brown' and 'green' ingredients?	Other important information

STEM Investigations, MP, ISBN 978 1 4202 4319 2 © Macmillan Science and Education Australia 2018

Name: ....

Date: ....

List the dos and don'ts of composting. What symbols could you use to tell people this information?

Do ...	Symbols
Don't ...	**Symbols**

STEM Investigations, MP, ISBN 978 1 4202 4319 2

EMPATHISE

STEM INVESTIGATIONS

Name: ....

Date: ....

Watch the video clip with your teacher and then answer these questions.

- What does food waste become when it decomposes?

- What gas is produced when food waste is composted?

- Why is composting different to throwing away food waste?

- Why do you think this video clip was created?

EMPATHISE

STEM INVESTIGATIONS

Name: ....

Date: ....

These questions will help you to do your survey. There is space at the end to write your own questions.

Question	Answer
Do you know what composting is?	
Do you use a compost system at home? Why or why not?	
Do you think composting is important? Why or why not?	
If a community compost system was available, would you use it?	

SORT THE BULLS FROM THE CHICKENS

INTRODUCTION

Millions of different animal species exist around the world, along with several hundred thousand plant species. Less than 20 per cent of animals have been formally described, with most of these being land animals. Animals have been classified into five major groups: mammals, birds, fish, reptiles and amphibians.

This investigation provides students with the opportunity to learn about the differences between animal and plant classification, with a specific focus on vertebrate animals. Students are challenged to create a map or diorama that demonstrates the different classifications of plants and animals that might be included in an agricultural show. They consider the different features of animals and plants through observation and research. This task can be differentiated by incorporating a digital component, such as an interactive flowchart or online questionnaire.

THE CHALLENGE

Your town's agricultural show is happening soon. Hundreds of people enter their animals or plants into the show competitions. This year, you are a volunteer on the show committee. They want a quick way to sort all the entries, so that similar things are kept safely together.

Your challenge is to design a questionnaire and flowchart to sort living things into groups for judging. You will create a map or diorama of the exhibition area, showing the locations of the plant and animal groups, for the committee. As part of your investigation, you will have to consider the needs of each group of living thing.

KEY UNDERSTANDINGS

- Things can be living or non-living.
- Animals and plants are living things.
- Living things can be grouped by what they have in common.
- All living things need energy, and they grow and reproduce.
- Vertebrate animals have a backbone.

KEY SKILLS

- Identify the different features of plants and animals.
- Classify plants and animals.
- Explain the similarities and differences between different plant or animal groups.
- Create labelled diagrams, sketches and models for an agricultural show competition.

KEY VOCABULARY

classify – group things with similar features

feature – something that can be seen, such as skin or egg-laying

living – grows, and needs food and water

non-living – has never lived

vertebrate – an animal with a backbone

KEY ACTIONS

- Explore features of different plants and animals.
- Create a flowchart to help identify different types of plants and animals.
- Consider how to organise plants and animals for a competition.
- Create a map or diorama.

→ OVERVIEW OF STAGES

TUNE IN:

Students consider what they know about plants and animals. They learn about the features of living things. They compare different living things and consider similarities and differences. They explore the five major types of vertebrate animals.

EMPATHISE

Students find out about the different types of animals and plants found at agricultural shows. They learn more about the features of the five major vertebrate animal groups: reptiles, mammals, birds, fish and amphibians. They also learn about different plant classifications.

DEFINE

Students learn how to create a flowchart to differentiate between different plants and animals. They decide which features need to be considered when classifying. They decide which plants and animals will be included in the agricultural show as well as the constraints of the investigation.

IDEATE

Students come up with creative ideas for how to organise animals and plants, using scientific classification, as well as how to organise them in an agricultural show. Students also think about the type of end product they will create, such as a map, diorama or other suggestion.

PROTOTYPE

Students draw, label and present the design of their plant and animal competition space. This may include flowcharts showing how animals are classified, and what space the animal is assigned, presented as a map or diorama.

TEST

Students test the design of the map or diorama. They make changes depending on the results. This may include feedback from others as well as modifications to the arrangement of animal and plant spaces.

SHARE AND EVALUATE:

Students create a flowchart or series of flowcharts to explain how they classified the animals and plants in their agricultural competition. They display this alongside their map or diorama. Students are provided with opportunities to self-evaluate and receive feedback from their peers.

→ SUGGESTED SCHEDULE

LESSON	STAGE
1–4	**Tune in:** Share knowledge about living and non-living things; explore the five major vertebrate animal groupings
5–7	**Empathise:** Research features of vertebrate animal groups and learn about different plants; write in journal
8–10	**Define:** Learn how to create a flowchart, considering different questions to include; consider the features to be included when classifying; decide which plants and animals to include in the investigation; write in journal
11–12	**Ideate:** Come up with creative ideas for organising animals and plants, using scientific classification, as well as how to organise them in an agricultural show; think about the format of the end product; write in journal
1–17	**Prototype** and **Test:** Draw, label and present the design for the organisation of an agricultural competition; build a model or develop a map; write in journal
18–21	**Share and evaluate:** Provide time to create flowcharts to explain classification of plants and animals; share final designs; evaluate self and others

CURRICULUM LINKS

SCIENCE

YEAR	STRAND	SUB-STRAND AND CONTENT
3	Science Understanding	Biological sciences: • Living things can be grouped on the basis of observable features and can be distinguished from non-living things
	Science as a Human Endeavour	Nature and development of science: • Science involves making predictions and describing patterns and relationships
3 & 4	Science Inquiry Skills	Communicating

TECHNOLOGIES

YEAR	STRAND	CONTENT
3 & 4	Design and Technologies Knowledge and Understanding	• Investigate the suitability of materials, systems, components, tools and equipment for a range of purposes
	Design and Technologies Processes and Production Skills	• Select and use materials, components, tools, equipment and techniques and use safe work practices to make designed solutions • Generate, develop and communicate design ideas and decisions using appropriate technical terms and graphical representation techniques • Evaluate design ideas, processes and solutions based on criteria for success developed with guidance and including care for the environment and communities

MATHEMATICS

YEAR	STRAND	SUB-STRAND AND CONTENT
3	Measurement and Geometry	Location and transformation: • Create and interpret simple grid maps to show position and pathways Shape: • Make models of three-dimensional objects and describe key features

This investigation also links to the General Capabilities:

AC

- Literacy
- Numeracy
- Information and Communication Technology (ICT) Capability
- Critical and Creative Thinking.

ASSESSMENT

The following resources are provided for assessing students at different stages of the STEM investigations:

- Generic reproducible 1 (Key vocabulary table), for assessing understanding of vocabulary
- Generic reproducible 2 (Self-evaluation), for student self-evaluation of the learning process
- Generic reproducible 3 (Responding to the investigation)
- Generic reproducible 5 (Design thinking assessment rubric), for evaluating student engagement in the design thinking stages
- Learning journal templates 1, 2, 3 and 4, incorporating student reflection and evaluation.

→ GETTING READY FOR THE INVESTIGATION

You can prepare yourself and students for this STEM investigation in the following ways:

- Identify groups of students who will work well together.
- Review the **Key science knowledge** that supports this investigation, and look at the **Useful links**.
- Investigate the **Useful apps**.
- Gather materials for the science activities about animal and plant classification during the Tune-in session, including pictures of animals and plants, and lists of animals and plants, grouped according to classification.
- Start collecting additional materials for prototyping (as shown on the **Materials needed** list).
- Determine where prototypes will be kept between lessons.
- Create a wall space where students can share their ideas in the Ideate stage.
- Organise the class into pairs.
- Start thinking about:
  - » sourcing information about different animals and plants, as well as agricultural shows
  - » making connections with plant and animal experts as well as people with experience in agricultural shows or similar
  - » time constraints for the task
  - » how, when and where the designs will be shared and evaluated
  - » whether students will select animals and plants to be included (from a list or open choice) or if they will be provided with a list of animals and plants to include.

USEFUL APPS

- App for creating semantic maps (links between different words and/or concepts), such as Popplet or Kidspiration
- App for creating multimedia presentations, such as Adobe Spark Video (via a teacher-created class account), Prezi or iMovie
- App for sharing ideas, thoughts, questions and images, such as Padlet or Lino
- Website for creating flowcharts, such as Draw.io
- App for engaging in collaborative tasks, such as OneNote Class Notebook

USEFUL LINKS

- Information about plants and animals for students, such as at mea.digital/sm50
- General information about plants and animals, such as at mea.digital/sm51
- Interactive animal classification game, such as at mea.digital/sm52
- Video clip of animal facts, such as at mea.digital/sm53
- Animal classification video clip, such as at mea.digital/sm54
- Plant classification video clip, such as at mea.digital/sm245
- List of plants, such as at mea.digital/sm55
- Agricultural show websites, such as at mea.digital/sm56, mea.digital/sm57, mea.digital/sm58, mea.digital/sm59

RESOURCES PROVIDED

- Generic reproducibles 1, 2, 3, 5, 7, 10, 12
- Reproducibles 9.1, 9.2, 9.3
- Learning journal templates 1, 2, 3, 4

MATERIALS NEEDED

- Recycled materials, such as assorted cardboard boxes, cardboard offcuts, tubes, string, ribbon
- Boxes, if making a diorama
- Matchsticks
- Cellophane, tissue paper, coloured paper
- Plasticine or other modelling clay
- Scissors
- Tape – different widths, strengths, materials
- PVA glue
- Hot glue guns and glue (optional)
- Staplers and staples
- Pictures of plants and animals from different categories
- Tape measures or rulers

Hot glue guns can be dangerous. Make sure students are supervised at all times.

KEY SCIENCE KNOWLEDGE

This section provides an overview of the key science concepts and vocabulary needed for this unit.

LIVING AND NON-LIVING THINGS

We **classify** everything as either **living** or **non-living**. Living things have particular **features** that identify them as living. For example, they have cells, and they can breathe, grow, develop and reproduce. Also, they need energy (including plants, animals and sunlight), and they respond to stimuli (for example, plants lean towards a light source).

Non-living things do not display the features of living things. They do not respond to stimuli or adapt to their environment.

CLASSIFICATION OF LIVING THINGS

Living things are classified into groups according to shared characteristics. There are seven levels of traditional scientific classification: kingdom, phylum, class, order, family, genus and species, and subgroupings of these classifications. The five kingdoms are animals, plants (green plants), fungi, prokaryotes (bacteria) and protoctists (other single- and multicelled organisms).

Plants can be broadly classed as vascular or non-vascular. Vascular plants have roots and stems. Non-vascular plants, such as algae, don't have these features. Vascular plants are seed bearing (such as flowering plants) or spore bearing (such as ferns). Seed-bearing plants are either angiosperms (flowering plants) or gymnosperms (non-flowering plants such as conifers).

Animals can be classified into **vertebrates** (with a backbone) and invertebrates (without a backbone). The five major groups of vertebrate animals are mammals, fish, birds, amphibians and reptiles. Within these groups are families of animals, genus groups and species groups.

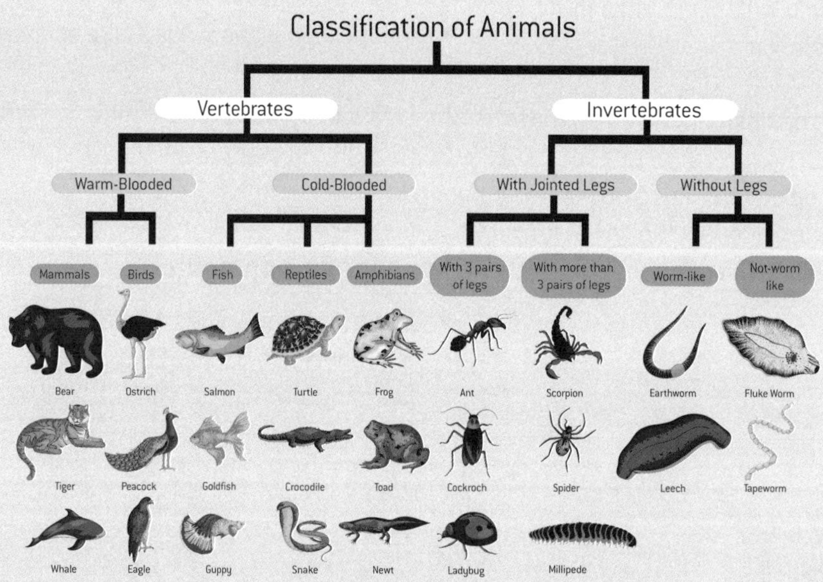

Animal species can be grouped and differentiated by asking key questions, for example, 'Does it have a backbone?' If yes, 'Is its body temperature constant?' and, if yes, 'Does it have feathers?'

KEY VOCABULARY

classify – group things with similar features
feature – something that can be seen, such as skin or egg-laying
living – grows, and needs food and water
non-living – has never lived
vertebrate – an animal with a backbone

→ TUNE IN

1. Ask students to complete **Generic reproducible 1 (Key vocabulary table)** using the key vocabulary for this unit. This reproducible will also be used at the end of the unit, to demonstrate changes in understanding.
2. Ask students to share interesting information about animals. Watch a video clip with interesting information about animals (see **Useful apps/links**). The class might like to create a display with interesting facts or an interactive document using an app such as Padlet or OneNote Class Notebook.
3. Create a set of animal 'Who am I?' cards. Have groups of students take turns reading the clues on the cards. The other students in the group guess what animal is being described and explain the important clues.
4. Students need to understand the difference between living and non-living things. They also need to understand the different characteristics of animals and plants that are used for classification. Set up the following three activities or similar.

ACTIVITY 1: PLANT AND ANIMAL CLASSIFICATION

1. Provide students with sets of pictures of animals. Ask students to group the pictures according to like characteristics and then have them explain their groupings. Compare the ways that each group of students has classified the plants and animals.
2. Watch a video clip about classification of animals (see **Useful apps/links**).
3. Provide students with time to review the groupings of their animal pictures and explain any changes they made.
4. Repeat the activity with sets of plant pictures and view a plant classification video clip (see **Useful apps/links**).

ACTIVITY 2: ANIMAL CHARACTERISTICS

1. Provide students with a link to an animal classification game (see **Useful apps/links**).
2. Discuss the different terms used in the game prior to beginning.

ACTIVITY 3: ANIMAL COMPARISON

1. Provide **Generic reproducible 7 (Double bubble)** to pairs of students.
2. Randomly assign two different animals to each pair and have them research each animal. Students record the similarities and differences between the two animals.
3. Have students share some of the interesting facts they found out about the animals.

5. Introduce the STEM investigation and challenge to the students. Provide them with the student card and read the information together.
6. Introduce the design thinking process by reviewing the stages on the student card. Explain that students will keep a journal about their learning at the different stages of the design.

TOP TIP! When providing pairs of animals for students to compare, make sure there are examples from different animal groups, such as a panda (mammal) and budgerigar (bird) or a whale (mammal) and a shark (fish).

USEFUL APPS/LINKS

- App for sharing ideas, thoughts, questions and images, such as Padlet or Lino
- App for engaging in collaborative tasks, such as OneNote Class Notebook
- Interactive animal classification game, such as at mea.digital/sm52
- Video clip with facts about animals, such as at mea.digital/sm53
- Animal classification video, such as at mea.digital/sm54
- Plant classification video, such as at mea.digital/sm245

→ EMPATHISE

During the Empathise stage of the design thinking process, students focus on finding out about different points of view. To empathise with others, they need to research some of the points of view associated with agricultural shows. This includes finding out about different plants and animals. Students will take notes, ask questions, draw diagrams and take photos where relevant.

ACTIVITY 1: AGRICULTURAL SHOWS

1. Have students investigate what happens at agricultural shows. If there is a local show that can be visited, then organise an excursion.
2. Have students research the types of activities that occur at agricultural shows, as well as the plants and animals on display. Provide them with **Reproducible 9.1 (Agricultural shows)** to collate their information.
3. Demonstrate how to navigate different official show websites, looking for tabs that signpost useful information, such as 'animals', and skimming headlines.
4. Have students explore at least three different websites and compare the types of activities and produce that can be exhibited (see **Useful apps/links**).

Students can update **Learning journal template 3 (Ideate page)**.

ACTIVITY 2: ALL ABOUT PLANTS AND ANIMALS

1. Provide students with **Reproducible 9.2 (Plant classification)** and **Reproducible 9.3 (Animal classification)** to record their findings.
2. Provide pairs of students with the name of one plant and one animal to investigate. They should work through the flowchart on the relevant reproducible to find out the classification of the animal or plant name they have been given.
3. Some useful examples are apple, fir tree, grass, orchid, protea, lily, fern, cycad, sunflower (for plants); cockatoo, brown bear, trout, green tree frog, sting ray (for animals). Note that there are some exceptions (such as the platypus).
4. Provide students with time to explain how they found out the information and the usefulness of the flowcharts.

PROMPTS

- What were some of the different types of animals/plants you found?
- What sorts of animals/plants are exhibited at agricultural shows?
- What was one interesting thing you found out?

MORE VOCABULARY

- empathise – understand and consider another person or group's point of view
- point of view – an opinion, attitude or judgement considered in a particular way

JOURNAL TIP

Ask students to complete **Learning journal template 1 (Empathise page)** while they are completing the different tasks. Remind them to date their notes and include photos of relevant information or pictures.

USEFUL APPS/LINKS

- List of plants, such as at mea.digital/sm55
- List of common plant names, such as at mea.digital/sm60
- Agricultural show websites, such as at mea.digital/sm56, mea.digital/sm57, mea.digital/sm58, mea.digital/sm59

ASSESSMENT

This stage of the design thinking process offers opportunities to observe students collecting information, developing questions, and recording their notes and thinking in their journal.

TOP TIP! When investigating agricultural shows, begin with shows in the local area, then perhaps compare shows with other regions or countries.

EMPATHISE DEFINE IDEATE PROTOTYPE TEST

→ DEFINE

The main focus of this stage of the design thinking process is to reframe the challenge and define what needs to be done. This includes noting insights that have been generated.

ACTIVITY 1: CONSIDER INFORMATION ABOUT SHOWS

1. Have students share their observations about the different agricultural shows that they researched.
2. Discuss the information that was collected:
   - What are some of the activities that people can do at shows?
   - Which types of animals are at most shows?
   - Which animals are not so common?
   - Are there any shows with plant exhibits or competitions?
   - What types of plants are at the shows?
   - How could you find out about other shows?

ACTIVITY 2: SELECT ANIMALS AND PLANTS

1. Have students think about the selection of plants and animals for their map or diorama.
2. Students make a collaborative list of plants and animals based on their research. Use a large piece of paper or collaborative app such as Padlet, Lino or OneNote Class Notebook. Decide whether other plants and animals can be added to the list and if there are selection criteria for their inclusion.

Students can update **Learning journal template 2 (Define page)**.

ACTIVITY 3: CREATE A CLASS CHECKLIST

1. Have students create a class checklist. Have them consider:
   - number of animals and plants to include (highlighting compulsory ones)
   - options for the end product, such as static map, interactive map or diorama
   - inclusion of flowcharts demonstrating classification of animals and plants included in the design.
2. After the initial checklist has been created, have students review it and make suggestions for inclusions, changes or deletions.
3. Provide students with easy access to the checklist so that it can guide their investigation. If using a collaborative tool, it can be modified during the investigation.

PROMPTS

- Do agricultural shows in different countries have similar activities?
- What are some of the more unusual activities found at shows?
- What are some of the activities that animals in shows are asked to do?

MORE VOCABULARY

- define – state the meaning of something
- insight – an accurate understanding of someone or something
- point of view – an opinion, attitude or judgement considered in a particular way

JOURNAL TIP

Discuss the term 'insight' and explain that it relates to something students have learned from the information gathered through research or excursions. You could refer to **Learning journal template 2**.

USEFUL APPS/LINKS

- App for sharing ideas, thoughts, questions and images, such as Padlet or Lino
- App for engaging in collaborative tasks, such as OneNote Class Notebook

EMPATHISE DEFINE IDEATE PROTOTYPE TEST

→ IDEATE

The Ideate stage of the design thinking process is all about generating lots of ideas. Students need to be flexible in their thinking and be able to move beyond obvious ideas. At this stage, ideas are not judged, just generated and gathered.

ACTIVITY 1: EXPLORE AGRICULTURAL SHOW PLANS

1. Provide students with some plans from agricultural shows, or explore the interactive maps provided by many of the shows, if available.
2. Have students consider the different plans, then brainstorm their own ideas in a concept map for what they might like to include in their map. They could use an app such as Popplet to help them organise their ideas.
3. Have students return to browsing the official maps before adding more ideas to their original concept map.

ACTIVITY 2: PLAN FLOWCHARTS

1. Review how to use and create a flowchart. These could be drawn using a small whiteboard, on paper or using an app such as Popplet, Kidspiration or Draw.io. Focus on initially creating 'big questions' with yes/no responses, such as 'Does the animal have a backbone? Does the plant have flowers?'
2. Organise the class into groups. Each group considers ideas for a flowchart for one particular plant or animal classification, such as bird, mammal, fish, amphibian, reptile, flowering plant, spore-bearing plant, non-flowering plant.
3. Students should create a range of questions that could be incorporated into the flowcharts.

PROMPTS

- How might these suggestions be included in a map for an agricultural show?
- How might you use the flowcharts to make sure the animals and plants are organised in the correct places?
- How can you make your ideas interactive?
- What types of materials or apps might be good to use?

MORE VOCABULARY

- feedback – information about, for example, a person's performance or the design of a product, which can be used to make improvements
- ideate – generate many ideas without making judgements about the ideas

JOURNAL TIP

When choosing three ideas to include in the journal, try to choose three ideas about the show map that aren't related.

USEFUL APPS/LINKS

- App for creating semantic maps (links between different words and/or concepts), such as Popplet or Kidspiration
- App for creating flowcharts, such as Draw.io

ASSESSMENT

At the Ideate stage, assessment could include observations about the number and diversity of student ideas, and their ability to provide feedback and create additional ideas. Reflection in the journal should provide an insight into some of the reasoning behind student choices.

EMPATHISE | DEFINE | IDEATE | PROTOTYPE | TEST

→ PROTOTYPE

At this stage of the design thinking process, students are asked to create a physical prototype of a solution. It is the stage where students need to get their ideas out of their heads and present them in a way that engages other students and helps them to understand the concept. When students create, it helps them to think and solve problems and disagreements.

Encourage students to photograph or film during the Prototype and Test stages. This information can be used to show the learning behind the design thinking process in action.

ACTIVITY 1: CREATE FLOWCHARTS

1. Have students select any additional, non-compulsory animals and plants that they will include in their design.
2. Students create flowcharts for classifying plants and animals. They should include all the important features on the two flowcharts (one for animals and one for plants).
3. Students discuss and draw how they might use the flowcharts to show how the animals and plants are to be grouped.

ACTIVITY 2: TRANSFORM IDEAS INTO PROTOTYPES

1. Have students start designing the layout of the judging area.
2. Students draw a design that incorporates all the animals and plants chosen.
3. Students use simple materials such as building blocks or containers to create their first prototype, such as a map or diorama.
4. Remind students to think about where animals and plants will be located, and why.

ACTIVITY 3: REFINE DESIGNS

1. Provide students with time to refine elements of their map or diorama.
2. Provide students with **Generic reproducible 10 (Group task organiser)** to help them plan the final construction.
3. Encourage students to photograph or video the different prototypes so they can demonstrate the learning process.

Ask students to fill in the Prototype part of **Learning journal template 4 (Prototype and test page)**. See the Journal tip for further student guidance.

PROMPTS

- Have you included all the animals and plants?
- Which part needs to be made first?
- How will you label the different parts?
- How will you include the flowcharts to show how the plants and animals were classified?

MORE VOCABULARY

- feedback – information about, for example, a person's performance or the design of a product, which can be used to make improvements
- prototype – an initial version of a model of a product or process that is used to develop a final model

JOURNAL TIP

Remind students to highlight the main features of their prototype. If students are creating an electronic journal, they can insert a photo of their prototype and annotate it.

USEFUL APPS/LINKS

- App for taking photographs or video, such as Adobe Spark Video or iMovie

ASSESSMENT

Observe students as they make changes to their designs. Are they able to consider feedback, make modifications and move rapidly through this process, or do they have difficulties with holding on to an idea and accepting feedback?

TOP TIP! When asking for feedback, students could ask each other:

- What are the types of animals being judged?
- What do animals in the judging area need?
- Which parts of your design work best?
- What do you need to change?
- What other materials might you need?

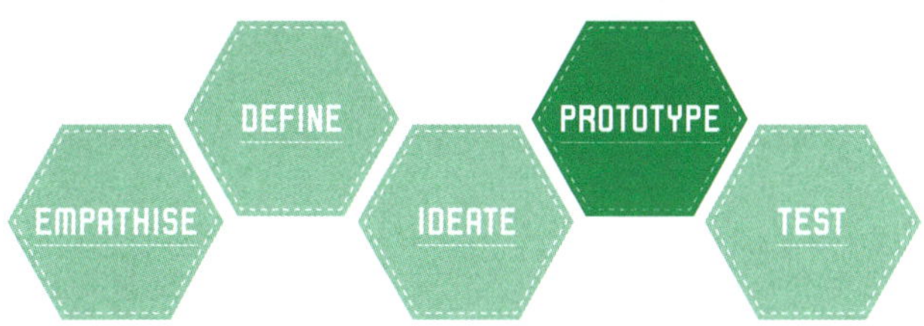

→ TEST

At this stage of the design thinking process, students test their prototype to see how it meets the criteria in the challenge.

ACTIVITY: TEST FEEDBACK

1. Have students gather feedback about the prototypes. Provide them with **Generic reproducible 12 (Prototype and test)** to record the ideas.
2. When providing feedback, students should consider if all the items or actions on the original checklist have been included, if the classification process for the animals and plants is clear and whether the animals' needs have been taken into account.
3. Students continue to cycle through the Prototype and Test stages until they have completed their design.

Ask students to fill in **Learning journal template 4 (Prototype and test page)**. See the **Journal tip** for further student guidance.

PROMPTS

- Does your prototype do what you wanted it to do?
- Did your design feature the animals people expect to see at a show?

MORE VOCABULARY

- evaluate – assess something, perhaps considering what worked and what didn't
- feature – a specific aspect of something, such as size, shape, colour or quality
- feedback – information about, for example, a person's performance or the design of a product, which can be used to make improvements
- prototype – an initial version of a model of a product or process that is used to develop a final model
- review – consider an idea, process or product and assess what works and what needs to be changed

JOURNAL TIP

Ask students to think about why it is important to test their ideas before they build their final design.

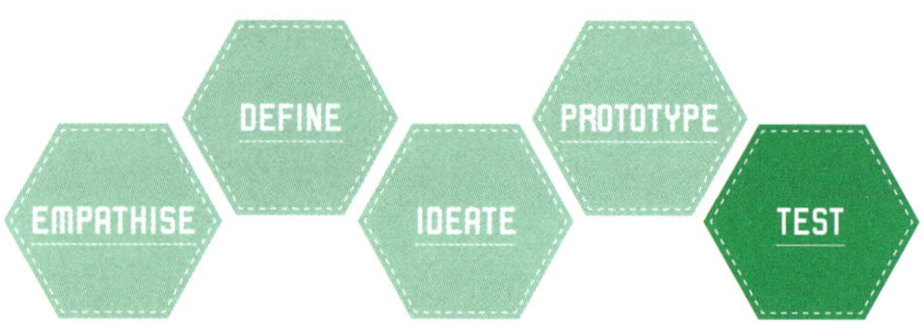

→ SHARE AND EVALUATE

At this stage of the investigation, students are provided with an opportunity to share their final design, as well as the processes involved in the investigation. Students evaluate their learning journals as well as their solutions.

ACTIVITY 1: FINALISE DESIGNS

1. Allow students to finalise their designs, including creating the map or diorama. They also need to provide examples of the flowcharts they created for classifying the plants and animals.
2. Set up a time for other people to see the different designs and provide feedback. This could include someone from the local community who is involved in agricultural shows or similar.
3. Students should include their learning journals with the display so others can see the different stages of the design process.

ACTIVITY 2: EVALUATE AND GIVE FEEDBACK

1. Provide students with **Generic reproducible 2 (Self-evaluation)** to complete.
2. During the sharing session, provide participants with tokens or stickers so they can vote for the design they would want to see at a show, or create an online survey for others to vote.

ASSESSMENT

Ask students to again complete **Generic reproducible 1 (Key vocabulary table)** using the key vocabulary for this unit. Compare their table with the one they completed at the Tune-in stage, to demonstrate changes in understanding.

Students complete **Generic reproducible 3 (Responding to the investigation)**. Compare their responses to their responses to **Generic reproducible 2**.

Teachers complete **Generic reproducible 5 (Design thinking assessment rubric)** for each student. Students compare the feedback they are given by the teacher with their self-assessment of how they used the design thinking process to solve problems **(Generic reproducible 3)**.

EMPATHISE

STEM INVESTIGATIONS

Name: ....

Date: ....

Find out some information about different agricultural shows. Your teacher will provide you with some useful links to get started.

Show name	
Location	
Activities	
Animals	
Other interesting information	
Plants	

EMPATHISE

STEM INVESTIGATIONS

Name: ....

Date: ....

Use this flowchart to find out what sort of plant you are investigating.

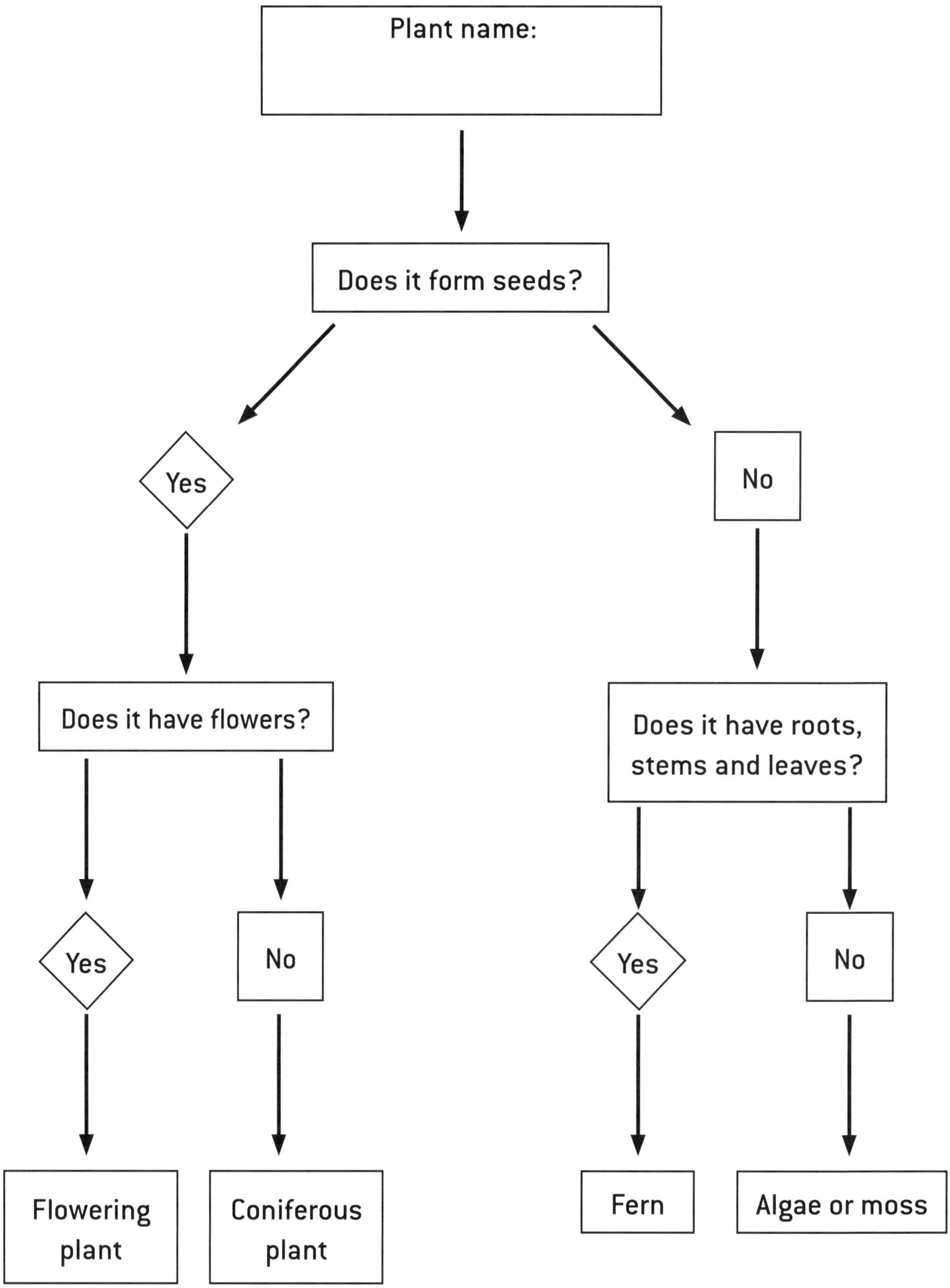

STEM Investigations, MP, ISBN 978 1 4202 4319 2

EMPATHISE

STEM INVESTIGATIONS

Name: ....

Date: ....

Use this flowchart to find out what sort of animal you are investigating.

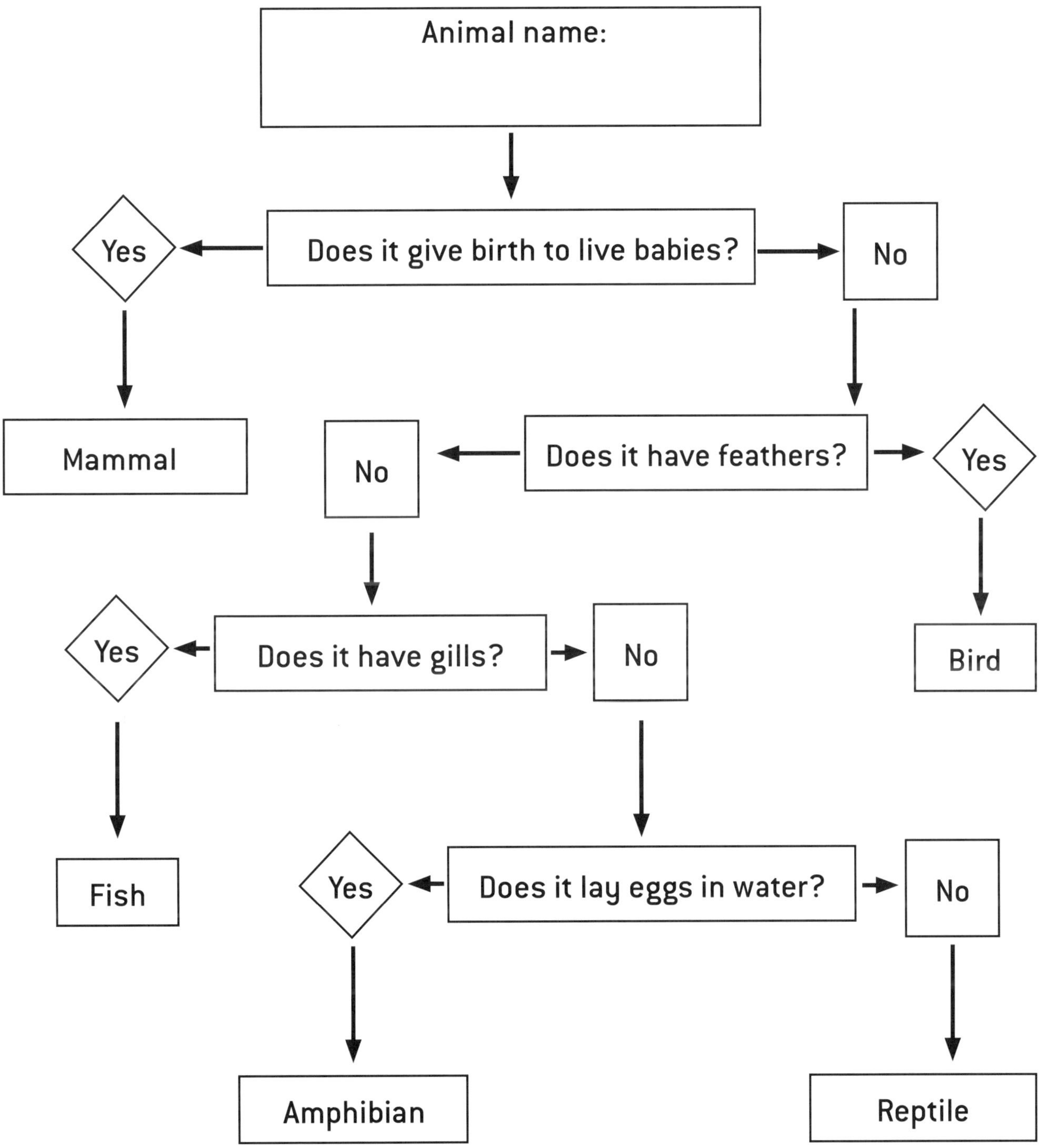

MAKE A MOVIE ABOUT THE EARTH'S MOVEMENT

→ INTRODUCTION

In many ancient cultures, people believed the Earth was flat. As more scientific evidence was gathered, this idea was shown to be false. Over time, scientists showed that the Earth is a like a sphere, but slightly flattened at the poles and bulging at the equator. It takes 24 hours to rotate on its axis, which gives us day and night. The seasons are caused by the Earth's revolutions (often called orbits) around the Sun.

In this STEM investigation, students are asked to produce a movie that shows that the Earth is a sphere that rotates on its axis and revolves around the Sun. The audience is a class of younger students who think the Earth is flat. Movies could be live action or animated. Students will need to demonstrate either how night and day happen or why we have seasons. As part of their investigation, they will learn how the Earth's rotation on its axis causes regular changes.

This STEM challenge is easily differentiated for students by encouraging different groups to use different degrees of complexity when creating their movies.

THE CHALLENGE

Someone has told the younger students at your school that the Earth is flat! Many believe it because they say that the ground looks and feels flat. Your teacher wants you to help convince the younger students of the truth.

Your challenge is to produce a movie that shows that the Earth is a sphere that rotates on its axis and orbits the Sun. You should show either how night and day happen or why we have seasons. As part of your investigation, you will learn how the Earth's rotation on its axis causes regular changes.

KEY UNDERSTANDINGS

- The Earth rotates on its axis, which causes night and day.
- The Earth's axis is tilted to the side.
- The Earth moves in an orbit around the Sun.
- The Earth's orbit and axis cause seasons.

KEY SKILLS

- Make careful observations by exploring the effect of the Earth's movement on our environment.
- Consider different points of view and develop empathy.
- Work together as a team, develop collaborative skills and consider different ideas and opinions.
- Think creatively to transform an idea into something that can be seen.

KEY VOCABULARY

axis – an imaginary line that something spins around, such as the line between the north pole and the south pole

orbit – move or revolve in a repeating pattern around another object in space

rotate – spin around a central point

sphere – a round, three-dimensional object

KEY ACTIONS

- Find out information about the rotation and orbit of the Earth, day and night, and the seasons.
- Explore movie-making and what makes an engaging movie.
- Interview students to find out about movie preferences.
- Produce a movie.

→ OVERVIEW OF STAGES

TUNE IN:

Students find out about the Earth's movement and what causes day and night and the seasons. They research the science behind effective movie making.

EMPATHISE

Students interview younger students about what makes an engaging movie. They find out if animated or live action films are preferred.

DEFINE

Students determine the main issues that relate to the production of a movie – the equipment required and the process of making a movie.

IDEATE

Students come up with creative ideas for making the movie engaging and interesting while also communicating the science. Sound effects and narration should complement the images.

PROTOTYPE

Students transform some of their ideas into storyboards. They make changes and try new ways of creating their idea.

TEST

Students check which ideas work best. They choose a final format and begin shooting their film. They test it with a sample audience from the targeted group of younger students. A journal with storyboard and scripts needs to be completed.

SHARE AND EVALUATE:

Final prototypes are shared with the school community. Feedback is provided.

→ SUGGESTED SCHEDULE

LESSON	STAGE
1–4	**Tune in:** Find out about the Earth's movement and what causes night and day and the seasons; research effective movie making
5–7	**Empathise:** Interview young students to find out what makes an engaging movie; research ways of making movies effective; write in journal
8–9	**Define:** Consider observations and insights; define main issues; write in journal
10–11	**Ideate:** Develop ideas; write in journal
12–14	**Prototype** and **Test:** Conduct prototyping and testing cycles; write in journal
15–16	**Share and evaluate:** Share and evaluate designs and prototypes

CURRICULUM LINKS

SCIENCE

YEAR	STRAND	SUB-STRAND AND CONTENT
3	Science Understanding	Earth and space sciences: • Earth's rotation on its axis causes regular changes, including night and day
3 & 4	Science as a Human Endeavour	Use and influence of science: • Science knowledge helps people to understand the effect of their actions
	Science Inquiry Skills	Questioning and predicting Planning and conducting Processing and analysing data and information Evaluating

TECHNOLOGIES

YEAR	STRAND	CONTENT
3 & 4	Design and Technologies Processes and Production Skills	• Critique needs or opportunities for designing and explore and test a variety of materials, components, tools and equipment and the techniques needed to create designed solutions • Generate, develop, and communicate design ideas and decisions using appropriate technical terms and graphical representation techniques • Select and use materials, components, tools and equipment using safe work practices to produce designed solutions • Evaluate design ideas, processes and solutions based on criteria for success developed with guidance and including care for the environment and communities • Plan a sequence of production steps when making designed solutions
	Digital Technologies Processes and Production Skills	• Collect, access and present different types of data using simple software to create information and solve problems • Define simple problems, and describe and follow a sequence of steps and decisions (algorithms) needed to solve them • Individually and with others, plan, create and communicate ideas and information safely, applying agreed ethical and social protocols
	Digital Technologies Creating Digital Solutions	• Explain how student-developed solutions and existing information systems meet common personal, school or community needs

MATHEMATICS

YEAR	STRAND	SUB-STRAND AND CONTENT
3 & 4	Measurement and Geometry	Location and transformation: • Create symmetrical patterns, pictures and shapes with and without digital technologies Shape: • Make models of three-dimensional objects and describe key features

This investigation also links to the General Capabilities:

- Literacy
- Numeracy
- Information and Communication Technology (ICT) Capability
- Critical and Creative Thinking.

This investigation also links to the Cross-Curriculum Priority of Sustainability.

ASSESSMENT

The following resources are provided for assessing students at different stages of the STEM investigations:

- Generic reproducible 1 (Key vocabulary table), for assessing understanding of vocabulary
- Generic reproducible 2 (Self-evaluation), for student self-evaluation of the learning process
- Generic reproducible 3 (Responding to the investigation)
- Generic reproducible 5 (Design thinking assessment rubric), for evaluating student engagement in the design thinking stages
- Learning journal templates 1, 2, 3 and 4, incorporating student reflection and evaluation.

GETTING READY FOR THE INVESTIGATION

You can prepare yourself and students for this STEM investigation in the following ways:

- Gather technology that will support learning about film production and producing a movie (see **Useful apps**).
- Gather materials for Activity 2 of the Tune-in session (see **Materials needed** list).
- Review information about the Earth's shape, rotation and orbit (see **Useful apps/links**).
- Determine where storyboards will be kept between lessons and where movies will be saved on computers (if relevant).
- Create a vocabulary wall/space to be added to throughout the investigation.
- Create a wall space where students can share their ideas during the Ideate stage.
- Organise the class into small groups.
- Start thinking about:
  - » how the movie design ideas will be evaluated
  - » inviting younger students to be interviewed about their film preferences
  - » who will view the prototypes and storyboards and provide feedback (such as a class of younger students)
  - » how, when and where the storyboards and/or movies will be presented and evaluated.

USEFUL APPS

- Apps for creating and organising ideas, such as Popplet, Inspiration, Padlet and Ideament
- App for sharing ideas, such as Air Sketch
- Apps for creating multimedia presentations, such as Adobe Spark Video (via a teacher-created class account) and iMovie
- Movie-making computer software, such as Windows Movie Maker and iMovie

USEFUL LINKS

- Information about the Earth's rotation and how it moves, such as at mea.digital/sm167
- Video clip about the Earth's rotation and revolution, such as at mea.digital/sm168
- Video clip or model explaining day and night, such as at mea.digital/sm169, mea.digital/sm170, mea.digital/sm171
- Video clip about how the seasons occur, such as at mea.digital/sm172
- Information about seasons and the Earth's tilt, such as at mea.digital/sm173
- Activity about the seasons and day and night, such as at mea.digital/sm174

RESOURCES PROVIDED

- Generic reproducibles 1, 2, 3, 4, 5, 6
- Reproducibles 10.1, 10.2, 10.3
- Learning journal templates 1, 2, 3, 4

MATERIALS NEEDED

- Sticky notes
- Paper
- Cardboard
- Pens and markers
- Sticky tape
- Whiteboards and markers
- Pencils
- Compass
- iPads and/or computers with movie-making technology
- Reading lamp or lantern that sheds 360-degree light

KEY SCIENCE KNOWLEDGE

This section provides an overview of the key science concepts and vocabulary needed for this unit.

SPHERICAL EARTH

When viewed from outer space, the Earth looks like a bright blue marble. It is similar to a **sphere**, except slightly flattened at the poles and bulging at the equator. The northern hemisphere (half-sphere) is above the equator and the southern hemisphere is below.

NIGHT AND DAY

The Earth **rotates** around its **axis**, the imaginary line that runs through its centre from the north pole to the south pole. One rotation takes 24 hours (a full day). At any one time, half of the Earth is facing the Sun and is experiencing day. The half facing away from the Sun is experiencing night. If the Earth were flat, all parts of the Earth would experience day and night at the same time.

REASONS FOR THE SEASONS

The Earth **orbits** the Sun in a regular path, completing one revolution in 365.25 days. Because the Earth is tilted on its axis, parts of the Earth receive different amounts of sunlight at different times of the year. This causes the seasons. For example, in June the northern hemisphere is tilted towards the Sun and experiences summer. Its daylight hours are longer and it is hotter, because the sunlight hits it directly. The opposite is true for the southern hemisphere at this time, and we call this winter. At the equator, daylight hours do not change throughout the year and these places have two seasons (wet and dry). If the Earth were flat, we would all have the same amount of daylight time and there would be no change or seasons.

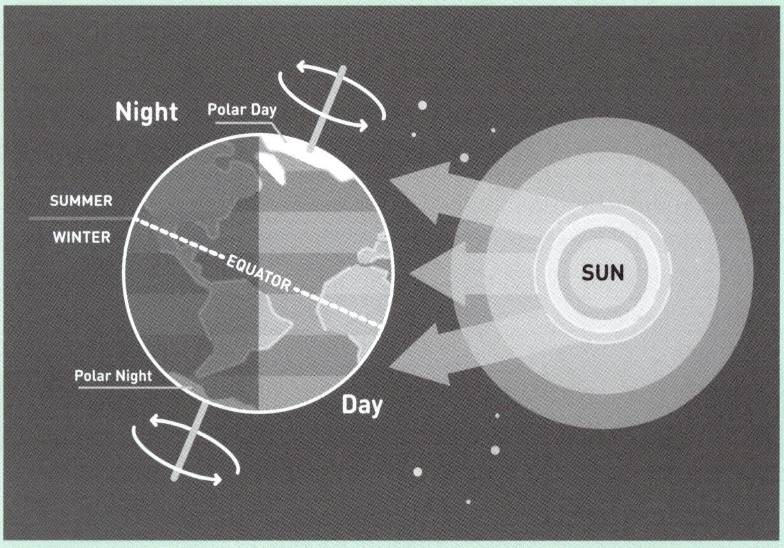

Day and night are caused by the rotation of the Earth and the seasons are caused by the Earth's tilt.

THE NIGHT SKY

The night sky looks different depending on where you are on the Earth. People in the southern hemisphere see mostly different constellations (patterns of stars) than people in the northern hemisphere. The Moon looks different to people in the northern and southern hemispheres.

KEY VOCABULARY

axis – an imaginary line that something spins around, such as the line between the north pole and the south pole

orbit – move or revolve in a repeating pattern around another object in space

rotate – spin around a central point

sphere – a round, three-dimensional object

→ TUNE IN

1. Ask students to complete **Generic reproducible 1 (Key vocabulary table)** using the key vocabulary for this unit. This reproducible will be used at the end of the unit to demonstrate changes in understanding.
2. Provoke thought with questions: 'What causes day and night to occur? What causes the seasons to occur?' Record students' understandings.
3. Watch video clips about the Earth's rotation and revolution (see **Useful apps/links**), or similar introductions to night and day and the seasons. Discuss observations and new learning.
4. Before engaging in the challenge, students need to understand how the Earth's rotation on its axis causes regular changes such as day and night and how the seasons occur. Set up the following three activities (or similar) for students.

ACTIVITY 1: SHAPE OF THE EARTH

1. Discuss the Big Picture fact on the student challenge card. Discuss why people thought the Earth was flat.
2. Provide students with **Reproducible 10.1 (Shape of the Earth)**. Students record reasons for the historical belief that the Earth was flat.
3. View a video clip about the shape of the Earth (see **Useful apps/links**).
4. Provide students with links to information about how we know the Earth is sphere-like. Record findings on **Reproducible 10.1**.

During the Tune-in sessions, conduct vocabulary activities to highlight and develop key vocabulary knowledge. Activities could include drawing semantic webs, creating a word wall or paired discussions. Check **Key vocabulary definitions** or read the **Key science knowledge** for a refresher on the key terms and concepts.

TOP TIP!

ACTIVITY 2: REASONS FOR THE SEASONS AND DAY AND NIGHT

1. Students suggest why we have regular patterns such as day and night and the seasons.
2. Use a globe to introduce the words 'tilt' and 'axis'. Explain that the Earth rotates on an axis that is tilted.
3. Encourage students to suggest how this tilt causes seasons. Discuss misconceptions and allow students time to understand the link between tilt and the seasons in the different hemispheres (see **Useful apps/links**).
4. Give each student a copy of **Reproducible 10.2 (Modelling the Earth's seasons)** and materials needed for the modelling activity. Clear a space and guide the class through the steps.
5. Students create an infographic explaining the Earth's rotation and revolution and how it causes night and day and the seasons. They could draw and annotate this on paper, create digital diagrams, or use an app such as ThingLink to annotate an image.

5. Introduce the STEM investigation and challenge to the students. Provide them with the student card and read the information together.
6. Introduce the design thinking process by reviewing the stages on the student card. Explain that students will keep a journal about their learning at the different stages of the design.

USEFUL APPS/LINKS

- Information about the Earth's rotation and how it moves, such as at mea.digital/sm167
- Video clip about the Earth's rotation and revolution, such as at mea.digital/sm168
- Video clip or model explaining day and night, such as at mea.digital/sm169, mea.digital/sm170
- Video clip about the shape of the Earth, such as at mea.digital/sm242
- Video clip about how the seasons occur, such as at mea.digital/sm172
- Information about seasons and the Earth's tilt, such as at mea.digital/sm173

→ EMPATHISE

During the Empathise stage of the design thinking process, students focus on finding out about different points of view. To empathise with others, they need to research some of the challenges associated with getting the desired message across in movie making and people's preferences for movie type.

ACTIVITY 1: MOVIE LIKES AND DISLIKES

1. Students write a list of their favourite films. Are these live-action or animated films?
2. Organise students into small groups to compare and contrast live-action and animated films. They should share their own preferences for film type.

ACTIVITY 2: INTERVIEWING YOUNGER STUDENTS

1. Provide students with **Reproducible 10.3 (Movie preferences survey)**.
2. Explain to students that they will be interviewing younger students to find out if they prefer live-action or animated films.
3. Invite younger students to class. Show some video clips of live-action and animated films.
4. Survey younger students to find out their preferences. Note whether the younger students' preferences are different from those of the older students.

ACTIVITY 3: WHAT MAKES A GOOD MOVIE?

1. Have students share favourite movies and what they like about them (regardless of whether they are live action or animated).
2. Ask students to share their understanding about storyboards: 'What are they? Why are they an important part of movie making?'
3. View a storyboard video clip and information about storyboarding and its importance to movie making (see **Useful apps/links**).

PROMPTS

- What is your best memory connected to a movie you have watched? Why do you think it is your best movie memory?
- What were the preferences of the younger students you interviewed?
- Are the younger students' preferences different from yours?
- What is important to consider when making movies?

MORE VOCABULARY

- empathise – understand and consider another person or group's point of view

JOURNAL TIP

Ask students to complete **Learning journal template 1 (Empathise page)** while they are doing the different tasks. Remind them to date their notes and include photos of relevant information or pictures.

USEFUL APPS/LINKS

- App for storyboarding, such as Storyboard That
- Storyboard video clip, such as at mea.digital/sm175
- How to storyboard, such as at mea.digital/sm176

ASSESSMENT

This stage of the design thinking process offers opportunities to observe students collecting information, developing questions, and recording their notes and thinking in their journal.

EMPATHISE DEFINE IDEATE PROTOTYPE TEST

DEFINE

The main focus of this stage of the design thinking process is to reframe the challenge. The initial challenge is quite open, so at this stage students learn how to define what needs to be done. This includes noting insights that have been generated.

ACTIVITY 1: CONSIDER OBSERVATIONS

1. Students consider the information they gathered in the Tune-in and Empathise stages. They may work in pairs or small groups. Provide them with a whiteboard, large sheet of paper and/or sticky notes to collate some of their key information. They should refer to their information on **Reproducible 10.1 (Investigating the Earth)** and **Reproducible 10.3 (Movie preferences survey)**. Students should transfer their main findings to **Learning journal template 2 (Define page)**.
2. Students should discuss one section of **Learning journal template 2** at a time, write their responses and then continue discussing their ideas for the next section, until the task is complete. This provides students with opportunities to hear others' responses and it also provides the teacher with input points.
3. Provide students with the opportunity to research further. Ask them to write other information they would like to know. Provide them with **Generic reproducible 4 (Key question table)** to assist them to record their questions, findings and sources.

ACTIVITY 2: CONSIDER INSIGHTS

Students should think of at least one insight they have gained from the process; for example, people have different preferences for movies. Students should add this insight to **Learning journal template 2**. They should then explain how this will affect their movie.

When considering insights, students could think about the following:

- What was something unexpected that you observed or found out? How was it unexpected?
- How will you decide on the most important aspect of your movie?
- Is there any other information that you need or would like to know? How will you find out?

PROMPTS

- What did you discover?
- What were the most important pieces of information that you gathered?
- What was something new that you learned?
- What other information do you need?

MORE VOCABULARY

- define – state the meaning of something
- insight – an accurate understanding of someone or something
- point of view – an opinion, attitude or judgement considered in a particular way

JOURNAL TIP

Discuss the term 'insight' and explain that it relates to something students have learned about the people and their responses to the surveys as well as information gathered through research or excursions. You could refer to **Learning journal template 2**.

USEFUL APPS/LINKS

- App for creating and organising ideas, such as Popplet, Inspiration, Padlet or Ideament
- App for storyboarding, such as Storyboard That

EMPATHISE DEFINE IDEATE PROTOTYPE TEST

→ IDEATE

The Ideate stage of the design thinking process is all about generating lots of ideas. Students need to be flexible in their thinking and be able to move beyond obvious ideas. At this stage, ideas are not judged, just generated and gathered.

ACTIVITY 1: INVESTIGATE MOVIE-MAKING

1. Provide students with links to information about making films and have them explore different effects used (see **Useful apps/links**).
2. Provide students with links to videos explaining how animated videos are made. Students record ideas and information. Consider differences between creating animated movies and live-action films.
3. Introduce students to movie-making technology available within the classroom.

ACTIVITY 2: GENERATE IDEAS

1. Ask groups of students to draw, write or storyboard their ideas for their movie.
2. Each new idea should be drawn or written on a separate piece of paper or sticky note and set out in storyboard style.
3. Ask students to group ideas on a wall or board.
4. Ask students to look at the different ideas and provide feedback to each other. It is important that students don't defend their ideas at this stage. They should just be listening to the feedback.
5. After the initial feedback, ask students to come up with more ideas. Encourage them to be creative and even radical.
6. Ask students to choose three of their ideas for a movie to show that the Earth is a sphere to write in their journal. Students use **Learning journal template 3 (Ideate page)** to do this. Ask students to choose one idea to explore further and explain the reasoning behind their choice.

PROMPTS

- How do your chosen ideas relate to the understanding that the Earth is a sphere that rotates on its axis and orbits the Sun?
- How might you test your movie idea?
- How can you make it more informative?
- What if you had different technology to use?

MORE VOCABULARY

- feedback – information about, for example, a person's performance or the design of a product, which can be used to make improvements
- ideate – generate many ideas without making judgements about the ideas

JOURNAL TIP

When choosing three ideas to include in the journal, try to choose three ideas that aren't related.

USEFUL APPS/LINKS

- Information about how a film is made, such as at mea.digital/sm177
- Sites for exploring kids' movie-making, such as mea.digital/sm178
- Online videos about animated movies, such as at mea.digital/sm179, mea.digital/sm180
- App for creating multimedia presentations, such as Adobe Spark Video or iMovie
- Movie-making computer software, such as Windows Movie Maker or iMovie
- Tools for creating ideas, such as at mea.digital/sm181
- Tips to achieve creativity and innovation, such as at mea.digital/sm182
- App for creating and organising ideas, such as Popplet, Inspiration, Padlet or Ideament
- App for storyboarding, such as Storyboard That

ASSESSMENT

At the Ideate stage, assessment could include observations about the number and diversity of student ideas, and their ability to provide feedback and create additional ideas. Reflection in the journal should provide an insight into some of the reasoning behind student choices.

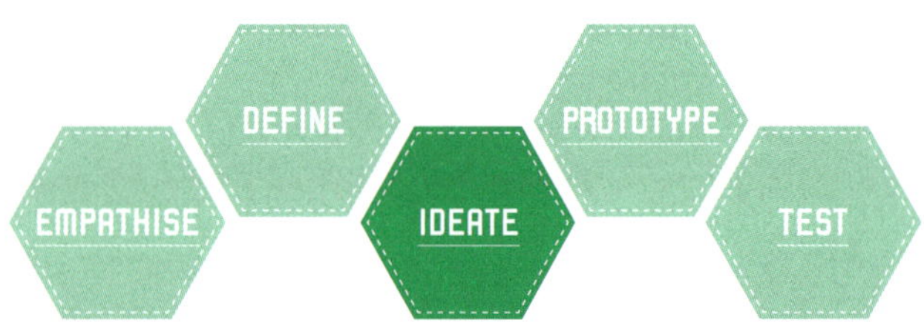

→ PROTOTYPE

At this stage of the design thinking process, students are asked to create a physical prototype of a solution. It is the stage where students need to get their ideas out of their heads and presented in a way that engages other students and helps them to understand the concept. When students create, it helps them to think and solve problems and disagreements. Students can role-play, make a storyboard or use sticky notes when they prototype. The most important feature is that viewers can interact with whatever is produced.

Encourage students to photograph or film during the Prototype and Test stages. This information can be used to show the learning behind the design thinking process in action.

ACTIVITY: TRANSFORM IDEAS INTO PROTOTYPES

1. Students review the ideas generated at the Ideate stage. Provide them with an A3 copy of **Generic reproducible 6 (In the frame)** so they can organise their ideas into two sections: least relevant and most relevant. Provide students with some question prompts to help support discussion of the ideas; for example:
   » Why do you think this idea could be used?
   » What parts of this idea could be improved?
   » What would need to be changed for this idea to be used?
   » Why do you think this idea is not so relevant to the challenge?
2. Provide students with storyboard materials/apps to use to create their prototype. Remind students that a prototype should be created rapidly and is not meant to look 'nice'.
3. After prototype has been created, ask students to see if it works and effectively presents information about the Earth's shape, rotation and orbit. Students give feedback by writing one thing that worked well and one thing that could be improved on sticky notes.
4. Students then use feedback to prototype again.

Ask students to fill in the Prototype part of **Learning journal template 4 (Prototype and test page)**. See the **Journal tip** for further student guidance.

PROMPTS

- What worked?
- How could it be improved?
- What else do you need to know, do or have?
- What other suggestions do you have?
- Does your prototype present information about the shape of the Earth, its rotation on its axis and its orbit?

MORE VOCABULARY

- feedback – information about, for example, a person's performance or the design of a product, which can be used to make improvements
- prototype – an initial version of a model of a product or process that is used to develop a final model

JOURNAL TIP

Remind students to highlight the main features of their prototype. If students are creating an electronic journal, they can insert a photo of their prototype and annotate it.

USEFUL APPS/LINKS

- App that can be used for a learning journal, allowing students to draw, link, type and record information, such as Notability

ASSESSMENT

Observe students as they make changes to their designs. Are they able to consider feedback, make modifications and move rapidly through this process, or do they have difficulties with holding on to an idea and accepting feedback?

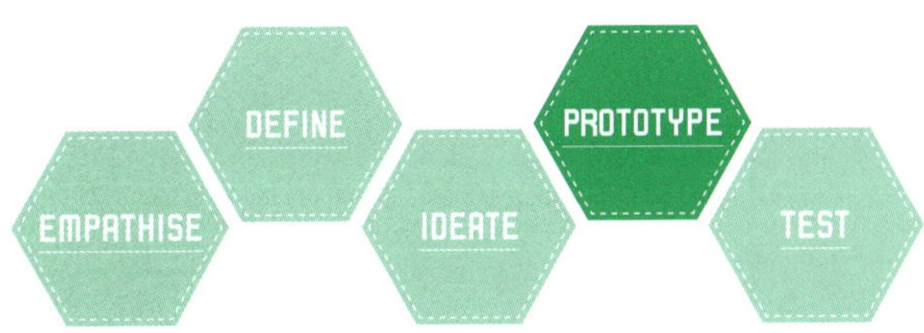

→ TEST

At this stage of the design thinking process, students test their prototype to see how it meets the criteria in the challenge. Students check to see if their prototype meets the criteria set at the start of the design process.

ACTIVITY: TEST FEEDBACK

1. Students take their last prototype and consider the original design challenge.
2. Invite younger students back to view prototypes.
3. Students consider feedback to determine if their ideas will be effective in convincing younger students of the Earth's shape and giving information about its orbit and rotation.
4. Provide the opportunity to cycle through the Prototype and Test stages again.

Ask students to fill in **Learning journal template 4 (Prototype and test page)**. See the **Journal tip** for further student guidance.

PROMPTS

- Does your prototype do what you wanted it to do?
- Are there other features that need to be added?

MORE VOCABULARY

- evaluate – assess something, perhaps considering what worked and what didn't
- feature – a specific aspect of something, such as size, shape, colour, quality
- feedback – information about, for example, a person's performance or the design of a product, which can be used to make improvements
- prototype – an initial version of a model of a product or process that is used to develop a final model
- review – consider an idea, process or product and assess what works and what needs to be changed

JOURNAL TIP

Ask students to think about why it is important to test their ideas before they build their final design.

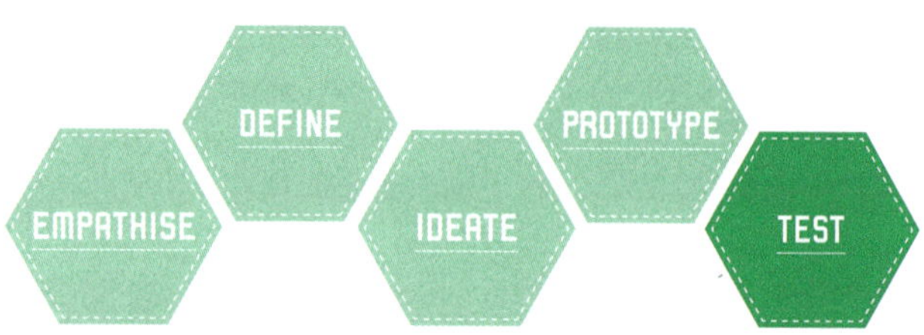

→ SHARE AND EVALUATE

At this stage of the investigation, students are provided with an opportunity to share their final design, as well as the processes involved in the investigation. Students evaluate their learning journals as well as their solutions.

ACTIVITY 1: BRING THE DESIGNS TOGETHER

1. Provide students with time to create their final movies.
2. Students should include their learning journals and storyboards with the movie so others can see the different stages of the design process.

ACTIVITY 2: EVALUATE AND GIVE FEEDBACK

1. Provide students with **Generic reproducible 2 (Self-evaluation)** to complete.
2. Ask students to provide feedback to each other about the most interesting features, the aspects that were most difficult and the changes that they would make if they repeated the task.
3. Provide students with an opportunity to share their storyboards and movies with younger students. Journals and other information relevant to the design process could be displayed as well.

ASSESSMENT

Ask students to again complete **Generic reproducible 1 (Key vocabulary table)** using the key vocabulary for this unit. Compare their table with the one they completed at the Tune-in stage, to demonstrate changes in understanding.

Students complete **Generic reproducible 3 (Responding to the investigation)**. Compare their responses to their responses to **Generic reproducible 2**.

Teachers complete **Generic reproducible 5 (Design thinking assessment rubric)** for each student. Students compare the feedback they are given by the teacher with their self-assessment of how they used the design thinking process to solve problems **(Generic reproducible 3)**.

TUNE IN

STEM INVESTIGATIONS

Name: ....

Date: ....

Write the reasons why people thought the world was flat. For each reason, write next to it the proof that it is untrue.

Reasons people thought the world was flat	Proof that the world is not flat and is like a sphere

STEM Investigations, MP, ISBN 978 1 4202 4319 2

Name: ....

Date: ....

In this activity you will model the seasons of the Earth.

What you need

- Polystyrene foam ball
- Permanent marker
- Reading lamp or battery-powered lantern

What to do

1. As a class, draw a circle around the middle of the 'Earth' (foam ball) to show the equator. Draw large dots on the north pole and south pole.

2. Place the 'Sun' (lamp or lantern) in the centre of the room and switch it on. The teacher holds the Earth, standing a metre away from the Sun.

3. The teacher tilts the Earth a little bit, so that the top dot is pointing to the top of a wall, rather than straight up to the ceiling.

4. The Earth now moves slowly around the Sun, with the top dot always staying pointed to the top of the same wall.

5. Ask your teacher to stop moving when the Sun is shining straight at the middle of the northern hemisphere. What season is it in the northern hemisphere?

6. The Earth again orbits the Sun, keeping its tilt towards the same wall. Ask your teacher to stop when the Sun is shining straight at the middle of the southern hemisphere. What season is it in the southern hemisphere? What about the northern hemisphere?

EMPATHISE

STEM INVESTIGATIONS

Name: ....

Date: ....

Use this table to write the survey answers you receive. You can use the space at the bottom of the page for your own questions or comments.

Question	Answer
What is your favourite movie? Why do you like it?	
Do you like watching animated films or live-action films? Why?	
What movies have you watched that have taught you something?	
I'm going to make a short movie that teaches you about the shape of the Earth and how the seasons and day and night happen. What do you think will be important for me to include in the movie?	

STEM Investigations, MP, ISBN 978 1 4202 4319 2

HELP TOURISTS SLEEP IN THE 'MIDNIGHT SUN'

INTRODUCTION

Humans need to sleep to remain healthy, and most humans sleep when it is dark. However, daytime and night-time are not the same everywhere. Some parts of Antarctica have constant daylight during summer, and during winter the sun doesn't rise. Some scientists spend months there. During summer, tourists can visit this remote continent of extreme weather conditions.

The student challenge is to design a portable living pod that could be used by visitors to Antarctica. This pod's shape must withstand the extreme Antarctic winds. It must be made of materials that will keep out the cold, and include design elements that allow visitors to get some sleep during the continuous summer sunshine, and make the most of the sunlight during the 'day'. As part of this investigation, students will learn about the rotation of the Earth and how it causes night and day.

This STEM challenge could be extended by getting students to complete further prototypes, including a 'skin' for the living pod. Students could try different materials and use a thermometer to test the internal temperature when exposed to heat and cold. They could also measure the light within the structure.

THE CHALLENGE

Far south in Antarctica, in the area around the south pole, there is constant daylight for a few months in summer. This is called the midnight sun. For a few months during the Antarctic winter, the sun does not even rise!

Your challenge is to design a living pod for summer visitors to Antarctica. The pod must withstand extreme winds and cold. The design must include features that allow visitors to escape the sunlight to sleep and to make the most of the sunlight when they are awake. As part of this investigation, you will learn about the Earth's rotation and its orbit around the Sun.

KEY UNDERSTANDINGS

- The Earth rotates (spins) on a tilted axis, and it orbits the Sun.
- The Earth's spin causes day and night.
- Because of the Earth's spin, the Sun seems to move across the sky.
- In summer at the poles, the Sun does not set and in winter it does not rise.

KEY SKILLS

- Interpret and use scientific data – read bar and line graphs.
- Research using the internet – use links provided to access videos explaining the Earth's rotation and axis tilt.
- Make careful observations from multimedia resources.
- Design experiments to test your ideas.
- Build a three-dimensional model using knowledge of shapes and nets.

KEY VOCABULARY

axis – an imaginary line that something spins around, such as the line between the north pole and the south pole

orbit – move or revolve in a repeating pattern around another object in space

rotate – spin around a central point

KEY ACTIONS

- Create a model or diagram showing night and day.
- Explain the midnight sun in polar regions.
- Research weather conditions in Antarctica.
- Experiment with shapes and materials.
- Design a model for a living pod.

OVERVIEW OF STAGES

TUNE IN:

Students discuss reasons for day and night. They build scientific understandings of the Earth's rotation and orbit around the Sun, and meet the concept of a midnight sun. They brainstorm and discuss sleep disruptions, and life in Antarctica.

EMPATHISE

Students discuss personal preferences for the things that make living and sleeping areas comfortable. They discuss the living condition compromises that would be made by scientists in Antarctica.

DEFINE

Students link personal understandings of ideal living and sleeping conditions with life in Antarctica. They discuss the challenges including space, availability of furniture, climate, continual daylight, extreme winds and the noise associated with the climate.

IDEATE

Students design an accommodation pod that uses strong shapes and provides comfort. They look at shapes in nature and building designs for inspiration.

PROTOTYPE

Students create a 'skeleton' model of their designs. Students test the strength of their designs, exploring which shapes are more structurally sound. Students include design elements that eliminate the daylight when people are trying to sleep.

TEST

Using a strong fan at different speeds, students test their designs for strength against wind.

SHARE AND EVALUATE:

Student designs could be shared with scientists working in Antarctica or other experts, as well as the school community.

SUGGESTED SCHEDULE

LESSON	STAGE
1–4	**Tune in:** Learn about the Earth's rotation on its axis; explore how day and night occur; discuss different activities during day and night; focus on night and the perfect conditions for a good night's sleep
5–6	**Empathise:** Investigate life in Antarctica; identify the challenges; research data to understand the extreme nature of the environment; write in journal
7–8	**Define:** Identify the challenges observed and implied through accessing blogs written by people living in Antarctica; write in journal
9–10	**Ideate:** Design solutions to the accommodation problem for visitors to Antarctica; write in journal
11–15	**Prototype and Test:** Revisit design criteria; use digital tools to record testing process; identify concrete data that can be used to compare designs for strength; develop data recording processes; write in journal
16–17	**Share and evaluate:** Peer evaluate using design criteria; vote on success of each design to meet the brief; possibly submit design brief to online forum linked to life in Antarctica

CURRICULUM LINKS

SCIENCE

YEAR	STRAND	SUB-STRAND AND CONTENT
3	Science Understanding	Earth and space sciences: • Earth's rotation on its axis causes regular changes, including night and day
		Physical sciences: • Heat can be produced in many ways and can move from one object to another

TECHNOLOGIES

YEAR	STRAND	CONTENT
3 & 4	Design and Technologies Processes and Production Skills	• Critique needs or opportunities for designing and explore and test a variety of materials, components, tools and equipment and the techniques needed to produce designed solutions • Generate, develop, and communicate design ideas and decisions using appropriate technical terms and graphical representation techniques • Select and use materials, components, tools, equipment and techniques and use safe work practices to make designed solutions • Evaluate design ideas, processes and solutions based on criteria for success developed with guidance and including care for the environment • Plan a sequence of production steps when making designed solutions individually and collaboratively
	Design and Technologies Knowledge and Understanding	• Investigate how forces and the properties of materials affect the behaviour of a product or system • Investigate the suitability of materials, systems, components, tools and equipment for a range of purposes

MATHEMATICS

YEAR	STRAND	SUB-STRAND AND CONTENT
3	Statistics and Probability	Chance: • Conduct chance experiments, identify and describe possible outcomes and recognise variation Data representation and interpretation: • Identify questions or issues for categorical variables. Identify data sources and plan methods of data collection and recording in results • Collect data, organise into categories and create displays using lists, tables, picture graphs and simple column graphs, with and without the use of digital technologies • Interpret and compare data displays
	Measurement and Geometry	Shape: • Make models of three-dimensional objects and describe key features

This investigation also links to the General Capabilities:

- Literacy
- Information and Communication Technology (ICT) Capability
- Numeracy
- Critical and Creative Thinking.

This investigation also links to the Cross-Curriculum Priority of Sustainability.

ASSESSMENT

The following resources are provided for assessing students at different stages of the STEM investigations:

- Generic reproducible 1 (Key vocabulary table), for assessing understanding of vocabulary
- Generic reproducible 2 (Self-evaluation), for student self-evaluation of the learning process
- Generic reproducible 3 (Responding to the investigation)
- Generic reproducible 5 (Design thinking assessment rubric), for evaluating student engagement in the design thinking stages
- Learning journal templates 1, 2, 3 and 4, incorporating student reflection and evaluation.

→ GETTING READY FOR THE INVESTIGATION

You can prepare yourself and students for this STEM investigation in the following ways:

- Identify groups of students who will work well together.
- Review the **Key science knowledge** that supports this investigation, and look at the **Useful links**.
- Investigate the **Useful apps**.
- Gather materials for all activities and start collecting additional materials for prototyping (as shown on the **Materials needed** list).
- Use a globe to familiarise students with geographical features and location.
- Explore Google Earth to understand and engage interactively with day and night concepts as well as geographical and climate regions.
- View online video clips explaining the Earth's rotation.
- Investigate the **Useful links** and select video footage that will support students to understand other concepts being taught in this investigation.

USEFUL APPS

- App for a virtual globe, such as Google Earth
- App for designing three-dimensional models, such as SketchUp
- App for simulating wind resistance, such as at mea.digital/sm247
- App for generating brainstorms, group ideas such as Padlet or Popplet

USEFUL LINKS

- Video clip about the Earth's rotation and orbit, such as at mea.digital/sm183
- Explanation of continual daylight at the south pole, such as at mea.digital/sm184
- Climate data for teachers, such as at mea.digital/sm185
- Verifiable scientific facts about Antarctica, such as at mea.digital/sm186
- Tourist camping in Antarctica, such as at mea.digital/sm187
- Multimedia resource about Antarctica, such as at mea.digital/sm188
- The Australian Antarctic Division, such as at mea.digital/sm189
- The midnight sun, such as at mea.digital/sm190
- Polar seasons, such as at mea.digital/sm191
- Life in Antarctica, such as at mea.digital/sm192, mea.digital/sm193, mea.digital/sm194
- Article for teachers about design thinking with children, such as at mea.digital/sm195

RESOURCES PROVIDED

- Generic reproducibles 1, 2, 3, 4, 5, 7, 9
- Reproducibles 11.1, 11.2, 11.3
- Learning journal templates 1, 2, 3, 4

MATERIALS NEEDED

- Pipe-cleaners
- Matchsticks
- Putty
- Icypole sticks
- Drinking straws
- Variety of materials if covering the frame of the pod, such as flexible plastic, rubber offcuts, fabric, foil, cardboard
- Variety of fans, torches, thermometers, portable heaters (hairdryers)
- Tape
- Glue and hot glue guns

Hot glue guns can be dangerous. Make sure students are supervised at all times.

KEY SCIENCE KNOWLEDGE

This section provides an overview of the key science concepts and vocabulary needed for this unit.

THE EARTH'S ROTATION CAUSES DAY AND NIGHT

In most places on the Earth, the 24 hours of each day have two visually distinct periods: day and night. Daytime is identified by sunlight, whilst night-time occurs as the Sun sets below the horizon and darkness arrives.

Day and night are caused by the Earth **rotating** on its **axis**, the imaginary line that runs through the Earth's centre from the north pole to the south pole. One rotation takes 24 hours (a full day). The half of the Earth that is facing the Sun at any one time is experiencing daytime; the half of the Earth that is not facing the Sun is experiencing night-time. Viewed from the Earth, the Sun appears to move across our sky each day, rising in the east and setting in the west. It is the Earth that is moving, not the Sun.

THE EARTH'S TILT AND ORBIT CAUSE SEASONS

As well as spinning on its axis, the Earth **orbits** the Sun, completing one revolution in 365.25 days. Because the Earth is tilted on its axis, parts of the Earth receive different amounts of sunlight at different times of the year. This causes the seasons. For example, in January the southern hemisphere is tilted towards the Sun and experiences summer. Its daylight hours are longer and it is hotter, because the sunlight hits it directly. The opposite is true for the northern hemisphere at this time, and we call this winter.

At the equator, daylight hours do not change throughout the year and these places have two seasons (wet and dry). The north pole and the south pole always point in the same directions in space, so these places have a different experience of the seasons.

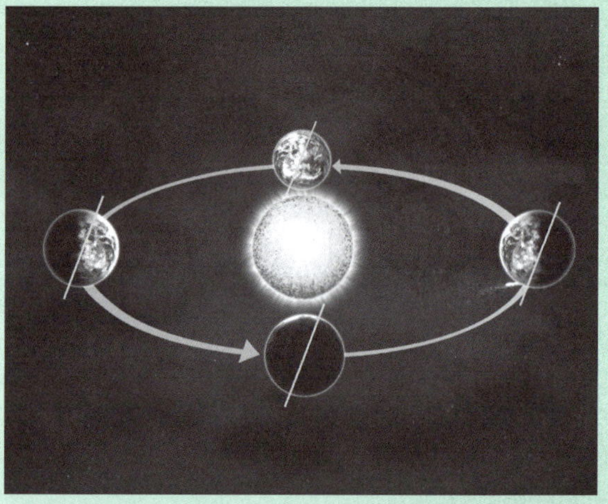

The Earth takes 365 days, 5 hours, 48 minutes and 46 seconds (one solar year) to make one revolution around the Sun.

THE MIDNIGHT SUN AND POLAR NIGHTS

Places near the poles experience continuous sunlight in certain months and no sunlight during others. Times of continuous sunlight are called the midnight sun, and times of constant night are called polar nights. This poses a challenge for humans, who are diurnal (they sleep during darkness and are awake during the day).

STRONG SHAPES

Different geometric shapes can be used to create outdoor structures. Structures need to be strong enough to withstand forces, for example, the roof of a building withstanding strong winds or earthquakes.

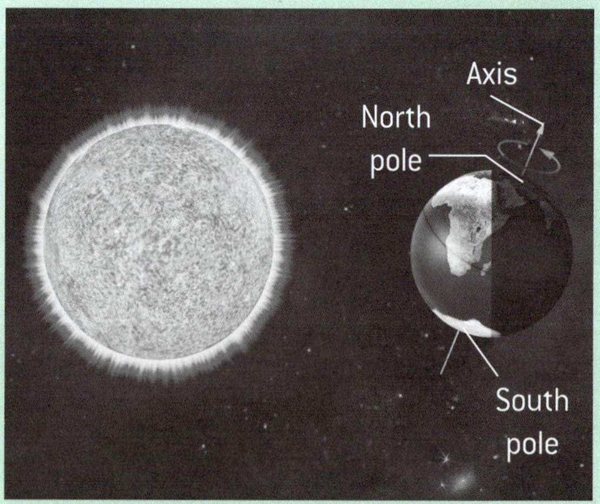

When a polar region is tilted towards the Sun, there is 24 hours of sunlight each day. At the same time, the other pole is experiencing 24 hours of darkness.

KEY VOCABULARY

axis – an imaginary line that something spins around
orbit – move or revolve in a repeating pattern around another object in space
rotate – spin around a central point

TUNE IN

1. Ask, 'What is the difference between day and night?' to develop key vocabulary and establish prior knowledge. Students could work in small groups to brainstorm on large paper their responses to this question.
2. Use **Generic reproducible 7 (Double bubble)** to categorise the responses, highlighting similarities and differences. Provide time to discuss, debate, clarify and reach consensus.
3. Ask students to complete **Generic reproducible 1 (Key vocabulary table)** using the key vocabulary for this unit. This reproducible will also be used at the end of the unit, to demonstrate changes in understanding.
4. Ask, 'How do night and day occur?' Students record their ideas individually in their learning journals, using both diagrams and words. If students are unsure, ask them to record questions they have about the transition from day to night. These questions can be displayed on a 'wonder wall', with sticky notes added as students develop understandings.
5. Ask students to share their ideas in small groups. Add any further questions to the wonder wall.

ACTIVITY 1: DAY AND NIGHT

1. Watch a video clip that demonstrates the Earth's rotation and orbit (see **Useful apps/links**).
2. Ask students to record at least one point, idea or fact in each column in **Generic reproducible 4 (Key question table)**. You may need to watch the video clip twice to allow students to complete this task.
3. Ask students to consider their new knowledge and how they would explain it. Propose the building of a simple model or use of digital tools. As a class, devise a list of essential elements for inclusion in this presentation.
4. Students can share their work with each other and peer review against the checklist developed.

ACTIVITY 2: A BAD NIGHT'S SLEEP

1. Ask students, 'What stops you from getting a good night's sleep?' Brainstorm responses as a class. Responses could be recorded as a bar graph, to establish the most annoying interferences.
2. Ask students to consider what it would be like to sleep if there was no night-time. What would be the disadvantages/advantages?
3. Watch a video clip about summer in Antarctica that highlights the continuous sunlight (see **Useful apps/links**).
4. Ask why the Sun might still be visible at midnight. Students generate hypotheses. Responses can be displayed or recorded in learning journals.

6. Introduce the STEM investigation and challenge to the students. Provide them with the student card and read the information together.
7. Introduce the design thinking process by reviewing the stages on the student card. Explain that students will keep a journal about their learning at the different stages of the design.

USEFUL APPS/LINKS

- Video clip about the Earth's rotation and orbit, such as at mea.digital/sm183
- Time-lapse video clip of 24 hours during the summer solstice in Antarctica, such as at mea.digital/sm196

→ EMPATHISE

During the Empathise stage of the design thinking process, students focus on finding out about different points of view. To empathise with others, they need to research some of the challenges associated with living in Antarctica during the summer months.

ACTIVITY 1: MY PERFECT BEDROOM

1. Refer to class discussion from the Tune-in stage, asking, 'What is the most annoying thing when you are trying to get to sleep?' Discuss personal preferences for comfortable living and sleeping areas. Students design or draw their perfect bedroom space, considering the elements required for a good night's sleep. This design phase could be completed in hard copy, or digital tools such as SketchUp could be introduced, with some discussion about two- and three-dimensional shapes/solids.
2. Compare bedroom designs and make a list of elements that are repeated frequently. This could be recorded as a tally and turned into a graph.

ACTIVITY 2: LIVING IN ANTARCTICA

1. Explore blogs or video clips that highlight the challenges of sustaining human life in polar regions (see **Useful apps/links**).
2. As students view the video clips or read the blogs they can use **Generic reproducible 9 (See, think, wonder)** to record their observations, questions and wonderings.
3. Discuss the living condition compromises that would be made by scientists in Antarctica. View images or video clips of staff quarters at the research stations (see **Useful apps/links**). Look at data identifying temperatures and wind strengths in different parts of the south pole (see **Useful apps/links**). Use **Reproducible 11.1 (Living in Antarctica)** to list the positives, negatives and related elements.

PROMPTS

- What effect might the Antarctic climate have on sleeping?
- How might wind impact life for humans in Antarctica?
- What are some things from home that people staying in Antarctica would have to do without?
- Looking at your bedroom design, what things would you miss if you had to relocate to Antarctica?

MORE VOCABULARY

- climate – weather patterns over a long period of time
- empathise – understand and consider another person or group's point of view
- point of view – an opinion, attitude or judgement considered in a particular way

JOURNAL TIP

Ask students to complete **Learning journal template 1 (Empathise page)** while they are doing the different tasks. Remind them to date their notes and include photos of relevant information or pictures.

ASSESSMENT

This stage of the design thinking process offers opportunities to observe students collecting information, developing questions, and recording their notes and thinking in their journal.

USEFUL APPS/LINKS

- App for designing three-dimensional models, such as SketchUp
- Challenges of living in polar regions, such as at mea.digital/sm197
- Images or a video clip of staff quarters at the research stations, such as at mea.digital/sm193
- Data identifying temperatures and wind strengths in different parts of the south pole, such as at mea.digital/sm199

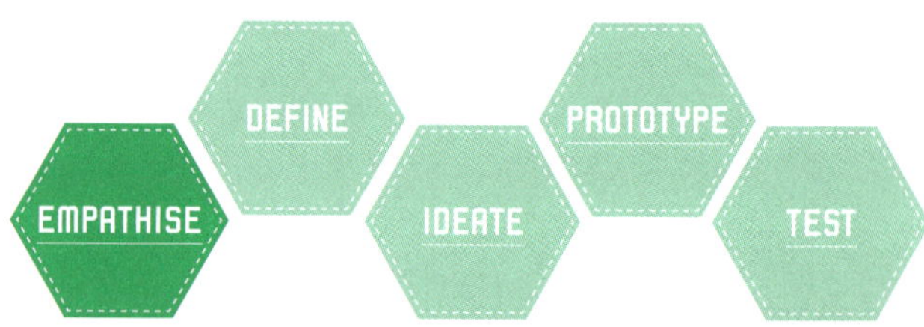

DEFINE

The main focus of this stage of the design thinking process is to reframe the challenge. The initial challenge is quite open, so at this stage students learn how to define what needs to be done. This includes noting insights that have been generated.

ACTIVITY 1: IDENTIFY WHAT TOURISTS WANT

1. Explore the tourism options available in Antarctica (see **Useful apps/links**). Draw attention to the fact that visitors to Antarctica have access only during the summer months, because Antarctica is ice-bound through winter. Reflect on the discussions about the summer solstice and extended periods of daylight, linking this with requirements for a good night's sleep.
2. Consider the accommodation expectations of tourists to Antarctica and view current available options (see **Useful apps/links**). Brainstorm the things tourists would expect when paying lots of money for the experience in Antarctica. Why would people choose Antarctica as a holiday destination?

ACTIVITY 2: DEFINE THE CHALLENGE

1. Set up class expectations of how the challenge will be undertaken. Explain to students time allocation, resource distribution, design thinking processes and associated language such as ideation, prototyping and testing. Establish expectations for recording processes, which could include digital record keeping through time-lapse, photos and video, a digital diary or a class blog.
2. Establish success criteria for this challenge. What are the expected outcomes? How can students extend themselves? Refer to **Generic reproducible 5 (Design thinking assessment rubric)**.

Students can update **Learning journal template 2 (Define page)** to record initial ideas about the challenge. Encourage students to reflect back to their ideas about an ideal bedroom as well as refer to the insights gained through learning about life in Antarctica.

PROMPTS

- What are the challenges when designing accommodation in Antarctica? (Discuss concepts such as space, availability of furniture, climate, continual daylight, extreme winds and noise, and transport of building materials.)
- Where in nature do we see strong structures? Could we use design ideas from nature?

MORE VOCABULARY

- define – state the meaning of something
- insight – an accurate understanding of someone or something
- point of view – an opinion, attitude or judgement considered in a particular way

JOURNAL TIP

An alternative to the learning journal could be a class blog. Students could follow the model of the blogs written by scientists in Antarctica. Through this blog you could provide prompts similar to those on the learning journal templates.

USEFUL APPS/LINKS

- Information on tourism in Antarctica, such as at mea.digital/sm200, mea.digital/sm201
- A class blog, such as at mea.digital/sm202
- How to use blogs in the classroom, such as at mea.digital/sm203

EMPATHISE DEFINE IDEATE PROTOTYPE TEST

→ IDEATE

The Ideate stage of the design thinking process is all about generating lots of ideas. Students need to be flexible in their thinking and be able to move beyond obvious ideas. At this stage, ideas are not judged, just generated and gathered.

ACTIVITY 1: GENERATE IDEAS

1. Ask students to design solutions to the accommodation problem for visitors to Antarctica. Record ideas on sticky notes (this limits the ideation detail and encourages small, quick sketches). The challenge is to generate as many unusual ideas as possible in a 'five-minute frenzy'.
2. Students generate a basic outline sketch of an accommodation pod.
3. After five minutes, provide students with another five minutes to consider the designs generated, and expand or re-invent.
4. Students choose three designs to explore further. Use **Learning journal template 3 (Ideate page)** to record these initial ideas.

ACTIVITY 2: THINK ABOUT SHAPES

1. In small groups, students share their three design ideas.
2. In these groups, students record the shapes used in the designs to determine the most popular shapes for building.
3. Consider the shapes of structures in nature. For example, a beehive uses hexagons and this produces an extremely strong structure. Ask, 'Where else do we see shapes used for building?' Explore shapes in nature as well as in the 'built world' through a walk around the school grounds or an online image search.
4. Identify shapes used in building that may not have been considered in the original ideation (see **Useful apps/links**). Identify shapes that are easily tessellated (repeated in a pattern), such as tiles.
5. Ask students to revisit their designs and consider the strength of the shapes chosen. Remind students of the importance of the accommodation being able to withstand extreme wind.

ACTIVITY 3: REMEMBER *THE THREE LITTLE PIGS*

1. In *The Three Little Pigs*, three houses were built, using different materials. Ask, 'What materials did the pigs use for the "skin" of their homes?' Discuss the advantages and disadvantages of these choices. Add thoughts to the first table on **Reproducible 11.2 (Materials for Antarctic living)**.
2. Consider the building materials that would suit the Antarctic environment and your design ideas. Brainstorm and complete the second table on **Reproducible 11.2**.

PROMPTS

- What things need to be considered when thinking about building in Antarctica?
- How could we learn more about the types of building materials that can withstand extreme weather conditions?
- What shapes are strong and tessellate well?
- What are our limitations when testing materials?

MORE VOCABULARY

- feedback – information about, for example, a person's performance or the design of a product, which can be used to make improvements
- ideate – generate many ideas without making judgements about the ideas

USEFUL APPS/LINKS

- Apps that support brainstorming/ideation, such as at mea.digital/sm204
- Information on strong shapes in structures, such as at mea.digital/sm205, mea.digital/sm206

ASSESSMENT

At the Ideate stage, assessment could include observations about the number and diversity of student ideas, and their ability to critically appraise and create additional ideas. Reflection in the journal should provide an insight into some of the reasoning behind student choices.

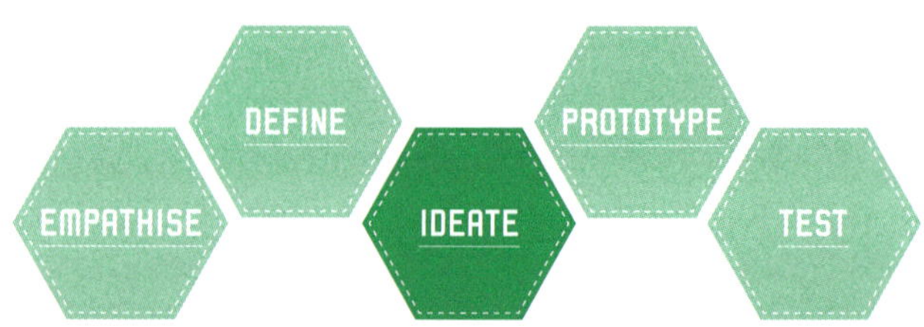

→ PROTOTYPE

At this stage of the design thinking process, students are asked to create a physical prototype of the skeleton of the accommodation pod, plus detailed sketches of the external and internal design.

Encourage students to photograph or film during the Prototype and Test stages. This information can be used to show the learning behind the design thinking process in action.

ACTIVITY: TRANSFORM IDEAS INTO PROTOTYPES

1. Refer students to their Ideate designs and discuss how these could be constructed in three dimensions to test the strength of the internal structure ('skeleton').
2. Provide students with construction materials that will allow them to build the 'skeleton'. Some students may prefer to use digital tools such as SketchUp.
3. Get students to build three different skeletons, and draw detailed sketches or digital diagrams of the anticipated external and internal designs on three copies of **Learning journal template 4 (Prototype and test page)**. These designs should be annotated to show the different features.

PROMPTS

- What do we know about tessellations? How could this knowledge help when prototyping?
- What is the priority when prototyping?
- What are we trying to construct during this phase?

TOP TIP!

Remind students that the fun part of prototyping is the 'fail quickly' aspect. Find out sooner rather than later if the idea will work. They should focus on the element of 'constructing and modifying' rather than making it look 'pretty'.

MORE VOCABULARY

- feedback – information about, for example, a person's performance or the design of a product, which can be used to make improvements
- prototype – an initial version of a model of a product or process that is used to develop a final model

JOURNAL TIP

Remind students to highlight the main features of their prototype. If students are creating an electronic journal, they can insert a photo of their prototype and annotate it.

USEFUL APPS/LINKS

- App for digital journalling, such as Keynote, PowerPoint or Explain Everything
- Article about design thinking processes, such as at mea.digital/sm208
- Introduction to structural engineering through shapes, such as at mea.digital/sm209
- Construction for kids, such as at mea.digital/sm210

ASSESSMENT

Observe students as they make changes to their designs. Are they able to consider feedback, make modifications and move rapidly through this process, or do they have difficulties with holding on to an idea and accepting feedback? Refer to students' annotated notes to support assessment. Consider video-recording the process so you can observe all students.

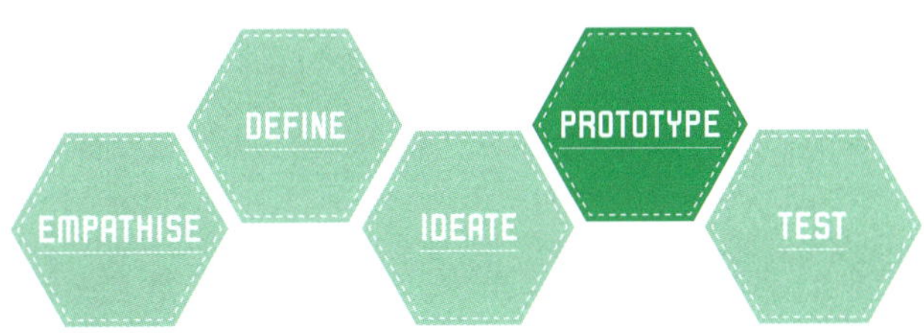

→ TEST

Students test their prototype to see how it meets the criteria in the challenge.

ACTIVITY 1: TEST THE 'SKELETON'

1. Use the fan to test each prototype at three different fan speeds. Students use **Reproducible 11.3 (Testing the 'skeleton')** to record results. Testing digital designs could use apps that simulate wind resistance (see **Useful apps/links**).
2. Have students draw a bar chart of their results and present it to the class. They select one design and justify the selection.

ACTIVITY 2: GET DESIGN FEEDBACK

1. Have students display sketches/diagrams of the external and internal designs.
2. Students discuss which designs and materials would attract most tourists.

Ask students to fill in **Learning journal template 4 (Prototype and test page)**. See the **Journal tip** for further student guidance.

PROMPTS

- What surprised you about your design?
- What are the most attractive or exciting parts?

MORE VOCABULARY

- feedback – information about, for example, a person's performance or the design of a product, which can be used to make improvements
- prototype – an initial version of a model of a product or process that is used to develop a final model

JOURNAL TIP

Ask students to think about why it is important to test their ideas before they build their final design.

USEFUL APPS/LINKS

App for simulating wind resistance, such as at mea.digital/sm211

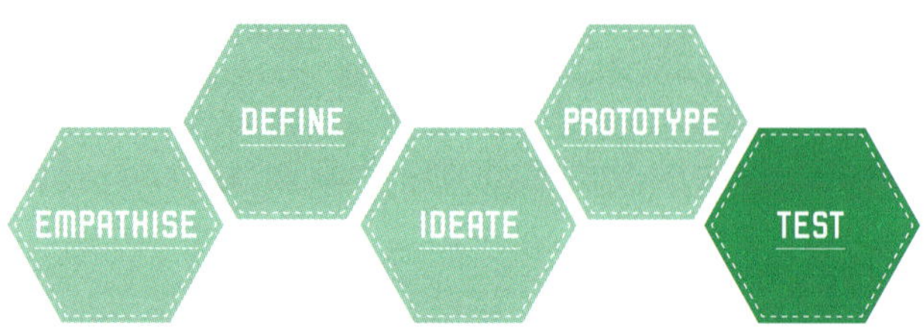

→ SHARE AND EVALUATE

Students are provided with an opportunity to share their final design, as well as the processes involved in the investigation. They evaluate their learning journals as well as their solutions.

ACTIVITY 1: 'SELL' IDEAS

1. Revisit the original challenge. Reflect on the design criteria and ask students to evaluate their success using their learning journals.
2. Ask students to consider how they will convince their classmates that their design is the best option. Students develop an advertising campaign to 'sell' their idea. Students can use digital tools, create a role-play, design a poster or other form of communication that highlights the elements of their new design.
3. Students provide feedback or vote, using success criteria as agreed upon as a class. Designs could be shared with scientists through the web feedback page of an Antarctic blog/forum or on your class blog, at an assembly or in a school newsletter.

ACTIVITY 2: REVIEW THINKING

1. Students complete a review of their personal learning throughout the investigation by completing **Generic reproducible 2 (Self-evaluation)**.
2. Ask students, 'If you were to undertake another investigation like this, what would you do differently? Why?'

ASSESSMENT

Ask students to again complete **Generic reproducible 1 (Key vocabulary table)** using the key vocabulary for this unit. Compare their table with the one they completed at the Tune-in stage, to demonstrate changes in understanding.

Students complete **Generic reproducible 3 (Responding to the investigation)**. Compare their responses to their responses to **Generic reproducible 2**.

Teachers complete **Generic reproducible 5 (Design thinking assessment rubric)** for each student. Students compare the feedback they are given by the teacher with their self-assessment of how they used the design thinking process to solve problems **(Generic reproducible 3)**.

EMPATHISE

STEM INVESTIGATIONS

Name: ....

Date: ....

What would it be like to live in Antarctica? Brainstorm this as a class and make notes about positive things, negative things and interesting things.

Positives of living in Antarctica	Negatives of living in Antarctica	Interesting things about living in Antarctica

IDEATE

STEM INVESTIGATIONS

Name: ....

Date: ....

Fill in the table with information from the story *The Three Little Pigs*.

Pig	House material	Advantages	Disadvantages
1			
2			
3			

What materials could you use in your design that would suit Antarctica? Write three materials, and list any advantages and disadvantages of each material.

Design idea	Living pod material	Advantages	Disadvantages
1			
2			
3			

STEM Investigations, MP, ISBN 978 1 4202 4319 2 © Macmillan Science and Education Australia 2018

TEST

STEM INVESTIGATIONS

Name: ....

Date: ....

Draw or add a photograph of each prototype in the first column.

Use the fan to test each prototype. Write what happens at each speed.

Picture of prototype	Results		
	Low fan	Medium fan	High fan

STEM Investigations, MP, ISBN 978 1 4202 4319 2 © Macmillan Science and Education Australia 2018

BRING BEES BACK TO THE CITY

NATURAL WORLD 12

INTRODUCTION

Bees play a role in pollinating the plants that produce the many vegetables and fruits we eat, and the animals we eat that are then eaten by us. Bee numbers are declining due to pesticides, parasites, disease and habitat loss. What would we do if these insects, which help produce so much of our food, vanish?

In this STEM investigation, students are asked to show how cities could be transformed to attract bees and to create a paper or digital brochure showing people how they could 'bring back the bees'. They need to demonstrate their understanding of the relationship between bees and flowering plants and how living things depend on each other.

This STEM challenge is easily differentiated for students by encouraging different groups to use different degrees of complexity when creating their city transformations. Students could test their designs or processes.

THE CHALLENGE

Bees have disappeared from some parts of your city. This is bad news because bees play an important role in the environment, including in growing food. Your city council wants people to think about bees and how to get them to return.

Your challenge is to show how your city could welcome bees. Find out why bees are important and why bee numbers might be low. Map part of your city, showing your changes. Design a brochure about 'bringing back the bees'. As part of your investigation, you will learn about bees and flowering plants, life cycles and how living things depend on each other.

KEY UNDERSTANDINGS

- Living things have life cycles.
- Living things depend on each other and their environment to survive.
- Bees pollinate plants, which allows the plants to make fruits or seeds.
- Bees are important to human food production.
- Human actions affect bee numbers.

KEY SKILLS

- Develop research skills by identifying key words and formulating questions.
- Improve your communication skills, through interviewing people and designing a convincing brochure.
- Use creative thinking to design solutions and present information.
- Develop evaluative skills, such as reflecting on the process and making suggestions for improvement.

KEY VOCABULARY

colony – a group of living things of the same species living closely together

life cycle – different stages of life that living things pass through

pollination – transfer of pollen to the female part of a flower

population – a group of animals of the same species that live in the same place

KEY ACTIONS

- Explore the role of bees in plant life cycles.
- Find out about beehives and threats to bees.
- Research city beekeeping.
- Find out ways to attract bees to cities.
- Design a brochure to show people how to 'bring back the bees'.

OVERVIEW OF STAGES

TUNE IN:

Students explore the life cycle of bees and how living things depend on each other. They share introductory information and watch a video clip about bees and their importance, as well as threats they are facing. They explore the needs of bees, and urban beekeeping.

EMPATHISE

Students find out about threats to bee populations and consider the impact on all living things. They explore what action some people are taking to address declining bee populations and why action is needed.

DEFINE

Students consider the main issues with transforming sections of cities to encourage bees back to the city. They consider the key components of the design challenge, including materials available and how to viably test prototypes.

IDEATE

Students generate creative ideas for transforming sections of the city to encourage bees and for making brochures to show people how to bring back the bees.

PROTOTYPE

Students transform some of their ideas into physical representations. These are created rapidly, using simple materials. Students can make storyboards, sketches, simple models or use sticky notes.

TEST

Students share their prototypes and provide feedback to each other about their ideas and also check the relevance and usability of their designs. They are given the opportunity to cycle through the Prototype and Test stages again.

SHARE AND EVALUATE:

Final prototypes are shared and evaluated, with opportunities for feedback from local beekeepers or local council members.

SUGGESTED SCHEDULE

LESSON	STAGE
1–4	**Tune in:** Find out about the life cycle of bees and how living things depend on bees and how bees depend on living things
5–7	**Empathise:** Explore threats to bee populations and urban beekeeping; write in journal
8–9	**Define:** Consider observations and insights; define main issues; write in journal
10–11	**Ideate:** Develop ideas; write in journal
11–14	**Prototype** and **Test:** Conduct prototyping and testing cycles; write in journal
15–16	**Share and evaluate:** Share and evaluate designs and prototypes

CURRICULUM LINKS

SCIENCE

YEAR	STRAND	SUB-STRAND AND CONTENT
4	Science Understanding	Biological sciences: • Living things have life cycles • Living things depend on each other and the environment to survive
	Science as a Human Endeavour	Use and influence of science: • Science knowledge helps people to understand the effect of their actions

TECHNOLOGIES

YEAR	STRAND	CONTENT
3 & 4	Design and Technologies Processes and Production Skills	• Critique needs or opportunities for designing, and explore and test a variety of materials, components, tools and equipment and the techniques needed to produce designed solutions • Generate, develop and communicate design ideas and decisions for audiences using appropriate technical terms and graphical representation techniques • Evaluate design ideas, processes and solutions based on criteria for success developed with guidance and including care for the environment • Plan a sequence of production steps when making designed solutions individually and collaboratively

MATHEMATICS

YEAR	STRAND	SUB-STRAND AND CONTENT
3	Measurement and Geometry	Location and transformation: • Create and interpret simple grid maps to show position and pathways
4	Measurement and Geometry	Location and transformation: • Use simple scales, legends and directions to interpret information contained in basic maps

This investigation also links to the General Capabilities:

- Literacy
- Numeracy
- Information and Communication Technology (ICT) Capability
- Critical and Creative Thinking.

This investigation also links to the Cross-Curriculum Priority of Sustainability.

ASSESSMENT

The following resources are provided for assessing students at different stages of the STEM investigations:

- Generic reproducible 1 (Key vocabulary table), for assessing understanding of vocabulary
- Generic reproducible 2 (Self-evaluation), for student self-evaluation of the learning process
- Generic reproducible 3 (Responding to the investigation)
- Generic reproducible 5 (Design thinking assessment rubric), for evaluating student engagement in the design thinking stages
- Learning journal templates 1, 2, 3 and 4, incorporating student reflection and evaluation.

GETTING READY FOR THE INVESTIGATION

You can prepare yourself and students for this STEM investigation in the following ways:

- Identify groups of students who will work well together.
- Review the **Key science knowledge** that supports this investigation, and look at the **Useful apps** and **Useful links**.
- Start collecting useful information for making paper or digital brochures, including images and maps.
- Gather materials for Activity 2 of the Prototype session (see **Materials needed** list).
- Determine where prototypes will be kept between lessons.
- Create a vocabulary wall.
- Create a wall space where students can share their ideas during the Ideate stage.
- Organise the class into pairs or small groups.
- Start thinking about:
  - » how the paper or digital brochures will be evaluated
  - » who will view the designs and brochures
  - » if there are local beekeepers, local council members or other experts who can give feedback about the designs, and whether feedback will be provided in person or digital form.

USEFUL APPS

- App for creating and organising ideas, such as Popplet, Inspiration, Padlet or Ideament
- App for sharing ideas, such as Air Sketch
- App for locating places and mapping, such as Google Earth or MapTrace
- App exploring locations, such as ArcGIS
- App for drawing maps, such as Drawing Maps

USEFUL LINKS

- Article about bees and their importance, such as at mea.digital/sm243
- Video clip about the importance of bees and children wanting to protect bees, such as at mea.digital/sm213
- Video clip about threats to bees, such as at mea.digital/sm214
- Video clip about bees in cities, such as at mea.digital/sm215
- Information about urban beehives, such as at mea.digital/sm216
- Information about backyard beekeeping, such as at mea.digital/sm217
- Information about urban beekeeping, such as at mea.digital/sm218

RESOURCES PROVIDED

- Generic reproducibles 1, 2, 3, 4, 5, 6, 11
- Reproducibles 12.1, 12.2, 12.3
- Learning journal templates 1, 2, 3, 4

MATERIALS NEEDED

- Sticky notes
- Paper
- Cardboard
- Sticky tape
- Other building materials, such as recyclable packaging, boxes, tubes, plastic bottles
- Rubber bands
- Scissors
- Glue
- Paint
- Large sheets of paper
- Fake grass and other plant-like materials that could be used for models of city transformations
- Matchboxes or other small boxes
- Large boxes
- Coloured paper
- Cellophane

KEY SCIENCE KNOWLEDGE

This section provides an overview of the key science concepts and vocabulary needed for this unit.

BEES, POLLINATION AND FOOD SUPPLY

Bees are a type of flying insect. The most common bee is the honey bee. For around 4000 years, honey bees have been kept for their honey and beeswax, a substance used to make candles, ointments and other products. But the most important thing that bees do is pollinate.

Pollination is an essential part of a flowering plant's **life cycle**. When a bee collects nectar and pollen from the flower of a plant, some pollen from the stamens – the male reproductive organ of the flower – sticks to the hairs of her body. When she visits the next flower, some of the pollen is rubbed off onto the stigma, or tip of the pistil – the female reproductive organ of the flower.

When pollination happens, fertilisation is possible, and seeds can develop.

Without pollination by bees and other insects, seed plants cannot produce these seeds and therefore reproduce. These plants produce the many vegetables and fruits we eat, and they are food for the animals that we consume.

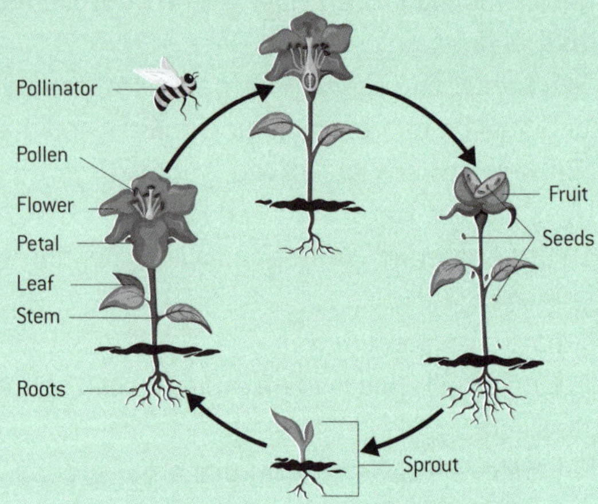

A pollinator such as a bee is an essential part of a flowering plant's life cycle.

HONEY BEEHIVES

Honey bees live in hives and have complex societies. Individual honey bees in a **colony** have different roles:

- The queen is a female that produces eggs.
- Workers are females that don't produce eggs. They have jobs such as cleaning and looking for food.
- Drones are males who mate with the queen.

In just one hive, there may be 50 000 workers and 300 drones, and there is just one queen.

The queen bee (left), worker bee (middle) and drone (right) all have different roles in a hive.

THREATS TO BEE POPULATIONS

Human actions affect honey bee numbers. The greatest threat to honey bee **populations** is habitat loss, such as when cities are built and green spaces are lost.

Colony collapse disorder is a syndrome that began to strike honey bee colonies this century. It is characterised by a sudden colony death, with a lack of adult bees, or bodies of dead bees inside the hive. Colony collapse disorder appears to affect the ability of bees to navigate. They leave the hive to find pollen and never return.

The cause of colony collapse disorder is not known but researchers suspect that a number of factors could be responsible, including pesticides, parasites and environmental stress.

KEY VOCABULARY

colony – a group of living things of the same species living closely together
life cycle – different stages of life that living things pass through
pollination – transfer of pollen to the female part of the flower
population – a group of animals of the same species that live in the same place

→ TUNE IN

1. Ask students to complete **Generic reproducible 1 (Key vocabulary table)** using the key vocabulary for this unit. This reproducible will also be used at the end of the unit to demonstrate changes in understanding.
2. Provide students with information about honey bees (not bumble bees), such as an introductory video clip (see **Useful apps/links**). Discuss the life cycle of honey bees, their role within a hive, how they depend on living things and how living things depend on them.
3. Discuss new learning. Provide space for students to record and display key information.

ACTIVITY 1: THE IMPORTANCE OF BEES

1. Provide students with links to information about the importance of bees (see **Useful apps/links**).
2. Ask students to create infographics that show an understanding of bees, their role and their importance to all living things. They could draw their diagrams and add information or use an app such as ThingLink to annotate images found online, then add information.
3. Have pairs of students share the information they gather.

ACTIVITY 2: THE PROCESS OF POLLINATION

1. Have students share what they already know or believe about the process of pollination. Explain that it is part of the life cycle of most flowering plants.
2. Provide students with links to information about pollination and the role of bees (see **Useful apps/links**).
3. Students create a visual display to show their understanding of how bees pollinate.

TOP TIP!

During the Tune-in sessions, conduct vocabulary activities to highlight and develop key vocabulary knowledge. Activities could include drawing semantic webs, creating a word wall or paired discussions. Check **Key vocabulary** definitions or read the **Key science knowledge** for a refresher on the key terms and concepts.

ACTIVITY 3: DECLINING BEE POPULATIONS

1. Provide students with **Reproducible 12.1 (Ideas about declining bee populations)**. Record prior knowledge or thinking about declining bee populations. Watch a video clip or read an article together about threats to bees (see **Useful apps/links**).
2. Students record threats to bees that are mentioned (such as pesticides, habitat loss, diseases, climate change, varroa parasite). Make sure they include individual threats, not just colony collapse disorder.
3. Organise students into small groups and have them find out more about each of the threats to bees. Fill in the first part of **Reproducible 12.1**.
4. Students use information gathered from activities 1, 2 and 3 to formulate hypotheses about why bee populations in cities are declining. They write their hypotheses on **Reproducible 12.1**.
5. Research declining bee populations in cities.
6. Invite each group to share information about the threats to bees and their hypotheses about population decline in cities.

4. Introduce the STEM investigation and challenge to the students. Provide them with the student card and read the information together.
5. Introduce the design thinking process by reviewing the stages on the student card. Explain that students will keep a journal about their learning at the different stages of the design.

USEFUL APPS/LINKS

- Introduction to bees for children, such as at mea.digital/sm219
- Information about the role of bees, such as at mea.digital/sm220
- Information about bees and their hives, such as at mea.digital/sm221
- Video clip about declining bee populations or information about threats to bees, such as at mea.digital/sm214, mea.digital/sm222
- App for mind mapping, such as iThoughts
- App to gather information when making observations, such as Popplet or ThingLink

EMPATHISE

During the Empathise stage of the design thinking process, students focus on finding out about different points of view. To empathise with others, they need to research some of the challenges associated with beekeeping. This includes finding out about how human activity affects bees and the success of beekeeping in cities. Students will take notes, ask questions, draw diagrams and take photos where relevant.

ACTIVITY 1: WHAT DO BEES NEED?

1. Organise students into pairs and provide them with **Reproducible 12.2 (Bees and their needs)**.
2. Students note information they already know or have learned in the Tune-in stage about the basic needs of bees. They might need to research further (see **Useful apps/links**).
3. Have students discuss the information collected. Can a city provide these needs?
4. Look at a map of a section of your city or a local city and consider what it has that could support bee populations and what may need to be changed. Discuss.
5. Fill in the rest of the table in **Reproducible 12.2**.
6. Record any questions students have about bees and their needs.

ACTIVITY 2: BEES IN THE CITY

1. Organise a visit to or from an urban beekeeper, or visit a website that encourages urban beekeeping (see **Useful apps/links**). Have students ask any questions from Activity 1 and record answers, or research further. Encourage students to take this opportunity to ask all they can about keeping bees in urban areas.
2. Watch a video clip about backyard beekeeping (see **Useful apps/links**).
3. Record all student findings on **Reproducible 12.3 (Beekeeping in cities)**.

ACTIVITY 3: ATTITUDES TOWARDS BEES

1. Find out about city people's attitudes towards bees in the city and the suggestion to 'bring bees back to the city'. Use **Generic reproducible 11 (Student interview)** to come up with questions.
2. Discuss findings as a class.

PROMPTS

- What human activities cause the biggest problems for bees?
- What are some difficulties of city beekeeping?
- Do cities need to change to accommodate bees?
- What is being done about declining bee numbers?

MORE VOCABULARY

- empathise – understand and consider another person or group's point of view
- point of view – an opinion, attitude or judgement considered in a particular way

JOURNAL TIP

Ask students to complete **Learning journal template 1 (Empathise page)** while they are doing the different tasks. Remind them to date their notes and include photos of relevant information or pictures.

USEFUL APPS/LINKS

- App for locating places and mapping, such as Google Earth, MapTrace or Drawing Maps
- App for exploring locations, such as ArcGIS
- Article about things bees need, such as at mea.digital/sm223
- Beekeeping supplies, such as at mea.digital/sm224
- Video clip about backyard beekeeping, such as at mea.digital/sm215
- Information about urban beekeeping, such as at mea.digital/sm218

ASSESSMENT

This stage of the design thinking process offers opportunities to observe students collecting information, developing questions, and recording their notes and thinking in their journal.

EMPATHISE | DEFINE | IDEATE | PROTOTYPE | TEST

DEFINE

The main focus of this stage of the design thinking process is to reframe the challenge. The initial challenge is quite open, so at this stage students learn how to define what needs to be done. This includes noting insights that have been generated.

ACTIVITY 1: CONSIDER OBSERVATIONS

1. Students consider the information gathered in the Tune-in and Empathise stages. They may work in pairs or small groups. Provide them with a whiteboard, large sheet of paper and/or sticky notes to collate some of their key information. They should refer to **Reproducible 12.2 (Bees and their needs)**, **Reproducible 12.3 (Beekeeping in cities)** and their filled-in **Generic reproducible 11 (Student interview)**. Students should transfer their main findings to **Learning journal template 2 (Define page)**.
2. Students should discuss one section of **Learning journal template 2** at a time, write their responses and then continue discussing their ideas for the next section, until the task is complete. This provides students with opportunities to hear others' responses and it provides the teacher with input points.
3. Provide students with the opportunity to research further. Ask them to write other information they would like to know, and their findings and sources, on **Generic reproducible 4 (Key question table)**.

ACTIVITY 2: CONSIDER INSIGHTS

1. Students should think of at least one insight they have gained from the process; for example, we depend on bees for much of the food we eat. Students should add this insight to **Learning journal template 2**. They should then explain how this will inform their transformation suggestions and the creation of a paper or digital brochure.
2. When considering insights, students could think about the following:
   - What was something unexpected that you observed or found out? How was it unexpected?
   - How will you decide on the most important aspects?
   - Is there any other information you need or would like to know? How will you find out?

ACTIVITY 3: CONSIDER CONSTRAINTS

At this stage, let students know the constraints of the challenge by describing the types of technology/materials that will be available to prototype the city transformations and create the paper or digital brochures. Also advise how students will evaluate their work.

Students can update **Learning journal template 2**.

PROMPTS

- What did you discover?
- What were the most important pieces of information that you gathered?
- What was something new that you learned?
- What other information do you need?

MORE VOCABULARY

- define – state the meaning of something
- insight – an accurate understanding of someone or something

JOURNAL TIP

At this stage, students should define the area of the city that they will be transforming. They could print satellite maps of the area or draw their own map and include this with **Learning journal template 2**.

USEFUL APPS/LINKS

- App for creating and organising ideas, such as Popplet, Inspiration, Padlet or Ideament
- App for sharing ideas, such as Air Sketch

EMPATHISE DEFINE IDEATE PROTOTYPE TEST

→ IDEATE

The Ideate stage of the design thinking process is all about generating lots of ideas. Students need to be flexible in their thinking and be able to move beyond obvious ideas. At this stage, ideas are not judged, just generated and gathered.

ACTIVITY: GENERATE IDEAS

1. Ask groups of students to draw or write ideas for their transformation of a section of the city to encourage bees. They should also note ideas that they could use for their brochure.
2. Each new idea should be drawn or written on a separate piece of paper or sticky note.
3. Ask students to group ideas on a wall or board.
4. Ask students to look at the different ideas and provide feedback to each other. It is important that students don't defend their ideas at this stage. They should just be listening to the feedback.
5. After the initial feedback, ask students to come up with more ideas. Encourage them to be creative and even radical.
6. Ask students to choose three of their ideas. Students use **Learning journal template 3 (Ideate page)** to do this.

PROMPTS

- How do your chosen ideas relate to the needs of bees and encouraging bees to live in urban areas?
- How might you evaluate your design?
- How can you make your paper or digital brochure more convincing?
- What if you had other digital tools available?

MORE VOCABULARY

- feedback – information about, for example, a person's performance or the design of a product, which can be used to make improvements
- ideate – generate many ideas without making judgements about the ideas

JOURNAL TIP

When choosing three ideas to include in the journal, try to choose three ideas that aren't related.

USEFUL APPS/LINKS

- Tools for creating ideas, such as at mea.digital/sm225
- Tips for creativity and innovation, such as at mea.digital/sm226

ASSESSMENT

At the Ideate stage, assessment could include observations about the number and diversity of student ideas, and their ability to provide feedback and create additional ideas. Reflection in the journal should provide an insight into some of the reasoning behind student choices.

TOP TIP!

At this stage, students may have produced a series of annotated drawings. They may have a collection of sticky notes, which they can organise into related ideas.

Encourage students to view and read others' ideas before giving feedback. Feedback could be within small groups or between partners. Considering others' ideas is an important part of this process, so students can build on their own ideas as they continue to ideate.

At each stage of this activity, ask students to discuss their thoughts before writing their responses. This will help them think through their ideas and select their final ideas to develop.

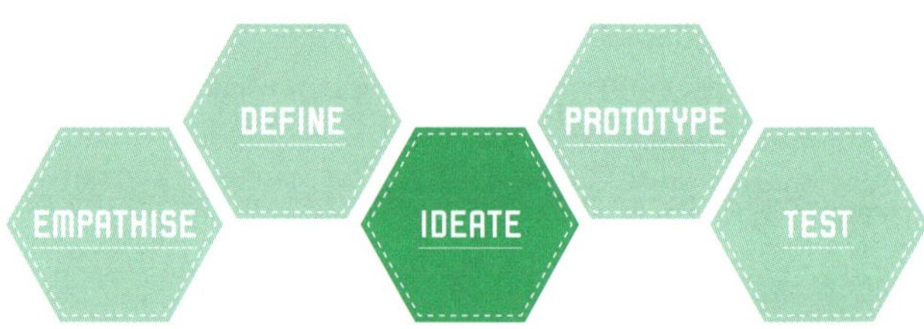

→ PROTOTYPE

At this stage of the design thinking process, students are asked to create a physical prototype. It is the stage where students need to get their ideas out of their heads and presented in a way that engages other students and helps them to understand the concept.

ACTIVITY 1: MAP THE CITY AREA

1. Students create a simple grid map of the section of the city they want to transform. They could hand-draw the map or use an app for drawing maps. The map should include a north arrow, grid lines with numbers and/or letters, and a simple scale. All buildings and roads should be marked.
2. Students should identify areas that could be transformed. They should make a list of the grid references for these areas.

ACTIVITY 2: TRANSFORM IDEAS INTO PROTOTYPES

1. Students review the ideas generated at the Ideate stage. Provide them with an A3 copy of **Generic reproducible 6 (In the frame)** so they can organise their ideas into two sections: least relevant and most relevant. Provide students with some question prompts to help support discussion of the ideas; for example:
   » Why do you think this idea could be used?
   » Where do you think this idea could be used? (Give a grid reference for your map.)
   » What aspects of this idea could be improved?
   » What would need to be changed for this idea to be used?
   » Why do you think this idea is not so relevant to the challenge?
2. Provide students with a range of materials to use to create a prototype. This prototype could include one or two aspects of their city transformation or one or two blocks. Remind students that a prototype should be created rapidly and is not meant to look 'nice'. Students could photograph their prototype to include in their brochure.

Ask students to fill in the Prototype part of **Learning journal template 4 (Prototype and test page)**. See the **Journal tip** for further student guidance.

PROMPTS

- What other suggestions do you have?
- What is the main feature of your prototype?
- How does it work?
- Which parts work best? What will you keep?
- Which parts need changing? How might you do this?
- What other materials might you need?

TOP TIP! Students may add labels to prototypes to explain some of the main features. Photographing and annotating pictures of prototypes can be useful.

MORE VOCABULARY

- feedback – information about, for example, a person's performance or the design of a product, which can be used to make improvements
- prototype – an initial version of a model of a product or process that is used to develop a final model

JOURNAL TIP

Remind students to highlight the main features of their prototype. If students are creating an electronic journal, they can insert a photo of their prototype and annotate it.

ASSESSMENT

Observe students as they make changes to their designs. Are they able to consider feedback, make modifications and move rapidly through this process, or do they have difficulties with holding on to an idea and accepting feedback?

EMPATHISE DEFINE IDEATE PROTOTYPE TEST

→ TEST

At this stage of the design thinking process, students test their prototype to see how it meets the criteria in the challenge. Students check to see if their prototype meets the criteria set at the start of the design process.

ACTIVITY: TEST FEEDBACK

1. Students take their last prototype and brochure and consider the original design challenge.
2. Invite local beekeepers or council members to view and evaluate prototypes. Have them offer feedback about what works well and what could be improved, and any suggestions they may have.
3. Ask students to consider feedback to determine if their suggested transformations to encourage bee colonies are viable. If not, what do they need to do to make it work?
4. Provide the opportunity to cycle through the Prototype and Test stages again.

Ask students to fill in **Learning journal template 4 (Prototype and test page)**. See the **Journal tip** for further student guidance.

PROMPTS

- Does your prototype do what you wanted it to do?
- Are there other features to be added or considered?

MORE VOCABULARY

- evaluate – assess something, perhaps considering what worked and what didn't
- feature – a specific aspect of something, such as size, shape, colour, quality
- feedback – information about, for example, a person's performance or the design of a product, which can be used to make improvements
- prototype – an initial version of a model of a product or process that is used to develop a final model

JOURNAL TIP

Ask students to think about why it is important to test their ideas before they build their final design.

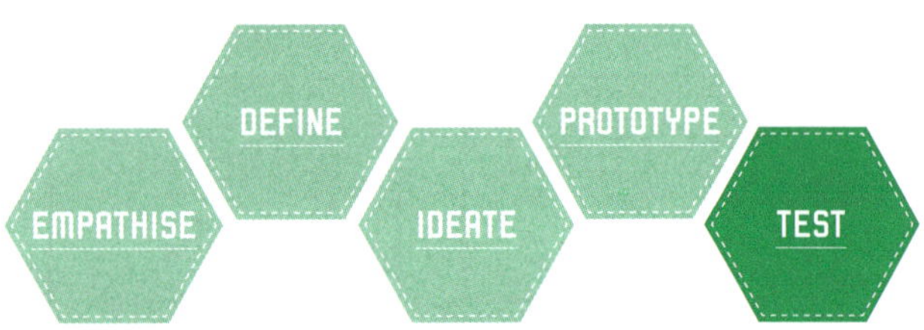

→ SHARE AND EVALUATE

At this stage of the investigation, students are provided with an opportunity to share their final design, as well as the processes involved in the investigation. Students evaluate their learning journals as well as their solutions.

ACTIVITY 1: BRING THE DESIGNS TOGETHER

1. Provide students with time to create their final designs.
2. Encourage them to film the process during prototyping and testing.
3. Students should create a paper or digital brochure to accompany their prototype.
4. Students should include their learning journals with their work so others can see the different stages of the design process.

ACTIVITY 2: EVALUATE AND GIVE FEEDBACK

1. Provide students with **Generic reproducible 2 (Self-evaluation)** to complete.
2. Ask students to provide feedback to each other about the most interesting features, the aspects that were most difficult and the changes that they would make if they repeated the task.
3. Provide students with opportunities to share their designs and brochure. This could include inviting the local beekeepers and council members back, or displaying their work for the school community.

ASSESSMENT

Ask students to again complete **Generic reproducible 1 (Key vocabulary table)** using the key vocabulary for this unit. Compare their table with the one they completed at the Tune-in stage, to demonstrate changes in understanding.

Students complete **Generic reproducible 3 (Responding to the investigation)**. Compare their responses to their responses to **Generic reproducible 2**.

Teachers complete **Generic reproducible 5 (Design thinking assessment rubric)** for each student. Students compare the feedback they are given by the teacher with their self-assessment of how they used the design thinking process to solve problems **(Generic reproducible 3)**.

TUNE IN

STEM INVESTIGATIONS

Name: ....

Date: ....

Why are bee populations in cities declining (getting smaller)?
Watch a video clip or read an article, and take notes.

Threats to bees – what I already think or know	Threats to bees – information from the video clip or article

Consider what you learned in the activities you have completed.

Write your final ideas about why bee populations in cities are declining.

Threats to bees – what I think now

EMPATHISE

STEM INVESTIGATIONS

Name: ....

Date: ....

Think about what you have learned so far. Consider what kinds of food, water and shelter a bee needs to survive. These are called its basic needs. List all the basic needs in the table.

Basic need	Available in a city? (✓ or ✗)	Changes that could be made to provide basic need

Write any questions you have about bees and their needs.

....

....

....

STEM Investigations, MP, ISBN 978 1 4202 4319 2

Name: ....

Date: ....

Interview a city beekeeper or do some research online. Find out the answers to these questions.

1. Why do some people keep bees?

....

....

....

2. Why do beekeepers think bees are important?

....

....

....

3. Where do beekeepers get their bees from?

....

....

4. How do beekeepers stay safe?

....

....

....

5. What are some rules about keeping bees in cities?

....

....

6. Other questions:

....

....

....

....

....

....

....

STEM Investigations, MP, ISBN 978 1 4202 4319 2

HELP PROTECT A SPECIES FROM EXTINCTION

→ INTRODUCTION

Scientists estimate that humans are contributing to a rate of extinction that is 1000 to 10 000 times the natural extinction rate (the rate at which extinctions would occur without humans). All over the world, scientists are exploring small and large methods to conserve species, habitats and biodiversity. One such example is the creation of small areas of natural, protected habitats such as parks, conservation zones, protected habitats and other natural reserves.

In this STEM Investigation, students are able to delve into the conservation of a local species by investigating the life and environment of an endangered animal, and create a conservation 'bubble' that could help the animal survive. The options available for the prototyping allow teachers to tailor the task to the needs, skills and interests of students.

THE CHALLENGE

The government wants to help protect endangered animal species using conservation 'bubbles'. These are safe areas for a species to live in. The government wants major towns to design their own bubbles. You want to make a difference to the environment so you have joined a team.

Your challenge is to design a small protected area where an endangered species can live. Choose an endangered species from your local area or another chosen area. As part of the investigation, you will learn about different life cycles and how living things depend on each other and the environment to survive.

KEY UNDERSTANDINGS

- Living and non-living things are different from each other.
- All living things have a life cycle.
- All living things need energy to live and they belong in a food chain.
- Living things need living and non-living things for food, shelter and safety.

KEY SKILLS

- Identify living and non-living features of an environment, using observable features to identify and group the features.
- Describe life cycles and food chains in an environment accurately, using correct terms and flowcharts.
- Create habitat maps and models in two and/or three dimensions, describing key features and elements of the habitat.
- Search for information using key words, locating accurate and appropriate sources to assist with research.
- Transform an idea into something that can be seen and shared with a defined audience for a particular purpose, using multimedia to enhance communication.

KEY VOCABULARY

food chain – a set of living things that transfer energy between them by eating or being eaten

habitat – where an animal or plant lives

life cycle – different stages of life that living things pass through

species – a group of closely related living things that can reproduce

KEY ACTIONS

- Learn about a local endangered animal.
- Plan for a conservation bubble to help the animal survive.
- Create a prototype of your conservation bubble.
- Share your ideas with others and get feedback.

OVERVIEW OF STAGES

TUNE IN:

Students learn about endangered animals in their local area or other chosen area. They identify living and non-living things, explore the life cycles of living things and identify the living and non-living features of a habitat and the interdependence within habitats.

EMPATHISE

Students develop an awareness of the importance of the environment. They empathise with a change in their own environment. They develop a list of the endangered species in their chosen area.

DEFINE

Students work in groups to select an animal as their focus for a conservation bubble. They investigate the life cycle, habitat and behaviours of their focus animal to define the key features of a successful conservation bubble.

IDEATE

Students organise their ideas and research to identify key features to include in a successful conservation bubble. They obtain feedback from other groups to assist them to refine their ideas and reflect on their thinking.

PROTOTYPE

Students select a two-dimensional map or three-dimensional model for their conservation bubble. They will finalise the design and create a physical or digital prototype, including annotations and explanations.

TEST

Students work as a group to reflect on their research and knowledge of their chosen animal and ensure that the basic features of a successful conservation bubble for their animal has been included.

SHARE AND EVALUATE:

Students share the final prototypes with physical and/or digital presentations of the proposed conservation bubble. Audiences could include other students, teachers, local park rangers, council representatives or other wildlife conservation groups.

SUGGESTED SCHEDULE

LESSON	STAGE
1–4	**Tune in:** Learn about living and non-living things and the relationships between these
5–6	**Empathise:** Empathise with the experience of habitat change; develop a list of local endangered animals; write in journal
7–9	**Define:** Investigate the habitat, life cycle and behaviours of their chosen animal; write in journal
10–11	**Ideate:** Develop several possibilities for the inclusions and organisation of features in a conservation bubble; write in journal
12–14	**Prototype** and **Test:** Create a physical or digital prototype with annotations and evaluate the inclusion of the key features; write in journal
15–16	**Share and evaluate:** Share ideas with an audience and evaluate the design thinking process

CURRICULUM LINKS

SCIENCE

YEAR	STRAND	SUB-STRAND AND CONTENT
3	Science Understanding	Biological sciences: • Living things can be grouped on the basis of observable features and can be distinguished from non-living things
4	Science Understanding	Biological sciences: • Living things have life cycles • Living things depend on each other and the environment to survive
3 & 4	Science as a Human Endeavour	Nature and development of science: • Science involves making predictions and describing patterns and relationships Use and influence of science: • Science knowledge helps people to understand the effect of their actions

TECHNOLOGIES

YEAR	STRAND	CONTENT
3 & 4	Design and Technologies Knowledge and Understanding	• Recognise the role of people in design and technologies occupations and explore factors, including sustainability, that impact on the design of products, services and environments to meet community needs
	Design and Technologies Processes and Production Skills	• Generate, develop, and communicate design ideas and decisions using appropriate technical terms and graphical representation techniques • Select and use materials, components, tools, equipment and techniques and use safe work practices to make designed solutions • Evaluate design ideas, processes and solutions based on criteria for success developed with guidance and including care for the environment • Plan a sequence of production steps when making designed solutions individually and collaboratively
	Digital Technologies Processes and Production Skills	• Collect, access and present different types of data using simple software to create information and solve problems • Plan, create and communicate ideas and information independently and with others, applying agreed ethical and social protocols

MATHEMATICS

YEAR	STRAND	SUB-STRAND AND CONTENT
3	Measurement and Geometry	Using units of measurement: • Measure, order and compare objects using familiar metric units of length, mass and capacity Location and transformation: • Create and interpret simple grid maps to show position and pathways
4	Measurement and Geometry	Using units of measurement: • Compare objects using familiar metric units of area and volume Location and transformation: • Use simple scales, legends and directions to interpret information contained in basic maps

This investigation also links to the General Capabilities:

- Literacy
- Information and Communication Technology (ICT) Capability
- Numeracy
- Critical and Creative Thinking.

This investigation also links to the Cross-Curriculum Priority of Sustainability.

ASSESSMENT

The following resources are provided for assessing students at different stages of the STEM investigations:

- Generic reproducible 1 (Key vocabulary table), for assessing understanding of vocabulary
- Generic reproducible 2 (Self-evaluation), for student self-evaluation of the learning process
- Generic reproducible 3 (Responding to the investigation)
- Generic reproducible 5 (Design thinking assessment rubric), for evaluating student engagement in the design thinking stages
- Learning journal templates 1, 2, 3 and 4, incorporating student reflection and evaluation.

GETTING READY FOR THE INVESTIGATION

You can prepare yourself and students for this STEM investigation in the following ways:

- Research endangered animals in your local area (see **Useful links**, your local zoo website and local and state government websites).
- Collect images of living and non-living things, ensuring that you have images of insects, birds, reptiles, mammals, plants and fungi, as well as correctly labelled images of life cycles of these (see **Useful links**).
- Collect relevant articles, reading resources and library books about habitats, food chains, predation and animal behaviours for the jigsaw activity in the Tune-in session. Ensure that the resources cater for the diverse learning needs of students.
- Review the activities for the investigation and decide how to group students for the design thinking process. Would your students work better in mixed ability groups, ability groups or interest groups?
- Contact local park rangers, local councils or wildlife organisations to identify opportunities for a local excursion or for a guest speaker to share their knowledge or give feedback on the final prototypes.

USEFUL APPS

- Apps for note-taking and collaboration such as Notability or OneNote Class Notebook
- App for creating interactive links between the prototype and descriptions, images, videos and images, such as ThingLink or Aurasma
- App for recording short narrated videos, such as Adobe Spark Video (via a teacher-created class account)
- Apps for mapping and modelling, such as DrawIsland or SketchUp
- App for blocking advertising on websites and saving text, such as Evernote

USEFUL LINKS

- Images of living and non-living things, such as at mea.digital/sm61
- Lists of endangered animals, such as at mea.digital/sm62, mea.digital/sm63, mea.digital/sm64
- Interactive activities for sorting living and non-living things, such as at mea.digital/sm65
- International and local endangered species, such as at mea.digital/sm66
- Insect life cycles, such as at mea.digital/sm67
- Examples of living and non-living classification, such as at mea.digital/sm68
- Articles for teachers about lesson plans for additional activities, such as at mea.digital/sm69, mea.digital/sm70, mea.digital/sm71
- Video clips about habitats, food chains and life cycles, such as at mea.digital/sm72

RESOURCES PROVIDED

- Generic reproducibles 1, 2, 3, 4, 5, 6, 10
- Reproducibles 13.1, 13.2, 13.3
- Learning journal templates 1, 2, 3, 4

MATERIALS NEEDED

- Collections of animal images (see **Getting ready for the investigation**)
- *The Very Hungry Caterpillar* by Eric Carle, or a similar picture storybook showing the life cycle of an animal
- Hula hoops for creating a Venn diagram in the Tune-in session, or chalk or masking tape to use on the carpet or on tables
- Poster paper, markers, highlighters, sticky notes (half a pad per group)
- Variety of construction and recycled materials for creating a prototype

KEY SCIENCE KNOWLEDGE

This section provides an overview of the key science concepts and vocabulary needed for this unit.

LIVING AND NON-LIVING THINGS

We can distinguish between living things (animals, plants, fungi, bacteria), previously living things (dead animals and plants, shed skin and exoskeletons, shells) and non-living things (rocks, water, human-made objects) by looking at their features. To be characterised as living (or previously living), the following characteristics are required: movement, respiration (the release of energy from food), sensitivity, growth, reproduction, excretion and nutrition (use of nutrients). Useful mnemonics for these are MRS GREN or MRS NERG.

LIFE CYCLES

All living things have **life cycles**, also referred to as development stages. As a living thing moves through its life cycle, it moves from immature to mature and becomes capable of reproducing. At different stages of their life cycles, living things often display differing characteristics of life such as changes in their nutritional needs.

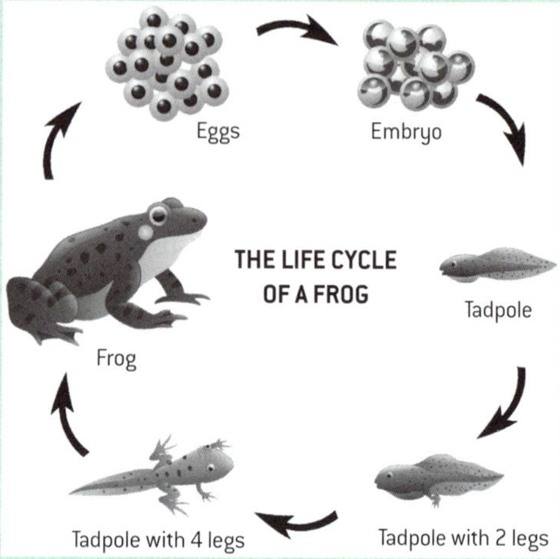

A life cycle is usually presented as a cycle diagram showing the different stages.

WHAT LIVING THINGS NEED TO SURVIVE

All living things depend on their habitat (the living and non-living features) to survive. They must obtain their food, shelter, mates and other needs from their local environment or **habitat**. Often, they are very sensitive to changes in their environment – sometimes, these changes can reduce a population or **species** so that it is endangered or extinct.

Within a habitat, living things are part of **food chains**. Energy flows along a food chain from a producer such as a plant (which obtains its energy from the sun), through a herbivore to a carnivore and eventually a top-level predator. Decomposers such as fungi have a special role to play as they feed on dead and decaying matter. As we move along the food chain, fewer species occupy each level. Relationships between multiple species in each level, and with their environments, are called food webs. When these food chains and webs are disturbed by things such as climate change, hunting, land clearing and introduced species, this can have a devastating effect on living things. Within a conservation area, it is important that the entire food chain is represented to ensure that energy is able to successfully flow through the system. The size and complexity of the food chain will influence the area needed to successfully house endangered species.

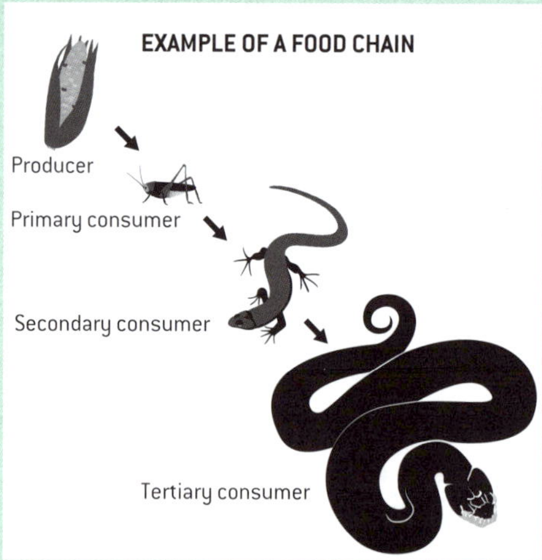

Within a food chain, each species has a role in the flow of energy.

KEY VOCABULARY

food chain – a set of living things that transfer energy between them by eating or being eaten

habitat – where an animal or plant lives

life cycle – different stages of life that living things pass through

species – a group of closely related living things that can reproduce

→ TUNE IN

1. Ask students to complete **Generic reproducible 1 (Key vocabulary table)** using the key vocabulary for this unit. This reproducible will also be used at the end of the unit, to demonstrate changes in understanding.
2. Introduce the challenge and brainstorm names of endangered and extinct species.
3. Ask students to estimate the number of endangered species in their country. Compare to an accurate list (see **Useful apps/links**).
4. Watch a video clip about a locally extinct or endangered species that has been successfully rehabilitated. Ask, 'What do the terms "extinct" and "endangered" mean? How did these scientists use a conservation bubble?'

ACTIVITY 1: IDENTIFYING LIVING AND NON-LIVING THINGS

1. Play an interactive sorting game of living and non-living things (see **Useful apps/links**), discussing observable features.
2. Have students make a large Venn diagram and sort images of living and non-living things into living, non-living and previously living. Use hula hoops to create the Venn diagram, or use chalk or masking tape on the carpet or a large table.
3. Share the simple mnemonic MRS GREN or MRS NERG for the seven characteristics of life (see **Key science knowledge**).

ACTIVITY 2: LIFE CYCLES OF LIVING THINGS

1. Read *The Very Hungry Caterpillar* by Eric Carle. Discuss the life cycle of the butterfly as shown in the book and compare this to the life cycle of a frog (as shown in **Key science knowledge**).
2. Create a visual representation of the life cycle of a butterfly either using diagrams or a creative activity.
3. Set up rotation stations of the labelled life cycle images collected in the preparation stage and distribute **Reproducible 13.1 (Life cycles)**. Have students review the images and record the life cycles.

ACTIVITY 3: DEPENDING ON EACH OTHER AND THE ENVIRONMENT

1. Watch a video clip about the relationships between living and non-living things.
2. Explain that students are going to work together to research a topic. They will summarise their understanding on **Reproducible 13.2 (Living things and their environment)**.
3. Explain the jigsaw procedure and have the groups complete **Generic reproducible 10 (Group task organiser)** and allocate expert topics (habitat, food chains, prey and predators, behaviours).
4. Allow time for students to work in expert topic groups to learn more about their topic from previously gathered resources.
5. Return students to their original groups to share their expertise and create a summary of their understandings for display.

5. Introduce the STEM investigation and challenge to the students. Provide them with the student card and read the information together.
6. Introduce the design thinking process by reviewing the stages on the student card. Explain that students will keep a journal about their learning.

USEFUL APPS/LINKS

- List of endangered species by country, such as at mea.digital/sm63
- Video clip about species rehabilitation, such as at mea.digital/sm73
- Sorting living and non-living things, such as at mea.digital/sm68
- Video, song or article about the characteristics of life, such as at mea.digital/sm74, mea.digital/sm75
- Printables of a butterfly life cycle, such as at mea.digital/sm76 or mea.digital/sm77
- Video clip about the relationships within a habitat, such as at mea.digital/sm78
- The jigsaw strategy, such as at mea.digital/sm79
- Video clip about a conservation bubble, such as at mea.digital/sm80

→ EMPATHISE

During the Empathise stage of the design thinking process, students focus on an awareness of the needs of other living things. To empathise with endangered species, they need to recognise that not all endangered animals are appealing, and develop some awareness of the scope of the endangered species list. This includes developing a list of the endangered animals from their local area and more broadly. Students will take notes, ask questions, and reflect on their own experiences and interests where relevant.

ACTIVITY 1: EXPERIENCING EMPATHY

1. Before class or during a break, remove something that students value from the classroom environment, such as water bottles, chairs or pencil cases.
2. Continue teaching as though the missing items have not vanished; ignore or feign disinterest in student concerns about the missing items.
3. After an appropriate length of time, 'notice' the missing items and then debrief students about their experiences, frustrations and discomfort. Ask them to consider how animals might be affected when their environment changes.

ACTIVITY 2: DEVELOPING AWARENESS

1. Clarify the distinction between extinct and endangered animals (see **Useful apps/links**).
2. Show a video clip to assist students to develop empathy for not-so-cute animals and discuss their responses (see **Useful apps/links**).
3. Group students into pairs or similar to identify the names of endangered species from your chosen area.
4. Collate the list on a poster for later reference. Consider creating a table of animal habitats and locations, or an image, to assist students.

PROMPTS

- Why is this animal endangered?
- What role does this animal play in their habitat?
- How might you feel if you were this animal?

MORE VOCABULARY

- empathise – understand and consider another person or group's point of view
- endangered – a species at risk of becoming extinct
- extinct – no more living members of that species exist
- point of view – an opinion, attitude or judgement considered in a particular way

JOURNAL TIP

Ask students to complete **Learning journal template 1 (Empathise page)** while they are doing the different tasks. Remind them to date their notes and include photos of relevant information or pictures.

USEFUL APPS/LINKS

- Presentation about extinct and endangered species, such as at mea.digital/sm70
- Video clip about the limited funding for research into less attractive animals, such as at mea.digital/sm82
- Article about endangered species, such as at mea.digital/sm66 or from your local authorities

ASSESSMENT

This stage of the design thinking process offers opportunities to observe students collecting information, developing questions, and recording their notes and thinking in their journal.

TOP TIP! The students may be very frustrated by the removal of their personal items in Activity 1. This is the point of the activity: to develop empathy for an animal's experience of the loss of habitat and safety. Take the time to thoroughly debrief the students and validate their feelings.

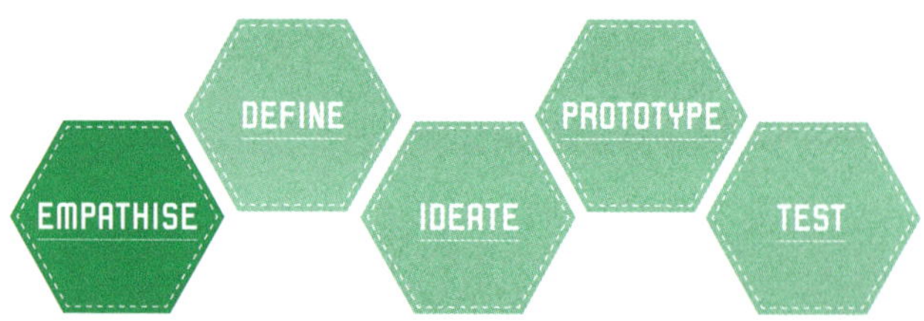

→ DEFINE

The main focus of this stage of the design thinking process is to reframe the challenge. The initial challenge is quite open, so at this stage students learn how to define what needs to be done. This includes noting insights that have been generated and challenges identified.

ACTIVITY 1: LEARN MORE ABOUT AN ANIMAL

1. Having decided how to group students for this investigation, negotiate with the students to ensure that each group is going to create a conservation bubble for a different animal.
2. Distribute one new copy of each of **Reproducibles 13.1 (Life cycles)**, **13.2 (Living things and their environment)** and **Generic reproducible 10 (Group task organiser)** to each group, and **Generic reproducible 4 (Key question table)** to each student.
3. Ask each group to complete **Generic reproducible 10** and allocate research tasks to locate information about the habitat, food chains, prey and predators, behaviours and life cycles of their selected animal.
4. Individual students or pairs locate relevant information by using micro-questions and **Generic reproducible 4**.
5. Have groups discuss and summarise their findings on **Reproducibles 13.1** and **13.2**.

ACTIVITY 2: DEFINE KEY FEATURES

1. Have students gather their group copies of **Reproducibles 13.1** and **13.2** and distribute **Reproducible 13.3 (Features of a conservation bubble)**.
2. Students use their notes from Activity 1 to reflect on their knowledge of their chosen animal and to define the key features to include in their design.

Students can update **Learning journal template 2 (Define page)**.

PROMPTS

- What are the key words of your micro-questions?
- What is your animal going to need to survive?
- Can you identify the habitat/life cycle/food chain for this animal?

MORE VOCABULARY

- define – state the meaning of something
- insight – an accurate understanding of someone or something
- point of view – an opinion, attitude or judgement considered in a particular way

JOURNAL TIP

Discuss the term 'insight' and explain that it relates to something students have learned about the animal and the other living and non-living things they need in their environment. You could refer to **Learning journal template 2**.

USEFUL APPS/LINKS

- App for collating notes, such as Notability or OneNote Class Notebook
- Articles about endangered animals relevant to your area (as identified in **Getting ready for the investigation**)

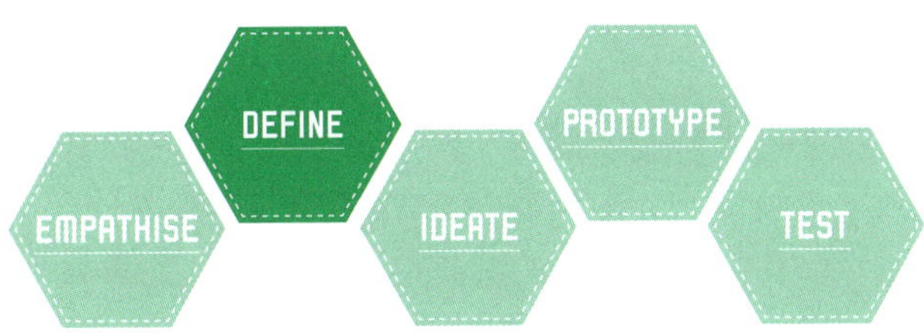

→ IDEATE

The Ideate stage of the design thinking process is all about generating lots of ideas. Students need to be flexible in their thinking and be able to move beyond obvious ideas. At this stage, ideas are not judged, just generated and gathered.

ACTIVITY 1: ORGANISE IDEAS

1. Using the completed **Reproducible 13.3 (Features of a conservation bubble)** and **Generic reproducible 6 (In the frame)**, students organise the features identified into more and less relevant for the success of their conservation bubble.
2. Organise students to share their ideas with another group, receiving feedback on their choices.
3. Allow time for the groups to reflect on their feedback and reconsider their placement of features on the frame.

ACTIVITY 2: SKETCH CONSERVATION BUBBLE IDEAS

1. Having identified the key features to be included in their conservation bubbles, students create a series of rough sketches of possible layouts for their habitats.
2. Organise a gallery walk for students to give feedback on the plans, using sticky notes to record their observations, questions and suggestions.

Students can update **Learning journal template 3 (Ideate page)**.

PROMPTS

- Have you included all the features to help your animal survive?
- How do these features appear in natural habitats?
- How could you improve the way you have grouped features?

MORE VOCABULARY

- feedback – information about, for example, a person's performance or the design of a product, which can be used to make improvements
- ideate – generate many ideas without making judgements about the ideas
- natural habitats – habitats that appear in nature with a diversity of species and non-living features

JOURNAL TIP

When choosing three ideas to include in the journal, try to choose three ideas that aren't related or that show different ways of thinking about the problem.

USEFUL APPS/LINKS

- App for creating a simple bird's-eye view map, such as DrawIsland
- App for recording the Ideate process, using text, drawings, images, weblinks and audio, such as Notability or OneNote Class Notebook

ASSESSMENT

At the Ideate stage, assessment could include observations about the number and diversity of student ideas, and their ability to provide feedback and create additional ideas. Reflection in the journal should provide an insight into some of the reasoning behind student choices.

EMPATHISE · DEFINE · IDEATE · PROTOTYPE · TEST

→ PROTOTYPE

At this stage of the design thinking process, students are asked to create a physical prototype of a solution. It is the stage where students need to get their ideas out of their head and presented in a way that engages other students and helps them to understand the concept. The most important feature is that viewers can interact with whatever is produced.

Encourage students to photograph or film during the Prototype and Test stages. This information can be used to show the learning behind the design thinking process in action.

ACTIVITY 1: FINALISE DESIGNS

1. Distribute a new copy of **Generic reproducible 10 (Group task organiser)** and allow time for the group to discuss the form their prototype will take and how they will explain their choices to an audience. Have them consider two-dimensional or three-dimensional models and the use of annotations or an explanatory text.
2. Ask the students to create a sketch of their final design, noting any key materials or details that will need to be remembered as they construct the prototype.

ACTIVITY 2: TRANSFORM IDEAS INTO PROTOTYPES

1. Provide students with relevant materials and technology to allow them to construct their prototype.
2. Allow time for students to share their prototypes and seek feedback from their peers to allow them to adjust or change their prototype. Encourage them to use the prompt questions when seeking feedback from peers and teachers.

Ask students to fill in the Prototype part of **Learning journal template 4 (Prototype and test page)**. See the **Journal tip** for further student guidance.

PROMPTS

- How will this prototype help you to communicate your ideas to other people?
- Are all the key features you identified earlier included in your prototype?
- What is obvious to an audience and what needs extra explanations (for example with extra notes)?

TOP TIP! Several options are included here for the prototyping of the conservation bubble. How many and which choices you present to the students will depend on their previous learning and personal preferences.

MORE VOCABULARY

- feedback – information about, for example, a person's performance or the design of a product, which can be used to make improvements
- prototype – an initial version of a model of a product or process that is used to develop a final model

JOURNAL TIP

Remind students to highlight the main features of their prototype. If students are creating an electronic journal, they can insert a photo of their prototype and annotate it.

USEFUL APPS/LINKS

- App for recording the progress of their design development, such as Adobe Spark Video
- Notetaking and collaboration app, such as Notability or OneNote Class Notebook
- Mapping and modelling software, such as DrawIsland or SketchUp

ASSESSMENT

Observe students as they make changes to their designs. Are they able to consider feedback, make modifications and move rapidly through this process, or do they have difficulties with holding on to an idea and accepting feedback?

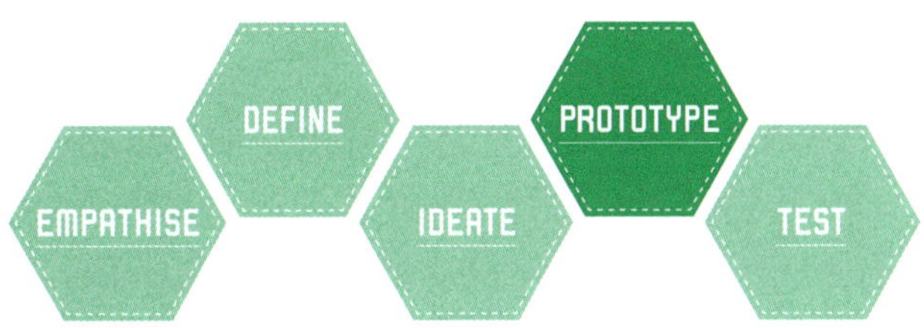

TEST

At this stage of the design thinking process, students test their prototype to see how it meets the criteria in the challenge. Students check to see if their prototype meets the criteria set at the start of the design process.

ACTIVITY: EVALUATE PROTOTYPES

1. Ask the students to gather all of their research and planning reproducibles and their finished prototype.
2. Have them reread their notes and tick, highlight or check off that their prototype reflects all of the needs they identified for their animal.
3. Allow time for the groups to make adjustments or expand their annotations and explanations based on their testing, including creating digital components to their prototype.

Ask students to fill in **Learning journal template 4 (Prototype and test page)**. See the **Journal tip** for further student guidance.

PROMPTS

- Does your prototype do what you wanted it to do?
- Are there other features that need to be added?

MORE VOCABULARY

- evaluate – assess something, perhaps considering what worked and what didn't
- feature – a specific aspect of something, such as size, shape, colour or quality
- feedback – information about, for example, a person's performance or the design of a product, which can be used to make improvements
- prototype – an initial version of a model of a product or process that is used to develop a final model

JOURNAL TIP

Ask students to think about why it is important to test their ideas before they build their final design.

EMPATHISE DEFINE IDEATE PROTOTYPE TEST

SHARE AND EVALUATE

At this stage of the investigation, students are provided with an opportunity to share their final design, as well as the processes involved in the investigation. Students evaluate their learning journals as well as their solutions.

ACTIVITY: SHARE PROTOTYPES

1. Ask groups to present their final ideas to the class, another year level or a visiting expert such as a local park ranger through oral presentations or a gallery walk.

ASSESSMENT

Ask students to again complete **Generic reproducible 1 (Key vocabulary table)** using the key vocabulary for this unit. Compare their table with the one they completed at the Tune-in stage, to demonstrate changes in understanding.

Students complete **Generic reproducible 3 (Responding to the investigation)**. Compare their responses to their responses to **Generic reproducible 2 (Self-evaluation)**.

Teachers complete **Generic reproducible 5 (Design thinking assessment rubric)** for each student. Students compare the feedback they are given by the teacher with their self-assessment of how they used the design thinking process to solve problems **(Generic reproducible 3)**.

TUNE IN

STEM INVESTIGATIONS

Name: ....

Date: ....

Record the life cycles of two living things from the stations created by your teacher. Be sure to record the names of each stage in the life cycle.

Life cycle of a ....

Name of stage:

....
....
....

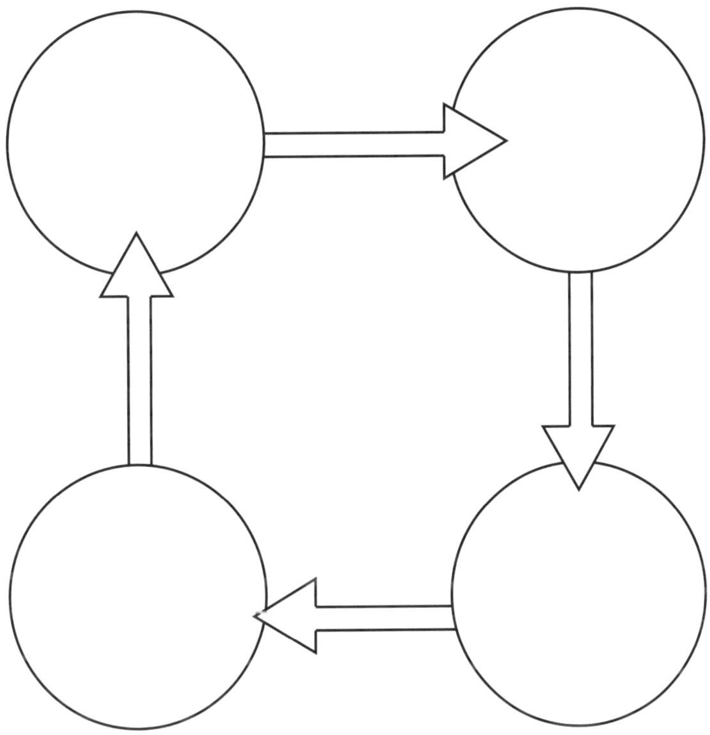

Name of stage:

....
....
....

Name of stage:

....
....
....

Name of stage:

....
....
....

Life cycle of a ....

Name of stage:

....
....
....

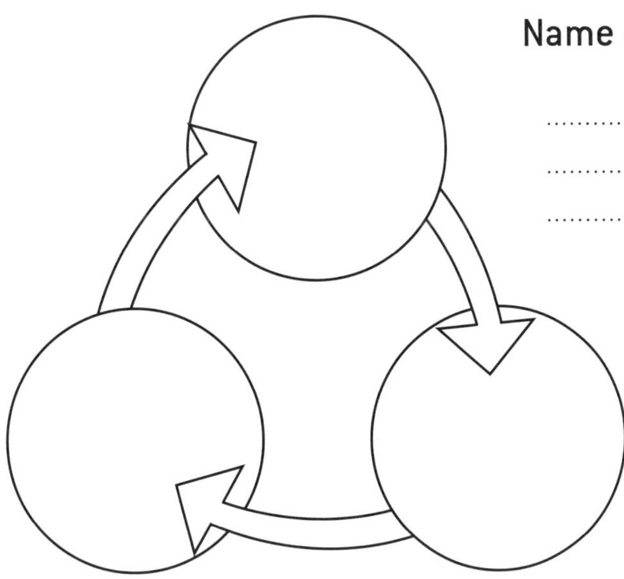

Name of stage:

....
....
....

Name of stage:

....
....
....

TUNE IN

STEM INVESTIGATIONS

Name: ....

Date: ....

Complete this table to summarise your research.

Topic	Notes
Habitat The home of an animal or plant – part of a community of living things	
Food chain The way energy moves from living thing to living thing within an environment	
Prey and predators Prey are animals that are eaten. Predators are animals that eat another animal.	
Behaviours The things that all members of a species normally do and how they act, including how they act towards each other	

STEM Investigations, MP, ISBN 978 1 4202 4319 2 © Macmillan Science and Education Australia 2018

Group names: ....

Date: ....

Complete this table to summarise all you have learned about your endangered animal. This sheet will help you plan for all the features needed in your conservation bubble.

Animal name: ....

Living things your animal needs What living things do you need to include in your bubble? Consider the animal's habitat, life cycle, food chain and behaviours.	
Non-living things your animal needs What non-living things do you need to include? Consider the animal's habitat, life cycle, food chain and behaviours.	
Other features What other living things and non-living things will help make your conservation bubble successful?	
Size Look at all of the features that you have listed. Think about what you know about your animal's behaviours. How much space does your conservation bubble need?	

CREATE AN ARCADE GAME BY REUSING MATERIALS

SUSTAINABLE WORLD 14

INTRODUCTION

The world's population wastes enormous amounts of resources every year, with much of it ending up in landfill. Many materials and products can be reused or recycled. Recycling often results in creative new products or materials.

This investigation combines awareness of waste, creativity connected with reuse, and an exploration of materials and forces. Students have the opportunity to reuse materials that otherwise may end up in landfill, such as cardboard boxes. Using the short film *Caine's Arcade* as inspiration, they are challenged to build a cardboard games arcade to demonstrate their understanding of the properties of different materials, simple machines and forces. While exploring different scientific concepts, they are also encouraged to consider the potential of recycling and reusing waste materials.

THE CHALLENGE

People say we live in a 'throw-away world'. When something gets old, people often throw it away and buy something new. We need to use the Earth's resources wisely and 'reduce, reuse, recycle'. Your class wants to spread this message. You think the best way to do this is to make a game of it!

Your challenge is to create an arcade game to show others that materials can be reused creatively. What materials would be best to make games such as pinball machines or moving clown heads? As part of this investigation you will learn about the properties of materials and how forces work.

KEY UNDERSTANDINGS

- A force is a push or pull on an object.
- Forces can be contact or non-contact.
- Properties of materials include strength, hardness and flexibility.
- Properties of a material affect its use.
- Many materials can be recycled and reused.

KEY SKILLS

- Interview and survey people to find out what they think and generate useful questions.
- Explain the properties of different materials, considering properties such as strength, flexibility, hardness and magnetism.
- Describe different forces, such as friction and magnetism.
- Create labelled diagrams, sketches and models of ideas for an arcade game.
- Transform ideas into something that can be seen – discuss, write, draw and build ideas.

KEY VOCABULARY

contact force – a force that acts on an object by touching it

force – a push or pull on an object

non-contact force – a force that acts on another object without touching it

simple machine – one of six tools that make pushing or pulling an object easier

KEY ACTIONS

- Interview and survey others.
- Research arcade games and forces.
- Create a labelled diagram of an arcade game.
- Explore the properties of materials.
- Reuse materials to build an arcade game.

OVERVIEW OF STAGES

TUNE IN:

Students will discuss issues with waste and the importance of reducing, reusing and recycling. They will watch a short film about a young boy, Caine, who created a games arcade by reusing materials. Students explore forces and properties of materials.

EMPATHISE

Students interview others to find out about the types of games they like to play. They research arcade games to find out more about different games. They survey others to find out which arcade games they are familiar with.

DEFINE

Students consider different arcade games and investigate forces that could be used. They think about different materials that could be reused. They explore different simple machines that might be incorporated, such as ramps and levers.

IDEATE

Students come up with creative ideas for different arcade games. They choose one or two different games to consider before choosing their final game type. They start thinking of catchy names to help people think about reusing and recycling.

PROTOTYPE

Students draw, label and present their design for their arcade game before building a model. Initial prototypes may include developing one or two components of the game before completing the final model.

TEST

Students test the different components of the game. They make changes depending on the results. This may include feedback from others as well as modifications to different elements of the game.

SHARE AND EVALUATE:

Students create a fun arcade by combining the different games created. They create a campaign to raise awareness of 'reduce, reuse, recycle'. They evaluate their own and each other's designs. Opportunities for expert feedback are investigated.

SUGGESTED SCHEDULE

LESSON	STAGE
1–4	**Tune in:** Discuss the issues with waste; watch *Caine's Arcade*, about creating a cardboard games arcade; explore forces and properties of materials
5–7	**Empathise:** Find out about the games others like to play; research different arcade games; survey others about their knowledge of different arcade games; write in journal
8–9	**Define:** Investigate useful forces and simple machines that can be used in arcade games; consider different recycled materials that could be used; discuss constraints of the challenge; write in journal
10–11	**Ideate:** Come up with creative ideas for different arcade games; start thinking of catchy names that make people think about recycling; write in journal
12–17	**Prototype** and **Test:** Draw, label and present a design for the arcade game; build a model using recycled materials; test components of the game and gather feedback from others; write in journal
18–21	**Share and evaluate:** Create a fun arcade with all the arcade games; create a campaign to raise awareness of the need to reduce, reuse and recycle; evaluate self and others

CURRICULUM LINKS

SCIENCE

YEAR	STRAND	SUB-STRAND AND CONTENT
4	Science Understanding	Physical sciences: • Forces can be exerted by one object on another through direct contact or from a distance Chemical sciences: • Natural and processed materials have a range of physical properties that can influence their use
	Science as a Human Endeavour	Nature and development of science: • Science involves making predictions and describing patterns and relationships
	Science Inquiry Skills	Communicating

TECHNOLOGIES

YEAR	STRAND	CONTENT
3 & 4	Design and Technologies Knowledge and Understanding	• Investigate how forces and the properties of materials affect the behaviour of a product or system • Investigate the suitability of materials, systems, components, tools and equipment for a range of purposes
	Design and Technologies Processes and Production Skills	• Select and use materials, components, tools, equipment and techniques and use safe work practices to make designed solutions • Generate, develop and communicate design ideas and decisions using appropriate technical terms and graphical representation techniques

MATHEMATICS

YEAR	STRAND	SUB-STRAND AND CONTENT
4	Measurement and Geometry	Using units of measurement: • Use scaled instruments to measure and compare lengths Geometric reasoning: • Compare angles and classify them as equal to, greater than, or less than, a right angle
	Number and Algebra	Money and financial mathematics: • Solve problems involving purchases and the calculation of change to the nearest five cents with and without digital technologies

This investigation also links to the General Capabilities:

- Literacy
- Numeracy
- Information and Communication Technology (ICT) Capability
- Critical and Creative Thinking.

This investigation links to the Cross-Curriculum Priority of Sustainability.

ASSESSMENT

The following resources are provided for assessing students at different stages of the STEM investigations:

- Generic reproducible 1 (Key vocabulary table), for assessing understanding of vocabulary
- Generic reproducible 2 (Self-evaluation), for student self-evaluation of the learning process
- Generic reproducible 3 (Responding to the investigation)
- Generic reproducible 5 (Design thinking assessment rubric), for evaluating student engagement in the design thinking stages
- Learning journal templates 1, 2, 3 and 4, incorporating student reflection and evaluation.

→ GETTING READY FOR THE INVESTIGATION

You can prepare yourself and students for this STEM investigation in the following ways:

- Identify groups of students who will work well together.
- Review the **Key science knowledge** that supports this investigation, and look at the **Useful links**.
- Investigate the **Useful apps**.
- Gather materials for the science activities about forces and materials during the Tune-In session.
- Start collecting additional materials for prototyping (as shown on the **Materials needed** list).
- Determine where prototypes will be kept between lessons.
- Create a wall space where students can share their ideas in the Ideate stage.
- Organise the class into pairs.
- Start thinking about:
  - » sourcing information about arcade games or providing games to play at school
  - » visiting a games arcade
  - » making connections with games designers, mechanical engineers and recycling places
  - » time constraints for the task
  - » gathering a panel of advisors or mentors to assist students
  - » finding experts to provide feedback to students
  - » how, when and where the designs will be shared and evaluated
  - » whether or not a budget will be provided for non-reused materials, such as tape and glue.

USEFUL APPS

- App for creating semantic maps (links between different words and/or concepts), such as Popplet or Kidspiration
- App for making notes using text, drawings, images, weblinks and audio, such as Notability
- App for creating multimedia presentations, such as Adobe Spark Video (via a teacher-created class account), Prezi or iMovie
- App for creating surveys, such as SurveyMonkey or Typeform
- App for creating augmented reality presentations, such as Aurasma
- App for making podcasts, such as Podbean
- App for sharing ideas, thoughts, questions and images, such as Padlet or Lino
- App for engaging in collaborative tasks, such as OneNote Class Notebook
- App for creating quizzes, such as Kahoot

USEFUL LINKS

- Video clip about cardboard arcade games, such as at mea.digital/sm18
- Information about ramps and friction, such as at mea.digital/sm19
- Information about the Global Cardboard Challenge, such as at mea.digital/sm20
- Information about tools and machines, such as at mea.digital/sm21
- The history of arcade games, such as at mea.digital/sm22 or mea.digital/sm23
- Information for teachers about the properties of materials, such as at mea.digital/sm24

RESOURCES PROVIDED

- Generic reproducibles 1, 2, 3, 4, 5, 7, 9, 10, 12
- Reproducibles 14.1, 14.2, 14.3
- Learning journal templates 1, 2, 3, 4

MATERIALS NEEDED

- Recycled materials, such as assorted cardboard boxes, cardboard offcuts, tubes, string, ribbon
- Scissors
- Tape – different widths, strengths, materials
- PVA glue
- Hot glue guns and glue (optional)
- Split pins
- Staplers and staples
- Different materials for exploration of the properties of materials, such as plastic, metal, fabric
- Toy cars
- Planks of wood or strong cardboard for ramps
- Stopwatch or other timing device
- Paint
- Coloured paper
- Scraps of material
- Marbles
- Ping-pong balls

Hot glue guns can be dangerous. Make sure students are supervised at all times.

KEY SCIENCE KNOWLEDGE

This section provides an overview of the key science concepts and vocabulary needed for this unit.

FORCES

A **force** is a push or pull on an object. A force can make an object change shape, such as a car if it hits a pole. It can make something speed up, such as a swing when it is pushed, or make it slow down, such as gravel on a road. It can also make an object stay in the same place. There are different types of forces, including friction, electromagnetism and elasticity. The direction of a force can be shown on a diagram by using an arrow.

A **contact force** is one that acts on an object by touching it, such as a bat hitting a ball. A **non-contact force** acts on another object from a distance and without touching it, such as a magnet attracting some iron filings.

LAWS OF MOTION

There are three laws of motion.

- An object will continue at the same speed or direction unless a force acts on it.
- The effect of a force on a smaller mass will be greater than on a bigger mass.
- For every action, there is always an equal and opposite reaction.

A bat hitting a ball involves a contact force.

PROPERTIES OF MATERIALS

Materials have different properties , including:

- strength – the amount of force needed to break a material
- hardness – the ease with which a material can be scratched
- flexibility – the ability of a material to change shape without breaking
- absorbency – the ability of a material to soak up a liquid
- waterproofness – the ability of a material to repel water
- elasticity – the ability of a material to return to its original shape after a force has been removed
- plasticity – the ability of a material to keep its shape after a force has been removed.

SOME PROPERTIES OF MATERIALS	
Metal	conductor, strong, hard, shiny, sometimes magnetic
Plastic	strong, waterproof, can change shape, can be transparent
Glass	transparent, strong if thick
Wood	strong, flexible, long-lasting, insulator
Fabric	flexible, absorbent, insulator

The properties of materials determine how they can be used. For example, metals are strong, hard and shiny. Some metals are magnetic and they are good conductors of heat and electricity. Based on this, metals are a good choice for cooking equipment.

SIMPLE MACHINES

Simple machines are used to magnify force. This means that less work (effort or energy) can be done to exert a greater force. We use simple machines every day to make our lives easier. The six simple machines are a lever, a wheel and axle, an inclined plane, a wedge, a pulley and a screw.

KEY VOCABULARY

contact force – a force that acts on an object by touching it
force – a push or pull on an object
non-contact force – a force that acts on another object without touching it
simple machine – one of six tools that make pushing or pulling an object easier

→ TUNE IN

1. Ask students to complete **Generic reproducible 1 (Key vocabulary table)** using the key vocabulary for this unit. This reproducible will also be used at the end of the unit, to demonstrate changes in understanding.
2. Provide students with **Generic reproducible 7 (Double bubble)**. Ask students to choose two of the terms 'reduce', 'reuse', 'recycle' to compare. Share ideas.
3. Introduce the challenge to students by showing them a short film such as *Caine's Arcade*, which is about a boy who created a cardboard games arcade (see **Useful apps/links**). Provide them with **Generic reproducible 9 (See, think, wonder)** to respond to the film.
4. Students need to understand forces and properties of materials. Set up the following activities or similar for students to explore these concepts.

ACTIVITY 1: FRICTION IN ACTION

1. As a class, record the time a toy car takes to run down a wooden ramp and then stop. Measure the distance from the start of the ramp to where it stops.
2. Put some material on the ramp. Ask students to predict what will happen to the car: will it speed up or slow down? Will it travel as far? Record the speed and distance the car travels.
3. Discuss the term 'friction'.
4. Ask students to experiment with different materials. Provide them with **Reproducible 14.1 (Friction of different materials)** to record the time and distance travelled by their cars for each type of material.
5. If there is time, have students change the angle of the ramp and repeat the experiment.

TOP TIP!

Before beginning the science explorations, ensure safety precautions have been discussed first, especially where throwing and bouncing are required.

ACTIVITY 2: PROPERTIES OF MATERIALS

1. Provide each student with a scrap of material. Have student pairs describe the texture.
2. Introduce the terms 'hardness', 'absorbency', 'flexibility', 'strength', 'magnetism', 'waterproofness' and 'transparency'.
3. Provide pairs or small groups of students with a range of materials including metals, plastics, fabric and wood. Provide them with **Reproducible 14.2 (Properties of materials)** and ask them to explore the properties of each material. Then have students create a rating scale for each property so they are able to compare the materials.
4. Students consider at least one use for each material they have explored.

ACTIVITY 3: EFFECTS OF FORCE

1. Provide groups of students with four examples of the same material. Ask them to observe and discuss what happens when different forces are applied through dropping, bouncing, throwing and rolling.
2. Use a group document or record information on a shared whiteboard or piece of paper.
3. After the information has been collated, discuss as a class how the different materials could be best used.

5. Introduce the STEM investigation and challenge to the students. Provide them with the student card and read the information together.
6. Introduce the design thinking process by reviewing the stages on the student card. Explain that students will keep a journal about their learning at the different stages of the design.

USEFUL APPS/LINKS

- App for engaging in collaborative tasks, such as OneNote Class Notebook
- Video clip about *Caine's Arcade*, such as at mea.digital/sm18

→ EMPATHISE

During the Empathise stage of the design thinking process, students focus on finding out about different points of view. To empathise with others, they need to research some of the points of view associated with games. This includes finding out about arcade games. Students will take notes, ask questions, draw diagrams and take photos where relevant.

ACTIVITY 1: TYPES OF ARCADE GAMES

1. Provide students with some pictures or video clips of arcade games.
2. Have students find out about different arcade games and make a class list.
3. Create a Padlet or use another collaborative tool to collate pictures and descriptions of different arcade games.
4. Have pairs of students choose one arcade game to investigate further. They should find out the aim of the game, any rules and how the game works and include the information in the collaborative tool.

ACTIVITY 2: GAMES INTERVIEW

1. As a class, generate a series of questions to be incorporated into an interview about games in general and arcade games in particular. Provide students with at least four question starters such as 'What types of ...?' and 'Why do you ...?'
2. Have pairs of students create questions, then share them with the class.
3. Students interview other students, friends or family to find out their opinions about games in general.
4. Have students share the responses to their interviews, then identify common patterns in the answers.

ACTIVITY 3: ARCADE GAME SURVEY

1. Show students how to use a survey tool such as Typeform or SurveyMonkey, or create a pen-and-paper survey.
2. Create a short survey about the different arcade games that were researched. Ask participants to indicate whether they have heard of the game, played it and whether or not they enjoyed playing it.
3. Discuss the results of the survey.

PROMPTS

- What were some of the different types of games that people like to play?
- What are some of the reasons that people play arcade games?
- Which was the most well known game?
- What was one interesting thing you found out?

MORE VOCABULARY

- empathise – understand and consider another person or group's point of view
- point of view – an opinion, attitude or judgement considered in a particular way

JOURNAL TIP

Ask students to complete **Learning journal template 1 (Empathise page)** while they are doing the different tasks. Remind them to date their notes and include photos of relevant information or pictures.

USEFUL APPS/LINKS

- App for sharing ideas, thoughts, questions and images, such as Padlet or Lino
- App for creating surveys, such as Survey Monkey or Typeform
- Article about arcade games, such as at mea.digital/sm22

ASSESSMENT

This stage of the design thinking process offers opportunities to observe students collecting information, developing questions, and recording their notes and thinking in their journal.

TOP TIP! When creating the class interview questions, write the information students want to find out. Then model how to create different types of questions to find out this information. Discuss the difference between open and closed questions. Provide examples of different types of answers, such as yes/no and multiple choice.

EMPATHISE – DEFINE – IDEATE – PROTOTYPE – TEST

→ DEFINE

The main focus of this stage of the design thinking process is to reframe the challenge. The initial challenge is quite open, so at this stage students learn how to define what needs to be done. This includes noting insights that have been generated.

ACTIVITY 1: CONSIDER OBSERVATIONS

1. Make a table to collate the information collected by the students through their interviewing, surveying and researching. Use a collaborative tool such as Google Docs.
2. Discuss the information that was collected.
   » Which new games did people mention?
   » Did some people have similar points of view to you? If yes, how?
   » Which was the most/least popular type of game?
   » Were there any people who hadn't played arcade games before?
   » Have you played arcade games?

Students can update **Learning journal template 2 (Define page)**.

ACTIVITY 2: EXPLORE FORCES AND SIMPLE MACHINES

1. Provide students with an arcade game, such as a pinball machine, or watch a video clip of a pinball machine in action.
2. Discuss the terms 'lever', 'spring' and 'ramp'. Discuss which of these simple machines have been incorporated in the pinball machine and how they work.
3. Review forces (see **Useful apps/links**) and consider whether or not the pinball machine incorporates a push or pull force.
4. Discuss contact and non-contact forces, considering which type of force is used in the pinball machine.
5. Explain that students will need to identify the simple machines and forces in the arcade game that they design and build.

ACTIVITY 3: PREPARE DESIGN BRIEFS

1. Organise students into small groups.
2. Define the parameters of the challenge, including the timeframe, available materials, and how and when the designs will be shared. Decide whether or not students will be given a budget for non-reused materials such as glue and tape. If they are not budgeting, consider limiting the amount of these materials provided to each group.
3. Provide students with **Reproducible 14.3 (Arcade game design brief)**. They should use this as a guide to the challenge and add details at relevant stages in the design process.

PROMPTS

- Do most traditional arcade games use contact or non-contact forces?
- How are levers sometimes used in arcade games?
- What was something new that you learned?
- What other information do you need?

MORE VOCABULARY

- define – state the meaning of something
- insight – an accurate understanding of someone or something
- point of view – an opinion, attitude or judgement considered in a particular way
- review – consider an idea, process or product and assess what works and what needs to be changed

JOURNAL TIP

Discuss the term 'insight' and explain that it relates to something students have learned about the people and their responses to the surveys as well as information gathered through research or excursions. You could refer to **Learning journal template 2**.

USEFUL APPS/LINKS

- App for engaging in collaborative tasks, such as OneNote Class Notebook or Google Docs
- Information about forces, such as at mea.digital/sm7

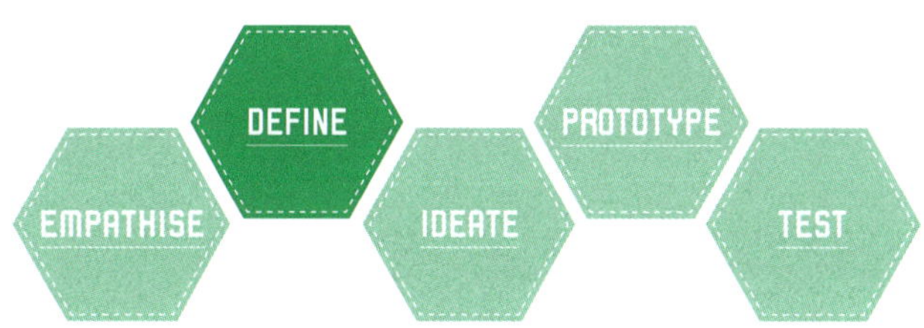

IDEATE

The Ideate stage of the design thinking process is all about generating lots of ideas. Students need to be flexible in their thinking and be able to move beyond obvious ideas. At this stage, ideas are not judged, just generated and gathered.

ACTIVITY 1: GENERATE IDEAS

1. Have students choose two different arcade games, such as a pinball machine and ball toss.
2. Students start with one game and write as many ideas relating to the game as possible. They could use sticky notes for each idea, write the ideas on a large piece of paper or use a collaborative app such as Padlet. Provide students with some questions to consider as they ideate:
   - What is the aim of the game?
   - How does the game start?
   - What are the moving parts?
   - Are there any obstacles?
   - What types of materials could be useful?
   - Does the game use contact forces, non-contact forces or both?
   - Is the game a single-person or multi-person game?
3. Ask students to write as many ideas as they can relating to the second arcade game.
4. Briefly compare the two games, discussing similarities and differences.
5. Have students return to the first arcade game and generate more ideas. Finally, add ideas to the second arcade game.

ACTIVITY 2: FURTHER EXPLORE IDEAS

1. Have students choose one of the arcade games to explore further. Provide them with further prompts: 'How could this game cater for different ages? How could this game be made more difficult? What are some possible names for this game?'
2. Students continue to add ideas about their arcade game, perhaps incorporating features from other arcade games.

PROMPTS

- How do these ideas include forces and simple machines?
- How might you test your design?
- How can you make it more exciting?
- What types of materials might be good to reuse?
- What are some catchy names for these games that will remind people about reusing and recycling?

MORE VOCABULARY

- feedback – information about, for example, a person's performance or the design of a product, which can be used to make improvements
- ideate – generate many ideas without making judgements about the ideas

USEFUL APPS/LINKS

- App for sharing ideas, thoughts, questions and images, such as Padlet or Lino

ASSESSMENT

At the Ideate stage, assessment could include observations about the number and diversity of student ideas, and their ability to provide feedback and create additional ideas. Encourage students to take notes and reflect in their learning journal, as needed.

Reflection in the journal should provide an insight into some of the reasoning behind student choices.

EMPATHISE DEFINE IDEATE PROTOTYPE TEST

→ PROTOTYPE

At this stage of the design thinking process, students are asked to create a physical prototype of a solution. It is the stage where students need to get their ideas out of their heads and present them in a way that engages other students and helps them to understand the concept. When students create, it helps them to think and solve problems and disagreements. Students can role-play, make a storyboard or use sticky notes when they prototype. The most important feature is that viewers can interact with whatever is produced.

ACTIVITY 1: COMPLETE THE DESIGN BRIEF

1. Have students return to **Reproducible 14.3 (Arcade game design brief)** and fill out details about the game they are creating, including the forces and simple machines incorporated.
2. Students create and annotate a detailed drawing of their first design. Students could use an app that creates interactive links, such as ThingLink, to highlight the key features.

ACTIVITY 2: TRANSFORM IDEAS INTO PROTOTYPES

1. Provide students with **Generic reproducible 10 (Group task organiser)** to help them plan the construction of the game. Have students choose one component of their game to create, such as a lever to move a ball, or a spring to propel a marble.
2. Have students start building other components and combining them.
3. After a prototype has been created, ask students to get feedback from others and give feedback, too.

Ask students to fill in the Prototype part of **Learning journal template 4 (Prototype and test page)**. See the **Journal tip** for further student guidance.

PROMPTS

- What is the aim of your arcade game?
- What part needs to be made first?
- How are the different parts attached?
- Which parts of the game need to move?

TOP TIP!

The Prototype stage is often very messy. It is important that students are focusing on their ideas, rather than the end product. Provide them with lots of materials – recycling depots can be a useful source of resources. Students may add labels to prototypes to explain some of the main features. Photographing and annotating pictures of prototypes can be useful.

When asking for feedback, students could ask each other some of the following questions:

- What is the aim of your arcade game?
- How does it work?
- Which parts work best? What will you keep?
- Which parts need changing? How might you do this?
- What other materials might you need?

MORE VOCABULARY

- feedback – information about, for example, a person's performance or the design of a product, which can be used to make improvements
- prototype – an initial version of a model of a product or process that is used to develop a final model

JOURNAL TIP

Remind students to highlight the main features of their prototype. If students are creating an electronic journal, they can insert a photo of their prototype and annotate it.

USEFUL APPS/LINKS

- App for creating interactive links (for example, between descriptions, videos, images and websites and a main image), such as ThingLink

ASSESSMENT

Observe students as they make changes to their designs. Are they able to consider feedback, make modifications and move rapidly through this process, or do they have difficulties with holding on to an idea and accepting feedback?

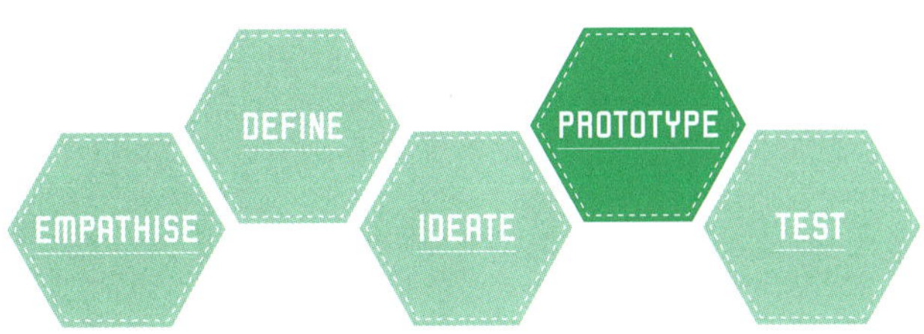

TEST

At this stage of the design thinking process, students test their prototype to see how it meets the criteria in the challenge.

ACTIVITY: TEST FEEDBACK

1. Have students gather feedback about the prototypes. Provide them with **Generic reproducible 12 (Prototype and test)** to record the ideas.
2. When providing feedback, students should consider ease of use, purpose of the game and materials used.
3. Students continue to cycle through the Prototype and Test stages until they have completed their design.

Ask students to fill in **Learning journal template 4 (Prototype and test page)**. See the **Journal tip** for further student guidance.

PROMPTS

- Does your prototype do what you wanted it to do?
- Are there features that need to be added or removed?

MORE VOCABULARY

- evaluate – assess something, perhaps considering what worked and what didn't
- feature – a specific aspect of something, such as size, shape, colour, quality
- feedback – information about, for example, a person's performance or the design of a product, which can be used to make improvements
- prototype – an initial version of a model of a product or process that is used to develop a final model
- review – consider an idea, process or product and assess what works and what needs to be changed

JOURNAL TIP

Ask students to think about why it is important to test their ideas before they build their final design.

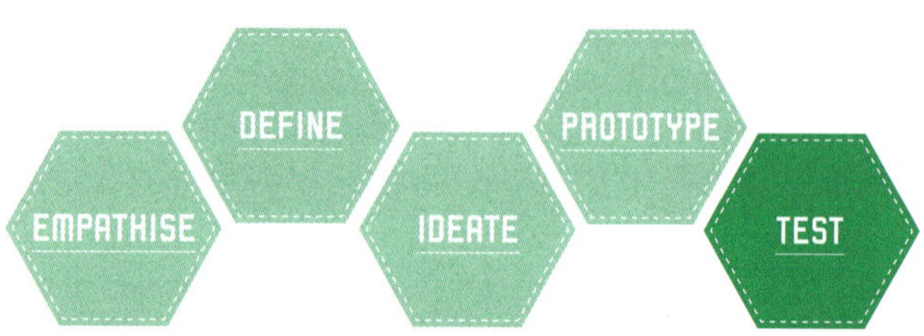

SHARE AND EVALUATE

At this stage of the investigation, students are provided with an opportunity to share their final design, as well as the processes involved in the investigation. Students evaluate their learning journals as well as their solutions.

ACTIVITY 1: BRING THE DESIGNS TOGETHER

1. Allow students to finalise their designs, decide the game name and set up the arcade. They also need to provide information about reducing, reusing and recycling waste. This could be in the form of a podcast, short video clip, survey or quiz.
2. Students should include their learning journals with the display so others can see the different stages of the design process.

ACTIVITY 2: EVALUATE AND GIVE FEEDBACK

1. Provide students with **Generic reproducible 2 (Self-evaluation)**.
2. During the arcade expo, provide participants with tokens so they can vote for their favourite arcade game.
3. Students could share their designs with the wider community, through events such as the Global Cardboard Challenge, and raise money for recycling programs.

ASSESSMENT

Ask students to again complete **Generic reproducible 1 (Key vocabulary table)** using the key vocabulary for this unit. Compare their table with the one they completed at the Tune-in stage, to demonstrate changes in understanding.

Students complete **Generic reproducible 3 (Responding to the investigation)**. Compare their responses to their responses to **Generic reproducible 2**.

Teachers complete **Generic reproducible 5 (Design thinking assessment rubric)** for each student. Students compare the feedback they are given by the teacher with their self-assessment of how they used the design thinking process to solve problems **(Generic reproducible 3)**.

Name: ....

Date: ....

- Make some ramps using different materials.
- Write the materials in the first column.
- Underline the material you think will produce the most friction (make the car travel the least).
- Circle the material you think will produce the least friction (make the car travel the farthest).
- Time how fast a toy car travels down the ramp and how far it travels from the top of the ramp to where it stops. Record your observations in the table. Were your predictions correct?

Material	Speed (seconds)	Distance (centimetres)

TUNE IN

STEM INVESTIGATIONS

Name: ....

Date: ....

Explore the properties of different materials. Find out if they are magnetic, flexible or waterproof. Write your observations in the table. An example is shown.

Material	Magnetic?	Flexible?	Waterproof?	Elastic?	Hard?
Thin plastic	no	yes	yes	no	difficult to scratch

DEFINE

STEM INVESTIGATIONS

Name: ....

Date: ....

Use this design brief to help you plan your arcade game.

Type of game	
Name of game	
Forces used	☐ contact force ☐ non-contact force ☐ magnetism ☐ throwing ☐ rolling ☐ bouncing ☐ dropping
Simple machines included	☐ lever ☐ spring ☐ ramp ☐ wheel ☐ other:
Materials to be reused	
New materials to be used	
Time allowed to complete	
How information about 'reduce, reuse, recycle' will be shared	☐ podcast ☐ survey ☐ quiz ☐ video ☐ other:

SHOW HOW ENGINEERING HELPS SAVE HABITATS

INTRODUCTION

A habitat is a home or environment of an animal or other living thing. Trees, rocks, plants, soil and water provide habitats for many animals. Habitats are destroyed when humans build cities, homes, roads and highways and when forests are cleared for timber or to create more farmland. Natural disasters and climate change can also destroy habitats. When plants and animals lose their habitats, they may become endangered or extinct.

In this STEM investigation, students are asked to invent and present one design or process to help stop the destruction of one habitat. They need to demonstrate their understanding of how living things depend on each other and the environment to survive.

This STEM challenge is easily differentiated for students by encouraging different groups to use different degrees of complexity when creating their inventions or testing their designs or processes.

THE CHALLENGE

You are a member of a young engineers club. Your club wants to attract new members. You decide to make a display to show how engineers can help protect the environment, including animals and plants.

Your challenge is to invent and present a device or process to help protect a habitat. Choose a habitat, learn about the animals and plants there and find out what threatens the habitat. What could stop this threat? As part of this investigation, you will learn how living things depend on each other and the environment.

KEY UNDERSTANDINGS

- Living things depend on each other and the environment to survive.
- A habitat is a home or environment of an animal or other living thing.
- Human activity, natural disasters and changing climate can destroy habitats.
- Habitat destruction affects different things in different ways.

KEY VOCABULARY

habitat – where an animal or plant lives

environment – all the living and non-living things on the Earth

engineer – a person who uses science and maths to create new things or to improve a product

survive – continue living and reproducing

KEY SKILLS

- Develop research skills, including formulating questions to help find information.
- Make observations and identify patterns relating to human activity and habitats.
- Use creative thinking to generate a range of diverse ideas and solutions.
- Develop evaluative skills, such as reflecting on the process and making suggestions for improvement.

KEY ACTIONS

- Find out how living things depend on each other to survive.
- Explore habitats and habitat threats.
- Consider the work of engineers.
- Invent and present a device or process to help stop habitat destruction.

→ OVERVIEW OF STAGES

TUNE IN:

Students explore how living things depend on each other. Share introductory information and a video clip on a habitat under threat and discuss students' understandings of habitats and what can destroy them. Students will choose one habitat to study.

EMPATHISE

Students find out about habitat destruction and consider the impact on living things. They explore motivations of engineers to help protect habitats.

DEFINE

Students consider the main issues with designing devices or processes to help stop the destruction of a habitat. They consider the key components of the design challenge, including materials available and how to test prototypes.

IDEATE

Students generate creative ideas for devices or processes to help stop habitat destruction.

PROTOTYPE

Students transform some or part of their ideas into physical representations. These are created rapidly, using simple materials. Students can make storyboards, sketches, simple models or use sticky notes.

TEST

Students share their prototypes and provide feedback to each other about their ideas, and check the relevance and usability of their designs. They are given the opportunity to cycle through the Prototype and Test stages again.

SHARE AND EVALUATE:

Final prototypes are shared and evaluated, with opportunities for feedback from engineers, animal conservationists or young people interested in engineering.

→ SUGGESTED SCHEDULE

LESSON	STAGE
1–4	**Tune in:** Share information about habitats and threats to them
5–7	**Empathise:** Find out about habitat destruction and impact on living things; write in journal
8–9	**Define:** Consider observations and insights; define main issues; write in journal
10–11	**Ideate:** Develop ideas; write in journal
11–13	**Prototype** and **Test:** Conduct prototyping and testing cycles; write in journal
14–15	**Share and evaluate:** Share and evaluate designs and prototypes

CURRICULUM LINKS

SCIENCE

YEAR	STRAND	SUB-STRAND AND CONTENT
4	Science Understanding	Biological sciences: • Living things depend on each other and the environment to survive
3 & 4	Science as a Human Endeavour	Use and influence of science: • Science knowledge helps people to understand the effect of their actions

TECHNOLOGIES

YEAR	STRAND	CONTENT
3 & 4	Design and Technologies Processes and Production Skills	• Critique needs or opportunities for designing, and explore and test a variety of materials, components, tools and equipment and the techniques needed to produce designed solutions* • Generate, develop and communicate design ideas and decisions for audiences using appropriate technical terms and graphical representation techniques • Evaluate design ideas, processes and solutions based on criteria for success developed with guidance and including care for the environment • Plan a sequence of production steps when making designed solutions individually and collaboratively

* If students are making a model of their device.

MATHEMATICS

YEAR	STRAND	SUB-STRAND AND CONTENT
3 & 4	Statistics and Probability	Data representation and interpretation: • Interpret and compare data displays

This investigation also links to the General Capabilities:

- Literacy
- Numeracy
- Information and Communication Technology (ICT) Capability
- Critical and Creative Thinking.

This investigation also links to the Cross-Curriculum Priority of Sustainability.

ASSESSMENT

The following resources are provided for assessing students at different stages of the STEM investigations:

- Generic reproducible 1 (Key vocabulary table), for assessing understanding of vocabulary
- Generic reproducible 2 (Self-evaluation), for student self-evaluation of the learning process
- Generic reproducible 3 (Responding to the investigation)
- Generic reproducible 5 (Design thinking assessment rubric), for evaluating student engagement in the design thinking stages
- Learning journal templates 1, 2, 3 and 4, incorporating student reflection and evaluation.

→ GETTING READY FOR THE INVESTIGATION

You can prepare yourself and students for this STEM investigation in the following ways:

- Identify groups of students who will work well together.
- Review the **Key science knowledge** that supports this investigation, and look at the **Useful apps** and **Useful links**.
- Start collecting useful materials for designing devices or processes to help stop habitat destruction (as shown in the **Materials needed** list).
- Determine where prototypes will be kept between lessons.
- Create a vocabulary wall.
- Create a wall space where students can share their ideas during the Ideate stage.
- Organise the class into pairs or small groups.
- Start thinking about:
  - » sourcing information about specific habitats (local, national or international) and their destruction
  - » how the devices or processes will be evaluated
  - » who will view the designs
  - » who will provide expert feedback about the designs (for example, local engineers and/or conservationists), and whether it will be provided in person or in digital form.

USEFUL APPS

- App for creating and organising ideas, such as Popplet, Inspiration, Padlet or Ideament
- App for sharing ideas, such as Air Sketch
- App for creating multimedia presentations, such as Adobe Spark Video (via a teacher-created class account) or iMovie

USEFUL LINKS

- Article about habitat loss and its impact, such as at mea.digital/sm120
- Video clip about habitats and living things depending on each other, such as at mea.digital/sm121
- Article about rainforests of Sumatra and Borneo, such as at mea.digital/sm122
- Article or video clip about orangutans and the threat to their habitat, such as at mea.digital/sm123, mea.digital/sm124
- Information on different engineering jobs, such as at mea.digital/sm125
- Information for teachers about reducing habitat loss, such as at mea.digital/sm126

RESOURCES PROVIDED

- Generic reproducibles 1, 2, 3, 5, 6
- Reproducibles 15.1, 15.2, 15.3
- Learning journal templates 1, 2, 3, 4

MATERIALS NEEDED

- Sticky notes
- Paper
- Cardboard
- Sticky tape
- Other building materials, such as recyclable packaging, boxes, tubes, plastic bottles
- Rubber bands
- Scissors
- Glue
- Paint

KEY SCIENCE KNOWLEDGE

This section provides an overview of the key science concepts and vocabulary needed for this unit.

LIVING THINGS, HABITATS AND ECOSYSTEMS

Living things need each other and non-living things to **survive**. Without food, water and oxygen, living things die. Sunlight, shelter and soil are also essential for the survival of living things.

A **habitat** provides an animal or plant with food, shelter, water and safety. Often, many species share habitats. For example, the Sumatran rainforests are the habitat of many thousands of animal and plant species, including the Sumatran tiger, orangutan and rhinoceros, and a plant that has the biggest flower in the world.

Living things get what they need from the living and non-living things within their habitat. This system of living things and non-living things that interact with each other and their **environment** is called an ecosystem.

All living things within ecosystems are part of food chains. A food chain describes the order in which organisms, or living things, depend on each other for food. Each food chain starts with a producer (plant), which is eaten by a consumer (animal). Another important link in a food chain is decomposers such as bacteria.

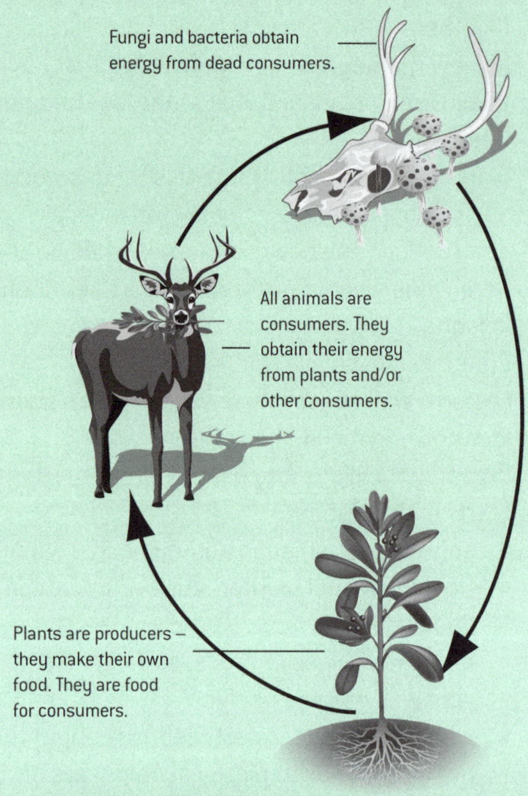

Food chains show the flow of energy and nutrients in ecosystems.

PROTECTING HABITATS

Sometimes a natural habitat is affected in such a way that it can no longer support the species within it. This habitat destruction is the biggest threat to wildlife. It can happen because of urban development, road building, water development, pollution, forest fires and some recreational activities.

In some places, people are working to conserve, protect and restore habitats. **Engineers** can help by developing ways to protect biological habitats:

- Materials engineers develop materials that mimic the qualities of wood to be used instead of rainforest timber.
- Chemical engineers have developed a way to lessen the harmful effects of starfish on coral reefs.
- Environmental engineers are developing ways to combat global warming, which affects coral reefs.
- Agricultural engineers are working on farming techniques that limit depletion of soil nutrients and maintain soil health.

Engineers consider both scientific and ethical issues as they create their designs.

KEY VOCABULARY

habitat – where an animal or plant lives

environment – all the living and non-living things on the Earth

engineer – a person who uses science and maths to create new things or to improve a product

survive – continue living and reproducing

TUNE IN

1. Ask students to complete **Generic reproducible 1 (Key vocabulary table)** using the key vocabulary for this unit. This reproducible will also be used at the end of the unit to demonstrate changes in understanding.
2. Students consider the statement 'Living things depend on each other and the environment to survive'. Research living things and their dependence on each other (see **Useful apps/links**) and use an interactive game on food chains in different habitats to explore further (see **Useful apps/links**). Record information on paper or use a mind-mapping app (see **Useful apps/links**).
3. Discuss what students observed and learned. Have them reread their information and use a sticky note to record their own statement explaining how living things depend on each other and the environment to survive.
4. Use students' statements to determine they all understand that living things depend on each other and the environment to survive.

ACTIVITY 1: HABITATS

1. Provide students with a link to information about habitats (see **Useful apps/links**).
2. Ask students to create an infographic explaining habitats. They will also need to find a physical description of one habitat, examples of that habitat (geographical locations) and examples of animals and plants that live in that habitat.
3. Ask pairs of students to take turns explaining different habitats and their features.

ACTIVITY 2: HABITAT DESTRUCTION

1. Provide students with **Reproducible 15.1 (Habitat destruction)**. Have students work in small groups to explore a wildlife conservation website (see **Useful apps/links**). Choose one habitat and record what is destroying it and/or how it is being destroyed, and what is affected by its destruction, on **Reproducible 15.1**.
2. Students regroup and present findings to others.
3. Provide students with coloured paper, scissors, coloured markers, pencils and glue. Have them create the habitat they have researched and creatively organise what they have learned about the habitat, what lives there and how it is being affected.

ACTIVITY 3: ENGINEERING SOLUTIONS

1. Explore the word 'engineering' to ensure students understand that engineers use science and maths to figure out the best way to create new things or to improve a product.
2. Provide students with links to information on engineering solutions (see **Useful apps/links**).
3. Students use sticky notes to create a wall of ways and things that are currently used to protect habitats.

5. Introduce the STEM investigation and challenge. Provide them with the student card and read through the information together.
6. Introduce the design thinking process by reviewing the stages on the student card.
7. Explain that students will keep a journal about their learning at the different stages of the design.

TOP TIP! During the Tune-in sessions, conduct vocabulary activities to highlight and develop key vocabulary knowledge. Activities could include drawing semantic webs, creating a word wall or paired discussions. Check **Key vocabulary** or read the **Key science knowledge** for a refresher on the key terms and concepts.

USEFUL APPS/LINKS

- App for mind mapping, such as iThoughts
- Online information about different habitats, such as at mea.digital/sm127
- Video clip about food chains, such as at mea.digital/sm128
- Interactive game about food chains in different habitats, such as at mea.digital/sm129
- Wildlife conservation website, such as at mea.digital/sm130
- Information about engineering solutions to habitat loss, such as at mea.digital/sm131
- Information about solutions to saving habitats, such as at mea.digital/sm132

→ EMPATHISE

During the Empathise stage of the design thinking process, students focus on finding out about different points of view. To empathise with others, they need to research some of the challenges associated with preventing habitat destruction. This includes finding out about threats to habitats and who/what is at risk. Students will take notes, ask questions, draw diagrams and take photos where relevant.

ACTIVITY 1: ORANGUTANS AND THEIR HABITAT

1. Provide students with links to information about the rainforests in Sumatra and Borneo, a large sheet of paper and coloured markers. Students read through the information in small groups.
2. Provide students with **Reproducible 15.2 (Rainforest current events)** to record key information about the rainforests in Sumatra and Borneo.

ACTIVITY 2: PERCEPTIONS

1. Provide students with **Reproducible 15.3 (Orangutan senses)**.
2. View video clips or read an article about orangutans (see **Useful apps/links**) and the threat to their habitat. Students record perceptions on **Reproducible 15.3**.
3. Organise students into pairs and have them share their responses.
4. As a whole class, students brainstorm what they consider to be the major issues for the orangutans and their habitat. Display these, to be referred to throughout the Define and Ideate stages.

ACTIVITY 3: WHAT IS BEING DONE TO HELP?

1. Provide students with links to information about ideas and incentives for protecting the rainforests of Sumatra and Borneo (see **Useful apps/links**).
2. Students use sticky notes to record ideas and incentives for protecting rainforest habitats.

PROMPTS

- What information about the rainforests in Borneo and Sumatra made the most impact on you?
- What are some of the words people use to describe the habitat and the orangutans?
- What were people concerned about?

MORE VOCABULARY

- empathise – understand and consider another person or group's point of view

JOURNAL TIP

Ask students to complete **Learning journal template 1 (Empathise page)** while they are doing the different tasks. Remind them to date their notes and include photos of relevant information or pictures.

USEFUL APPS/LINKS

- App for creating and organising ideas, such as Popplet, Inspiration, Padlet or Ideament
- App for sharing ideas, such as Air Sketch
- Online article about the rainforests of Sumatra and Borneo, such as at mea.digital/sm122
- Article or video clip about orangutans and the threat to their habitat, such as at mea.digital/sm123, mea.digital/sm124
- Information about incentives for protecting habitats, such as at mea.digital/sm241

ASSESSMENT

This stage of the design thinking process offers opportunities to observe students collecting information, developing questions, and recording their notes and thinking in their journal.

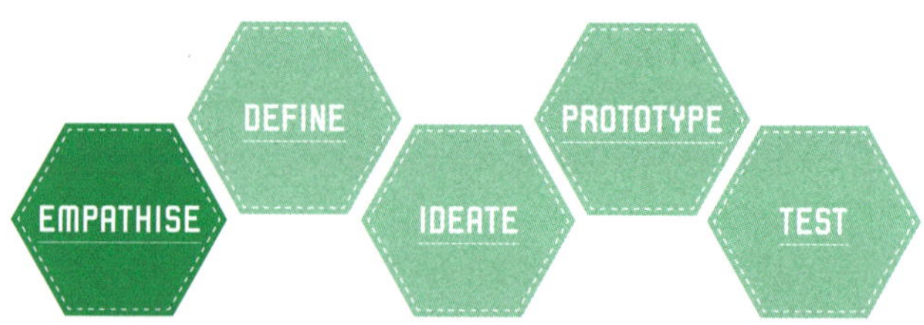

DEFINE

The main focus of this stage of the design thinking process is to reframe the challenge. The initial challenge is quite open, so at this stage students learn how to define what needs to be done. This includes noting insights that have been generated.

ACTIVITY 1: CONSIDER OBSERVATIONS

1. Students consider the information they gathered at the Tune-in and Empathise stages. They may work in pairs or small groups. Provide them with a whiteboard, large sheet of paper and/or sticky notes to collate some of their key information. They should refer to their information on **Reproducible 15.1 (Habitat destruction)** and **Reproducible 15.2 (Rainforest current events)**. Students should transfer their main findings to **Learning journal template 2 (Define page).**
2. Students should discuss one section of **Learning journal template 2** at a time, write their responses and then continue discussing their ideas for the next section, until the task is complete. This provides students with opportunities to hear others' responses and it provides the teacher with input points.
3. Provide students with the opportunity to research further. Ask them to write other information they would like to know. Provide them with **Generic reproducible 4 (Key question table)** to assist them to record their questions, findings and sources.

ACTIVITY 2: CONSIDER INSIGHTS

1. Students should think of at least one insight they have gained from the process; for example, the desire for palm oil is destroying habitats. Students should add this insight to **Learning journal template 4 (Prototype and test page)**. They should then explain how this will affect the invention of a device or process to help stop the destruction of the rainforests.
2. When considering insights, students could think about the following:
   » What was something unexpected that you observed or found out? How was it unexpected?
   » How will you decide on the most important aspect of your invention?
   » Is there any other information that you need or would like to know? How will you find out?

PROMPTS

- What did you discover?
- What were the most important pieces of information that you gathered?
- What was something new that you learned?
- What other information do you need?

MORE VOCABULARY

- define – state the meaning of something
- insight – an accurate understanding of someone or something
- point of view – an opinion, attitude or judgement considered in a particular way

JOURNAL TIP

Discuss the term 'insight' and explain that it relates to something students have learned about the people and their responses. You could refer to **Learning journal template 2**.

USEFUL APPS/LINKS

- App for creating and organising ideas, such as Popplet, Inspiration, Padlet or Ideament
- App for sharing ideas, such as Air Sketch

EMPATHISE DEFINE IDEATE PROTOTYPE TEST

IDEATE

The Ideate stage of the design thinking process is all about generating lots of ideas. Students need to be flexible in their thinking and be able to move beyond obvious ideas. At this stage, ideas are not judged, just generated and gathered.

ACTIVITY: GENERATE IDEAS

1. Ask groups of students to draw or write ideas for their invention.
2. Each new idea should be drawn or written on a separate piece of paper or sticky note.
3. Ask students to group ideas on a wall or board.
4. Ask students to look at the different ideas and provide feedback to each other. It is important that students don't defend their ideas at this stage. They should just be listening to the feedback.
5. After the initial feedback, ask students to come up with more ideas. Encourage them to be creative and even radical.
6. Ask students to choose three of their ideas for an invention of a device or process to protect the rainforest habitat. Students use **Learning journal template 3 (Ideate page)** to do this. Ask students to choose one idea to explore further and explain the reasoning behind their choice.

TOP TIP!

At this stage, students may have produced a series of drawings that are annotated. They may have a collection of sticky notes, which they can organise into related ideas.

Encourage students to view and read others' ideas before giving feedback. Feedback could be within small groups or between partners. Considering others' ideas is an important part of this process, so students can build on their own ideas as they continue to ideate.

At each stage of this activity, ask students to discuss their thoughts before writing their responses. This will help them think through their ideas and select their final ideas to develop.

PROMPTS

- How do your chosen ideas relate to protecting habitats and the species that live there?
- How might you test your invention?
- How could you make it work for other habitats?
- What if you had different materials to use?

MORE VOCABULARY

- feedback – information about, for example, a person's performance or the design of a product, which can be used to make improvements
- ideate – generate many ideas without making judgements about the ideas

JOURNAL TIP

When choosing three ideas to include in the journal, try to choose three ideas that aren't related.

USEFUL APPS/LINKS

- App for creating and organising ideas, such as Popplet, Inspiration, Padlet or Ideament
- App for sharing ideas, such as Air Sketch

ASSESSMENT

At the Ideate stage, assessment could include observations about the number and diversity of student ideas, and their ability to provide feedback and create additional ideas. Reflection in the journal should provide an insight into some of the reasoning behind student choices.

→ PROTOTYPE

At this stage of the design thinking process, students are asked to create a physical prototype of all or part of the designed process or device. It is the stage where students need to get their ideas out of their heads and presented in a way that engages other students and helps them to understand the concept. When students create, it helps them to think and solve problems and disagreements. Students can role-play, make a storyboard, sketches or simple models, or use sticky notes. The most important feature is that viewers can interact with the design.

The process could be filmed to show the learning behind the design thinking process in action.

ACTIVITY: TRANSFORM IDEAS INTO PROTOTYPES

1. Students review the ideas generated at the Ideate stage. Provide them with an A3 copy of **Generic reproducible 6 (In the frame)** so they can organise their ideas into two sections: least relevant and most relevant. Provide students with some question prompts to help support discussion of the ideas; for example:
   » Why do you think this idea could be used?
   » What parts could be improved?
   » What would need to be changed?
   » Why do you think this idea is not so relevant to the challenge?
2. Provide students with a range of materials to use to create their prototype. Remind students that a prototype should be created rapidly and is not meant to look 'nice'.
3. Ask students to see if their prototypes work as planned and if they play an effective part in protecting the rainforest habitat. Feedback could be given by writing one thing that worked well, and one thing that could be improved.
4. Students then use feedback to prototype again.

Ask students to fill in the Prototype part of **Learning journal template 4 (Prototype and test page)**. See the **Journal tip** for further student guidance.

PROMPTS

- What worked?
- How could it be improved?
- What else do you need to know, do or have?
- What other suggestions do you have?

TOP TIP!

Provide students with lots of materials – recycling depots can be a useful source of resources. Students may add labels to prototypes to explain some of the main features. Photographing and annotating pictures of prototypes can be useful.

When asking for feedback, students could ask each other some of the following questions:

- What is the main feature of your prototype?
- How does it work?
- Which parts work best? What will you keep?
- Which parts need changing? How might you do this?
- What other materials might you need?

MORE VOCABULARY

- feedback – information about, for example, a person's performance or the design of a product, which can be used to make improvements
- prototype – an initial version of a model of a product or process that is used to develop a final model

JOURNAL TIP

Remind students to highlight the main features of their prototype. If students are creating an electronic journal, they can insert a photo of their prototype and annotate it.

USEFUL APPS/LINKS

- App that can be used to create an interactive annotation of the prototype, such as ThingLink
- App for sharing ideas, such as Air Sketch

ASSESSMENT

Observe students as they make changes to their designs. Are they able to consider feedback, make modifications and move rapidly through this process, or do they have difficulties with holding on to an idea and accepting feedback?

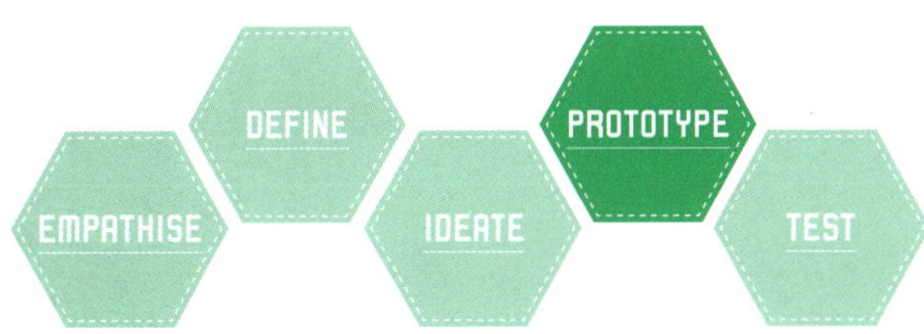

TEST

At this stage of the design thinking process, students test their prototype to see how it meets the criteria set at the start of the design process.

ACTIVITY: TEST FEEDBACK

1. Students take their last prototype and consider the original design challenge.
2. Invite local engineers and/or conservationists to view prototypes and designs, if possible. Have them offer feedback about what works well and what could be improved, and any suggestions they may have.
3. Ask students to consider feedback to determine if their invention works to protect the habitat. If not, what do they need to do to make it work?
4. Provide the opportunity to cycle through the Prototype and Test stages again.

Ask students to fill in **Learning journal template 4 (Prototype and test page)**. See the **Journal tip** for further student guidance.

PROMPTS

- Does your prototype and design do what you wanted it to do?
- Are there other features that need to be added?

MORE VOCABULARY

- evaluate – assess something, perhaps considering what worked and what didn't
- feature – specific aspect of something, such as size, shape, colour or quality
- feedback – information about, for example, a person's performance or the design of a product, which can be used to make improvements
- prototype – an initial version of a model of a product or process that is used to develop a final model
- review – consider an idea, process or product and assess what works and what needs to be changed

JOURNAL TIP

Ask students to think about why it is important to test their ideas before they build their final designs.

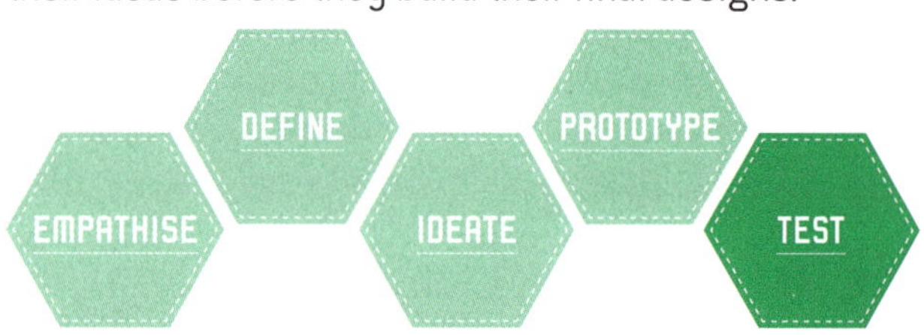

SHARE AND EVALUATE

At this stage of the investigation, students are provided with an opportunity to share their final design, as well as the processes involved in the investigation. Students evaluate their learning journals as well as their solutions.

ACTIVITY 1: BRING THE DESIGNS TOGETHER

1. Provide students with time to create their final designs.
2. Encourage them to film the process during prototyping and testing.
3. Students can create an iMovie or use Adobe Spark Video to demonstrate the process and thinking behind designs if technology is available. This audience for the presentation could be young people interested in engineering.
4. Students should include their learning journals with the display so others can see the different stages of the design process.

ACTIVITY 2: EVALUATE AND GIVE FEEDBACK

1. Provide students with **Generic reproducible 2 (Self-evaluation)** to complete.
2. Ask students to provide feedback to each other about the most interesting features, the aspects that were most difficult and the changes that they would make if they repeated the task.
3. Provide students with opportunities to share their designs with the wider community. This could include inviting the local engineers and conservationists back.

ASSESSMENT

Ask students to again complete **Generic reproducible 1 (Key vocabulary table)** using the key vocabulary for this unit. Compare their table with the one they completed at the Tune-in stage, to demonstrate changes in understanding.

Students complete **Generic reproducible 3 (Responding to the investigation)**. Compare their responses to their responses to **Generic reproducible 2**.

Teachers complete **Generic reproducible 5 (Design thinking assessment rubric)** for each student. Students compare the feedback they are given by the teacher with their self-assessment of how they used the design thinking process to solve problems (**Generic reproducible 3**).

TUNE IN

STEM INVESTIGATIONS

Name: ....

Date: ....

Habitat: ....

Question	**What I already know**	**New information I have found**	**Where I found the information**
Where is it?			
What species live within it?			
How is it being destroyed?			
What impact does this have on the species that live there?			
What are some other interesting facts?			

EMPATHISE

STEM INVESTIGATIONS

Name: ....

Date: ....

Record some key information about the rainforests in Sumatra and Borneo in the boxes.

What is happening?

Where is it happening?	Habitat threats	How long has it been happening?

Who is involved?	Why is it happening?

STEM Investigations, MP, ISBN 978 1 4202 4319 2 © Macmillan Science and Education Australia 2018

Name: ....

Date: ....

Identify threats to the habitats of the orangutans. Use the boxes to describe what this might look, feel, smell, taste and sound like for orangutans.

Threats to the habitat of the orangutans

Looks like ...

Feels like ...

Sounds like ...

Tastes like ...

Smells like ...

STEM Investigations, MP, ISBN 978 1 4202 4319 2 © Macmillan Science and Education Australia 2018

HELP PROTECT A RIVER FOR YEARS TO COME

SUSTAINABLE WORLD 16

→ INTRODUCTION

Both natural processes and human activity cause changes to the Earth's surface over time. Human activities, such as irrigation, can have major effects on the Earth's surface. Irrigation is what farmers do when they add water to their fields to help crops grow. Irrigation can cause reduced water flow and can increase the amount of salt in the water. Over time, farming and irrigation can cause riverbank erosion and increased water and soil salinity (salt in the water). This affects the plants and wildlife of a river area.

In this STEM investigation, students are asked to map a section of a river and design devices or processes to stop riverbank erosion, improve the soil quality and reduce water wastage on a farm so that less water needs to be taken from the river. They need to demonstrate their understanding of how human activities, such as irrigation, can have major effects on the Earth's surface.

This STEM challenge is easily differentiated for students by encouraging different groups to use different degrees of complexity when creating their solutions.

THE CHALLENGE

Your cousins live on a farm beside a major river. For 100 years, farms along the river have been taking water from it for their animals and crops. Over time, farming and irrigation have caused riverbank erosion and salty soil. This affects plants and wildlife.

Your challenge is to create a plan to protect the river. As a team, map a section of the river. Design devices or processes to stop erosion, improve soil quality or reduce the farm's water wastage. As part of your investigation, you will learn how the Earth's surface changes over time as a result of natural processes and human activity.

KEY UNDERSTANDINGS

- Human activities, such as irrigation, can have major effects on the Earth's surface.
- Irrigation can reduce water flow and increase salinity (salt in the water).
- Less water flow and more salinity can affect plants and wildlife.
- Loss of native plants on riverbanks can cause erosion.

KEY SKILLS

- Develop flexible thinking skills by considering research and feedback and being willing to change ideas, opinions and solutions.
- Make careful observations.
- Combine two or more different ideas to make something new – use synthesising skills.
- Work together to solve problems and design new devices and processes.

KEY VOCABULARY

catchment area – the area from which rainfall flows into a river or lake

erosion – movement of soil and weathered rock, usually by wind and water

irrigation – supply of water to land or crops

salinity – saltiness of a body of water or soil

KEY ACTIONS

- Find out about irrigation, riverbank erosion and salty soil, and the effects of farming on rivers.
- Explore ways of preventing riverbank erosion and reducing water wastage.
- Design processes or devices to help.

OVERVIEW OF STAGES

TUNE IN:

Students consider vocabulary and find definitions. They explore how the Earth's surface changes over time as a result of natural processes and human activity, and discuss farming practices and their impacts on water wastage, riverbank erosion and increased salinity.

EMPATHISE

Students find out about farming and irrigation and how it causes riverbank erosion and salinity, and the impact on plants and wildlife of the river area. Students consider the points of view of various affected groups, including farmers.

DEFINE

Students consider some issues with designing devices or processes to prevent riverbank erosion, improve soil quality or reduce water wastage. They consider the key components of the design challenge, including materials available and viable ways to test prototypes.

IDEATE

Students generate creative ideas for designing devices or processes to stop riverbank erosion, improve soil quality or reduce water wastage.

PROTOTYPE

Students transform some of their ideas into physical representations. These are created rapidly, using simple materials. Students can make storyboards, sketches or simple models, or use sticky notes.

TEST

Students share their prototypes and provide feedback to each other about their ideas and also check the relevance and usability of their designs. They are given the opportunity to cycle through the Prototype and Test stages again.

SHARE AND EVALUATE:

Final prototypes are shared and evaluated, with opportunities for feedback from local farmers and/or land conservationists.

SUGGESTED SCHEDULE

LESSON	STAGE
1–4	**Tune in**: Explore how the Earth's surface changes over time as a result of natural processes and human activity
5–7	**Empathise**: Find out how human activity affects a local river and catchment area and points of view of different people within the catchment; write in journal
8–9	**Define**: Consider different ways of designing processes to protect the river and catchment area; write in journal
10–11	**Ideate**: Generate creative ideas for designing devices or processes to stop riverbank erosion with consideration to reducing water wastage; write in journal
11–13	**Prototype** and **Test**: Conduct prototyping and testing cycles; write in journal
14–15	**Share and evaluate**: Share and evaluate designs and prototypes

CURRICULUM LINKS

SCIENCE

YEAR	STRAND	SUB-STRAND AND CONTENT
4	Science Understanding	Earth and space sciences: • Earth's surface changes over time as a result of natural processes and human activity
	Science as a Human Endeavour	Use and influence of science: • Science knowledge helps people to understand the effect of their actions

TECHNOLOGIES

YEAR	STRAND	CONTENT
4	Design and Technologies Processes and Production Skills	• Critique needs or opportunities for designing, and explore and test a variety of materials, components, tools and equipment and the techniques needed to produce designed solutions • Generate, develop and communicate design ideas and decisions for audiences using appropriate technical terms and graphical representation techniques • Evaluate design ideas, processes and solutions based on criteria for success developed with guidance and including care for the environment • Plan a sequence of production steps when making designed solutions individually and collaboratively*

* If students are making a model of their device or process.

MATHEMATICS

YEAR	STRAND	SUB-STRAND AND CONTENT
4	Measurement and Geometry	Location and transformation: • Use simple scales, legends and directions to interpret information contained in basic maps Using units of measurement: • Compare objects using familiar metric units of area and volume

This investigation also links to the General Capabilities:

AC

- Literacy
- Numeracy
- Information and Communication Technology (ICT) Capability
- Critical and Creative Thinking
- Ethical Understanding.

This investigation also links to the Cross-Curriculum Priority of Sustainability.

ASSESSMENT

The following resources are provided for assessing students at different stages of the STEM investigations:

- Generic reproducible 1 (Key vocabulary table), for assessing understanding of vocabulary
- Generic reproducible 2 (Self-evaluation), for student self-evaluation of the learning process
- Generic reproducible 3 (Responding to the investigation)
- Generic reproducible 5 (Design thinking assessment rubric), for evaluating student engagement in the design thinking stages
- Learning journal templates 1, 2, 3 and 4, incorporating student reflection and evaluation.

GETTING READY FOR THE INVESTIGATION

You can prepare yourself and students for this STEM investigation in the following ways:

- Identify groups of students who will work well together.
- Review the **Key science knowledge** that supports this investigation, and look at the **Useful apps** and **Useful links**.
- Start collecting useful materials for making models of a mapped river section and designing devices or processes to stop riverbank erosion (as shown in the **Materials needed** list).
- Determine where prototypes and models will be kept between lessons.
- Create a vocabulary wall.
- Create a wall space where students can share their ideas during the Ideate stage.
- Organise the class into pairs or small groups.
- Start thinking about:
  - » sourcing information about riverbank erosion
  - » how the devices or processes will be evaluated
  - » who will view the designs
  - » who will provide expert feedback about the designs (for example, a farmer to assess the practicality of the designs and processes), and whether it will be provided in person or digitally.

USEFUL APPS

- App for locating places and mapping, such as Google Earth or MapTrace
- App for exploring locations, such as ArcGIS
- App for drawing maps, such as Drawing Maps
- App for creating multimedia presentations, such as Adobe Spark Video (via a teacher-created class account) or iMovie

USEFUL LINKS

- Article for teachers about farming practices, water use and weathering and erosion, such as at mea.digital/sm133, mea.digital/sm134
- Article about soil erosion and how to prevent it, such as at mea.digital/sm135
- Information about causes of riverbank erosion, such as at mea.digital/sm136
- Information about salinity, such as at mea.digital/sm137
- Video clip about weathering and erosion, such as at mea.digital/sm138
- Online erosion game, such as at mea.digital/sm139
- Slideshow of erosion, such as at mea.digital/sm140
- Erosion experiment, such as at mea.digital/sm141
- Mapping activities, such as at mea.digital/sm142
- Mapping tools, such as at mea.digital/sm143

RESOURCES PROVIDED

- Generic reproducibles 1, 2, 3, 4, 5, 6
- Reproducibles 16.1, 16.2, 16.3
- Learning journal templates 1, 2, 3, 4

MATERIALS NEEDED

- Sticky notes
- Paper
- Cardboard
- Sticky tape
- Other building materials, such as recyclable packaging, boxes, tubes, plastic bottles
- Rubber bands
- Scissors

KEY SCIENCE KNOWLEDGE

This section provides an overview of the key science concepts and vocabulary needed for this unit.

WHAT IS IRRIGATION?

The supply of water to land or crops, such as through pipes, canals and sprinklers, is called **irrigation**. In places that do not have reliable rainfall, farming is either not possible or very difficult unless there is irrigation. Irrigation can help improve the quality and growth of crops. In some cases, farmers use their local river's water supply to irrigate their fields.

IRRIGATION AND SALINITY

Irrigation can cause environmental problems such as increased salt in the soil. The concentration of salt in soil is called **salinity**. It happens when large volumes of irrigation water cause the level of the local groundwater (that is, water held underground in the soil or in crevices of rock), and the salts in it, to rise. Irrigation salinity is worsened when the water used to irrigate crops is from a salty source. High levels of salts in soil can cause poor plant health, and native plant species can become dominated by salt-tolerant species. It also affects wildlife.

Irrigation is common in places where rainfall is unreliable.

Irrigation salinity can be controlled by using irrigation water efficiently. Crops should only be given the amount of water they can actually use. Reducing water usage in irrigated areas usually means changes to irrigation infrastructure and technology.

Gated channels can be used to control the supply of water for irrigation.

RIVERS AND EROSION

As salty water from **catchment areas** affected by irrigation flows into creeks and rivers, the concentration and volume of salt increase. Over time, as salinity increases, the quality of river water declines.

Erosion occurs when weathered rock and sediments are picked up and moved to another place by ice, water, wind or gravity. Weathering is the process where rock is dissolved, worked away or broken down into smaller pieces. Weathering can be caused by water, air, chemicals, plants and animals. Moving water can be a major cause of erosion of riverbanks. Riverbank erosion is increased in areas where native vegetation has been removed or lost – sometimes due to increased soil salinity.

KEY VOCABULARY

catchment area – the area from which rainfall flows into a river or lake
erosion – movement of soil and weathered rock, usually by wind and water
irrigation – supply of water to land or crops
salinity – saltiness of a body of water or soil

→ TUNE IN

1. Ask students to complete **Generic reproducible 1 (Key vocabulary table)** using the key vocabulary for this unit. This reproducible will also be used at the end of the unit to demonstrate changes in understanding.
2. Watch a video clip on weathering and erosion (see **Useful apps/links**). Students create mindmaps/infographics to record information.
3. Discuss what students observed and learned, and research erosion and farming practices that contribute to erosion.
4. Introduce the term 'irrigation' and ask students to share what their current understanding of irrigation is. Research irrigation and other farming practices and their contribution to erosion, water wastage and salinity.
5. Before engaging in the challenge, students need to have an understanding of how the Earth's surface changes over time as a result of natural processes and human activity, including farming.

ACTIVITY 1: WATER EROSION

1. Put a bucket of soil on a covered desk (outside if possible). Pick up a full watering can and ask students to predict what would happen if the water was steadily poured onto the soil pile.
2. Tell students they are going to perform an experiment that demonstrates how water has the power to shape land (see the erosion experiment in **Useful apps/links**). Set up a table with three different 'land' types (bare soil, soil with dead leaves on top, and soil with plants growing in it) and explain that you will pour water on the three types to see what happens. Students record the aim and their predictions on **Reproducible 16.1 (Water erosion experiment)**. Share predictions.
3. Perform the experiment. Students complete **Reproducible 16.1** and share conclusions about water erosion.
4. Students record new wonderings about water and erosion. Refer back to online articles and other information about erosion.
5. Research ways to prevent soil erosion and create infographics to record findings.

ACTIVITY 2: IRRIGATION AND ITS EFFECTS

1. Discuss key information about irrigation and why it is necessary in some places.
2. Group students into pairs and have them research irrigation, especially impacts on the environment. Students record information on paper.
3. Share and display findings.
4. Students suggest connections between erosion and irrigation and formulate ideas about the effect of human activities.
5. Explore efficient ways of preventing water wastage in small groups and share findings.

ACTIVITY 3: MAPPING

1. Students think–pair–share what they know of mapping. Discuss coordinates and compass points. Review scales, legends and directions.
2. Explore local areas on Google Earth. Have students explore different landforms.
3. Ask students where they may see erosion.
4. Experiment with mapping local areas on paper or online (see **Useful apps/links**).

6. Introduce the STEM investigation and challenge to the students. Provide them with the student card and read the information together.
7. Introduce the design thinking process by reviewing the stages on the student card. Explain that students will keep a journal about their learning at the different stages of the design.

USEFUL APPS/LINKS

- Apps for locating, exploring and mapping, such as Google Earth or MapTrace, Drawing Maps and ArcGIS
- Article about soil erosion and how to prevent it, such as at mea.digital/sm135
- Video clip about weathering and erosion, such as at mea.digital/sm138
- Online erosion game or experiment, such as at mea.digital/sm139, mea.digital/sm141
- Map activities/tools, such as at mea.digital/sm143

→ EMPATHISE

During the Empathise stage of the design thinking process, students focus on finding out about different points of view. To empathise with others, they need to research some of the challenges associated with farming practices and land conservation. This includes finding out about people's perspectives on irrigation, erosion and protecting rivers.

ACTIVITY 1: THE MURRAY-DARLING BASIN

1. View a video clip about the Murray-Darling basin and research farming practices that lead to water wastage and poor water quality (see **Useful apps/links**). Record information.
2. View a video clip that highlights different groups affected by changes to rivers (see **Useful apps/links**). Use **Reproducible 16.2 (Different points of view)** to identify the different opinions of different groups of people in any video clips you have watched, including the perspectives of Indigenous communities and farming communities.
3. Students discuss different perspectives and share ideas and thoughts. Have them think about who and what they need to consider when designing their devices or processes.

ACTIVITY 2: EFFECTS OF FARMING

1. If possible, students should go on an excursion to a local farm or area where erosion on a riverbank can be viewed and where they can discover more about soil quality and water wastage. They could also view irrigation practices on a local farm.
2. Students record observations on **Reproducible 16.3 (Effects of farming on rivers)**. If an excursion is not possible, get students to use the Murray-Darling issues in the video clips in Activity 1 to fill in the reproducible.

PROMPTS

- In what ways are rivers and their catchments important to different people?
- What are some of the words people used to describe the river?
- What were people concerned about?
- How were their different concerns related or connected?

MORE VOCABULARY

- empathise – understand and consider another person or group's point of view
- point of view – an opinion, attitude or judgement considered in a particular way

JOURNAL TIP

Ask students to complete **Learning journal template 1 (Empathise page)** while they are doing the different tasks. Remind them to date their notes and include photos of relevant information or pictures.

USEFUL APPS/LINKS

- App for recording ideas, such as Popplet
- Video about the Murray-Darling basin drying up, such as at mea.digital/sm144
- Video clip about the Murray-Darling basin that includes points of view of different groups, such as at mea.digital/sm145
- Article about river pollution, such as at mea.digital/sm146

ASSESSMENT

This stage of the design thinking process offers opportunities to observe students collecting information, developing questions, and recording their notes and thinking in their journal.

EMPATHISE DEFINE IDEATE PROTOTYPE TEST

DEFINE

The main focus of this stage of the design thinking process is to reframe the challenge. The initial challenge is quite open, so at this stage students learn how to define what needs to be done. This includes noting insights that have been generated.

ACTIVITY 1: CONSIDER OBSERVATIONS

1. Students consider the information they gathered in the Empathise stage. They may work in pairs or small groups. Provide them with a whiteboard, large sheet of paper and/or sticky notes to collate some of their key information. They should refer to their information on **Reproducible 16.2 (Different points of view)** and **Reproducible 16.3 (Effects of farming on rivers)** as well as other information recorded. Students should then transfer the main findings to **Learning journal template 2 (Define page)**.
2. Students should discuss one section of **Learning journal template 2** at a time, write their responses and then continue discussing their ideas for the next section, until the task is complete. This provides students with opportunities to hear others' responses and it provides the teacher with input points.
3. Discuss the terms 'device' and 'process' so students understand the options available for the solutions they may come up with.
4. Provide students with the opportunity to research further. Ask them to write other information they would like to know. Provide them with **Generic reproducible 4 (Key question table)** to assist them to record their questions, findings and sources.

PROMPTS

- What did you discover?
- What were the most important pieces of information that you gathered?
- What was something new that you learned?
- What other information do you need?

ACTIVITY 2: CONSIDER INSIGHTS

Students should think of at least one insight they have gained from the process; for example, rivers are important to different groups of people for different reasons. Students should add this insight to **Learning journal template 2**. They should then explain how this will affect the design of their device or process.

When considering insights, students could think about the following:

1. What was something unexpected that you saw or found out? How was it unexpected?
2. How will you decide on the most important aspect of your device or process?
3. Is there any other information that you need or would like to know? How will you find out?

ACTIVITY 3: CONSIDER CONSTRAINTS

At this stage, let students know the constraints of the challenge by describing the types of materials that will be available and how students will test their devices or processes.

MORE VOCABULARY

- define – state the meaning of something
- insight – an accurate understanding of someone or something
- point of view – an opinion, attitude or judgement considered in a particular way

JOURNAL TIP

Discuss the term 'insight' and explain that it relates to something students have learned about the people and their responses to the surveys as well as information gathered through research or excursions. You could refer to **Learning journal template 2**.

USEFUL APPS/LINKS

- App for creating and organising ideas, such as Popplet, Inspiration, Padlet or Ideament

EMPATHISE DEFINE IDEATE PROTOTYPE TEST

→ IDEATE

The Ideate stage of the design thinking process is all about generating lots of ideas. Students need to be flexible in their thinking and be able to move beyond obvious ideas. At this stage, ideas are not judged, just generated and gathered.

ACTIVITY: GENERATE IDEAS

1. Ask groups of students to draw or write their ideas for a device or process.
2. Each new idea should be drawn or written on a separate piece of paper or sticky note.
3. Ask students to group ideas on a wall or board.
4. Ask students to look at the different ideas and provide feedback to each other. It is important that students don't defend their ideas at this stage. They should just be listening to the feedback.
5. After the initial feedback, ask students to come up with more ideas. Encourage them to be creative and even radical.
6. Ask students to choose three of their ideas to write in their journal. Students use **Learning journal template 3 (Ideate page)** to do this. Ask students to choose one idea to explore further and explain the reasoning behind their choice.

TOP TIP!

At this stage, students may have produced a series of drawings that are annotated. They may have a collection of sticky notes, which they can organise into related ideas.

Encourage students to view and read others' ideas before giving feedback. Feedback could be within small groups or between partners. Considering others' ideas is an important part of this process, so students can build on their own ideas as they continue to ideate.

At each stage of this activity, ask students to discuss their thoughts before writing their responses. This will help them think through their ideas and select their final ideas to develop.

PROMPTS

- How do your chosen ideas relate to riverbank erosion and water wastage?
- How might you test your device or process for preventing riverbank erosion and water wastage?
- How can you make it something that benefits all users of the river?
- What if you had different materials to use?

MORE VOCABULARY

- feedback – information about, for example, a person's performance or the design of a product, which can be used to make improvements
- ideate – generate many ideas without making judgements about the ideas

JOURNAL TIP

When choosing three ideas to include in the journal, try to choose three ideas that aren't related.

USEFUL APPS/LINKS

- Tools for creating ideas, such as at mea.digital/sm147
- Tips to achieve creativity and innovation, such as at mea.digital/sm148

ASSESSMENT

At the Ideate stage, assessment could include observations about the number and diversity of student ideas, and their ability to provide feedback and create additional ideas. Reflection in the journal should provide an insight into some of the reasoning behind student choices.

EMPATHISE · DEFINE · **IDEATE** · PROTOTYPE · TEST

PROTOTYPE

At this stage of the design thinking process, students are asked to create a physical prototype of all or part of the designed process or device. It is the stage where students need to get their ideas out of their heads and presented in a way that engages other students and helps them to understand the concept. When students create, it helps them to think and solve problems and disagreements. Students can role-play, make a storyboard, sketches or simple models, or use sticky notes. The most important feature is that viewers can interact with the design.

The process could be filmed to show the learning behind the design thinking process in action.

ACTIVITY: TRANSFORM IDEAS INTO PROTOTYPES

1. Students review the ideas generated at the Ideate stage. Provide them with an A3 copy of **Generic reproducible 6 (In the frame)** so they can organise their ideas into two sections: least relevant and most relevant. Provide students with some question prompts to help support discussion of the ideas; for example:
   - Why do you think this idea could be used?
   - What parts of this idea could be developed?
   - What would need to be changed for this idea to be used?
   - Why do you think this idea is not so relevant to the challenge?
2. Provide students with a range of materials to use to create their prototype. Remind students that a prototype should be created rapidly and is not meant to look 'nice'.
3. After prototypes have been created, ask students to see if theirs work in the way they had planned and if they could be effective. Get feedback from others.
4. Students use feedback to prototype again.

Ask students to fill in the Prototype part of **Learning journal template 4 (Prototype and test page)**. See the **Journal tip** for further student guidance.

PROMPTS

- What worked?
- How could it be improved?
- What else do you need to know, do or have?
- What other suggestions do you have?
- Does your prototype consider the needs of different members of the community and care for landforms and wildlife?

TOP TIP! Students may add labels to prototypes to explain some of the main features. Photographing and annotating pictures of prototypes can be useful.

When asking for feedback, students could ask each other some of the following questions:

- What is the main feature of your prototype?
- How does it work?
- Which parts work best? What will you keep?
- Which parts need changing? How might you do this?
- What other materials might you need?

MORE VOCABULARY

- feedback – information about, for example, a person's performance or the design of a product, which can be used to make improvements
- prototype – an initial version of a model of a product or process that is used to develop a final model

JOURNAL TIP

Remind students to highlight the main features of their prototype. If students are creating an electronic journal, they can insert a photo of their prototype and annotate it.

ASSESSMENT

Observe students as they make changes to their designs. Are they able to consider feedback, make modifications and move rapidly through this process, or do they have difficulties with holding on to an idea and accepting feedback?

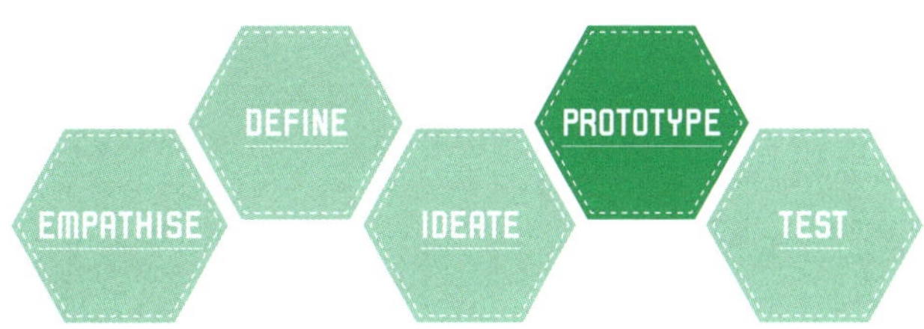

→ TEST

At this stage of the design thinking process, students test their prototype to see how it meets the criteria set at the start of the design process.

ACTIVITY: TEST FEEDBACK

1. Students take their last prototype and consider the original design challenge.
2. Ask students to check whether or not their design works. If not, what do they need to do to make it work?
3. Provide the opportunity to cycle through the Prototype and Test stages again.

Ask students to fill in **Learning journal template 4 (Prototype and test page)**. See the **Journal tip** for further student guidance.

PROMPTS

- Does your prototype do what you wanted it to do?
- Are there other features that need to be added?

MORE VOCABULARY

- evaluate – assess something, perhaps considering what worked and what didn't
- feature – specific aspect of something, such as size, shape, colour or quality
- feedback – information about, for example, a person's performance or the design of a product, which can be used to make improvements
- prototype – an initial version of a model of a product or process that is used to develop a final model
- review – consider an idea, process or product and assess what works and what needs to be changed

JOURNAL TIP

Ask students to think about why it is important to test their ideas before they build their final design.

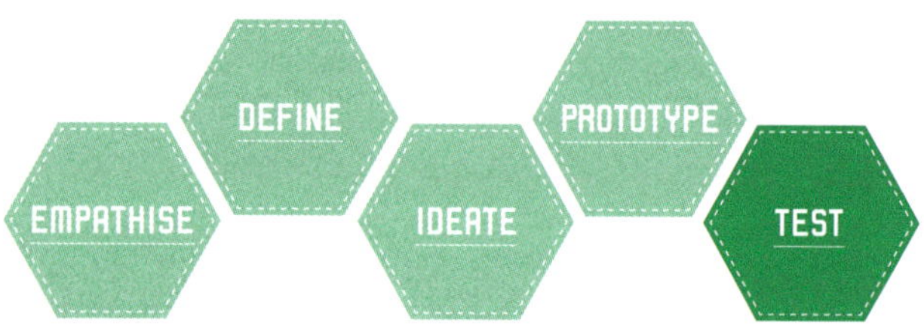

→ SHARE AND EVALUATE

At this stage of the investigation, students are provided with an opportunity to share their final design, as well as the processes involved in the investigation. Students evaluate their learning journals as well as their solutions.

ACTIVITY 1: BRING THE DESIGNS TOGETHER

1. Provide students with time to create their final designs.
2. Encourage them to film the process during prototyping and testing.
3. Students can create an iMovie or use Adobe Spark Video to demonstrate the process and thinking behind designs if possible.
4. Students should include their learning journals with the display so others can see the different stages of the design process.

ACTIVITY 2: EVALUATE AND GIVE FEEDBACK

1. Provide students with **Generic reproducible 2 (Self-evaluation)** to complete.
2. Ask students to provide feedback to each other about the most interesting features, the aspects that were most difficult and the changes that they would make if they repeated the task.
3. Provide students with opportunities to share designs with the wider community, such as local farmers/growers and land conservationists.

ASSESSMENT

Ask students to again complete **Generic reproducible 1 (Key vocabulary table)** using the key vocabulary for this unit. Compare their table with the one they completed at the Tune-in stage, to demonstrate changes in understanding.

Students complete **Generic reproducible 3 (Responding to the investigation)**. Compare their responses to their responses to **Generic reproducible 2**.

Teachers complete **Generic reproducible 5 (Design thinking assessment rubric)** for each student. Students compare the feedback they are given by the teacher with their self-assessment of how they used the design thinking process to solve problems **(Generic reproducible 3)**.

TUNE IN

STEM INVESTIGATIONS

Name: ....

Date: ....

Aim	Hypothesis/prediction

Materials	Method

Result	Labelled diagram
Conclusion	

STEM Investigations, MP, ISBN 978 1 4202 4319 2

EMPATHISE

STEM INVESTIGATIONS

Name: ....

Date: ....

Record information that helps you understand the points of view of different groups of people within the river catchment area.

Name of the river and catchment area: Location:
Name and describe the groups of people mentioned in the video clips.
What are their main concerns about the river?
What do they think could help protect the river and the catchment area?
Why do you think the river and its catchment area are important to each of the groups of people living and working there?

STEM Investigations, MP, ISBN 978 1 4202 4319 2 © Macmillan Science and Education Australia 2018

EMPATHISE

STEM INVESTIGATIONS

Name: ....

Date: ....

Use these questions to help you record relevant information.

As you use this sheet, keep this big question in your mind:

How does farming affect the river and its catchment area?

What did you first think when you saw this area or situation? (Think about erosion, soil and water wastage.)

....

....

....

What issues and concerns did people have?

....

....

....

What are people doing to help solve some of the problems?

....

....

....

Are these things working?

....

....

....

Use extra paper to note any other questions you think of, and any other important information and illustrations.

GIVE NEW LIFE TO OLD CLOTHES!

WHO WE ARE 17

INTRODUCTION

The production of cheap clothing with a limited life span has encouraged 'fast fashion': buying more clothes and throwing them away after a short time. The amount of clothing that is reused is increasing, but most unwanted clothing still ends up as landfill. This landfill has an impact on the environment, because some dyes contaminate soil and groundwater. Fast fashion also has a human toll, with large numbers of people making clothes for meagre wages and in poor conditions.

In this STEM investigation, students will learn about issues relating to fast fashion. They are challenged to consider different uses for everyday items of clothing, beyond their intended use. They explore the properties of clothing materials. They also create an awareness campaign to highlight some of the issues associated with fast fashion.

THE CHALLENGE

Each season, new fashions arrive in clothing stores. Many of the cheaper items are bought and then worn only a few times. This is sometimes called 'fast fashion'. Some people donate their clothes or sell them. But many clothes still end up in landfill.

Your challenge is to think of other uses for clothing and encourage people in your community to reduce their clothing waste. Choose an item of clothing such as a T-shirt and think of different ways to reuse it. As part of this investigation, you will learn about the different properties of materials and about sustainability.

KEY UNDERSTANDINGS

- Different materials have different properties.
- Some properties of materials are flexibility and strength.
- Clothing can be made from natural and processed materials.
- The properties of some materials can lead to waste.

KEY VOCABULARY

biodegradable – able to be broken down into very small parts by bacteria in soil

fibre – a natural or synthetic thread that may be made into products such as fabric

property – a feature of a material, such as strength or ability to change shape

synthetic – made by humans

KEY SKILLS

- Make careful observations.
- Describe the properties of different materials.
- Analyse information.
- Compare and contrast the properties of different materials.
- Transform an idea into something that can be seen, using measurement skills and knowledge of different shapes.

KEY ACTIONS

- Find out about clothing waste.
- Explore the properties of clothing materials, and explore two- and three-dimensional shapes.
- Create new uses for an item of clothing.
- Create an awareness campaign.

OVERVIEW OF STAGES

TUNE IN:

Students learn about the rise of fast fashion and the reasons that people like to buy new clothes. They find out about the impact of fast fashion on society and the environment. Students learn about the different properties of materials, and explore two- and three-dimensional shapes.

EMPATHISE

Students find out about the clothing habits of different people using surveys and interviews.

DEFINE

Students consider the different types of clothing that are typically worn and the materials they are made from. They consider the key components of the design challenge, including clothing type, the properties of materials being used and repurposing options.

IDEATE

Student generate ideas for the repurposing of an item of clothing such as a T-shirt or jeans.

PROTOTYPE

Students choose one or two ideas to transform into detailed sketches or models.

TEST

Students seek feedback about their ideas and check the strength and usability of their designs.

SHARE AND EVALUATE:

Final prototypes are shared and evaluated, with opportunities for expert feedback investigated. Students create a fast fashion awareness campaign using their repurposed clothing products to promote reuse and to reduce the negative impact of fast fashion.

SUGGESTED SCHEDULE

LESSON	STAGE
1–3	**Tune in**: Learn about fast fashion; explore properties of clothing materials; introduce the student challenge
4–7	**Empathise**: Learn about the clothing habits of different people; find out about attitudes to reusing and recycling clothing, fast fashion and its environmental and economic impacts; collate information; write in journal
8–9	**Define**: Define the main issues; write in journal
10–11	**Ideate**: Develop ideas about different ways to recycle clothing; write in journal
12–15	**Prototype** and **Test**: Conduct prototyping and testing cycles; write in journal
16–18	**Share and evaluate**: Share and evaluate designs and prototypes; create an awareness campaign

→ CURRICULUM LINKS

SCIENCE

YEAR	STRAND	SUB-STRAND AND CONTENT
4	Science Understanding	Chemical sciences: • Natural and processed materials have a range of physical properties; these properties can influence their use
3 & 4	Science as a Human Endeavour	Use and influence of science: • Science knowledge helps people to understand the effect of their actions

TECHNOLOGIES

YEAR	STRAND	CONTENT
3 & 4	Design and Technologies Knowledge and Understanding	• Recognise the role of people in design and technologies occupations and explore factors, including sustainability, that impact on the design of solutions to meet community needs • Investigate how forces and the properties of materials affect the behaviour of a product or system • Investigate the suitability of materials, systems, components, tools and equipment for a range of purposes
	Design and Technologies Processes and Production Skills	• Critique needs or opportunities for designing and explore and test a variety of materials, components, tools and equipment and the techniques needed to create designed solutions • Generate, develop, and communicate design ideas and decisions using appropriate technical terms and graphical representation techniques • Select and use materials, components, tools and equipment using safe work practices to produce designed solutions • Evaluate design ideas, processes and solutions based on criteria for success developed with guidance and including care for the environment and communities • Plan a sequence of production steps when making designed solutions

MATHEMATICS

YEAR	STRAND	SUB-STRAND AND CONTENT
4	Measurement and Geometry	Using units of measurement: • Measure, order and compare objects using familiar metric units of length, mass and capacity Shape: • Compare the areas of regular and irregular shapes by informal means
	Statistics and Probability	Data representation and interpretation: • Construct suitable data displays, with and without the use of digital technologies, from given or collected data. Include tables, column graphs and picture graphs where one picture can represent many data values

This investigation also links to the General Capabilities:

- Literacy
- Numeracy
- Information and Communication Technology (ICT) Capability
- Critical and Creative Thinking

This investigation links to the Cross-Curriculum Priority of Sustainability.

→ ASSESSMENT

The following resources are provided for assessing students at different stages of the STEM investigations:

- Generic reproducible 1 (Key vocabulary table), for assessing understanding of vocabulary
- Generic reproducible 2 (Self-evaluation), for student self-evaluation of the learning process
- Generic reproducible 3 (Responding to the investigation)
- Generic reproducible 5 (Design thinking assessment rubric), for evaluating student engagement in the design thinking stages
- Learning journal templates 1, 2, 3 and 4, incorporating student reflection and evaluation.

→ GETTING READY FOR THE INVESTIGATION

You can prepare yourself and students for this STEM investigation in the following ways:

- Identify groups of students who will work well together. Organise the class into pairs.
- Review the **Key science knowledge** that supports this investigation, and look at the **Useful links**.
- Investigate the **Useful software**.
- Gather materials for the exploration of different fabrics during the Tune-in session.
- Start collecting additional materials for prototyping (as shown on the **Materials needed** list).
- Determine where prototypes will be kept between lessons.
- Create a wall space where students can share their ideas in the Ideate stage.
- Source sewing machines and/or needles and thread. Find volunteers to assist with basic sewing skills.
- Start thinking about:
  - » sourcing information on impacts of fast fashion
  - » inviting someone to speak about clothing waste and ways of reusing clothing
  - » making connections with clothing manufacturers, retailers and recyclers
  - » time constraints for the task
  - » gathering a panel of advisors or mentors to assist students with modifying their designs
  - » how, when and where the designs will be shared and evaluated
  - » the types of awareness campaigns that students could read about and use.

USEFUL APPS

- App for creating semantic maps (links between different words and/or concepts), such as Popplet or Kidspiration
- App for creating interactive links (for example, between descriptions, videos, images and websites and a main image), such as ThingLink
- App for surveys, such as SurveyMonkey or Typeform
- App for creating multimedia presentations, such as Adobe Spark Video (via a teacher-created class account), Prezi or iMovie
- App for drawing shapes, inserting images and making annotations, such as DrawIsland
- App for sharing ideas, thoughts, questions and images, such as Padlet or Lino
- App for engaging in collaborative tasks, such as OneNote Class Notebook
- App for creating drawings, such as SketchUp

USEFUL LINKS

- Statistics about the garment industry, such as at mea.digital/sm25
- Facts about clothes consumption, such as at mea.digital/sm26
- Physical properties and characteristics of fabrics, such as at mea.digital/sm27
- Environmental impact of the clothing industry, such as at mea.digital/sm28
- Fast fashion video clip, such as at mea.digital/sm29
- Images or videos of repurposing clothes, such as at mea.digital/sm30, mea.digital/sm31
- Shape exploration tool, such as at mea.digital/sm32
- Resources for promoting creativity, such as at mea.digital/sm33

RESOURCES PROVIDED

- Generic reproducibles 1, 2, 3, 4, 5, 6
- Reproducibles 17.1, 17.2, 17.3
- Learning journal templates 1, 2, 3, 4

MATERIALS NEEDED

- Sticky notes (half a pad per pair)
- Paper
- Coloured card
- Pens and markers
- Sticky tape
- Multiple small samples of different natural and synthetic fabrics, such as cotton, denim, nylon, felt, fleece
- Needles, thread and/or sewing machine(s)
- Measuring tape
- Hot glue guns and glue
- Scissors
- String
- Ribbon
- Weights
- Cardboard and paper containers (for disassembling)
- Rulers

Hot glue guns can be dangerous. Make sure students are supervised at all times.

KEY SCIENCE KNOWLEDGE

This section provides an overview of the key science concepts and vocabulary needed for this unit.

TYPES OF CLOTHING MATERIALS

Clothing can be made from natural or **synthetic** materials. Examples of natural materials are cotton, wool, silk, leather, down (fine feathers) and bamboo. Polyester, nylon and spandex are some examples of synthetic materials. Some synthetic materials may have natural materials that are **biodegradable** but most synthetic materials are not biodegradable.

Some clothing materials are made from a type of recycled plastic. The plastic is melted, made into **fibre** and then woven into fabrics.

PROPERTIES OF CLOTHING MATERIALS

Physical **properties** of clothing fibres include type, size and length. Texture depends on how these fibres are combined (such as in weaving and knitting). Buyers want clothes to look good and feel comfortable, so colour, texture, weight and light permeability are important properties. Some clothes need to be durable, so manufacturers consider factors such as abrasive strength (tested by rubbing), bursting strength and tearing strength. Lastly, the quality of a material needs to be compared with the cost of creating it.

IMPACTS OF FAST FASHION

Mass clothing production has a social impact – millions of workers in clothing factories are paid below a living wage, work long hours, and many are under working age. The production of synthetic fibres usually uses a lot of energy and can generate hazardous waste. Even natural fibres have an impact; for example, the production of cotton includes considerable use of pesticides. When clothes are discarded in landfill, some of the dyes contaminate the soil and groundwater. Materials such as polyester can take up to 200 years to break down.

In response to the rise of fast fashion, some people are choosing to repurpose clothes, rather than throw them away after a few uses.

Children's clothing is often made of durable materials such as cotton.

Growing the cotton

A lot of water is used to grow cotton, and harmful chemicals are often used.

Making the fabric

Spinning and weaving cotton uses energy. Most electrical energy is generated using fossil fuels.Chemicals used in factories can pollute the environment.

Manufacturing the T-shirt

Sewing machines in clothing factories use energy.

Packaging the T-shirt

Packaging uses up natural resources and may use non-renewable materials.

Transporting the T-shirt to the store

Planes and trucks burn fossil fuels.

Cleaning the T-shirt

Washing clothes uses energy and water, and detergents can cause water pollution.

KEY VOCABULARY

biodegradable – able to be broken down into very small parts by bacteria in soil

fibre – a natural or synthetic thread that may be made into products such as fabric

property – a feature of a material, such as strength or ability to change shape

synthetic – made by humans

→ TUNE IN

1. Ask students to complete **Generic reproducible 1 (Key vocabulary table)** using the key vocabulary for this unit. This reproducible will also be used at the end of the unit, to demonstrate changes in understanding.
2. Throughout the investigation, quiz students about the important terms they are using. This could be through a quick chat or an online tool (see **Useful apps/links**).
3. Introduce the general challenge. Ask students to estimate the number of clothes items they have and to do a rough count at home. Were they surprised? Did they find any clothes that they don't wear very much? What do they do with clothes they no longer wear?
4. Watch a video clip about fast fashion (see **Useful apps/links**). Ask:
   » What did people do in the past when their clothes started to become worn out?
   » Why do you think people like new clothes?
   » What was something new or surprising that you learned?
   » Were you aware of the working and living conditions of people in some clothing factories?
   » What other information would you like to find out? How would you go about doing this?
5. Set up the following activities or similar for students to explore the properties of clothing materials as well as different shapes that can be made.

ACTIVITY 1: DIFFERENT TYPES OF MATERIALS

1. Discuss the terms 'natural' and 'synthetic'.
2. Provide students with a range of materials.
3. Students sort and categorise materials as natural or synthetic.
4. Have pairs of students explore the properties of one material. Provide them with **Reproducible 17.1 (Material properties)**. Ask students to find out its origin, how it is processed, common uses and properties. Create a class display for students to refer to during the investigation.

ACTIVITY 2: STRENGTHS OF MATERIALS

1. Provide groups of students with a range of materials. Have them design a way to test strength, for example, how many weights a fabric can hold before tearing.
2. Highlight the importance of a fair test (making sure that each material is tested under the same conditions).
3. Have students make predictions before creating a table to record their observations. Repeat the tests for greater reliability.

ACTIVITY 3: SHAPES EXPLORATION

1. Have students explore different two- and three-dimensional shapes, considering their potential for making new products.
2. Begin with a shape exploration activity (see **Useful apps/links**). Have students explore the ways that shapes can be connected and new shapes can be made.
3. Explore three-dimensional shapes by disassembling old paper or cardboard containers, and create nets for each shape.

6. Introduce the STEM investigation and challenge to the students. Provide them with the student card and read the information together.
7. Introduce the design thinking process by reviewing the stages on the student card. Explain that students will keep a journal about their learning at the different stages of the design.

TOP TIP! Try to make time to teach students some basic sewing skills. It may be useful to have some helpers during this activity, or to run small workshops.

USEFUL APPS/LINKS

- App for quizzing, such as Kahoot or Nearpod
- Video clip about fast fashion, such as at mea.digital/sm29
- Shape exploration activity, such as at mea.digital/sm32

→ EMPATHISE

During the Empathise stage of the design thinking process, students focus on finding out about different points of view. To empathise with others, they need to research some of the challenges associated with fast fashion. This includes finding out about people's shopping habits, and attitudes to recycling and new clothes. Students will take notes, ask questions, draw diagrams and take photos where relevant.

ACTIVITY 1: CLOTHING HABITS SURVEY

1. Students find out about the clothing habits of other people using a survey. Have students consider the types of information they would like to collect.
2. If using technology, demonstrate how to use a survey tool such as Typeform or SurveyMonkey. A class account may need to be set up due to the age of the students. The school learning management system may have an internal survey tool that could be accessed. If using a paper survey, provide students with examples of how to set out information.
3. After the survey has been created, have students survey as many different people as possible within a given timeframe. When the survey has been completed, ask students to create a spreadsheet, tables and/or graphs to present the information. Have students look for interesting information and patterns. Compare the information c ollected from different surveys.

ACTIVITY 2: CLOTHING HABITS INTERVIEW

1. Have students interview one person for a more in-depth insight into their clothing habits. Provide them with **Reproducible 17.2 (Clothing habits interview)** to record their information.
2. Ask students to consider the information they have collected and determine the most important insights they have found out.

PROMPTS

- What are the different amounts of clothing people owned?
- What are some of the attitudes people have to buying used clothes?
- What are some of the reasons for buying new clothes?
- What was one interesting thing you found out?

MORE VOCABULARY

- empathise – understand and consider another person or group's point of view
- point of view – an opinion, attitude or judgement considered in a particular way

JOURNAL TIP

- Ask students to complete **Learning journal template 1 (Empathise page)** while they are doing the different tasks. Remind them to date their notes and include photos of relevant information or pictures.

USEFUL APPS/LINKS

- App for creating surveys, such as Survey Monkey or Typeform
- App for making spreadsheets, graphs and tables, such as Excel or Numbers

ASSESSMENT

This stage of the design thinking process offers opportunities to observe students collecting information, developing questions, and recording their notes and thinking in their journal.

TOP TIP! When creating the interview questions, write the information students want to find out. Then model how to create different types of questions to find out this information. Discuss the difference between open and closed questions. Provide examples of different types of answers, such as yes/no and multiple choice.

EMPATHISE · DEFINE · IDEATE · PROTOTYPE · TEST

DEFINE

The main focus of this stage of the design thinking process is to reframe the challenge. The initial challenge is quite open, so at this stage students learn how to define what needs to be done. This includes noting insights that have been generated.

ACTIVITY 1: CONSIDER OBSERVATIONS

1. Students consider the information they gathered in the Empathise stage. They may work in pairs or small groups. Provide them with a whiteboard, large sheet of paper and/or sticky notes to collate key information. Ask them to consider some issues with the types of clothes that are discarded as well as the materials these clothes are made from.
2. Students should discuss one section of **Learning journal template 2 (Define page)** at a time, write their responses, then continue discussing their ideas for the next section, until the task is complete. This allows students to hear others' responses and provides the teacher with input points.
3. Discuss how the students will be repurposing an item of clothing – finding a new use for it.
4. Display a video clip that shows how clothing can be repurposed (see **Useful apps/links**).
5. Consider and list some of the clothing that people typically wear, such as jeans, shirts and socks.
6. Allow students to research further about fast fashion. Ask them to write other information they would like to know, such as how clothing can be reused, and issues with producing cheap clothing.
7. Provide students with **Generic reproducible 4 (Key question table)** to assist them to record their questions, findings and sources.

ACTIVITY 2: CONSIDER INSIGHTS

1. Students think of at least one insight they have gained so far; for example, material can be knotted to add strength.
2. Students add this to **Learning journal template 2** and then explain what needs to be created.
3. When considering insights, students could consider the following:
   » What was something unexpected that you saw or found out?
   » How was it unexpected?
   » How will you decide which item of clothing to repurpose?
   » Is there any other information that you need or would like to know? How will you find out?

ACTIVITY 3: CONSIDER CONSTRAINTS

At this stage, let students know the constraints of the challenge, by describing the timeframe, available materials, how and when designs will be shared, and whether or not products will be created or just designed. Provide students with **Reproducible 17.3 (Repurposing project planner)** for recording specifications.

PROMPTS

- What did you discover?
- What were the most important pieces of information that you gathered?
- What was something new that you learned?
- What other information do you need?

MORE VOCABULARY

- define – state the meaning of something
- insight – an accurate understanding of someone or something
- point of view – an opinion, attitude or judgement considered in a particular way

JOURNAL TIP

Discuss the term 'insight' and explain that it relates to something students have learned about the people and their responses to the surveys as well as information gathered through research or excursions. You could refer to **Learning journal template 2**.

USEFUL APPS/LINKS

- How to turn a T-shirt into a bag, such as at mea.digital/sm31

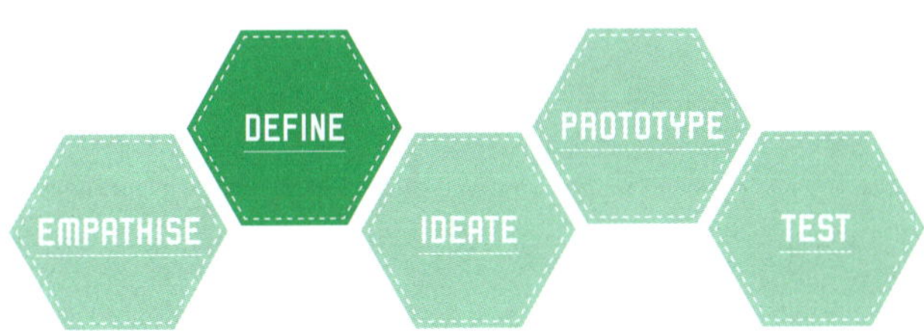

→ IDEATE

The Ideate stage of the design thinking process is all about generating lots of ideas. Students need to be flexible in their thinking and be able to move beyond obvious ideas. At this stage, ideas are not judged, just generated and gathered.

ACTIVITY: GENERATE IDEAS

1. Review some of the important vocabulary relating to the investigation. Write some of the key properties of materials onto coloured card and have students randomly choose a word to explain to their partner.
2. Ask groups of students to draw or write their ideas. Each new idea should be on a separate piece of paper or sticky note.
3. Ask students to group ideas on a wall or board.
4. Ask students to look at the different ideas and provide feedback to each other. It is important that students don't defend their ideas at this stage. They should just be listening to the feedback.
5. After the initial feedback, ask students to come up with more ideas. Encourage them to be creative and even radical.
6. Ask students to choose three of their ideas to write down in their journal. Students use **Learning journal template 3 (Ideate page)** to do this. Ask students to choose one idea to explore further and explain the reasoning behind their choice.

TOP TIP!

At this stage, students may have produced a series of drawings, showing some of the ways that clothing can be turned into another useful item. These drawings should be annotated with information about purpose, materials, colour and so on. They may have a collection of sticky notes, which they can organise into related ideas. Encourage students to view and read others' ideas before giving feedback. Feedback could be within small groups or between partners. Considering others' ideas is an important part of this process, so students can build on their own ideas as they continue to ideate.

At each stage of this activity, ask students to discuss their thoughts before writing their responses. This will help them to think through their ideas and select their final ideas to develop.

PROMPTS

- How do these ideas relate to creating a new purpose for the clothing you have selected?
- How might you test your design?
- How can you make it more useful?
- How can you change your design into something completely different?
- What if you had to use different materials?

MORE VOCABULARY

- feedback – information about, for example, a person's performance or the design of a product, which can be used to make improvements
- ideate – generate many ideas without making judgements about the ideas

JOURNAL TIP

When choosing three ideas to include in the journal, try to choose three ideas that aren't related. Remind students to think about ideas for their awareness campaign, too.

USEFUL APPS/LINKS

- Tools for creating ideas, such as at mea.digital/sm49
- Tips to achieve creativity and innovation, such as at mea.digital/sm99
- Resources for promoting creativity, such as at mea.digital/sm239

ASSESSMENT

At the Ideate stage, assessment could include observations about the number and diversity of student ideas, and their ability to provide feedback and create additional ideas. Reflection in the journal should provide an insight into some of the reasoning behind student choices.

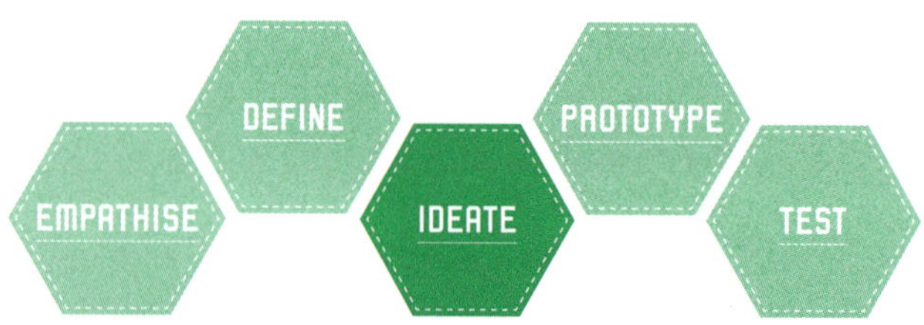

→ PROTOTYPE

At this stage, students are asked to create a physical prototype of a solution. Students need to get their ideas out of their heads and present them in a way that engages other students and helps them to understand the concept. When students create, it helps them to think and solve problems and disagreements. Students can role-play, make a storyboard or use sticky notes when they prototype. The most important feature is that viewers can interact with whatever is produced.

Encourage students to photograph or film during the Prototype and Test stages. This information can be used to show the learning behind the design thinking process in action.

ACTIVITY: TRANSFORM IDEAS INTO PROTOTYPES

1. Students review the ideas generated at the Ideate stage. Provide them with an A3 copy of **Generic reproducible 6 (In the frame)** so they can organise their ideas into two sections: least relevant and most relevant. Provide students with question prompts to support discussion of the ideas; for example:
   - » Why do you think this idea could be used?
   - » What would need to be changed for this idea to be used?
   - » Why do you think this idea is not so relevant to the challenge?

   Students continue until they have an idea to start prototyping.
2. Provide students with a range of materials to use to create their prototype. Remind students that a prototype should be created rapidly and it is not meant to look 'nice'.
3. After a prototype has been created, ask students to see if it works and get feedback from others.
4. Students then use the feedback to prototype again.

Ask students to fill in the Prototype part of **Learning journal template 4 (Prototype and test page)**. See the Journal tip for further student guidance.

PROMPTS

- What worked?
- How could it be improved?
- What else do you need to know, do or have?
- What other suggestions do you have?

TOP TIP!

The Prototype stage is often very messy. It is important that students are focusing on their ideas, rather than the end product. Provide them with lots of materials – recycling depots can be a useful source of resources. Student may add labels to prototypes to explain some of the main features. Photographing and annotating pictures of prototypes can be useful.

When giving feedback, students could ask:

- What is the main feature of your prototype?
- How does it work?
- Which parts work best? What will you keep?
- Which parts need changing?
- What other materials might you need?

MORE VOCABULARY

- feedback – information about, for example, a person's performance or the design of a product, which can be used to make improvements
- prototype – an initial version of a model of a product or process that is used to develop a final model

JOURNAL TIP

Remind students to highlight the main features of their prototype. If students are creating an electronic journal, they can insert a photo of their prototype and annotate it.

USEFUL APPS/LINKS

- App for creating interactive links (for example, between descriptions, videos, images and websites and a main image), such as ThingLink
- App for making notes using text, drawings, images, weblinks and audio, such as Notability
- App for drawing shapes, inserting images and making annotations or adding to the inserted image, such as DrawIsland

ASSESSMENT

Observe students as they make changes to their designs. Are they able to consider feedback, make modifications and move rapidly through this process, or do they have difficulties with holding on to an idea and accepting feedback?

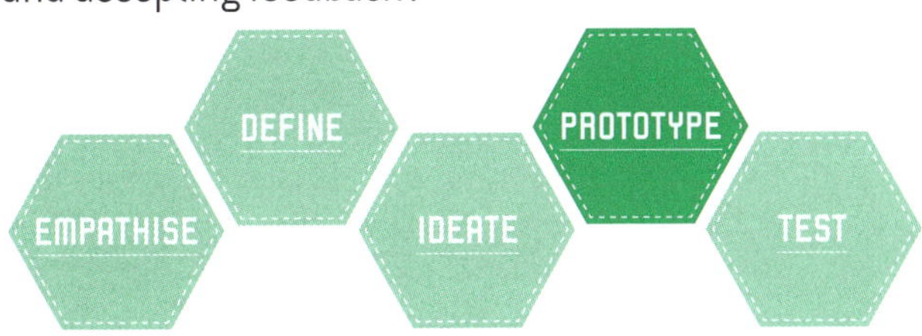

→ TEST

At this stage of the design thinking process, students test their prototype to see how it meets the criteria in the challenge.

ACTIVITY: TEST FEEDBACK

1. Students take their last prototype and consult with one of the people who completed their initial survey, or who they interviewed.
2. Ask students to check whether or not their design works and what they need to do to make it work if it doesn't.
3. Provide the opportunity to cycle through the Prototype and Test stages again.

Ask students to fill in **Learning journal template 4 (Prototype and test page)**. See the **Journal tip** for further student guidance.

PROMPTS

- Does your prototype do what you wanted it to do?
- Are there other features that need to be added?

MORE VOCABULARY

- evaluate – assess something, perhaps considering what worked and what didn't
- feature – a specific aspect of something, such as size, shape, colour, quality
- feedback – information about, for example, a person's performance or the design of a product, which can be used to make improvements
- prototype – an initial version of a model of a product or process that is used to develop a final model
- review – consider an idea, process or product and assess what works and what needs to be changed

JOURNAL TIP

Ask students to think about why it is important to test their ideas before they build their final design.

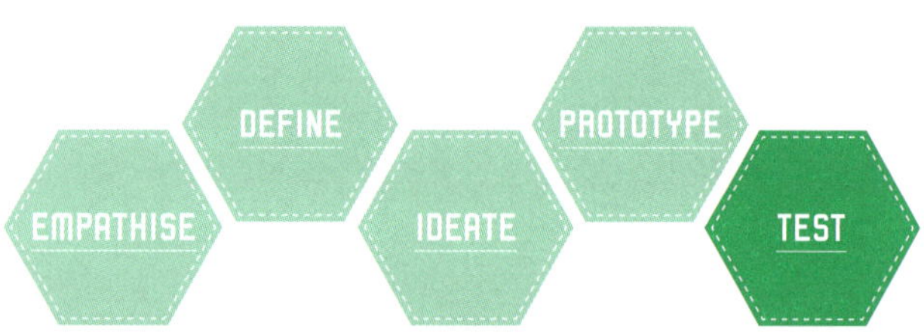

→ SHARE AND EVALUATE

At this stage of the investigation, students are provided with an opportunity to share their final design, as well as the processes involved in the investigation. Students evaluate their learning journals as well as their solutions.

ACTIVITY 1: BRING THE DESIGNS TOGETHER

1. Allow students time to create final designs.
2. Students can create an iMovie or use Adobe Spark Video (via a teacher-created class account) or Prezi to demonstrate the process and thinking behind the designs.
3. Provide students with time to create their awareness campaign. They will need to review their information and decide if any more is needed. They will need to make a decision about the format of their campaign.
4. Students should include their learning journals with the display so others can see the different stages of the design process.

ACTIVITY 2: EVALUATE AND GIVE FEEDBACK

1. Provide students with **Generic reproducible 2 (Self-evaluation)** to complete.
2. Ask students to provide feedback to each other about the most interesting features, the aspects that were most difficult and the changes that they would make if they repeated the task.
3. Provide students with opportunities to share their designs with the wider community. It may be possible to share some of the videos with an expert for design feedback.

ASSESSMENT

Ask students to again complete **Generic reproducible 1 (Key vocabulary table)** using the key vocabulary for this unit. Compare their table with the one they completed at the Tune-in stage, to demonstrate changes in understanding.

Students complete **Generic reproducible 3 (Responding to the investigation)**. Compare their responses to their responses to **Generic reproducible 2**.

Teachers complete **Generic reproducible 5 (Design thinking assessment rubric)** for each student. Students compare the feedback they are given by the teacher with their self-assessment of how they used the design thinking process to solve problems (**Generic reproducible 3**).

TUNE IN

STEM INVESTIGATIONS

Name: ....

Date: ....

Name of material:	This material is: ☐ natural ☐ synthetic
Picture or sample of material:	This material is used for:
This material feels:	Describe some of the properties of this material. Here are some useful words: strong, flexible, transparent, opaque, woven, knitted, waterproof, durable
This material is made in:	

STEM Investigations, MP, ISBN 978 1 4202 4319 2 © Macmillan Science and Education Australia 2018

EMPATHISE

STEM INVESTIGATIONS

Name: ....

Date: ....

Interview someone to find out about their clothing habits. The last two rows have been left blank for your own questions.

Question	Notes
How many different items of clothing do you think you own?	
How often do you buy new clothes?	
Have you ever bought clothes that are not brand new? Why/why not?	
What do you do with the clothes you no longer want to wear?	
What do you know about where your clothes are made and who makes them?	

DEFINE

STEM INVESTIGATIONS

Name: ....

Date: ....

Use this table to help plan and organise your repurposing investigation. Add information to it as you work through your challenge.

Item of clothing to repurpose	
Material(s) clothing is made from	
Time allowed to complete the task	
Final design idea	
Materials selected to use	
Reasons for choice of materials	
Equipment or tools needed	
Awareness campaign audience	
Format of awareness campaign (e.g. speaker, school social media release, poster, local newspaper)	

MAKE AN ATTRACTIVE TOY FOR CHILDREN

WHO WE ARE 18

INTRODUCTION

Some traditional children's games and toys have been played for centuries. While digital games have become very popular, there has been a rise in the sale of traditional games and toys in recent years. Traditional games and toys promote language development, turn-taking and other social interaction skills.

This investigation provides students with the opportunity to create a game or toy that incorporates at least one magnet. They are challenged to build a game or toy that demonstrates their understanding of magnetic forces and the properties of different materials. They consider the elements of an engaging game or toy, through interviewing and observation. This task can be differentiated by adding extra elements, such as specific actions for a toy, or more than one magnetic part for a game.

THE CHALLENGE

The Attractive Toy Company specialises in toys that work because of magnets. They have asked your school to help them with a charity project, making 'attractive' games and toys for children.

Your challenge is to work in a team to design and make a game or toy with at least one magnet. You will need to research, draw and create. Then you need to test your creation and make a poster explaining how it works. As part of this investigation, you will learn about forces that work from a distance.

KEY UNDERSTANDINGS

- A force is a push or pull on an object.
- Forces can be contact or non-contact.
- Forces affect the motion or behaviour of an object.
- Forces in magnets can attract or repel objects.
- Some materials are attracted to magnets.

KEY VOCABULARY

attract – pull something towards something else, such as a magnet attracting a paperclip

force – a push or pull on an object that makes it move, or change direction or shape

repel – push something away, such as the north pole of a magnet pushing away from the north pole of another magnet

KEY SKILLS

- Interview and observe people to find out what they think, including observing others as they play different games or play with toys.
- Explain how magnets behave, using terms such as 'attract' and 'repel'.
- Select materials for a specific use, based on their properties – they may need to be strong, transparent or opaque, or flexible.
- Create labelled diagrams, sketches and models for a magnetic game or toy.
- Transform an idea into something that can be seen – discuss, write, draw and build ideas.

KEY ACTIONS

- Interview and observe others.
- Research games and toys.
- Explore the properties of magnets.
- Create a labelled diagram of a game or toy.
- Build a game or toy with a magnetic component.

OVERVIEW OF STAGES

TUNE IN:

Students will consider what they know about games and toys and whether or not these games and toys have magnetic components. They will explore how magnets work and consider the different properties of materials that they might use in their design.

EMPATHISE

Students interview others to find out about the types of games or toys they like to play with. They observe others playing with different games or toys.

DEFINE

Students further investigate the properties of magnets. They find out about different issues to consider when using magnets, such as safety issues and the availability of different magnets. They think about different materials that could be used in their design.

IDEATE

Students come up with creative ideas for different magnetic toys or games. They think about the aim and how a magnet could be incorporated.

PROTOTYPE

Students draw, label and present their design of a magnetic game or toy before creating a model. Initial prototypes may include developing one or two components of the game or toy before completing the final model.

TEST

Students test the different components of the game or toy. They make changes depending on the results. This may include feedback from others as well as modifications to different elements of the game.

SHARE AND EVALUATE:

Students create a poster or interactive image explaining how to use their game or toy. Students provide others with the opportunity to play with their games or toys. They could observe other people's reactions to the different products and also ask for feedback. They evaluate their own and each other's designs.

SUGGESTED SCHEDULE

LESSON	STAGE
1–4	**Tune in**: Indicate knowledge of magnets associated with games and toys; watch videos about magnetism; explore magnets and properties of materials
5–7	**Empathise**: Find out about the games and toys others like to play with; research different games and toys; observe others playing with games and toys; write in journal
8–9	**Define**: Further investigate the properties of magnets; find out about different issues relating to magnets; think about materials to use in the design; write in journal
10–11	**Ideate**: Come up with ideas for magnetic games or toys; think about how a magnet could be incorporated; write in journal
12–17	**Prototype** and **Test**: Draw, label and present a design for a magnetic game or toy; build a model using recycled materials; test components of the game and gather feedback from others; write in journal
18–21	**Share and evaluate**: Provide the opportunity for others to play with the magnetic games and toys; observe others' interactions with the products and seek feedback; evaluate self and others

CURRICULUM LINKS

SCIENCE

YEAR	STRAND	SUB-STRAND AND CONTENT
4	Science Inquiry Skills	Questioning and predicting Processing and analysing data and information Evaluating Communicating
4	Science Understanding	Physical sciences: • Forces can be exerted by one object on another through direct contact or from a distance
3 & 4	Science as a Human Endeavour	Use and influence of science: • Science knowledge helps people to understand the effect of their actions

TECHNOLOGIES

YEAR	STRAND	CONTENT
3 & 4	Design and Technologies Knowledge and Understanding	• Investigate how forces and the properties of materials affect the behaviour of a product or system • Investigate the suitability of materials, systems, components, tools and equipment for a range of purposes
3 & 4	Design and Technologies Processes and Production Skills	• Select and use materials, components, tools, equipment and techniques and use safe work practices to make designed solutions • Generate, develop and communicate design ideas and decisions using appropriate technical terms and graphical representation techniques • Evaluate design ideas, processes and solutions based on criteria for success developed with guidance and including care for the environment and communities

MATHEMATICS

YEAR	STRAND	SUB-STRAND AND CONTENT
3	Measurement and Geometry	Shape: • Make models of three-dimensional objects and describe key features Using units of measurement: • Measure, order and compare objects using familiar metric units of length, area, mass and capacity
4	Measurement and Geometry	Using units of measurement: • Use scaled instruments to measure and compare lengths, masses, capacities and temperatures

This investigation also links to the General Capabilities:

- Literacy
- Numeracy
- Information and Communication Technology (ICT) Capability
- Critical and Creative Thinking.

ASSESSMENT

The following resources are provided for assessing students at different stages of the STEM investigations:

- Generic reproducible 1 (Key vocabulary table), for assessing understanding of vocabulary
- Generic reproducible 2 (Self-evaluation), for student self-evaluation of the learning process
- Generic reproducible 3 (Responding to the investigation)
- Generic reproducible 5 (Design thinking assessment rubric), for evaluating student engagement in the design thinking stages
- Learning journal templates 1, 2, 3 and 4, incorporating student reflection and evaluation.

GETTING READY FOR THE INVESTIGATION

You can prepare yourself and students for this STEM investigation in the following ways:

- Identify groups of students who will work well together.
- Review the **Key science knowledge** that supports this investigation, and look at the **Useful links**.
- Investigate the **Useful apps**.
- Gather materials for the science activities about magnets and materials during the Tune-in session, including pictures of magnetic and non-magnetic games and toys, and yes/no cards for each student.
- Start collecting additional materials for prototyping (as shown on the **Materials needed** list).
- Determine where prototypes will be kept between lessons.
- Create a wall space where students can share their ideas in the Ideate stage.
- Organise the class into pairs.
- Start thinking about:
  - sourcing information about magnetic games and toys
  - collecting some games and toys for students to engage with
  - making connections with game and toy designers or retailers
  - time constraints for the task
  - finding experts in the toy industry, board gamers or perhaps mechanical engineers to provide feedback to students
  - how, when and where the designs will be shared and evaluated
  - whether or not a budget will be provided for the project.

USEFUL APPS

- App for creating semantic maps (links between different words and/or concepts), such as Popplet or Kidspiration
- App for creating multimedia presentations, such as Adobe Spark Video (via a teacher-created class account), Prezi or iMovie
- App for creating augmented reality presentations, such as Aurasma
- App for sharing ideas, thoughts, questions and images, such as Padlet or Lino
- App for engaging in collaborative tasks, such as OneNote Class Notebook

USEFUL LINKS

- Video about some of the best magnetic games and toys, such as at mea.digital/sm34
- Video about magnetism, such as at mea.digital/sm35
- Information for teachers about the properties of materials, such as at mea.digital/sm36

RESOURCES PROVIDED

- Generic reproducibles 1, 2, 3, 5, 10, 12
- Reproducibles 18.1, 18.2, 18.3
- Learning journal templates 1, 2, 3, 4

MATERIALS NEEDED

- Recycled materials, such as assorted cardboard boxes, cardboard offcuts, tubes, string, ribbon
- Scissors
- Tape – different widths, strengths, materials
- PVA glue
- Hot glue guns and glue (optional)
- Split pins
- Staplers and staples
- Different materials for exploration of the properties of materials such as plastic, metal, fabric
- Ramps
- Different types of magnet, such as bar magnets and magnetic sticker strips – for exploration and use in designs
- Iron filings
- Coloured paper
- Marbles
- Ping-pong balls
- Wheels
- Metallic balls
- Tape measures/rulers

Hot glue guns can be dangerous. Make sure students are supervised at all times.

KEY SCIENCE KNOWLEDGE

This section provides an overview of the key science concepts and vocabulary needed for this unit.

FORCES

A **force** is a push or pull on an object. A force can make an object change shape, such as when a potter models clay, or it can make something speed up, slow down or stay in its place. Different types of forces include friction, electromagnetism and elasticity. Force has direction, which can be marked on a diagram with an arrow.

A contact force acts on an object by touching it, such as closing a door or kicking a ball. A non-contact force acts on an object without touching it, such as when hair stands on end due to static electricity.

MAGNETS

Magnetism is a type of force. All matter consists of atoms with negatively charged electrons spinning randomly around them. When the electrons spin in the same direction, they create a magnetic force.

Magnets have a north pole and a south pole. The poles are the strongest parts of the magnet. Magnets **attract** magnetic materials, such as many metals. When the same poles of two magnets are brought together, they will **repel** each other. When the north pole of a magnet is placed near the south pole of a magnet, the two will be attracted.

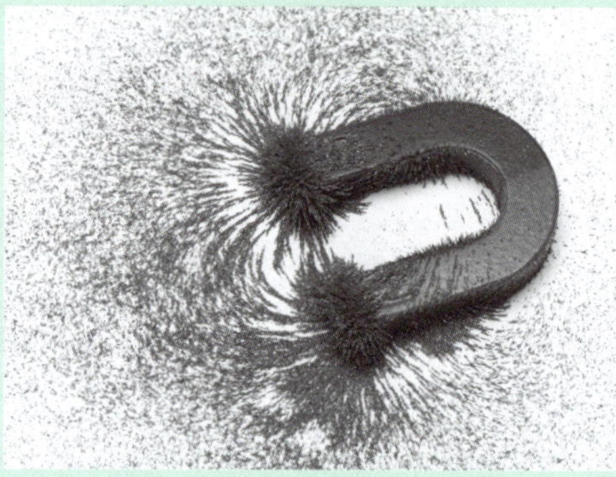

Metal filings near a magnet are influenced by its magnetic field.

Magnets can be used for many different purposes, including sorting of recycled materials, and in magnetically levitated (maglev) trains, vending machines and electric motors.

PROPERTIES OF MATERIALS

Materials have different properties, which affect how they can be used. These properties include strength, hardness, flexibility, absorbency, waterproofness, elasticity, plasticity and magnetism. It is important to consider the properties of materials when creating new products.

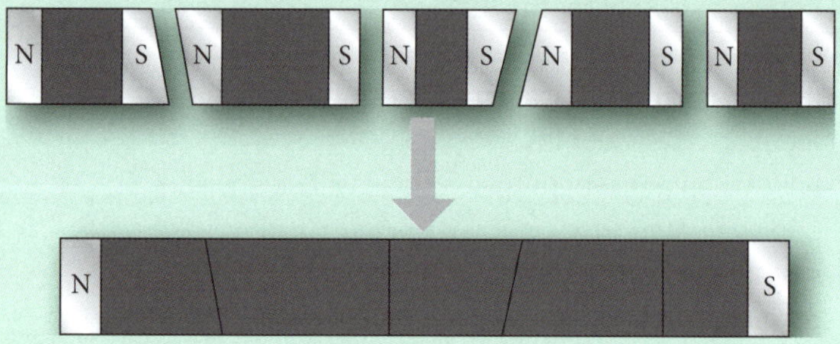

Magnets have a north pole and a south pole. The like poles of two magnets repel each other, and the opposite poles attract.

When making a game or toy that involves magnets, students should especially consider the magnetic properties of all other materials they are using. Is a material magnetic (attracted to a magnet)? Is this magnetism strong or weak? Does the material allow magnetic force to pass through it? Will the magnet be used as a contact or non-contact force?

KEY VOCABULARY

attract – pull something towards something else, such as a magnet attracting a paperclip

force – a push or pull on an object that makes it move, or change direction or shape

repel – push something away, such as the north pole of a magnet pushing away from the north pole of another magnet

TUNE IN

1. Ask students to complete **Generic reproducible 1 (Key vocabulary table)** using the key vocabulary for this unit. This reproducible will also be used at the end of the unit, to demonstrate changes in understanding.
2. Show students images of different games and toys. Ask them whether or not they think the game or toy uses magnets.
3. Introduce the challenge by providing students with some magnetic games or toys, such as the fishing rod game, magnetic construction blocks or travel board games. Alternatively, watch a video clip that shows some magnetic games and toys (see **Useful apps/links**). Have students discuss their responses.
4. Students need to understand the properties of magnets and materials. Set up the following activities or similar for students.

ACTIVITY 1: MAGNET PROPERTIES

1. Have students watch a short video clip about magnets (see **Useful apps/links**).
2. Discuss the terms 'repel' and 'attract' in relation to magnetism. Have students create a semantic map for each word (see **Useful apps/links**).
3. Provide students with magnets such as bar magnets and magnetic strips so that they can explore magnetic attraction and repulsion.
4. If possible, replicate the metallic ball and ramp demonstration in the video clip (see **Useful apps/links**) and have students discuss their observations.

ACTIVITY 2: MAGNETIC HUNT

1. Discuss the term 'magnetic' and how it is possible to test whether or not a material is magnetic.
2. Provide students with **Reproducible 18.1 (Magnetic materials)**. Give students a range of materials (magnetic and non-magnetic) and some magnets. Have them predict which materials are magnetic.
3. Students test the materials for magnetism, and record their observations on the reproducible.
4. Have students explore their surroundings with their magnets to find other magnetic materials.

ACTIVITY 3: MATERIAL SELECTION

1. Have pairs of students consider different materials that will be available for their investigation.
2. Challenge students to create an experiment to test a particular property of each material, such as strength or flexibility.
3. Provide students with **Reproducible 18.2 (Material properties testing plan)** to complete. Students then test the different materials and record their observations.
4. Have students discuss the results with their partner and write a summary of their discussion.
5. Have pairs of students investigating the same property share and compare their results.

5. Introduce the STEM investigation and challenge to the students. Provide them with the student card and read the information together.
6. Introduce the design thinking process by reviewing the stages on the student card. Explain that students will keep a journal about their learning at the different stages of the design.

TOP TIP! Before beginning the science explorations, discuss the safety issues associated with magnets. Make sure students are supervised at all times and that all magnets are accounted for at the end of each session.

USEFUL APPS/LINKS

- App for creating semantic maps (links between different words and/or concepts), such as Popplet or Kidspiration
- Video about top magnetic games and toys, such as at mea.digital/sm34
- Video clip about magnetism, including a demonstration with a metallic ball and ramp, such as at mea.digital/sm35

→ EMPATHISE

During the Empathise stage of the design thinking process, students focus on finding out about different points of view. To empathise with others, they need to research some of the points of view associated with games. Students will take notes, ask questions, draw diagrams and take photos where relevant.

ACTIVITY 1: FAVOURITE GAMES AND TOYS INTERVIEW

1. Have students interview others about their favourite games and toys.
2. To help students plan their interview questions, model the types of questions that students might wish to include.
3. After students have completed their interview questions, have them role-play an interview with a partner before carrying out the interview with their final interviewee.

ACTIVITY 2: GAME AND TOY OBSERVATION

1. As a class, collect a range of games and toys to play with. Include some magnetic games and toys. Invite some students from another class to play with the games and toys.
2. Provide students with **Reproducible 18.3 (Game and toy observations)** to record the observations they make about the people playing with the games and toys. Discuss the importance of observing carefully, focusing on people's reactions, their facial expressions and the parts of the games or toys that they seem to like best or dislike.

PROMPTS

- What were some of the different types of games and toys that people liked to play with?
- When people were playing with the games and toys, what sorts of facial expressions did you notice?
- What were some of the most commonly liked games or toys?
- What was one interesting thing you found out?

MORE VOCABULARY

- empathise – understand and consider another person or group's point of view
- point of view – an opinion, attitude or judgement considered in a particular way

JOURNAL TIP

Ask students to complete **Learning journal template 1 (Empathise page)** while they are doing the different tasks. Remind them to date their notes and include photos of relevant information or pictures.

USEFUL APPS/LINKS

- Video clip about good magnetic games and toys, such as at mea.digital/sm34

ASSESSMENT

This stage of the design thinking process offers opportunities to observe students collecting information, developing questions, and recording their notes and thinking in their journal.

TOP TIP! Before setting up the observation activity, find a short video clip for students to watch so they can learn some important observation skills. Have them focus on facial expressions, body language and what the people are saying.

EMPATHISE DEFINE IDEATE PROTOTYPE TEST

DEFINE

The main focus of this stage of the design thinking process is to reframe the challenge. The initial challenge is quite open, so at this stage students learn how to define what needs to be done. This includes noting insights that have been generated.

ACTIVITY 1: CONSIDER OBSERVATIONS

1. Have students share their observations about the different games and toys. Create a table with each of the games and toys and have students collate their observations. An app such as OneNote Class Notebook or Padlet could be used to make a collaborative document.
2. Discuss the information that was collected:
   - » What were some of the emotions that you observed?
   - » How did people's facial expressions change?
   - » What were some of the most popular features of the games or toys being played with?
   - » What were some of the parts of the games or toys that were not so well liked?
   - » Could you tell which people were used to playing games? How did you know this?

ACTIVITY 2: FIND OUT ABOUT WORKING WITH MAGNETS

1. Have students explore some of the issues involved with magnets and using them.
2. Provide students with some videos or links to articles about working with magnets (see **Useful apps/links**).
3. After students have finished researching, have them create a class list of things to be aware of with magnets, such as storage and keeping magnets away from certain items.

Students can update **Learning journal template 2 (Define page)**.

PROMPTS

- What are some of the safety issues when working with magnets?
- What types of materials might you want to use in your design?
- How might you explain your game or toy?
- What other information do you need?

ACTIVITY 3: CREATE DESIGN BRIEFS

1. Have students create a class criteria sheet. Explain that they will complete different sections during the investigation. They should include:
   - » location of the magnet
   - » use of the magnet
   - » name and purpose of the game or toy
   - » explanation of how to play the game or toy
   - » list of materials
   - » learning process, including changes to design (see **Learning journal template 4**).
2. After the initial criteria sheet has been created, have students review the contents and make suggestions for inclusions, changes or deletions.
3. When the criteria sheet is complete, provide students with easy access to a paper or electronic version. Remind students to refer to the criteria sheet regularly to ensure they remain on track with the investigation.

MORE VOCABULARY

- define – state the meaning of something
- insight – an accurate understanding of someone or something
- point of view – an opinion, attitude or judgement considered in a particular way

JOURNAL TIP

Discuss the term 'insight' and explain that it relates to something students have learned about the people and their responses to the surveys as well as information gathered through research or excursions. You could refer to **Learning journal template 2**.

USEFUL APPS/LINKS

- Article about uses of magnets, such as at mea.digital/sm240
- App for sharing ideas, thoughts, questions and images such as Padlet or Lino
- App for engaging in collaborative tasks, such as OneNote Class Notebook

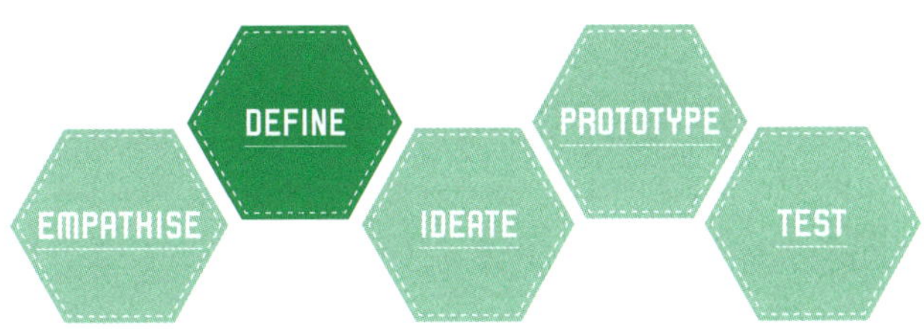

→ IDEATE

The Ideate stage of the design thinking process is all about generating lots of ideas. Students need to be flexible in their thinking and be able to move beyond obvious ideas. At this stage, ideas are not judged, just generated and gathered.

ACTIVITY 1: GENERATE GAME IDEAS

1. Make a class list of games that could be created as magnetic games.
2. Write each game onto a separate piece of card and place the cards on the wall, spread around the room. Alternatively, write each game onto a large piece of paper and place each paper on a separate table.
3. Provide students with pens or pencils and sticky notes, if using the wall display. Allocate each group to a different game. Provide them with 1–2 minutes to write down as many ideas as they can about the game they are thinking about.
4. After the time is up, have students move to a different game. Make sure they read others' ideas so they are not duplicating ideas. The other students' ideas may inspire new ideas.
5. Rotate the students every couple of minutes until they have written ideas for all games.
6. Repeat this activity, focusing on magnetic toy ideas.

ACTIVITY 2: EXTEND IDEAS

1. Allow groups of students to choose whether they want to create a magnetic game or a toy.
2. Provide them with time to read and reflect on the ideas generated by the class about the type of game or toy they wish to create.
3. Have students add further suggestions to their chosen game or toy.

PROMPTS

- How do these ideas use magnets?
- How might you check that a magnet can be used?
- How can you make it more exciting?
- What types of materials might be good to use?

MORE VOCABULARY

- feedback – information about, for example, a person's performance or the design of a product, which can be used to make improvements
- ideate – generate many ideas without making judgements about the ideas
- reflect – consider and evaluate

JOURNAL TIP

Ask students to add their three favourite ideas to **Learning journal template 3 (Ideate page)**. Encourage them to choose three ideas that aren't related.

USEFUL APPS/LINKS

- App for sharing ideas, thoughts, questions and images, such as Padlet or Lino

ASSESSMENT

At the Ideate stage, assessment could include observations about the number and diversity of student ideas, and their ability to provide feedback and create additional ideas. Reflection in the journal should provide an insight into some of the reasoning behind student choices.

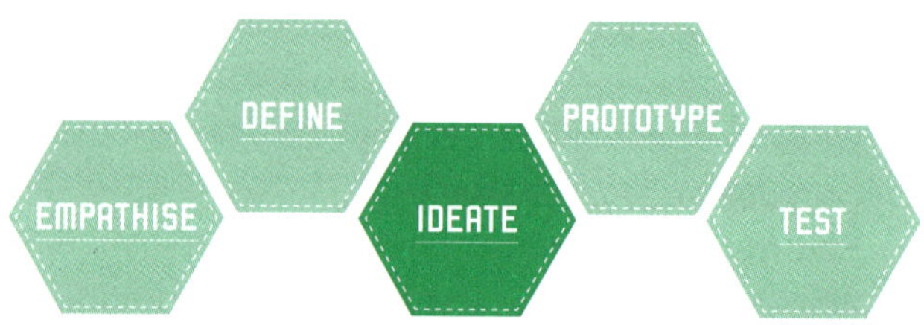

PROTOTYPE

At this stage of the design thinking process, students are asked to create a physical prototype of a solution. Students need to get their ideas out of their heads and present them in a way that engages other students and helps them to understand the concept. When students create, it helps them to think and solve problems and disagreements. Students can role-play, make a storyboard or use sticky notes when they prototype. The most important feature is that viewers can interact with whatever is produced.

Encourage students to photograph or film during the Prototype and Test stages. This information can be used to show the learning behind the design thinking process in action.

ACTIVITY 1: TRANSFORM IDEAS INTO PROTOTYPES

1. Have students consider their different ideas.
2. Students highlight one or two ideas they think are appealing.
3. Students discuss and draw how they might create their game or toy. Small whiteboards or drawing apps can be useful.
4. After students have drawn a design, they use simple materials to create their first prototype.
5. Remind students to think about where the magnet will be incorporated and how it will work.

ACTIVITY 2: REFINE DESIGNS

1. Once the design has been developed, provide students with time to refine elements of their game or toy.
2. Provide students with **Generic reproducible 10 (Group task organiser)** to help them plan the final construction of the game or toy. Have students choose one component of their game to create.
3. If possible, photograph or video the different prototypes to assist with reviewing.
4. When asking for feedback, students could ask each other some of the following questions:
   - » What is the aim of magnetic game or toy?
   - » How does it work?
   - » Which aspects work best? What will you keep?
   - » Which aspects need changing? How might you do this?
   - » What other materials might you need?

Ask students to fill in the Prototype part of **Learning journal template 4 (Prototype and test page)**. See the **Journal tip** for further student guidance.

PROMPTS

- How is a magnet included in your game or toy?
- Which part needs to be made first?
- How are the different parts attached?
- Which parts of the game or toy need to move?

TOP TIP! The Prototype stage is often very messy. It is important that students are focusing on their ideas, rather than the end product. Provide them with lots of materials – recycling depots can be a useful source of resources. Students may add labels to prototypes to explain some of the main features. Photographing and annotating pictures of prototypes can be useful.

MORE VOCABULARY

- feedback – information about, for example, a person's performance or the design of a product, which can be used to make improvements
- prototype – an initial version of a model of a product or process that is used to develop a final model

JOURNAL TIP

Remind students to highlight the main features of their prototype. If students are creating an electronic journal, they can insert a photo of their prototype and annotate it.

USEFUL APPS/LINKS

- App for taking photographs or video, such as Adobe Spark Video or iMovie

ASSESSMENT

Observe students as they make changes to their designs. Are they able to consider feedback, make modifications and move rapidly through this process, or do they have difficulties with holding on to an idea and accepting feedback?

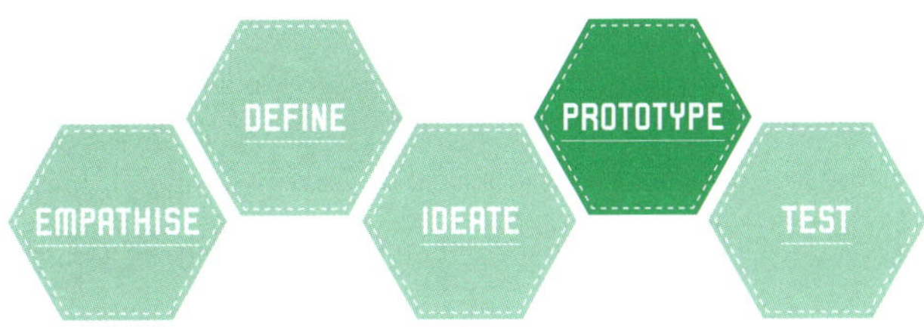

→ TEST

At this stage of the design thinking process, students test their prototype to see how it meets the criteria in the challenge.

ACTIVITY: TEST FEEDBACK

1. Have students gather feedback about the prototypes. Provide them with **Generic reproducible 12 (Prototype and test)** to record the ideas.
2. When providing feedback, students should consider ease of use, purpose of the game and materials used.
3. Students continue to cycle through the Prototype and Test stages until they have completed their design.

Ask students to fill in **Learning journal template 4 (Prototype and test page)**. See the **Journal tip** for further student guidance.

PROMPTS

- Does your prototype do what you wanted it to do?
- Are there features that need to be added or removed?

MORE VOCABULARY

- evaluate – assess something, perhaps considering what worked and what didn't
- feature – a specific aspect of something, such as size, shape, colour or quality
- feedback – information about, for example, a person's performance or the design of a product, which can be used to make improvements
- prototype – an initial version of a model of a product or process that is used to develop a final model
- review – consider an idea, process or product and assess what works and what needs to be changed

JOURNAL TIP

Ask students to think about why it is important to test their ideas before they build their final design.

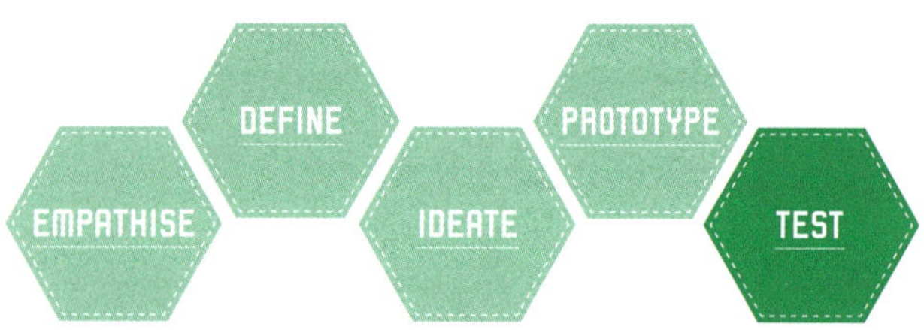

→ SHARE AND EVALUATE

At this stage, students are provided with an opportunity to share their final design, as well as the processes involved in the investigation. Students evaluate their learning journals as well as their solutions.

ACTIVITY 1: FINALISE DESIGNS

1. Allow students to finalise their designs, including creating a game or toy name. They also need to provide information about how the magnet has been included and how it works.
2. Provide them with time to create a poster or use an interactive app, such as ThingLink or Aurasma, to explain how the toy works or how the game is played.
3. Set up a time for other people to play with the different games and toys created.
4. Students should include their learning journals with the display so others can see the different stages of the design process.

ACTIVITY 2: EVALUATE AND GIVE FEEDBACK

1. Provide students with **Generic reproducible 2 (Self-evaluation)** to complete.
2. During the toy and game session, provide participants with tokens or stickers so they can vote for their favourite game or toy.
3. Have the creators observe other people interacting with the games and toys and describe the different reactions they see.

ASSESSMENT

Ask students to again complete **Generic reproducible 1 (Key vocabulary table)** using the key vocabulary for this unit. Compare their table with the one they completed at the Tune-in stage, to demonstrate changes in understanding.

Students complete **Generic reproducible 3 (Responding to the investigation)**. Compare their responses to their responses to **Generic reproducible 2**.

Teachers complete **Generic reproducible 5 (Design thinking assessment rubric)** for each student. Students compare the feedback they are given by the teacher with their self-assessment of how they used the design thinking process to solve problems **(Generic reproducible 3)**.

Name: ....

Date: ....

Look at some different materials and predict whether or not they are magnetic. Write your predictions in the table.

Use a magnet to test whether or not each material is magnetic. Write your observations in the table.

Material	Prediction		Observation	
	Magnetic	Non-magnetic	Magnetic	Non-magnetic

Name: ....

Date: ....

Choose one property to test (such as flexibility) and decide how to compare different materials.

Property to be tested: ....

Materials to be tested:

1. .... 2. .... 3. ....

The aim of the experiment is to find out: ....

....

Prediction: I think that: ....

....

Instructions for the experiment (what you need to do):

....

....

....

....

Write your observations in this table.

Material	Observations

STEM Investigations, MP, ISBN 978 1 4202 4319 2 © Macmillan Science and Education Australia 2018

GAME AND TOY OBSERVATIONS

EMPATHISE

STEM INVESTIGATIONS

Name: ....

Date: ....

Invite some people to play with different games or toys. Make some observations while they are playing.

Look carefully for clues about what other people think of the games or toys:

- What do you hear? (words, noises)
- What sorts of facial expressions do you see? (smiling, laughing, frowning, raising eyebrows)
- What are people doing with their hands?
- What are they doing with their bodies?

Record your observations in this table. An example has been done for you.

Observations	What these observations show
Laughing and smiling	*Enjoying playing with the game*

CREATE ART TO CELEBRATE THE PASSING OF TIME

→ INTRODUCTION

As the Earth rotates on its axis, we experience regular changes such as night and day. Earth also revolves around (orbits) the Sun. The Sun's light causes objects on Earth to cast shadows that change in both direction and length as the Earth rotates. Thousands of years ago, humans began exploring ways of recording time using shadows. A sundial can use the Earth's movement to track the passing of time.

In this STEM investigation, students are asked to demonstrate their understanding that the Earth's rotation on its axis causes regular changes such as the Sun's apparent movement across the sky, and day and night. They will also explore how objects in sunlight cast shadows. They will design an art installation that incorporates a sundial or other sun clock and that represents their community.

This STEM challenge is easily differentiated for students by encouraging different groups to use different degrees of complexity when creating their sundials or sun clocks.

THE CHALLENGE

Your town is turning 200 years old. To celebrate, town organisers are asking artists to create some temporary artworks in the town square. The theme is 'the passing of time'. Your art teacher thinks you could come up with something fun!

Your challenge is to create an art installation that includes a sun clock and that represents your community. Look at sundials from history for inspiration. Your prototype and presentation should explain how your sun clock works and why it should be chosen. You will learn how the Earth's rotation causes changes such as day and night.

KEY UNDERSTANDINGS

- The Sun is a source of light.
- The Earth's rotation on its axis causes regular changes, including day and night.
- The Earth's rotation on its axis is why the Sun appears to move across the sky.
- The Sun's position in the sky during the day means that shadows change.
- Sundials and sun clocks use shadows to show the time.

KEY SKILLS

- Develop research skills, including using key words, formulating relevant questions to research and collecting and organising data.
- Make careful observations, including what needs to be observed and recorded.
- Consider other people's points of view, by thinking about and understanding different perspectives.
- Present and communicate ideas and information, including choosing appropriate technology to represent ideas.

KEY VOCABULARY

axis – a real or imaginary line on which something rotates

rotation – the action of turning on an axis; one Earth rotation takes 24 hours

shadow – a dark area produced when light cannot pass through an object

sundial – an instrument that uses shadow to show the time

KEY ACTIONS

- Find out about the Earth's rotation, day and night, the 'movement' of the Sun, and shadows.
- Explore ways of recording time using sunlight and shadows.
- Design and create an artwork that includes a sundial.

→ OVERVIEW OF STAGES

TUNE IN:

Students find out what causes day and night and how time is measured. They explore how shadows are cast and they research sun clocks.

EMPATHISE

Students find out information about artistic representation and collect images about the history of their town through family or friends, local information sources and residents.

DEFINE

Students consider how they can create an art installation that represents the passing of time in their local community and incorporates an effective sundial or sun clock.

IDEATE

Students generate ideas for building sundials or sun clocks and how these can be incorporated into an art installation that represents the local community and the passing of time within that community.

PROTOTYPE

Students transform some of their ideas into physical representations using simple materials – sketches and/or models.

TEST

Students share their prototypes and provide feedback to each other. Sundials and/or sun clocks can be tested.

SHARE AND EVALUATE:

Final prototypes are shared with the school community and someone from the local community. Feedback is provided.

→ SUGGESTED SCHEDULE

LESSON	STAGE
1–4	**Tune in**: Share information about the Earth's movement, night and day, how shadows are cast by sunlight and how sundials use the 'movement' of the Sun to record time
5–7	**Empathise**: Learn about the history of the town from different perspectives; explore artistic representations of history and time; empathise and record responses; write in journal
8–9	**Define**: Consider observations and insights; define main issues; write in journal
10–11	**Ideate**: Develop ideas; write in journal
11–13	**Prototype** and **Test**: Conduct prototyping and testing cycles; write in journal
14–15	**Share and evaluate**: Share and evaluate designs and prototypes

CURRICULUM LINKS

SCIENCE

YEAR	STRAND	SUB-STRAND AND CONTENT
3	Science Understanding	Earth and space sciences: • Earth's rotation on its axis causes regular changes, including night and day
3 & 4	Science as a Human Endeavour	Nature and development of science: • Science involves making predictions and describing patterns and relationships

TECHNOLOGIES

YEAR	STRAND	CONTENT
3 & 4	Design and Technologies Processes and Production Skills	• Critique needs or opportunities for designing, and explore and test a variety of materials, components, tools, and equipment and the techniques needed to produce designed solutions • Generate, develop and communicate design ideas and decisions using appropriate technical terms and graphical representation techniques • Select and use materials, components, tools, equipment and techniques and use safe work practices to make designed solutions • Evaluate design ideas, processes and solutions based on criteria for success developed with guidance and including care for the environment • Plan a sequence of production steps when making designed solutions individually and collaboratively

MATHEMATICS

YEAR	STRAND	SUB-STRAND AND CONTENT
3	Measurement and Geometry	Using units of measurement: • Tell time to the minute and investigate the relationship between units of time
4	Statistics and Probability	Data representation and interpretation: • Select and trial methods for data collection, including survey questions and recording sheets

This investigation also links to the General Capabilities:

- Literacy
- Numeracy
- Information and Communication Technology (ICT) Capability
- Critical and Creative Thinking
- Personal and Social Capability.

ASSESSMENT

The following resources are provided for assessing students at different stages of the STEM investigations:

- Generic reproducible 1 (Key vocabulary table), for assessing understanding of vocabulary
- Generic reproducible 2 (Self-evaluation), for student self-evaluation of the learning process
- Generic reproducible 3 (Responding to the investigation)
- Generic reproducible 5 (Design thinking assessment rubric), for evaluating student engagement in the design thinking stages
- Learning journal templates 1, 2, 3 and 4, incorporating student reflection and evaluation.

GETTING READY FOR THE INVESTIGATION

You can prepare yourself and students for this STEM investigation in the following ways:

- Identify groups of students who will work well together.
- Review the **Key science knowledge** that supports this investigation, and look at the **Useful links**.
- Gather materials for creating sundials or sun clocks (as shown on the **Materials needed** list).
- Start collecting images and information about your local town throughout its history.
- Determine where prototypes will be kept between lessons.
- Create a vocabulary wall/space to be added to throughout the investigation.
- Create a wall space where students can share their ideas during the Ideate stage.
- Organise the class into small groups.
- Start thinking about:
  - » how the art installation with sundials/sun clocks ideas will be evaluated
  - » who will view the design ideas
  - » who will provide feedback about the ideas and how that feedback will be provided – in person or digitally
  - » inviting someone to speak about the local town's history for the Empathise stage
  - » how, when and where the design ideas will be presented and evaluated.

USEFUL APPS

- Apps for creating and organising ideas, such as Popplet, Inspiration, Padlet and Ideament
- Apps for sharing ideas, such as Airsketch
- App for creating multimedia presentations, such as Adobe Spark Video (via a teacher-created class account), Prezi or iMovie

USEFUL LINKS

- Information about the Earth's rotation and day and night, such as at mea.digital/sm83, mea.digital/sm246
- Video clip about the Earth's rotation and revolution, such as at mea.digital/sm84
- Resource for gathering information, such as at mea.digital/sm85
- Interactive information about the Earth's rotation and day and night, such as at mea.digital/sm86
- Explanation of seasons, such as at mea.digital/sm87
- Interactive information about light and shadow, such as at mea.digital/sm88, mea.digital/sm89
- A story about sundials, such as at mea.digital/sm90
- Keeping time and its history, such as at mea.digital/sm91
- How to make a simple sundial, such as at mea.digital/sm92, mea.digital/sm93
- Suitable images of artistic representations of the passing of time, such as at mea.digital/sm94, mea.digital/sm95, mea.digital/sm96

RESOURCES PROVIDED

- Generic reproducibles 1, 2, 3, 4, 5, 6
- Reproducibles 19.1, 19.2, 19.3, 19.4, 19.5
- Learning journal templates 1, 2, 3, 4

MATERIALS NEEDED

- Sticky notes
- Paper
- Cardboard
- Pens and markers
- Sticky tape
- Sticks
- Compass
- Photographs of local community over time
- Glue
- Paper plates
- Whiteboards and markers
- Paper
- Clipboards
- Pencils
- Paint brushes
- Paint
- Oil pastels
- Clay
- Other resources for building the art installation, such as glass jars, plastic containers, cardboard boxes, cellophane, beads, stones

KEY SCIENCE KNOWLEDGE

This section provides an overview of the key science concepts and vocabulary needed for this unit.

NIGHT AND DAY

The Earth **rotates** (spins on its own axis) once every 24 hours – the length of an Earth day. The **axis** is an imaginary line that runs through the centre of the Earth from the north pole to the south pole. It is daytime on the side facing the Sun, and night on the side facing away.

The Earth rotates from west to east, which makes the Sun look like it is rising in the east and setting in the west. This is because the Earth is spinning, not because the Sun is moving. The Sun's 'movement' across the sky causes objects to cast shadows. The shadows we see on Earth change depending on the position of the Sun in the sky during the day.

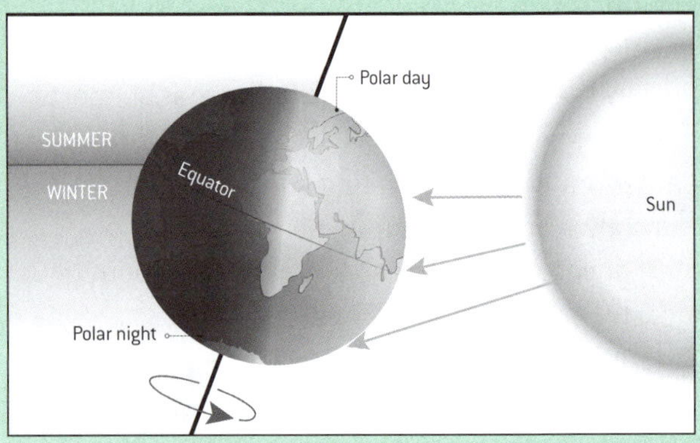

The Earth's rotation causes night and day, and the seasons change as the Earth orbits the Sun.

RECORDING THE PASSING OF TIME

People use time to measure how long it takes for something to happen. In the ancient world, people would measure time by looking at the sky and watching the Sun rise and set and the moon become full. They noticed the days becoming shorter and longer, and the cycle of the seasons.

The ancient Egyptians invented a type of clock called a **sundial**. The earliest sundials were very basic, simply a stick or pillar that cast a **shadow** on the ground. On sunny days, sundials cast shadows that move as the day passes.

Sundials can be made of various materials, including metal, wood and stone. The surface of a sundial is flat and called a dial plate. The lines on the dial plate, numbered to show the hours, are called hour lines. A structure called a gnomon sticks up at an angle from the dial plate. It has a sloping edge called a style. The gnomon's shadow moves around the dial as the day passes, and every hour it falls on a new hour line. The position of the shadow is then used to tell the time.

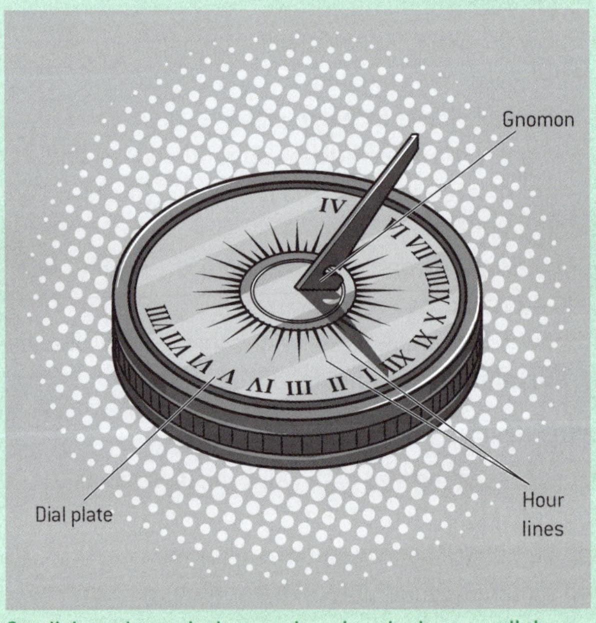

Sundials and sun clocks use changing shadows to tell the time of day.

KEY VOCABULARY

axis – a real or imaginary line on which something rotates
rotate – the action of turning on an axis; one Earth rotation takes 24 hours
shadow – a dark area produced when light cannot pass through an object
sundial – an instrument that uses shadow to show the time

→ TUNE IN

1. Ask students to complete **Generic reproducible 1 (Key vocabulary table)** using the key vocabulary for this unit. This reproducible will be used at the end of the unit to demonstrate changes in understanding.
2. Ask, 'What makes us think time is passing?' Record students' understandings of night and day.
3. Watch a video clip about the Earth's rotation (see **Useful apps/links**).
4. Discuss observations and new learning. Record student wonderings.
5. Before engaging in the challenge, students need to have an understanding of the Earth's movement, how shadows are cast and the history of sun clocks. Set up the following three activities (or similar) for students.

ACTIVITY 1: NIGHT AND DAY

1. Provide students with links to information about the Earth's rotation on its axis and its revolution (see **Useful apps/links**). Ask them how this relates to night and day.
2. Ask students to create an infographic explaining the Earth's rotation and how it causes night and day. They could draw and annotate this on paper, create diagrams on the computer, or use an app such as ThingLink.
3. Ask pairs of students to explain how the Earth's rotation causes night and day.

ACTIVITY 2: SHADOWS

1. View online interactive video clips about light and shadows (see **Useful apps/links**).
2. Clarify understandings: 'Is the Sun moving across the sky? What is really happening?'
3. Discuss key information presented in the video clip. Note that it discusses time in relation to shadows.
4. Provide students with clipboards, paper and pencils. Explore and sketch shadows in the environment and/or ones they create with pencils.

ACTIVITY 3: RECORDING TIME

1. Provide students with links to information about sundials (see **Useful apps/links**). On **Reproducible 19.1 (Making connections)**, students record new learnings about sundials and connections to their understanding of the Earth's movement, how the Sun casts shadows, and sundials.
2. Provide students with paper plates and pencils to construct a basic sundial.
3. Place sundials outside and have students sketch the sundials' shadows at different times of the day, preferably on the hour. Use **Reproducible 19.2 (Sundial shadows)** to record information.

6. Introduce the STEM investigation and challenge to the students. Provide them with the student card and read the information together.
7. Introduce the design thinking process by reviewing the stages on the student card. Explain that students will keep a journal about their learning at the different stages of the design.

TOP TIP! During the Tune-in sessions, conduct vocabulary activities to highlight and develop key vocabulary knowledge. Activities could include drawing semantic webs, creating a word wall or paired discussions. Check **Key vocabulary definitions** or read the **Key science knowledge** for a refresher on the key terms and concepts.

USEFUL APPS/LINKS

- Information about the Earth's rotation and day and night, such as at mea.digital/sm83
- Video clip about the Earth's rotation, such as at mea.digital/sm84
- Information about light and shadow, such as at mea.digital/sm86
- Information about changing shadows, such as at mea.digital/sm89
- Information about sundials, such as at mea.digital/sm97

→ EMPATHISE

During the Empathise stage of the design thinking process, students focus on finding out about different points of view. To empathise with others, they need to research some of the experiences and memories of members of the local community. Students will take notes, ask questions, and observe and take photos where relevant.

ACTIVITY 1: TOWN MEMORIES

1. Ask students to think about their local town. Provide students with paper to use illustrations and words to show their memories of their town and what has changed throughout their time there.
2. Organise students into small groups and have them share their memories or observations.
3. Discuss differences in what was shared and why different students have different memories and/or experiences of their town. Explain that this is their history and ask, 'How might it be different for others who live in the town?'

ACTIVITY 2: HISTORY OF MY TOWN

1. Have local community members share their experiences or memories of the local town and show photographs.
2. Provide students with **Reproducible 19.3 (Community member interview)** to record information and any questions.
3. Students form groups with students who interviewed a different local community member and share information.
4. Students consider and record ideas about how their experiences and memories are different to those interviewed, and suggest reasons why.
5. With permission, create an online album of photos shared by local community members.

PROMPTS

- What is your best memory connected to this town? Why?
- What were some of the memories of the local community members that you interviewed? What have they noticed has changed over time?
- How did different class members react to the artworks? What words did they use to describe how they felt?

ACTIVITY 3: USING ART TO PORTRAY HISTORY AND TIME

1. Students brainstorm art that they have noticed in the local community. Discuss what the artists may have wanted to portray.
2. Provide students with examples of art that shows history and/or the passing of time (see **Useful apps/links**). This may be as photocopies or as a digital slideshow. Students complete **Reproducible 19.4 (Artwork study)** to help consider the artist's point of view and message.
3. Students share responses to art and how they felt about different artworks. This should be modelled by the teacher first.

MORE VOCABULARY

- empathise – understand and consider another person's or group's point of view
- point of view – an opinion, attitude or judgement considered in a particular way

JOURNAL TIP

Ask students to complete **Learning journal template 1 (Empathise page)** while they are doing the different tasks. Remind them to date their notes and include photos of relevant information or pictures.

USEFUL APPS/LINKS

- App to organise information from interviews and responses to art, such as Popplet
- Suitable images of artistic representations of the passing of time, such as at mea.digital/sm94, mea.digital/sm95, mea.digital/sm96

ASSESSMENT

This stage of the design thinking process offers opportunities to observe students collecting information, developing questions, and recording their notes and thinking in their journal.

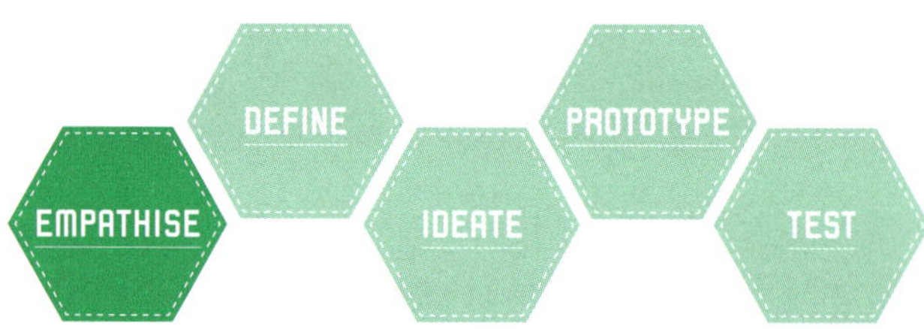

→ DEFINE

The main focus of this stage of the design thinking process is to reframe the challenge. The initial challenge is quite open, so at this stage students learn how to define what needs to be done. This includes noting insights that have been generated.

ACTIVITY 1: CONSIDER OBSERVATIONS

1. Students consider the information they gathered in the Tune-in and Empathise stages. They may work in pairs or small groups. Provide them with a whiteboard, large sheet of paper and/or sticky notes to collate some of their key information. They should refer to their information on **Reproducible 19.3 (Community member interview)** and **Reproducible 19.4 (Artwork study)**. Students should transfer their main findings to **Learning journal template 2 (Define page)**.
2. Students should discuss one section of **Learning journal template 2** at a time, write their responses and then continue discussing their ideas for the next section, until the task is complete. This provides students with opportunities to hear others' responses and it provides the teacher with input points.
3. Provide students with the opportunity to research further. Ask them to write other information they would like to know. Provide them with **Generic reproducible 4 (Key question table)** to assist them to record their questions, findings and sources.

ACTIVITY 2: CONSIDER INSIGHTS

1. Students should think of at least one insight they have gained from the process; for example, individuals have different personal histories based on their experiences and memories. They should then explain how this will affect the design of their art installation incorporating a sundial.
2. When considering insights, students could think about the following:
   - What was something unexpected that you observed or found out? How was it unexpected?
   - How will you decide on the most important aspect of your art installation?
   - Is there any other information that you need or would like to know? How will you find out?

ACTIVITY 3: CONSIDER CONSTRAINTS

1. Have students consider the constraints of the challenge by describing the types of materials that will be available. Discuss how students will test the sundial design and art installation to see that it meets the criteria.

Students can update **Learning journal template 2**.

PROMPTS

- What did you discover?
- What were the most important pieces of information that you gathered?
- What was something new that you learned?
- What other information do you need?

MORE VOCABULARY

- define – state the meaning of something
- insight – an accurate understanding of someone or something
- point of view – an opinion, attitude or judgement considered in a particular way

JOURNAL TIP

Discuss the term 'insight' and explain that it relates to something students have learned about the people they interviewed as well as information gathered through research. You could refer to **Learning journal template 2**.

USEFUL APPS/LINKS

- App for creating and organising ideas, such as Popplet, Inspiration, Padlet or Ideament

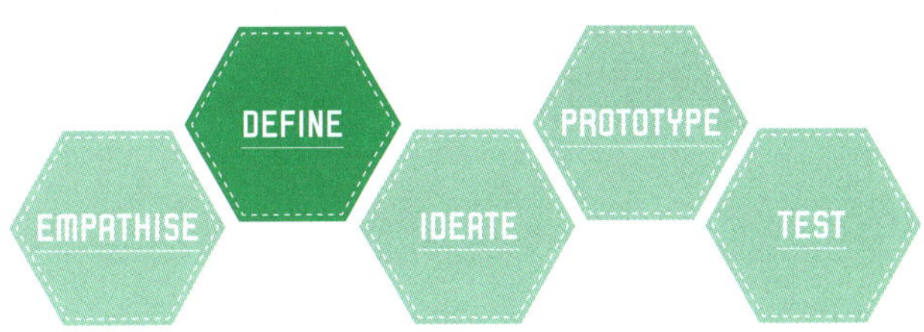

→ IDEATE

The Ideate stage of the design thinking process is all about generating lots of ideas. Students need to be flexible in their thinking and be able to move beyond obvious ideas. At this stage, ideas are not judged, just generated and gathered.

ACTIVITY: GENERATE IDEAS

1. Ask groups of students to draw or write their ideas for their sundial.
2. Each new idea should be drawn or written on a separate piece of paper or sticky note.
3. Ask students to group ideas on a wall or board.
4. Ask students to look at the different ideas and provide feedback to each other. It is important that students don't defend their ideas at this stage. They should just be listening to the feedback.
5. After the initial feedback, ask students to come up with more ideas. Encourage them to be creative and even radical.
6. Ask students to choose three of their ideas for an art installation, incorporating a sundial or sun clock to represent the passing of time, to write in their journal. Students use **Learning journal template 3 (Ideate page)** to do this. Ask students to choose one idea to explore further and explain the reasoning behind their choice.

TOP TIP!

At this stage, students may have produced a series of drawings that are annotated. They may have a collection of sticky notes, which they can organise into related ideas.

Encourage students to view and read others' ideas before giving feedback. Feedback could be within small groups or between partners. Considering others' ideas is an important part of this process, so students can build on their own ideas as they continue to ideate.

At each stage of this activity, ask students to discuss their thoughts before writing their responses. This will help them think through their ideas and select their final ideas to develop.

PROMPTS

- How do your chosen ideas relate to the 'passing of time'?
- How might you test your sundial design and artistic installation?
- How can you make it reflect more of your local community?
- What if you had different materials to use?

MORE VOCABULARY

- feedback – information about, for example, a person's performance or the design of a product, which can be used to make improvements
- ideate – generate many ideas without making judgements about the ideas

JOURNAL TIP

When choosing three ideas to include in the journal, try to choose three ideas that aren't related.

USEFUL APPS/LINKS

- Tools for creating ideas, such as at mea.digital/sm98
- Tips for creativity and innovation in education, such as at mea.digital/sm99

ASSESSMENT

At the Ideate stage, assessment could include observations about the number and diversity of student ideas, and their ability to provide feedback and create additional ideas. Reflection in the journal should provide an insight into some of the reasoning behind student choices.

EMPATHISE DEFINE IDEATE PROTOTYPE TEST

→ PROTOTYPE

At this stage of the design thinking process, students are asked to create a physical prototype of a solution. It is the stage where students need to get their ideas out of their heads and presented in a way that engages other students and helps them to understand the concept. When students create, it helps them to think and solve problems and disagreements. Students can role-play, make a storyboard or use sticky notes when they prototype. The most important feature is that viewers can interact with whatever is produced.

Encourage students to photograph or film during the Prototype and Test stages. This information can be used to show the learning behind the design thinking process in action.

ACTIVITY: TRANSFORM IDEAS INTO PROTOTYPES

1. Students review the ideas generated at the Ideate stage. Provide them with an A3 copy of **Generic reproducible 6 (In the frame)** so they can organise their ideas into two sections: least relevant and most relevant. Prompt students to help support discussion of the ideas, such as 'Why do you think this idea could be used? What aspects of this idea could be improved? What would need to be changed for this idea to be used?'
2. Provide students with a range of materials to create their prototype. Remind students that a prototype should be created rapidly and is not meant to look 'nice'.
3. Ask students to assess whether their prototypes effectively represent the passing of time in the local community.
4. Students continue to cycle through this activity until they have an idea to start prototyping.

Ask students to fill in the Prototype part of **Learning journal template 4 (Prototype and test page)**. See the **Journal tip** for further student guidance.

PROMPTS

- What worked?
- How could it be improved?
- What else do you need to know, do or have?
- What other suggestions do you have?
- Does your prototype represent the passing of time in your local community?

TOP TIP!

When asking for feedback, students could ask each other some of the following questions:

- What is the main feature of your prototype?
- How does it work?
- Which parts work best? What will you keep?
- Which parts need changing? How might you do this?
- What other materials might you need?

MORE VOCABULARY

- feedback – information about, for example, a person's performance or the design of a product, which can be used to make improvements
- prototype – an initial version of a model of a product or process that is used to develop a final model

JOURNAL TIP

Remind students to highlight the main features of their prototype. If students are creating an electronic journal, they can insert a photo of their prototype and annotate it.

USEFUL APPS/LINKS

- App that can be used for a learning journal, allowing students to draw, link, type and record information, such as Notability
- App that can be used to create an interactive annotation of the prototype, such as ThingLink

ASSESSMENT

Observe students as they make changes to their designs. Are they able to consider feedback, make modifications and move rapidly through this process, or do they have difficulties with holding on to an idea and accepting feedback?

EMPATHISE DEFINE IDEATE PROTOTYPE TEST

→ TEST

At this stage of the design thinking process, students test their prototype to see how it meets the criteria in the challenge. Students check to see if their prototype meets the criteria set at the start of the design process.

ACTIVITY: TEST FEEDBACK

1. Students take their last prototype and consider the original design challenge.
2. Invite local community members back to view the prototypes. Have them complete **Reproducible 19.5 (Prototype feedback)**.
3. Ask students to consider feedback to determine if their design works to represent the passing of time in the local community. If not, what could they do to make it represent this better?
4. Provide the opportunity to cycle through the Prototype and Test stages again.

Ask students to fill in **Learning journal template 4 (Prototype and test page)**. See the **Journal tip** for further student guidance.

PROMPTS

- Does your prototype do what you wanted it to do?
- Are there other features that need to be added?

MORE VOCABULARY

- evaluate – assess something, perhaps considering what worked and what didn't
- feature – a specific aspect of something, such as size, shape, colour, quality
- feedback – information about, for example, a person's performance or the design of a product, which can be used to make improvements
- prototype – an initial version of a model of a product or process that is used to develop a final model
- review – consider an idea, process or product and assess what works and what needs to be changed

JOURNAL TIP

Ask students to think about why it is important to test their ideas before they build their final design.

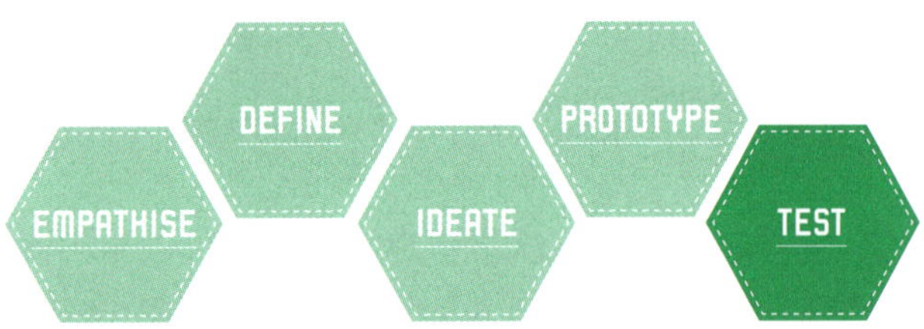

→ SHARE AND EVALUATE

At this stage of the investigation, students are provided with an opportunity to share their final design, as well as the processes involved in the investigation. Students evaluate their learning journals as well as their solutions.

ACTIVITY 1: BRING THE DESIGNS TOGETHER

1. Provide students with time to create their final designs.
2. Encourage them to film the process during prototyping and testing.
3. Students can create an iMovie or use Adobe Spark Video to demonstrate design process and thinking if technology is available.
4. Students should include their learning journals with the display so others can see the different stages of the design process.

ACTIVITY 2: EVALUATE AND GIVE FEEDBACK

1. Provide students with **Generic reproducible 2 (Self-evaluation)** to complete.
2. Ask students to provide feedback to each other about the most interesting features, the aspects that were most difficult and the changes that they would make if they repeated the task.
3. Have students share their designs and a summary of what it represents with the wider community. Journals and other information to show the research and design process could be displayed as well.

ASSESSMENT

Ask students to again complete **Generic reproducible 1 (Key vocabulary table)** using the key vocabulary for this unit. Compare their table with the one they completed at the Tune-in stage, to demonstrate changes in understanding.

Students complete **Generic reproducible 3 (Responding to the investigation)**. Compare their responses to their responses to **Generic reproducible 2**.

Teachers complete **Generic reproducible 5 (Design thinking assessment rubric)** for each student. Students compare the feedback they are given by the teacher with their self-assessment of how they used the design thinking process to solve problems **(Generic reproducible 3)**.

Name: ....

Date: ....

Facts about sundials What have you found out about sundials?	Connections to what you have learned How does this connect to what you have learned about the Earth's movement and how objects in sunlight cast shadows?

TUNE IN

STEM INVESTIGATIONS

Name: ....

Date: ....

Time	How long is the shadow?	Where is the Sun in the sky? (Remember to never look directly at the Sun!)

At what time was the shadow the longest on your sundial?

At what time was the shadow the shortest on your sundial?

EMPATHISE

STEM INVESTIGATIONS

Name: ....

Date: ....

Interview a member of the local community. Find out about their memories of this town. Learn about the things that have changed as time has passed.

Here are some questions to guide you. You can add your own question in the blank row.

Question	Notes
How long have you lived in this town?	
What are some of your favourite memories of this town?	
Does the town look different now to when you were first living here? If so, what has changed?	
What do you like the most about this town?	
What do you like the least about this town?	
If you could change something about this town, what would it be?	
Where did you play when you were young? What did you play with?	

EMPATHISE

STEM INVESTIGATIONS

Name: ....

Date: ....

Name of artist and artwork:	
Interesting facts about the artwork: 1. 2. 3.	Sketch something about the artwork that you like or could use for your own design.
What message do you think the artist is trying to give?	

STEM Investigations, MP, ISBN 978 1 4202 4319 2 © Macmillan Science and Education Australia 2018

TEST

STEM INVESTIGATIONS

Name: ....

Date: ....

Thank you for looking at my idea for an artwork. It needs to represent the passing of time in our local community. The design needs to include a sundial.

Please fill in your responses below.

The best part of the art installation idea is ...

....

....

....

....

A question that I have is ...

....

....

....

....

One suggestion is ...

....

....

....

....

STEM Investigations, MP, ISBN 978 1 4202 4319 2

KEEP PEOPLE COOL AT BIG EVENTS

INTRODUCTION

People around the world love sport, and they flock to stadiums to watch their favourite athletes compete. Because the chances of weather extremes due to climate change are more likely, adaptability has become an important stadium design consideration. Both athletes and spectators need to be healthy and comfortable all year round.

In this STEM investigation, students are asked to design an exciting stadium of the future. It should include features that make it suitable for sport and entertainment in all weather conditions.

This STEM challenge is easily differentiated for students by encouraging different groups to use different degrees of complexity when creating their stadiums.

THE CHALLENGE

Your national Olympic committee wants to build a new stadium. The stadium will be used by athletes and entertainers, and should keep spectators (the people watching) comfortable. The committee is holding a competition about its design, and you want to enter.

Your challenge is to design a stadium of the future. It should include features that make it usable in all weather conditions. It should keep people cool in hot weather and dry in wet weather. As part of your investigation, you will learn about predicting the effect of heat on different materials.

KEY UNDERSTANDINGS

- The effects of heat on different materials can be predicted.
- Materials have physical properties.
- Materials can be insulators or conductors.
- Materials are selected for use based on their properties.

KEY VOCABULARY

climate – weather patterns over a long period of time

conductor – a material that heat or other energy can travel through

heat – a form of energy

insulator – a material that heat or other energy cannot travel through

KEY SKILLS

- Make careful observations and predictions by exploring the effects of heat on different materials.
- Develop research skills, including using key words for searches, locating reliable sources and recording important information.
- Use creative thinking to design solutions and present information.
- Develop evaluative skills, such as reflecting on the process and making suggestions for improvement.

KEY ACTIONS

- Find out information about the properties of materials.
- Explore the needs of people at stadiums.
- Consider different examples of stadium design.
- Design a climate-proof stadium.

→ OVERVIEW OF STAGES

TUNE IN:

Explore sports stadiums and their purpose, consider materials used to build them and develop an understanding of the properties of materials that make them more suitable for a particular use. Research the effect of heat on different materials.

EMPATHISE

Students find out about who uses sports stadiums and how they use them, and why it would be beneficial to build them to be climate-proof.

DEFINE

Students consider the main issues with designing stadiums that need to be climate-proof. The parameters of the challenge are defined.

IDEATE

Students generate creative ideas for a stadium design that is climate-proof.

PROTOTYPE

Students transform some of their ideas into physical representations. These are created rapidly, using simple materials. Students can role-play, make storyboards or use sticky notes when they prototype.

TEST

Students share their prototypes and provide feedback to each other. They are given the opportunity to cycle through the Prototype and Test stages again.

SHARE AND EVALUATE:

Final prototypes are shared and evaluated, with opportunities for expert feedback from local scientists, athletes and/or entertainers.

→ SUGGESTED SCHEDULE

LESSON	STAGE
1–4	**Tune in**: Find out about building sports stadiums and properties of different materials and how they are affected by heat
5–8	**Empathise**: Explore different sports stadiums, who uses them and who could benefit from climate-proofing them; write in journal
9–10	**Define**: Consider observations and insights; define main issues; write in journal
11–12	**Ideate**: Develop ideas; write in journal
13–16	**Prototype** and **Test**: Conduct prototyping and testing cycles; write in journal
17–18	**Share and evaluate**: Share and evaluate designs and prototypes

CURRICULUM LINKS

SCIENCE

YEAR	STRAND	SUB-STRAND AND CONTENT
3	Science Understanding	Chemical sciences: • A change of state between solid and liquid can be caused by adding or removing heat
4	Science Understanding	Chemical sciences: • Natural and processed materials have a range of physical properties that can influence their use
3 & 4	Science as a Human Endeavour	Nature and development of science: • Science involves making predictions and describing patterns and relationships Use and influence of science: • Scientific understandings, discoveries and inventions are used to solve problems that directly affect people's lives

TECHNOLOGIES

YEAR	STRAND	CONTENT
3 & 4	Digital Technologies Processes and Production Skills	• Collect, access and present different types of data using simple software to create information and solve problems
	Design and Technologies Processes and Production Skills	• Critique needs or opportunities for designing, and explore and test a variety of materials, components, tools and equipment and the techniques needed to produce designed solutions • Generate, develop and communicate design ideas and decisions for audiences using appropriate technical terms and graphical representation techniques • Evaluate design ideas, processes and solutions based on criteria for success developed with guidance and including care for the environment • Plan a sequence of production steps when making designed solutions individually and collaboratively

MATHEMATICS

YEAR	STRAND	SUB-STRAND AND CONTENT
3 & 4	Statistics and Probability	Data representation and interpretation: • Identify questions or issues for categorical variables • Identify data sources and plan methods of data collection and recording
	Measurement and Geometry	Using units of measurement: • Use scaled instruments to measure and compare lengths, masses, capacities and temperatures • Compare objects using familiar metric units of area and volume

This investigation also links to the General Capabilities:

- Literacy
- Numeracy
- Information and Communication Technology (ICT) Capability
- Critical and Creative Thinking.

ASSESSMENT

The following resources are provided for assessing students at different stages of the STEM investigations:

- Generic reproducible 1 (Key vocabulary table), for assessing understanding of vocabulary
- Generic reproducible 2 (Self-evaluation), for student self-evaluation of the learning process
- Generic reproducible 3 (Responding to the investigation)
- Generic reproducible 5 (Design thinking assessment rubric), for evaluating student engagement in the design thinking stages
- Learning journal templates 1, 2, 3 and 4, incorporating student reflection and evaluation.

GETTING READY FOR THE INVESTIGATION

You can prepare yourself and students for this STEM investigation in the following ways:

- Identify groups of students who will work well together.
- Review the **Key science knowledge** that supports this investigation, and look at the **Useful apps** and **Useful links**.
- Start collecting useful materials for making a climate-proof stadium (as shown in the **Materials needed** list).
- Determine where prototypes will be kept between lessons.
- Create a vocabulary wall.
- Create a wall space where students can share their ideas during the Ideate stage.
- Organise the class into pairs or small groups.
- Start thinking about:
  - » inviting athletes, entertainers and/or season-ticket holders or frequent concertgoers to be interviewed about their experiences in stadiums
  - » ways to check or assess the prototypes at the Test stage
  - » who will provide expert feedback about the designs – for example, athletes, entertainers or scientists – and whether it will be provided in person or in digital form.

USEFUL APPS

- App for creating semantic maps (links between different words and/or concepts), such as Popplet
- App for creating multimedia presentations, such as Adobe Spark Video (via a teacher-created class account) or iMovie
- App for creating interactive links (for example, between descriptions, videos, images and websites and a main image), such as ThingLink
- App for creating infographics, such as Canva
- App for young architects, such as Skyscrapers

USEFUL LINKS

- Properties of materials, such as at mea.digital/sm227
- Video clip about materials and their properties, such as at mea.digital/sm228
- Information for teachers about chemistry in sport and materials used for sports equipment and stadiums, such as at mea.digital/sm229, mea.digital/sm230
- Climate-proofing sports stadiums, such as at mea.digital/sm231
- Stadiums of the future, such as at mea.digital/sm232, mea.digital/sm233
- Stadiums past and present, such as at mea.digital/sm234
- Online design tool, such as SketchUp

RESOURCES PROVIDED

- Generic reproducibles 1, 2, 3, 4, 5, 6, 12
- Reproducibles 20.1, 20.2, 20.3, 20.4
- Learning journal templates 1, 2, 3, 4

MATERIALS NEEDED

- Sticky notes
- Paper
- Cardboard
- Pencils
- Sticky tape
- Other building materials, such as recyclable packaging, boxes, tubes, plastic bottles, bubble wrap, wool, Styrofoam packaging pellets
- Aluminium foil
- Transparent plastic sheets
- Rubber bands
- Scissors
- Glue
- Paint
- Large sheets of paper
- Matchboxes or other small boxes
- Coloured paper
- Cellophane
- iPads or computers with online design tools

KEY SCIENCE KNOWLEDGE

This section provides an overview of the key science concepts and vocabulary needed for this unit.

MATERIALS AND THEIR PROPERTIES

Materials have different properties that make them suitable for different purposes. Examples are metals, which are **conductors** of heat, and rubber, which is an **insulator**. We can modify or process materials to make them more useful.

PROPERTY	EXAMPLE
Transparent (lets light through)	glass, clear plastic
Opaque (does not let light through)	porcelain, brick
Reflective (of heat and sunlight)	aluminium foil
Waterproof (does not let water through or absorb it)	plastic
Strong (difficult to break)	rock, diamond
Weak (breaks easily)	paper, tissue
Flexible (easy to bend)	rubber, clay
Rigid (difficult to bend)	glass
Hard (difficult to scratch)	diamond
Magnetic (strongly attracted to magnets)	metals such as iron
Conductor (of heat, electricity or sound)	metals such as copper
Insulator (of heat, electricity or sound)	rubber, porcelain, wool

Materials have many properties. For example, aluminium foil is reflective, opaque, waterproof, weak, flexible and insulative.

MATERIALS FOR BUILDING SPORTS STADIUMS

Stadiums usually consist of a field or stage that is completely or partly enclosed by a tiered structure designed to allow spectators to stand or sit when viewing an event. They need to be suitable for the **climate** of the area where they are located.

Modern construction materials have changed the design and performance of stadiums and other sports venues. Stadiums can now be built faster, last longer and have lower energy usage. For example, additives to cement can speed up or slow down the time it takes to set, special paints and coatings protect surfaces from the weather and other damage, and retractable and reflective roofs can be used to shade spectators and competitors in extreme **heat** or wet weather.

The roof of this stadium in Singapore can be closed to keep out the rain, and it reflects heat.

KEY VOCABULARY

climate – weather patterns over a long period of time
conductor – a material that heat or other energy can travel through
heat – a form of energy
insulator – a material that heat or other energy cannot travel through

→ TUNE IN

1. Ask students to complete **Generic reproducible 1 (Key vocabulary table)** using the key vocabulary for this unit. This reproducible will also be used at the end of the unit to demonstrate changes in understanding.
2. Before engaging in the challenge, students need to understand the effects of heat on different materials and that changes in state can occur by adding or removing heat. View a time-lapse video clip about adding heat to materials (see **Useful apps/links**) and share understandings about what happened and why.

ACTIVITY 1: EXPLORING MATERIALS THAT CONDUCT AND INSULATE

1. Students share ideas about the relationship between heat (as energy) and temperature (if heat is added, temperature rises; if heat is removed, temperature decreases).
2. Spread butter onto plastic, metal and wooden spoons. Have students record predictions about which material will be the best heat conductor.
3. Place the spoons in a glass, with their handles down, and carefully add hot water. Students observe which spoon the butter melts on. Have students record conclusions about the best heat conductor.
4. Students look at **Reproducible 20.1 (Conductors and insulators)** and research the materials.

ACTIVITY 2: MATERIALS FOR DIFFERENT PURPOSES

1. Watch video clips about materials and their properties and inventing new materials (see **Useful apps/links**).
2. Discuss key information, focusing on the fact that humans continue to change materials in order to improve them.
3. Provide students with information about materials and their properties and uses (see **Useful apps/links**).
4. Have students work in pairs to create an infographic containg key information about materials and their properties, and how this influences what they are used for.
5. Students share information with other pairs.

ACTIVITY 3: MATERIALS FOR STADIUMS

1. Provide students with links to information about the design and building of stadiums and innovative building materials (see **Useful apps/links**). Read this information together.
2. Have students record information about the materials used, important design elements and considerations for future stadium design on **Reproducible 20.2 (Stadium design)**.
3. Students share new information in groups.

3. Introduce the STEM investigation and challenge to the students. Provide them with the student card and read the information together.
4. Introduce the design thinking process by reviewing the stages on the student card. Explain that students will keep a journal about their learning at the different stages of the design.

TOP TIP! During the Tune-in sessions, conduct vocabulary activities to highlight and develop key vocabulary knowledge. Activities could include drawing semantic webs, creating a word wall or paired discussions. Check **Key vocabulary** definitions or read the **Key science knowledge** for a refresher on the key terms and concepts.

USEFUL APPS/LINKS

- 'Adding heat' experiment, such as at mea.digital/sm235
- Properties of materials, such as at mea.digital/sm227
- Video clip about materials (including new materials) and their properties, such as at mea.digital/sm244, mea.digital/sm228
- Climate-proofing sports stadiums, such as at mea.digital/sm231
- Stadiums of the future, such as at mea.digital/sm232, mea.digital/sm233
- Stadiums past and present, such as at mea.digital/sm234
- App for mind mapping, such as iThoughts
- App to gather information when making observations, such as Popplet

→ EMPATHISE

During the Empathise stage of the design thinking process, students focus on finding out about different points of view. To empathise with others, they need to research some of the challenges associated with stadium design from the perspectives of athletes, entertainers and spectators. Students will take notes, ask questions, draw diagrams and take photos where relevant.

ACTIVITY 1: WHAT ATHLETES AND ENTERTAINERS NEED

1. Students share their opinions about what athletes and entertainers need from a stadium.
2. Have students research athletes and what environmental factors affect peak performance.
3. Students consider other entertainments held at stadiums and the needs of the entertainers.
4. If possible, invite athletes and/or entertainers to visit the school. Students compile questions to find out about their sport/entertainment and requirements for a stadium. Record relevant information on **Reproducible 20.3 (Stadium likes and dislikes)**.
5. Record athlete and/or entertainer needs in **Reproducible 20.4 (Shared stadium needs)**.

ACTIVITY 2: WHAT SPECTATORS NEED

1. Students share experiences as spectators at a stadium. Use **Reproducible 20.3** to create a list of what worked well and what didn't work well for them as spectators.
2. Invite staff or community members who have been spectators at different stadiums to share their experiences of different stadiums. Add to the table in **Reproducible 20.3**.
3. Record the needs of spectators on **Reproducible 20.4.**
4. Encourage students to view different perspectives and realise the need for a climate-proof stadium.

PROMPTS

- What is the most important consideration for athletes, entertainers and spectators when considering stadium design?
- What were athletes, entertainers and spectators most concerned about?
- Are all points of view important when considering stadium design?

ACTIVITY 3: STADIUM EXCURSION

1. Organise an excursion to a stadium, where possible. This could be a stadium tour or as spectators at an event.
2. Students use paper and clipboards or tablets to sketch and record design ideas, materials used and wonderings about stadiums and improvements that could make them climate-proof.

MORE VOCABULARY

- empathise – understand and consider another person or group's point of view
- point of view – an opinion, attitude or judgement considered in a particular way

JOURNAL TIP

Ask students to complete **Learning journal template 1 (Empathise page)** while they are doing the different tasks. Remind them to date their notes and include photos of relevant information or pictures.

USEFUL APPS/LINKS

- App for young architects, such as Skyscrapers
- App for gathering information, such as Popplet

ASSESSMENT

This stage of the design thinking process offers opportunities to observe students collecting information, developing questions, and recording their notes and thinking in their journal.

TOP TIP! Students could also ask their interviewees about their favourite stadiums. Do they have a connection to a particular stadium? Why? In what ways are stadiums, as places of celebration, similar to places such as churches, community halls and town squares? How are they different?

EMPATHISE | DEFINE | IDEATE | PROTOTYPE | TEST

DEFINE

The main focus of this stage of the design thinking process is to reframe the challenge. The initial challenge is quite open, so at this stage students learn how to define what needs to be done. This includes noting insights that have been generated.

ACTIVITY 1: CONSIDER OBSERVATIONS

1. Students consider the information they gathered in the Tune-in and Empathise stages. They may work in pairs or small groups. Provide them with a whiteboard, large sheet of paper and/or sticky notes to collate some of their key information. They should refer to their information on **Reproducible 20.2 (Stadium design)** and information gathered by interviewing athletes and spectators. Students should transfer their main findings to **Learning journal template 2 (Define page)**.
2. Students should discuss one section of **Learning journal template 2** at a time, write their responses and then continue discussing their ideas for the next section, until the task is complete. This provides students with opportunities to hear others' responses and it provides the teacher with input points.
3. Provide students with the opportunity to research further. Ask them to write other information they would like to know. Provide them with **Generic reproducible 4 (Key question table)** to assist them to record their questions, findings and sources.

ACTIVITY 2: CONSIDER INSIGHTS

Students should think of at least one insight they have gained from the process; for example, extreme temperatures are dangerous for both athletes and spectators. Students should add this insight to **Learning journal template 2**. They should then explain how this may inform their design for a climate-proof stadium.

When considering insights, students could think about the following:

» What was something unexpected that you observed or found out? How was it unexpected?

» How will you decide on the most important part of your stadium design?

» Is there any other information that you need or would like to know? How will you find out?

ACTIVITY 3: CONSIDER CONSTRAINTS

1. Let students know the constraints of the challenge by describing the types of technology/materials that will be available and how students will evaluate design ideas.
2. Have students note these constraints in their journal.

PROMPTS

- What did you discover?
- What were the most important pieces of information that you gathered?
- What was something new that you learned?
- What other information do you need?
- How could you test if your design is climate-proof?

MORE VOCABULARY

- define – state the meaning of something
- insight – an accurate understanding of someone or something
- point of view – an opinion, attitude or judgement considered in a particular way

JOURNAL TIP

Discuss the term 'insight' and explain that it relates to something students have learned about the people and their responses to the surveys as well as information gathered through research or excursions. You could refer to **Learning journal template 2**.

USEFUL APPS/LINKS

- App for creating and organising ideas, such as Popplet, Inspiration, Padlet or Ideament
- App for sharing ideas, such as Air Sketch

EMPATHISE DEFINE IDEATE PROTOTYPE TEST

→ IDEATE

The Ideate stage of the design thinking process is all about generating lots of ideas. Students need to be flexible in their thinking and be able to move beyond obvious ideas. At this stage, ideas are not judged, just generated and gathered.

ACTIVITY: GENERATE IDEAS

1. Ask groups of students to draw or write ideas for their stadium of the future.
2. Each new idea should be drawn or written on a separate piece of paper or sticky note.
3. Ask students to group ideas on a wall or board.
4. Ask students to look at the different ideas and provide feedback to each other. It is important that students don't defend their ideas at this stage. They should just be listening to the feedback.
5. After the initial feedback, ask students to come up with more ideas. Encourage them to be creative and even radical.
6. Ask students to choose three of their ideas for a stadium of the future. Students use **Learning journal template 3 (Ideate page)** to do this.

TOP TIP

At this stage, students may have produced a series of drawings that are annotated. They may have a collection of sticky notes, which they can organise into related ideas.

Encourage students to view and read others' ideas before giving feedback. Feedback could be within small groups or between partners. Considering others' ideas is an important part of this process, so students can build on their own ideas as they continue to ideate.

At each stage of this activity, ask students to discuss their thoughts before writing their responses. This will help them think through their ideas and select their final ideas to develop.

PROMPTS

- How do your chosen ideas relate to the needs of athletes, entertainers and spectators?
- How might you evaluate your design?
- How can you make it more suitable for everyone?
- How can you make your design more climate-proof?
- What if you had other materials available?

MORE VOCABULARY

- feedback – information about, for example, a person's performance or the design of a product, which can be used to make improvements
- ideate – generate many ideas without making judgements about the ideas

JOURNAL TIP

When choosing three ideas to include in the journal, try to choose three ideas that aren't related.

USEFUL APPS/LINKS

- Tools for creating ideas, such as at mea.digital/sm236
- Tips for creativity and innovation, such as at mea.digital/sm237

ASSESSMENT

At the Ideate stage, assessment could include observations about the number and diversity of student ideas, and their ability to provide feedback and create additional ideas. Reflection in the journal should provide an insight into some of the reasoning behind student choices.

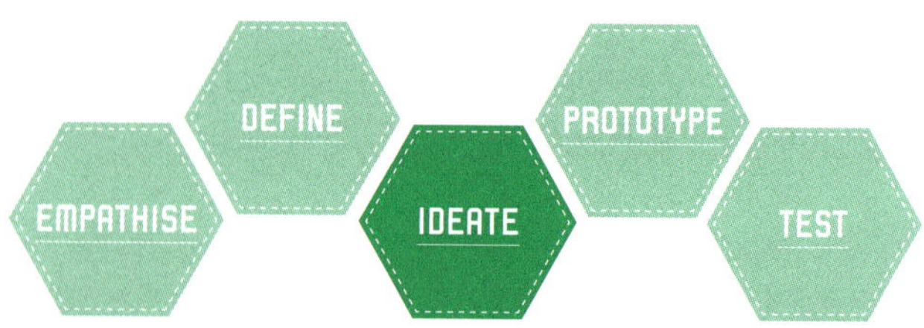

→ PROTOTYPE

At this stage of the design thinking process, students are asked to create a physical prototype of the stadium. It is the stage where students need to get their ideas out of their heads and presented in a way that engages other students and helps them to understand the concept. When students create, it helps them to think and solve problems and disagreements. Students can role-play, make a storyboard or use sticky notes when they prototype. The most important feature is that viewers can interact with whatever is produced.

Encourage students to photograph or film during the Prototype and Test stages. This information can be used to show the learning behind the design thinking process in action.

ACTIVITY: TRANSFORM IDEAS INTO PROTOTYPES

1. Students review the ideas generated at the Ideate stage. Provide them with an A3 copy of **Generic reproducible 6 (In the frame)** so they can organise their ideas into two sections: least relevant and most relevant. Provide students with some question prompts to help support discussion of the ideas; for example:
   » Why do you think this idea could be used?
   » What aspects of this idea could be improved?
   » What would need to be changed for this idea to be used?
   » Why do you think this idea is not so relevant to the challenge?
2. Provide students with a range of materials to use to create their prototype. Remind students that a prototype should be created rapidly and is not meant to look 'nice'.

Ask students to fill in the Prototype part of **Learning journal template 4 (Prototype and test page)**. See the **Journal tip** for further student guidance.

PROMPTS

- What other suggestions do you have?
- What is the main feature of your prototype?
- How does it work?
- Which parts work best? What will you keep?
- Which parts need changing? How might you do this?
- What other materials might you need?

TOP TIP! It is important that students are focusing on their ideas, rather than the end product. Provide them with lots of materials, including materials that are good conductors or insulators, such as aluminium foil and wool. Students may add labels to prototypes to explain some of the main features. Photographing and annotating pictures of prototypes can be useful.

MORE VOCABULARY

- feedback – information about, for example, a person's performance or the design of a product, which can be used to make improvements
- prototype – an initial version of a model of a product or process that is used to develop a final model

JOURNAL TIP

Remind students to highlight the main features of their prototype. If students are creating an electronic journal, they can insert a photo of their prototype and annotate it.

ASSESSMENT

Observe students as they make changes to their designs. Are they able to consider feedback, make modifications and move rapidly through this process, or do they have difficulties with holding on to an idea and accepting feedback?

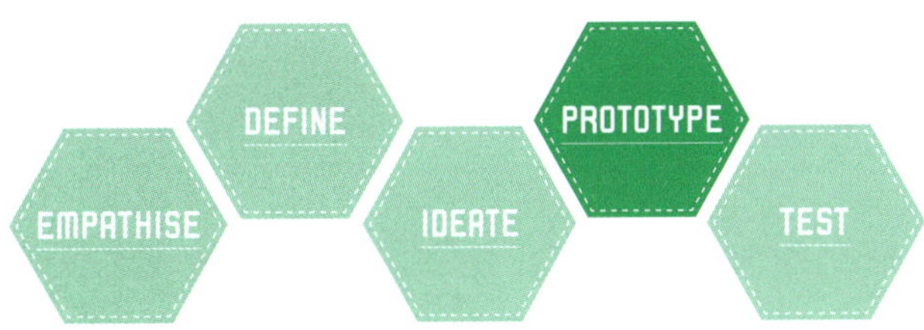

→ TEST

At this stage of the design thinking process, students test their prototype to see how it meets the criteria in the challenge.

ACTIVITY: TEST FEEDBACK

1. Students take their last prototype and consider the original design challenge. Provide them with **Generic reproducible 12 (Prototype and test)** to record their ideas.
2. Invite local scientists, athletes or entertainers to view the final designs. Students offer information from **Generic reproducible 12**. Remind students to explain how their stadium is climate-proof.
3. Have visitors offer feedback about what works well and what could be improved.
4. Ask students to consider if their suggested designs for future, climate-proof stadiums are viable. If possible, test some aspects. If not viable, what must they change?
5. Provide the opportunity to cycle through the Prototype and Test stages again.

Ask students to fill in the Prototype part of **Learning journal template 4 (Prototype and test page)**. See the **Journal tip** for further student guidance.

PROMPTS

- Does your prototype do what you wanted it to do?
- Are there other features that need to be added?

MORE VOCABULARY

- evaluate – assess something, perhaps considering what worked and what didn't
- feature – a specific aspect of something, such as size, shape, colour, quality
- feedback – information about, for example, a person's performance or the design of a product, which can be used to make improvements
- prototype – an initial version of a model of a product or process that is used to develop a final model

JOURNAL TIP

Ask students to think about why it is important to test their ideas before they build their final design.

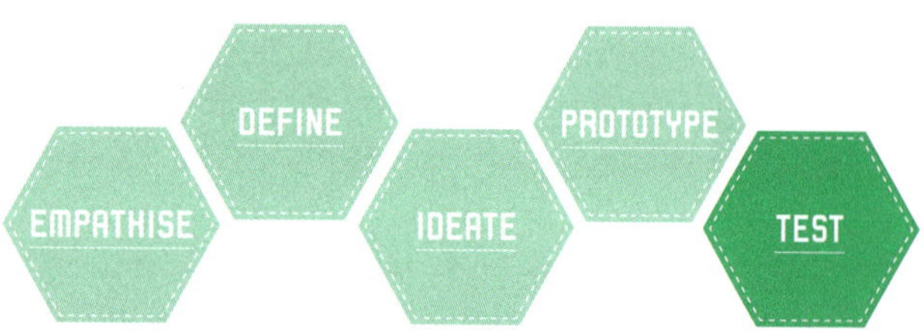

→ SHARE AND EVALUATE

At this stage of the investigation, students are provided with an opportunity to share their final design, as well as the processes involved in the investigation. Students evaluate their learning journals as well as their solutions.

ACTIVITY 1: BRING THE DESIGNS TOGETHER

1. Provide students with time to create their final designs.
2. Encourage them to film the process during prototyping and testing.
3. Students can create an iMovie or use Adobe Spark Video to demonstrate the process and thinking behind designs, if technology is available.
4. Students should include their learning journals with the display so others can see the different stages of the design process.

ACTIVITY 2: EVALUATE AND GIVE FEEDBACK

1. Provide students with **Generic reproducible 2 (Self-evaluation)** to complete.
2. Ask students to provide feedback to each other about the most interesting features, the aspects that were most difficult and the changes that they would make.
3. Provide students with opportunities to share their designs with the wider community.

ASSESSMENT

Ask students to again complete **Generic reproducible 1 (Key vocabulary table)** using the key vocabulary for this unit. Compare their table with the one they completed at the Tune-in stage, to demonstrate changes in understanding.

Students complete **Generic reproducible 3 (Responding to the investigation)**. Compare their responses to their responses to **Generic reproducible 2**.

Teachers complete **Generic reproducible 5 (Design thinking assessment rubric)** for each student. Students compare the feedback they are given by the teacher with their self-assessment of how they used the design thinking process to solve problems **(Generic reproducible 3)**.

Name: ....

Date: ....

Cut up this word list into cards. Sort the cards into 'insulators' and 'conductors'. Write these headings on a large sheet of paper and paste the cards onto it. Add the sheet to your learning journal.

wool	**aluminium foil**
copper	**plastic**
gold	**cardboard**
bubble wrap	**candle wax**
paper	**silver coin**
Styrofoam	**rock**
diamond	**iron**
rubber band	**modelling clay**
silver	**wood**

TUNE IN

STEM INVESTIGATIONS

Name: ....

Date: ....

Write some information about stadium materials and designs, now and in the future.

Materials used to build stadiums today	
Materials that could be used to build stadiums in the future	
Important design features of stadiums today	
Design features to think about for future stadiums	

STEM Investigations, MP, ISBN 978 1 4202 4319 2

EMPATHISE

STEM INVESTIGATIONS

Name: ....

Date: ....

Take this reproducible to your interview and make notes.

Name of person	Athlete, entertainer or spectator?	Name and location of stadium	What they liked about the stadium	What they didn't like about the stadium

STEM Investigations, MP, ISBN 978 1 4202 4319 2 © Macmillan Science and Education Australia 2018

EMPATHISE

STEM INVESTIGATIONS

Name: ....

Date: ....

After the interviews, write the stadium likes and dislikes of the different groups here, then work out which likes and dislikes they have in common. Write your learning in dot points.

Main things athletes and entertainers need in a stadium	Main things spectators need in a stadium	Things that everyone needs in a stadium

STEM Investigations, MP, ISBN 978 1 4202 4319 2 © Macmillan Science and Education Australia 2018

Name: ....

Date: ....

STEM INVESTIGATIONS

Read each of the topic words. Tick the column that applies to you. If you know the meaning of the word, write it in a sentence.

Topic word	I've never heard of this word.	I don't know the meaning of this word.	I know this word. (Write the word in a sentence to show its meaning.)

STEM Investigations, MP, ISBN 978 1 4202 4319 2 © Macmillan Science and Education Australia 2018

STEM INVESTIGATIONS

Name: ....

Date: ....

Write your challenge question here.

Write at least two things you already knew at the start of the investigation.

1.

2.

Write at least two things you have learned.

1.

2.

Write at least one improvement you could make.

Which part of your design do you like best? Explain why.

Write at least one question you still have about the challenge.

STEM Investigations, MP, ISBN 978 1 4202 4319 2 © Macmillan Science and Education Australia 2018

STEM INVESTIGATIONS

Name: ....

Date: ....

Statement	A LOT	A LITTLE	NOT MUCH
I enjoyed learning about this investigation topic. (Explain why.)			
I would like to learn more about this topic. (Explain why.)			
The activities in this investigation were interesting. (Explain why.)			
The group work in this investigation was enjoyable. (Explain why.)			
I can use the design thinking process to solve problems. (Explain why.)			

DEFINE

STEM INVESTIGATIONS

Name: ....

Date: ....

Use this table to create questions to help you find information that relates to your key (or main) question. Record where you found this information.

KEY QUESTION:		
Micro-question	**Notes**	**Source of information**

STEM Investigations, MP, ISBN 978 1 4202 4319 2

Name: ....

Date: ....

STEM INVESTIGATIONS

Design thinking stage/ associated skills		Established	Consolidating	Emerging
Empathise	**Observation skills**	Able to make detailed observations about people's points of view or world views. ☐	Makes some observations about people's points of view or world views. ☐	Needs assistance to make observations about people's points of view or world views. ☐
	Insights	Able to identify and describe insights that have been inferred from observations with no guidance. Demonstrates empathy. ☐	Able to identify and describe insights that have been inferred from observations with some guidance. Some evidence of empathy. ☐	Needs considerable guidance to identify and describe insights that have been inferred from observations. Little or no evidence of empathy. ☐
Define	**Describing task**	Able to describe the main features of the challenge in detail and include some original approaches. ☐	Able to describe the main features of the challenge – needs more detail and originality. ☐	Needs assistance to describe the main features of the challenge and include detail. ☐
	Reframing of challenge	Uses clear and precise language to reframe the challenge. Uses verbs to describe the actions. ☐	Needs some guidance to choose clear and precise language to reframe the challenge. ☐	Needs guidance to choose precise language to reframe the challenge. Unable to reframe without assistance. ☐
Ideate	**Range of ideas**	Clear evidence of divergent thinking. Able to generate more than ten original ideas without assistance. ☐	Some evidence of divergent thinking. Able to generate at least five original ideas without assistance. ☐	Divergent thinking not evident. Needs assistance to generate ideas. ☐
	Organisation of ideas	Ideas are well organised and clearly articulated. ☐	Ideas show some level of organisation and are able to be explained in simple terms. ☐	Ideas do not show evidence of organisation and guidance is needed to explain the ideas. ☐
Prototype	**Use of materials**	Uses a range of materials in novel ways. ☐	Uses a range of materials in expected ways. ☐	Uses a limited range of materials in expected ways. ☐
	Annotation of designs	Provides a detailed record of the development of prototypes, including annotation of designs. ☐	Provides some evidence of recording development of prototypes, including annotation of designs. ☐	Provides little or no evidence of recording development of prototypes, including annotation of designs. ☐
	Flexible thinking	Clear evidence of flexibility of thinking through changes made to prototypes. ☐	Some evidence of flexibility of thinking through changes made to prototypes. ☐	Little evidence of flexibility of thinking through minimal changes made to prototypes. ☐
Test	**Questioning and feedback**	Asks probing questions and tests prototypes thoroughly. Listens carefully to feedback and responds appropriately. ☐	Shows evidence of testing prototypes and responding to feedback. Needs prompting to ask questions for feedback. ☐	Needs guidance to test prototypes and prompting to ask questions for feedback. ☐
Teamwork	**Collaboration**	Able to work productively as part of a team. Listens to others' opinions, and understands and fulfils role within the group. ☐	Needs guidance to work productively as part of a team. Listens to others' opinions, and understands and fulfils role within the group, with prompting. ☐	Needs considerable supervision to work productively as part of a team. May have difficulties listening to and acknowledging others' opinions. Needs assistance to complete role in group. ☐
Sharing	**Narration**	Able to provide an engaging narrative that explains the challenge, points of view and insights gained, prototyping and the end solution. ☐	Able to provide a simple narrative that explains the challenge, points of view and insights gained, prototyping and the end solution. ☐	Needs guidance and scaffolding to provide a simple narrative that explains the challenge, points of view and insights gained, prototyping and the end solution. ☐

STEM INVESTIGATIONS

Name: ....

Date: ....

Brainstorm ideas. Write the most relevant ideas in the middle of the frame. Write the least relevant ideas in the outer part of the frame.

Least relevant ideas

Most relevant ideas

STEM Investigations, MP, ISBN 978 1 4202 4319 2

STEM INVESTIGATIONS

Name: ....

Date: ....

Differences

Similarities

Differences

Name: ....

Date: ....

Your teacher will provide you with a list of words to record on the hexagons or ask you to create your own words. Cut out the hexagons and use them to make connections between the important words, information and concepts for the issue you are investigating.

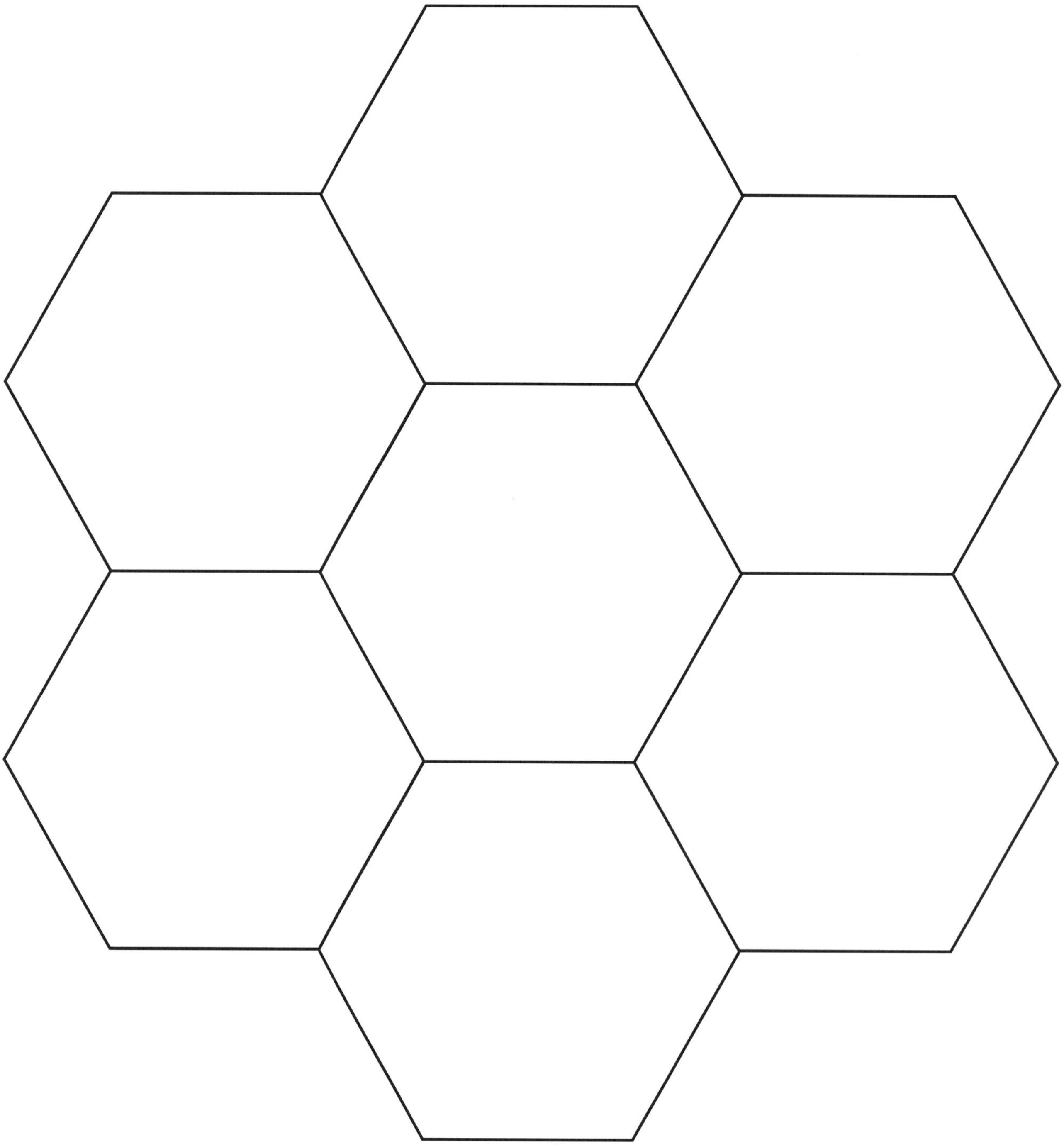

STEM Investigations, MP, ISBN 978 1 4202 4319 2 © Macmillan Science and Education Australia 2018

Name: ....

Date: ....

STEM INVESTIGATIONS

Think about these three questions in relation to your investigation:

- What do I see?
- What do I think about?
- What does it make me wonder?

I wonder ...

I think ...

I see ...

Name: ....

Date: ....

STEM INVESTIGATIONS

Group members:

Write the STEM challenge question here.

End product (This is what is going to be produced/made.):

Make a list of tasks to be done to complete the end product.

Give each person in the group tasks to do. Tick each task after it has been completed.

Task: ☐	→	Name:
Task: ☐	→	Name:
Task: ☐	→	Name:
Task: ☐	→	Name:

STEM Investigations, MP, ISBN 978 1 4202 4319 2 © Macmillan Science and Education Australia 2018

Name: ....

Date: ....

Interview a friend, family member or person in the community to find out their experiences, knowledge and opinions.

Question	Interviewee answer
What do you know about …?	
What is your experience with …?	
How do you feel about …?	
How would you …?	

STEM INVESTIGATIONS

Name: ....

Date: ....

What did you have to include in your prototype?

What did you do to check your prototype?

Write at least one change you made when you were prototyping.

What was the most important change you made? Why was it important?

STEM Investigations, MP, ISBN 978 1 4202 4319 2